FLOOR RULES

Floor Rules

Insider Culture in Financial Markets

MARK W. GEIGER

Yale

UNIVERSITY PRESS

New Haven and London

Yale University Press books may be purchased in quantity
for educational, business, or promotional use. For information,
please e-mail sales.press@yale.edu (U.S. office) or sales@yaleup.
co.uk (U.K. office).

Set in type by IDS Infotech, Ltd.
Printed in the United States of America.

Library of Congress Control Number: 2024931215
ISBN 978-0-300-21402-4 (hardcover : alk. paper)

A catalogue record for this book is available from the British
Library.

This paper meets the requirements of ANSI/NISO z39.48-1992
(Permanence of Paper).

10 9 8 7 6 5 4 3 2 1

People of the same trade seldom meet together, even for merriment and diversion, but the conversation ends in a conspiracy against the public, or in some contrivance to raise prices.

—ADAM SMITH, *Wealth of Nations*

Contents

Preface

FLOOR RULES: INFORMAL TERM used by traders on the Chicago exchanges in the 1970s to describe the unwritten standards they observed and held one another to. Also referred to as *pit discipline*.

This book is about the business culture of financial insiders, the group people have in mind when they speak of "Wall Street" or "the City." "Insider" here refers not only to inside traders but to the larger group to which they belong: money specialists who work with other money specialists and have little contact with customers or other outsiders. For all that is written about financial markets, the people who work in them remain poorly understood. This book tries to fill in some of the blank spaces in what we know about who these people are, what they do, and why.

Most of the vast literature on the markets concerns questions of mechanics; such coverage as financial insiders do get tends to be accusatory and polemical. But as common as marketplace villainy is, there is a larger picture. Financial insiders share a counterculture with customs, norms, and values different from those of the mainstream. Countercultures are typically fringe groups, but this one is at the very heart of capitalism. To misunderstand (or merely despise) the people who run world finance is unwise and potentially risky.

This book presents case studies of significant market episodes when the actions and strategies of the chief participants were more than usually visible. This book is pitched mainly to economists and historians, but sociologists may find some sections useful. A bunch of sharp operators double-crossing one another makes an entertaining spectacle, and I tried to keep analysis from interfering from a good story.

Acknowledgments

Support for this project was provided by the Department of Economics at the University of California, Los Angeles; the United States Studies Centre at the University of Sidney; and the John W. Kluge Center at the Library of Congress. To those institutions and the people there who provided helpful advice, my heartfelt thanks. The anonymous readers at Yale University Press who reviewed the manuscript gave many helpful suggestions. My wife, Lisa Ruddick, and my family have been supportive throughout. Special thanks to Wayne Baker at the University of Michigan and Ronald Burt at the University of Chicago for their advice and comments on the network analysis sections.

Abbreviations

BBA	British Bankers Association
CBOE	Chicago Board Options Exchange
CBOT	Chicago Board of Trade
CFTC	Commodity Futures Trading Commission
CNC	Connected noncore (one of three classes of members in the CBOT affiliation network)
FCA	Financial Conduct Authority
FFTR	Fed funds transfer rate
FICC	Fixed income, currency, and commodities
FINRA	Financial Industry Regulatory Authority
Forex	Foreign exchange
FSA	Financial Services Authority
FTE	Full-time equivalent (employee)
HFT	High-frequency trading
LIBOR	London Interbank Offered Rate
NAICS	North American Industry Classification System
NYSE	New York Stock Exchange
OIS	Overnight index swap (rate)
OTC	Over the counter
SEC	Securities Exchange Commission
SOFR	Secured Overnight Financing Rate
SWIFT	Society for Worldwide Interbank Financial Telecommunication
VIX	CBOE volatility index (also known as the fear index)
WFH	Work from home

FLOOR RULES

Introduction

As an MBA student in the middle 1970s, I worked briefly in the Bank of America trading room in San Francisco. I was in international money markets and foreign exchange, market areas then open to commercial banks. Around my third day, when I still had only the vaguest idea of what the department did, a great whoop went up a few workstations down from me. I looked up and saw a trader climbing onto his desk, shouting about some coup he had pulled off. Then he whipped off his clothes and streaked the trading room, bounding across the desktops. The traders (Googie, Stewball, Froggie, Milky, and Shadow, among others) hooted and cheered as he passed; some pelted him with pens, take-out cartons, and other trash. Then things settled down as quickly as they had started. Within minutes, everyone, including the star of the show, was back at work and hard at it. But now I saw the scene differently. Anything, it seemed, could happen at any moment. I felt I had learned an important lesson: *These people are different.*[1]

Later, when I had a full-time job on Wall Street, that difference came into clearer focus. My workmates and I had a guild outlook. We considered ourselves members of an elite group, with its own specialized language, orders, degrees, and trade secrets. (Looking back, our high opinion of ourselves seems odd, given the disapproval of everyone else.) When we saw financial rogues on the news, sometimes people we knew, a common sentiment was, *How do people think the market works, anyway?* We knew that few, if any, of the perpetrators felt guilty, though they doubtless regretted getting caught. We were not about to explain that to anybody; the guild was Our Thing and exclusive. Membership extended only to people in the front office (revenue-producing departments of investment firms), on exchange floors, and in a few management and executive positions. We thought ourselves raffish, edgy, in the know, part of something big. Anyone who has held one of these jobs will know what I mean. And in truth, to move huge sums of money around the world is no small thing. It is fast company, too; no one is dull or slow. A former floor trader once said to me, "I felt like the most alive man on the planet."

This book is about how members of the guild do business with one another, rather than with outsiders. High finance and the people who work there get much public attention, but mostly in connection with customers and the larger economy. Intragroup relations, the subject of this book, receive far less attention. "Insider," as the term is used here, does not refer just to insider traders but to the larger group to which they belong. Like many tightly knit groups in specialized occupations, financial insiders have unwritten rules, sometimes called an "industry mind-set." Anyone who has served in the military has seen the closed world of professional soldiers. So too in finance, a comparatively small number of lifers hold together a system where most people are short timers. The phrase in the book's title, "floor rules," is a now-obsolete slang term from the Chicago Board of Trade (CBOT) for these unwritten rules for the members' business dealings. "Pit discipline" is another CBOT term for the same thing.

The insider group goes back a long way, as does the term itself. "Insider" and "outsider" already had something close to their modern meanings in the New York stock market by the 1840s. "Insiders" are people who work primarily in financial markets as revenue producers, as well as the managers who supervise them. "Outsiders" work elsewhere and are customers of the insiders' services. Also, from the time of the earliest use of the term "insider," it has meant someone with inside information. The insider group is not uniform but comprises two distinct subgroups, described later in this chapter. Over the time span covered in this book, job titles and roles have changed several times, and contemporaries sometimes used terms inconsistently. To avoid confusion, I will use the term "market crowd" from now on to describe the entire insider group.[2]

The findings that emerged from the research for this book surprised me. What I call "floor rules" here—how insiders conduct business among themselves—have not changed at all over the nearly 160 years spanned by this book. The cultural persistence is striking since *everything else* about the market has changed. Regulation, technology, trading venues, communications, employment, financial instruments, market institutions—all are different, changed not once but several times. Compared to the markets of 1866, the time of the first case study, the markets of 2023 are like the two-hundred-year-old ax: the blade has been replaced twice, the handle three times. Still and all, the market crowd of 1866 would easily understand the game in 2023.

The case studies presented in this book will go into the specific behaviors of the crowd, but I will quickly note a few of the major findings. The crowd divides into two subgroups, an elite group of long-term survivors and high earners and a larger population of supporting players who do less well. The elite's social network holds the group together, and cliques are common but often short-lived. Deception between members, in their dealings with one another, is universal and expected. Every trading strategy employed by the different actors in the case studies involves some form of deception. Members' planning horizon and memory of past events are both very short term, and despite all the trickery, there are few grudges. (Grudges don't pay.) Contempt for clients is, if not universal, very common. Some of the findings were hard come by. In the first, 1866 case, written sources only gave brief and sometimes conflicting accounts of the key events. I filled in the picture by analyzing the stock prices and share volumes traded for the Erie Railway and other roads over several months in 1865–1866. First, though, I had to locate and transcribe the prices and number of shares traded from the New York newspapers.

While much of the subject matter of this book is historical, it is still relevant. Insider ways today are the same, and the group is very much a going concern. But for all the press coverage that "Wall Street" receives, the business remains poorly understood even by the educated public. The usual labels—"the banking industry," "the finance industry," "the financial sector," and the like—are too vague to explain much. Since 1997, the U.S., Canada, and Mexico have classified industries using the North American Industry Classification System (NAICS). In 2021, NAICS Sector 52, Finance and Insurance, employed an average of 6.1 million people in the U.S., 5 percent of the total labor force.[3] But Sector 52 covers thirty-nine separate industries, everything from central banks and claims adjusting to real estate investment trusts. "Wall Street" in the movie-villain sense spans two industries of the thirty-nine: NAICS codes 523110 and 523130. The first covers firms chiefly engaged in investment banking and securities dealing, and the second is for firms engaged in commodity contracts dealing. These two industries cover high finance, meaning finance involving very large sums of money. And it is workers in these two industries, not in the other thirty-seven, that get called unpleasant names—"banksters," for instance, a Depression-era epithet resurrected in the 1990s.[4]

The market crowd today consists of thirty to thirty-five thousand people worldwide. Historically, the crowd has worked in three principal locations: exchange floors, informal open-air curb markets, and the trading rooms of financial firms. Computerization has almost wiped out the first two. Nowadays the crowd works in the FICC section of the front office of banks, hedge funds, and other investment firms; FICC is the current acronym for fixed income, currency, and commodities. FICC is only one part of the modern front office; the other two are investment banking (corporate finance and mergers and acquisitions) and wealth management. Both are different enough from FICC to warrant a separate study. But trading is the root and heritage of the business, and the other parts are comparatively recent add-ons. Also, FICC, as currently defined, is the main profit center.[5]

Of the entire market crowd of thirty-five thousand, about half of them work for firms too small or in locations too obscure to count for much. The half that matters mainly works out of the top global banks in the world's most important financial centers. The Global Financial Centres Index (GFCI) ranks 119 world financial centers in order of importance. New York, London, Singapore, and Hong Kong head the list, in that order. Workers in locations ranked below Frankfurt (number eighteen) are on the fringes of the game. For the top twelve global investment banks, FICC has for years generated the most revenue of the three front-office divisions. In 2022, FICC produced over half of the twelve banks' total revenue with one-half the head count of the other two front-office divisions combined. FICC is also the most productive, and the gap is widening. In 2019, FICC revenue per employee was twice that of investment banking; in 2022, it was three times as large.[6]

The market crowd is worth taking some trouble to understand, since it runs the world financial system and plays a pivotal role in modern economies. The group is small, but it would be hard to exaggerate its importance. If these people vanished, the world economy would stop. The group is also the main source of marketplace innovation. Ideas originating in Wall Street and City of London firms have lowered interest costs, reduced risk, and improved capital efficiency and availability. Since the mid-1970s, the academic discipline of financial economics has emerged as a second major source of innovation; the Black-Scholes options pricing model and factor analysis are famous examples of theories that transformed practice. But in the same period, many more key developments came from practitioners, not theorists. Eurobonds exist because of Siegmund Warburg at S. G. Warburg, and financial derivatives because of Leo Melamed at the Chicago Mercantile Exchange (the Merc). Robert Dall and Steven Joseph at Salomon Brothers created modern, private-sourced mortgage-backed securities. Minos Zombanakis at Manufacturers Hanover invented the London Interbank Offered Rate, LIBOR. And so on. Before floating-rate loans and LIBOR existed, even resource-rich countries had trouble getting financing.[7]

At the same time, the crowd has a well-earned reputation for engaging in morally slippery scheming, cheating customers, and flouting the public interest. For all its useful contributions, the group has a high incidence of white-collar crime. Indeed, the crowd often uses its financial innovations to *commit* crimes. LIBOR has been immensely useful in finance, but the banks that managed LIBOR tilted it for years to reap billions of dollars in illegal profits. George Akerlof and Robert Shiller argue in their book *Phishing for Phools* that opportunistic behavior is a built-in flaw of free-market capitalism. The thinking is, "If we don't do it, somebody else will." But some industries are worse than others, and in finance the problem is of long standing. When Jesus drove the money changers from the temple, He said, "It is written, 'My house will be a house of prayer,' but you have made it a den of thieves!" We know nothing about the money changers except that they were there and what Jesus thought of them. A lesser but more recent critic of the business, William Armstrong, offered a similar assessment in his 1848 book *Stocks and Stock-Jobbing in Wall-Street.* "We by no means intend to say that, that there are not persons of high and unblemished honor, who may be trusted to any extent, but ... to one such in Wall Street, there are many of a precisely opposite character." The moral tone of the Street has probably improved since 1848, but the wrong kind are still around.[8]

Before I go any further, I want to stress that finance is not uniquely wicked, despite being one of the most disliked industries anywhere. This book aims to give a clear picture of how financial insiders behave toward one another and necessarily covers the industry's widespread and long-standing ethical problems. But other industries—notably, those that share certain features with finance—have had similar troubles. The best-known examples are large, multicompany price-fixing conspiracies by folding-paper carton manufacturers, school milk providers, and electrical equipment suppliers. In the paper carton case, in 1976, twenty-two companies were found guilty and forty-seven executives were fined, received jail terms, or were put on probation. Later, sociologists and the convicted executives themselves identified several reasons the industry had gone astray. First, the companies' products were so similar that they could compete only on price. Second, compensation for salespeople was based almost exclusively on profits and volume, and management's attitude reportedly was "get the numbers no matter what." Third, low-level supervisors and managers set prices, with little oversight. Fourth, salespeople had frequent contact with their competitors and therefore had many opportunities to make secret agreements. And last, the illegal practices were of such long standing that no one thought anything was wrong. All these conditions are present in finance. None of this excuses the guilty parties for the crimes they committed or the harm they caused.[9]

Just as the main outlines of the insider group have remained unchanged for the past 150 years, the same is true of the industry's clients. Insiders work at the market center, where money people deal only with others like themselves and are active participants, in that they control assets—that is, they buy and sell directly into the market. Outsiders are at one remove or more from the market, for which they are the source of fee revenue and capital. In the market, all insiders hold an advantage over all outsiders. The market not only brings together buyers and sellers but is also the collection point for information that affects prices. Success in trading depends on speed and timing, and insiders are the first to learn any news. Insiders and outsiders divide into two subgroups apiece, which, displayed graphically, form a series of concentric circles. Distance from the center corresponds to the level of market involvement and the number of connections among participants.

The outermost ring is the first of the two outsider groups, namely, long-term investors. This group is the largest of the four and has the weakest links to the marketplace. Members of this group buy financial instruments for use, either to yield income or to hedge against risk. Many long-term investors dislike the money business and avoid it if possible. They usually have few connections with other participants. Long-term investors were already a distinct group as far back as the era in which the very first book on the stock market was published, *Confusion of Confusions* (1688). There, Joseph de la Vega wrote of the business of the Amsterdam Stock Exchange, the world's oldest, founded in 1602. In terms that are

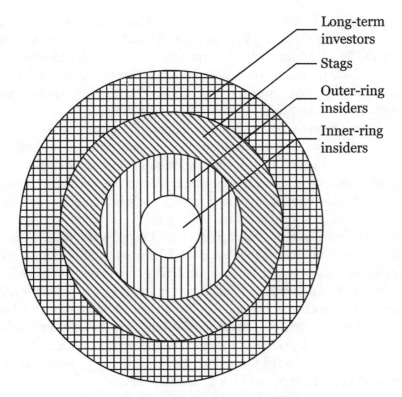

Long-term
investors

Stags

Outer-ring
insiders

Inner-ring
insiders

Fig. 1. Financial market insiders and outsiders.

still relevant, de la Vega described long-term investors as wealthy, risk-averse men who kept aloof from the market and who bought stable, income-yielding investments. In most ways, these long-term investors want the opposite of what the other three groups want. Unlike the other groups, long-term investors accept the market rate of return, want stable stocks, and trade seldom. Since they usually remain offstage and out of sight, the other three groups are the public face of the business. Long-term investors play a different game and do not figure in this book.[10]

Stags, the second of the two outsider/customer groups, are short-term speculators. The term "stag" has been in use at least since the 1860s, with slightly different meanings in New York and London. Like the insider groups, stags do not accept the market rate of return and do not buy financial instruments for use. Instead, they try to earn a higher return (alpha) by taking advantage of short-term price movements and so trade often and hold securities for short periods. Day traders fall into this category. Though stags play no direct part in the case studies presented in the following chapters, they are an important offstage presence because insider strategies routinely target them. Also, much financial journalism, which is an important primary source for the cases, caters to a stag readership. Stags aspire to be insiders but instead are the main source of what Wall Street nowadays calls "dumb money."[11]

Outer-ring insiders, the first and largest of the two insider groups, include most of the employees in the modern front office. Outer-ring insiders share the guild outlook; they aspire to be inner-ring insiders, but they are not. The group is the cannon fodder of the industry and turns over rapidly. Wall Street and City firms famously hire in good times and lay off in bad; that firms also lay off in good times is less well known. Even in a rising market, some products and services do badly. Then, a firm will probably lay off the entire working group and hire fresh staff later if conditions warrant. Mostly you don't get to know people well. In *Liquidated: An Ethnography of Wall Street*, Karen Ho writes that investment banks average one major layoff every eighteen months, with minor culls between. Ho herself worked for Bankers Trust for only six months before her entire department was cut. The industry does not keep turnover statistics, but when I worked on the Street, I had six bosses in four and a half years. Four of them got fired or laid off.[12]

At the center of the diagram—and the market itself—is the fourth and smallest group, what C. S. Lewis called "the inner ring." Members of this group hold the same positions as outer-ring insiders but are an elite minority in these occupations. Viewed from the outside, inner-ring insiders have two distinguishing traits: they earn more money than outer-ring insiders, and they last longer—much longer. Inner-ring insiders work in the market for decades, while outer-ring insiders are a floating, transient population. Inner-ring insiders do not control the market, but they exert disproportionate influence. More than anyone else, inner-ring insiders rule.[13]

In finance, inner-ring insiders play the money game best, and their earning power makes them the aspirational group for the rest of the crowd and for stags. To make money is the whole point, after all; people and firms that do not, don't count and don't last. The phrase "to make money in the market" is misleading. Instead, money comes from winning bets made with other players, and the flow is disproportionately to inner-ring insiders from the other groups. Even the best-connected insiders know only a tiny fraction of the entire crowd, but networks of personal connections hold the insider group together. Inner-ring insiders have more connections with other market participants than anybody else, partly because they have more time to connect. As a result, they hear news faster and get the earliest warnings of shifts in the collective mood. Getting the news before other players is critical because the pace of the work is so fast. Inner-ring insiders do not prosper through long-range planning. Long-term survival depends first on short-term survival, which takes a single-minded focus on the immediate present. Hindsight doesn't pay. For a successful trader, what happened last year might as well have happened in prehistoric Egypt.[14]

Inner- and outer-ring insiders all try to make money in much the same way, but the former are better at it. They do better not because they are smart, experienced, and decisive; the market is full of such people. What makes the inner ring special is the group's shared connections, which is to say social capital. "Social capital" refers to resources created by a social network and available in varying degrees to its members. The term "market crowd" that I use implies disorganization, but the crowd is anything but. The inner ring is an elite whose members help one another, as elites always do. The help can take many forms, for example, the exchange of privileged information, an interest-free loan, parked securities, or remaining silent. Inner-ring insiders work in the best firms and in the most important financial centers and are the keepers of institutional memory. Their long job tenure makes them arbiters of the unwritten rules, which counts for a lot.[15]

Market outsiders—sometimes called "noise traders" by insiders—may buy and sell according to a plan, well or poorly thought out, or to no plan at all. Insiders make *informed* decisions to buy and sell—which is to say, they act on information. But a problem in any dense network of expert, full-time professionals is that everyone will know the same things. If a market actor hears something and tells three friends, they each tell three friends, and so on, the news will spread fast. And if everyone knows something, there is no advantage in knowing it. Naïve outsiders, if you can find them, are easy money. But professionals competing against other professionals can find the field too level for comfort. Advantage comes to holders of closely held information. The information can be true but little known or false and planted to mislead. Either way, the information is valuable, either to make money or to share with someone as a favor. Information of this sort, used in this way, will pass via participants' personal, unofficial connections.

The value of having many personal connections in the market goes beyond the specific information that moves between parties; the connections are also valuable for judging the mood of the market. Making money often depends more on insight into the crowd mind than on external events. De la Vega says as much about the market of 1688; in 1936, J. M. Keynes made the same point in the famous "beauty contest" passage. Around the same time as Keynes, Benjamin Graham and David L. Dodd wrote in their classic *Security Analysis*, "the market is not a weighing machine ... [but] a voting machine, whereon countless individuals register choices which are the product partly of reason and partly of emotion." Sixty years on, in *Making Markets*, Mitchel Abolafia quotes a New York bond trader: "A lot of smart people don't do very well at trading because they know what information means. When you trade, you need to know what people *think* the information means." George Soros calls this two-way relationship between flawed perceptions and real events "reflexivity" and considers it the core of his own investment strategy.[16]

This book has three objectives: to explore insider culture and thinking, the group's self-organization, and the reasons for its long-term cultural persistence. The last topic, cultural persistence, is covered in the conclusion. This book will not address questions of public policy or market reform, topics off-point for this monograph. Market regulation mainly aims to protect the public from predatory practices and the larger economy from such events as bubbles and crashes. Rules to make insiders behave better toward one another are a second-tier priority at best, which suits the insider group: they prefer to resolve differences privately. And as in a gang war, no one cares much when gangsters shoot one another, nor do the gangsters call the police for help. Forces of law and order only really engage when innocent bystanders get hurt. Chapters follow in chronological order, from 1866 to 2022, and use two research approaches, case studies and quantitative network analysis. The perspective of the case studies is ground level; the network analysis gives an aerial view.

The case studies focus on important financial actors and market episodes with as much granularity as the source material allows. One case takes place in the stock market, two cases in derivatives markets, and one in the modern, mixed FICC market. Case studies are properly a type of exploratory research, used to gain a preliminary idea of what a more rigorous study would show. Case studies do not, therefore, support global claims or arguments, yet they are the best method available for the present topic. Financial markets are too large, too varied, and too old and the data are too fragmentary to conduct a statistically robust study. But the subject is too important to abandon for lack of an ideal study design.

Because of the closed-off nature of the market crowd, a major consideration in selecting cases was to find instances when the crowd's machinations were more visible than usual. The first case, set in 1866, is as far back as archival sources allow for detailed examination of the *group*, rather than individual operators. We know much about early, famous stock market figures such as John Law and William Duer but almost nothing about the larger crowd of speculators to which they belonged. Nor does enough market data survive to support a detailed study. A second consideration was to select cases in important locations. The four cases presented here, two in New York and one each in Chicago and London, are in only two countries. But they are enough. The U.S. and the U.K. are home to the world's top financial centers and, as of 2021, had between them 45 percent of world stock market capitalization. Customs and business ethics may be different in Kazakhstan; but a nation that wants a long-term infrastructure loan sends representatives to London, not Almaty.[17]

The first case, set in the New York stock markets in 1865 and 1866, shows a market environment dominated by cliques constantly sparring for advantage. In late 1865, a group of outer-ring insiders and stags pooled their money to manipulate Erie Railway Company stock. The principal actor in the events described was one of the best-known market figures of the era, Daniel Drew. Drew (with Jubilee Jim Fisk in a supporting role) used an innovative maneuver to make the first great stock coup of the Gilded Age. Drew's strategy became a model for the famous Erie War a few months later, a story told many times. Until now, this earlier period in the careers of Drew and Fisk has been passed over. The case introduces readers to the crowd's distinctive thinking and behavior and shows the difference between insiders' treatment of outsiders and their treatment of one another.

The second case takes place in 1888 and follows a struggle between two rival factions of inner-ring insiders. The action centers around a great wheat corner on the Chicago Board of Trade in 1888. Unlike the New York case, the conflict here was between equals. On one side was Benjamin P. Hutchinson, "Old Hutch," a famous speculator and the inspiration for several fictional financial villains. Opposing him was the most powerful clique on the exchange, the Big Four. Like the first, this case is a close-up description of a market episode infamous in its day and forgotten since. This case elaborates and adds to the outline of insider behavior presented earlier. By itself, the New York case could be read as a strictly local affair, starring a few obscure and long-forgotten fast-buck artists. Instead, we see the men of 1888 behaving just like the men of 1866—twenty-two years later, a thousand miles away and in a different marketplace altogether (derivatives). This case also introduces a broader theme explored in detail in chapter 3: network effects. Hutchinson and the Big Four not only battled each other but also brought their networks of supporters into the fight. Results were literally nearly fatal.[18]

The third case focuses on cartels of powerful institutions. The case concerns the world's largest banks' involvement in the LIBOR affair, the biggest financial scandal up to that time, and takes place chiefly in London. After remaining hidden for years, the banks' manipulation of LIBOR first came to the attention of regulators in 2007. The resulting investigations and court proceedings continued for years more, peaking in 2012. The sheer size of the LIBOR fraud is not its most important feature, for purposes of this book. Rather, the LIBOR case shows two important changes to the status of the market crowd and its shared culture that took place since the time frame of chapter 2. First, when this case takes place, the market crowd is no longer tethered to fixed geographical locations. Second, insider culture, once the crowd's sole property, has become the corporate culture of the crowd's current employers, the big banks.

The fourth and final case covers bankers' communications with one another via private chat applications, before and after the COVID pandemic. In September 2022 U.S. regulators penalized eight of the world's largest banks for massive breaches in the agencies' rules and the banks' own policies on such messaging. This case study locates the crowd's social network in a way the older cases could not, when communication was all by word of mouth. This case also points to a situation that has not been previously noted in this book but that comes up in the marketplace all the time: the market crowd has a choice between "good" and "bad" behavior that in fact is no choice. Crowd members can follow a set of externally imposed rules, lose money, and be forced out. Or they can break those rules, make money, and stay in the game. This case shows, as did the preceding one, the spread of insider culture to the big banks. This case also shows the most recent development of all: the growing separation between the market crowd and the banks. The crowd can now work independent of physical location and with less and less support from the banks, as the latter move toward all-electronic trading. The divorce, when it happens, may be a relief to both parties.

The network analysis, the second research approach used in this book, is applied to the membership of the Chicago Board of Trade from 1910 to 1940. As chapters of the book are presented chronologically, this material appears in chapter 3. Here, the goal is not to uncover patterns of individual behavior but patterns of connection within and between different subgroups of members. Network analysis reveals the extent to which the structural location of actors constrains their behavior. Put in more technical terms, the network position of a node fixes its opportunities and constraints and so affects outcomes as well. Here, the analysis aims to discover how the network locations of members correlated with their chances of long-term (ten-and twenty-year) survival on the exchange. For a time this long past, the network of primary interest, the members' social network, is lost and unrecoverable. We can make inferences about it, however, using the members' affiliation network, for which an excellent data set survives.[19]

I hope these chapters help fill in gaps in our knowledge about a small but important occupational group. A challenge of this topic is that many of the knowledge gaps are not vacant but occupied by stereotypes. The market crowd plays a key role in modern economies and is a moral puzzle that defies easy understanding. A simple mental short-cut is to typecast crowd members as stock characters from financial thrillers: thugs, swinish nouveau riche, and sinister masterminds. A comparatively innocuous stereotype shows in pictures of NYSE floor traders that often go with financial news stories. In truth, so little trading now takes place on the NYSE floor that in 2014 *MarketWatch* announced that the journal would no longer show pictures of it. To do so would, the editor wrote, distort the news rather than report it. Computers have all but ended floor trading, and computers photograph poorly.[20]

A more insidious, seductive stereotype involves glamour. Outsiders have strong opinions about the group and, for all the bad press, oddly and ambivalently view high finance as a glamour occupation and the turf of glamorous outlaws. The movie characters Gordon Gekko in *Wall Street* and Jordan Belfort in *The Wolf of Wall Street* are prominent examples, but a longer list could easily be drawn up. The inspiration for the Mephistophelian Gekko, played by Michael Douglas (whose performance won him an Academy Award) was the 1980s financial felon Ivan Boesky. The real-life Boesky was a shallow, false-front crook, smaller in every way than his screen avatar. Gekko, in contrast, was so magnetic that he *increased* public interest in financial careers, even though he was penitentiary bound when the film ended. The screenwriter, Terry Winter, later said he would have written the part differently if he had foreseen that result, dubbed "the Gekko Effect" by Andrew Lo of the Massachusetts Institute of Technology.[21]

And behind the public displays of exciting, high living is a harder reality: the world of the crowd is the world of the strong. The crowd is not the only such place; fraternities, high school cliques, police forces in their worse moments, cults, and urban gangs are much the same. The strong oppose rules and laws, which protect the weak and restrain the strong. The latter, of course, can take care of themselves. The strong fence off the group from outsiders and outside influences, which could upset the balance of power. Weak players fare poorly in these places, which nevertheless depend on them: the strong, to be strong, need followers. The weak must somehow persuade themselves that this arrangement benefits them. Gekko and Belfort make powerful recruiting posters, but recruiting posters are misleading. Nobody enters the business expecting to be one of the weak, but most people drawn to finance by Gordon Gekko will wind up as food. A common saying from my own Wall Street time was "Dodge City"—meaning, anything goes. Not everyone is suited for that.

CHAPTER ONE

New York, 1866
The Greatest Stock Operator
on Wall Street

THIS CASE IS SET in 1866 New York, immediately after the end of the U.S. Civil War. Securities trading was anarchic, conducted in five competing exchanges and an unknown number of anonymous, informal locations. The year 1866 is the start of the period when primary archival sources allow for an account of the whole crowd, rather than of a single famous individual. The action centers on one of the two leading speculators of the day, Daniel Drew (Cornelius Vanderbilt was the other). Of the four cases presented, this has the tightest focus on individual rather than group behaviors. The case gives a first look at some of the crowd's distinctive ways, such as pervasive deception and very short-term thinking, in dealings with both outsiders and insiders.

One of many unforeseen results of the U.S. Civil War was the expansion of U.S. securities markets. The market was not new; Americans speculated in financial instruments before the stock market or even the country existed. The Continental Congress and the states had issued a blizzard of debt paper to finance the Revolution, and a secondary market in these notes grew up before the war even ended. Forward contracts, short sales, margin purchases, stock loans, and arbitrage were all in use by 1790. By the early national period, the United States had a lively and sophisticated financial market, despite the primitive state of much of the country.[1]

SCENE AT THE STOCK EXCHANGE, NEW YORK.—SEE PAGE 207.

Fig. 2. New York Stock Exchange and Board before the Civil War, mid-1850s (*New-York Illustrated News*, October 15, 1853, 215). Between 1852 and 1854, the NYSE&B occupied rented rooms in the large hall over the reading room of the Merchants' Exchange (Eames, *The New York Stock Exchange*, 34). (Scan by the author)

From the start, New York was the main center, but securities traded actively in other U.S. cities as well. More business was done curbside than on exchanges. But street brokers do not keep records; except for scattered anecdotes, the curbside business and the names of the participants are lost to history. Records come from the exchanges, especially the ancestor of the NYSE, the New York Stock Exchange and Board. The Board, as it was called, started small and remained so before the Civil War. Twenty-four brokers signed the Buttonwood Agreement in 1792; by 1861, the Board had about 140 members. Trading rules were archaic, copied from the Philadelphia exchange in 1817 and little changed over the years. The rules scarcely mattered, though, with an average daily volume of about 160 transactions. On the eve of the war, a single meeting of two hours a day sufficed for trading and association business.[2]

The war changed all this. From 1861 to 1865, the Northern states built a huge military machine, and its supply needs pumped money into all levels of society. Inflation further fueled the war boom: consumer prices rose 75 percent during the war, and share prices more than doubled. New customers flooded the market, "tailors and barbers, and grocers and barkeepers, and a host of vagabonds and others who had accumulated a little money," as one newspaper sniffed. The curb market exploded. Men traded gold and securities in saloons, basements, hotel lobbies, and rented rooms. The new business overwhelmed the New York Stock Exchange and Board, and many of its members looked askance at the new, unwashed customers. In early 1861, New York had one securities exchange; by late 1865, there were five. The most vigorous of the new entrants was the Open Board of Stock Brokers, founded in 1862, and from then on, the original exchange was known as the Old Board. Most of the new customers left when the speculative fever subsided after the war, but financial markets reached deeper into American life than ever before. Twenty years later, *Harper's* commented, "The war for the preservation of the national Union largely converted the American people into a nation of speculators." In fact, speculators were simply more obvious, since the war had broadened the field of play. William Priest, an Englishman who lived in the United States in the 1790s, characterized the country as "the land of speculation."[3]

In the stock market, for all the changes the war wrought, in many ways the same game played out on a larger field. The stock market chicanery of the Gilded Age is now legendary, but it was heir to a long tradition. In the U.S. so-called stock-jobbing already had a reputation for sharp practices by the 1790s. The New York market had long-established customs and business practices by 1865, of which the many newcomers—customers and brokers alike—knew nothing. Daniel Drew was the most important crossover figure from the prewar period, and he had learned the business from a generation of operators who, except for Jacob Little, are virtually forgotten. John Ward, Samuel J. Beebe, and J. W. Bleecker were once great men in their little world, and Drew had known them all. As Drew had learned from them, the new arrivals now learned from veterans like Drew. By 1865, Drew was at the height of his power and influence—called "the greatest stock operator in Wall Street" by *The Nation*.[4]

In October of that year, five months after the war ended, seven New York speculators came to Drew with a proposition. The group had assembled

Fig. 3. The market crowd. Curbstone trading outside the two principal New York exchanges, 1864, at the intersection of William and Beaver, looking northeast toward William Street. The New York Stock Exchange and Board is in the building to the left ("Kerbstone Stockbrokers in New York," *Illustrated London News*, July 4, 1864, 8). In December 1865, the New York Stock Exchange and Board occupied Dan Lord's Building, at 25 William Street (H. Wilson, *Trow's New York City Directory*, 1865, 656). The street location can be precisely identified by the freight-forwarding business in the center of the engraving, Leech & Co., which was located at 1 William Street (H. Wilson, *Trow's New York City Directory*, 1863, 507; *Mitchell Map of New York City*, 1860).

a pool of ten thousand shares of Erie Railway stock to be used to run up the company's share price. If Drew would manage the pool, they would share the profits with him. On their own, the clique, as short-term alliances of speculators were called, would get nowhere, and they knew it. The seven were outer-ring insiders and stags—stockbrokers, bankers, a lawyer, and a merchant—and they lacked connections and access. Drew, though, was an inner-ring insider of the purest type, twenty-six years on Wall Street and a greater power there than anyone except Cornelius Vanderbilt. Drew agreed

Fig. 4. "Daniel Drew, Esq.—[Photographed by Brady]," 1867 ("Daniel Drew, Esq., of New York," *Harper's Weekly*, April 27, 1867, 1).

to the bargain. He would set strategy and trade for the clique for three months, until the end of January 1866, after which they would divide the profits. He pledged not to speculate in Erie himself during that time, though the others could do so.[5]

Unfortunately for the seven speculators, they were dumb money, to use the modern term. At the time, such individuals were called "lambs," a term then replacing the older "flunkies." The clique members should have wondered why such a prominent speculator would bother with them. Ten thousand shares made only a small stock pool, and it was to be a bull pool at that. Drew was nearly always a bear, and prospects for a bull pool were bad then for anybody. The costs of the war had been so high as to raise fears of federal bankruptcy. Postwar demobilization and restrictive fiscal and monetary policies were causing severe deflation in the civilian economy and putting great pressure on stock prices. The loss of the military business had slashed railroad profits, and railroad stocks accounted for almost three-fourths of the trading volume on New York's exchanges. The whole market was sinking, and no amount of insider cleverness would change that. But Drew had a use of his own for the pool.[6]

The clique underestimated Drew, as people often did at first. Twenty years later, in 1885, *Harper's* noted that most Wall Street titans came from "the lower walks of rural life." The writer was referring to the great men of the 1880s, but the description also fit Drew. He had grown up poor on a small farm in Putnam County, New York, and had spent his early years driving cattle down the Hudson Valley to New York City. He eventually worked all ends of the cattle trade, and from the 1820s on, he brokered sales, lent money, and discounted promissory notes for other stockmen. He branched out into steamboats in the middle 1830s and was successful there as well. In 1839, in what may have seemed a logical step, he opened a brokerage office at 53 Wall Street, when the Old Board had sixty-five members. In 1865, Drew was sixty-eight, strong and active still, tall and broad-shouldered and with piercing gray eyes. But his background had marked him. He was swarthy, with a pinched, heavily lined face, and his dress was rough and countrified. Strangers sometimes mistook him for a small farmer or a teamster, in town for the day to do some little business. His speech and manners were rude, but he had a rustic charm and was friendly, approachable, and democratic in manner. He once remarked, "I got to be a millionaire afore I know'd it, hardly." He was a devout Methodist and the principal benefactor of Drew Theological Seminary, later Drew University. He was illiterate and kept the details of his business affairs in his head.[7]

On the face of it, Drew was the ideal pool manager. He was an insider both in the stock market and in the Erie Railway Company. He had been on Erie's board of directors since 1853 and was the board's main spokesperson; he was also corporate treasurer and issued the annual report. He had never been company president, but he dominated the enterprise through intelligence, personal force, and money. Erie's management was notoriously inept and over the years had repeatedly borrowed money from Drew to get the company out of financial scrapes. Now, Erie owed him $2 million and had handed over twenty-eight thousand shares of the company's common stock as collateral. Erie had no cash to repay the loan, which was callable, so Drew effectively held the company hostage. The loan gave him control of one of the country's largest corporations for much less money than Vanderbilt later invested in the New York Central. Along with that railroad, Erie was one of two main rail lines connecting New York City with the West. Via connections with other roads, Erie's network reached as far as St. Louis and Cincinnati.[8]

In theory, Erie would eventually pay off the loan and reclaim the shares. There was little prospect of this, though, which suited Drew. The 28,000 shares he held were more than twice Erie's daily trading volume on the two main exchanges in November 1865. Desperate as usual, the company had let him have the stock cheap, at an effective cost to Drew of about 71 when the stock was selling for 95. He routinely bought, sold, and loaned the shares to move the price in a direction that suited him. Control over Erie in turn gave him great power in the stock market. With 160,000 shares outstanding, Erie common was one of the largest and most active issues traded. A price change in Erie could move the whole market. In November 1865 Erie shares made up 14 percent of *all* stock traded on the Old Board and the Open Board. Some months the percentage was higher. As company treasurer, Drew learned first about anything that would affect the share price, information he used to trade for his own account. He also timed news releases about Erie to suit his purposes; other times he floated rumors. He broke no laws, but the financial press, intending no compliment, called him "the speculative director."[9]

Drew's first move for the clique, in early November, was to try to push Erie's share price above par. The stock was trading at around 93 then, and at the time, par for most stocks, Erie included, was 100. Drew followed a conventional strategy, reliably successful in the hyperspeculative war years. A clique would put on a performance, or show, to make it look like the price of a stock would soon rise sharply. The clique would spread rumors of the coming rise, plant news stories, and make a flurry of wash (bogus) sales at advancing prices. If all went well, stags and outerring insiders would buy the stock and bid up the price. Briefly, the illusion would become reality. These engineered price rises only lasted a few days, long enough for the clique to sell its own shares. The Civil War–era name for this maneuver is lost, but the modern term is "pump-and-dump." Bear

cliques had tricks of their own to depress the price of a stock they had
sold short.[10]

Between the clique's contribution and loan collateral, Drew controlled a larger block of Erie shares than three days' average turnover of
the stock on the two main exchanges. But Drew would do little trading
on either one, except to mask his real aims. The market crowd watched
Drew's every move, and anything he did set off rumors and a wave of
trading. To trade on-exchange was to trade in public, and for that, Drew
did business through his long-time friend David Groesbeck, a popular
and respected member of the Old Board. But this was window dressing,
and Groesbeck's usefulness to Drew was limited. The New York Stock
Exchange and Board required its members to trade there and nowhere
else. Drew would do his real trading off-exchange and in multiple locations. The curb market, which met in the street outside the exchange,
had existed longer than the exchange itself. Brokers also bought and sold
shares in their offices. But there were many other options. In the speculative frenzy of the war years, informal trading venues had sprung up all
over the city.[11]

For clandestine trading, Drew used a series of cut-outs. He passed
trades first to his cashier, who sent them to Fisk & Belden, a one-client
brokerage firm that Drew had set up and financed for this purpose. Drew
had known James Fisk Jr. since 1863, when Fisk negotiated favorable
terms for him in a sale of several steamboats to some of Fisk's Boston
friends. Fisk was new to Wall Street and unknown there, but William
Belden, son of an old friend of Drew's, already had a bad name. Neither
Fisk nor Belden belonged to an organized exchange (which would have
refused to admit them). But they could trade where Groesbeck could
not, and vice versa. Besides, Groesbeck had scruples, and Fisk and Belden
had none. Accounts differ, but Drew may have started trading through
Jay Gould at this time, for the same reasons.[12]

Through the first days of November, Drew pushed up Erie's share
price, with middling success; the price rose two dollars, to 97 on November 7. But on the eighth, he suddenly ended his efforts, and the price
dropped sharply. The pump-and-dump was ineffective because it tar-
geted lambs, and these innocents were scarce on Wall Street in November 1865. The remaining players saw through the strategy. The market
was now a brokers' market, meaning without customers, where only brokers and a few full-time speculators remained. In 1864, the last full year
of the war, sixty-two new brokerage firms opened in New York. Now

they had to scrape by trading for their own accounts and, in the words of one commentator, could scarcely pay for their stationery. The pot was smaller too. A successful market coup would net less from a few full-time speculators than from a flock of lambs, and professional speculators then accounted for over two-thirds of exchange turnover in Erie shares.[13]

As unfamiliar as the marketplace of 1865 now appears, that was the business then. Insider trading was legal then and always had been, and railroad directors did so flagrantly. The *Chicago Tribune* derided them as being better at cornering the market in their own stocks than they were at running railroads. Sometimes every major railroad stock was "under clique management," as one newspaper put it, cliques often made up of the railroads' own executives. Cliques, too, had been around since the earliest days of stock markets. In 1688, Joseph de la Vega wrote that on the Amsterdam exchange, "cabals"—that is, cliques—worked to move share prices; 160 years after de la Vega, in 1848, William Armstrong made the same point: "The bold and enterprising broker is very far from confining his calculations to, and estimating his profits by, the unavoidable movements of securities. His talent is principally exercised in causing or bringing about fluctuations by every method that human ingenuity can invent, and he gains or loses according to the success of his plans or designs." In some ways, cliques resembled mutual funds, in that small investors pooled their money and hired professional financial managers. Unlike funds, though, cliques usually lasted only a few weeks to a few months. Also, cliques worked actively to manipulate a single stock— either to bull or to bear it, that is, to inflate or depress the price.[14]

After the failure of Drew's November plans, he next undertook to corner the short sellers—the bear speculators. But a corner was difficult when the bears were experienced speculators, as was the case now. Erie's share price was already falling, and the bears were cautious, only willing to make small short contracts of a few days' duration. Drew would have to trick the bears into thinking the stock would soon fall more sharply. If all went well, the bears would go heavily short on Erie, while Drew secretly bought up all the readily available stock. Then, when the bears' contracts fell due, they would have to buy the stock from Drew at whatever exorbitant price he set. On Wall Street at the time, such a maneuver was called a "scoop game."

In mid-November Drew started to buy again, on-exchange and off. The stock, which had steadily dropped into the low nineties, now reversed direction and began to rise. But as it did, the financial press started reporting rumors about the poor condition of the company. Erie had lost more business than the other roads, informed observers said. Its workers had gone unpaid for months (which was true) because the company was out of cash (which was also true). Dividends would be impossible this year. So things went until mid-December. By then, Drew owned most of the Erie cash stock, meaning the actual share certificates, of which only a few thousand circulated in the New York markets. In February 1866 daily on-exchange turnover of all stocks totaled just under seventy thousand shares and more than that on the street. But most trades were book-entry, and far more stock traded on paper than existed. Most stock of reputable corporations (as Erie still was, just) stayed in the portfolios of long-term investors and did not circulate much. For speculators who traded many times daily, such stock might as well not exist. Official exchange rules, though, required sellers in regular-way trades to deliver shares the next day. The rule was irrelevant for parties who agreed to settle by check, but buyers had the right to demand cash stock. In these latter transactions, the sellers would default if they could not deliver the stock. Bears were especially vulnerable, since they routinely borrowed stock to settle trades.[15]

While Drew quietly accumulated the cash stock, he also bought short contracts for Erie from anyone willing to sell one, and trading volume remained high. Short sales depended largely on borrowed stock, which allowed the seller to delay settlement in hopes of being able to buy the stock more cheaply later. While Drew kept his ownership hidden, he kept the market active by ordering his brokers to loan out his Erie shares on easy terms. Then suddenly on December 20, Drew ordered all the loaned stock recalled, due back the following day. But the corner did poorly. On the twentieth, Erie had opened at 95½, and over succeeding days, the price rose to 97⅞. But only a few bears settled at the jumped-up price. Some cash stock still circulated, and the wealthier bears borrowed it and delivered it to Drew's brokers. They had to pay around fifty dollars a day per hundred shares, but in the short term, that was cheaper than settling with Drew.[16]

The bears who held out hoped to make the corner so costly for Drew that he would abandon the effort and sell his stock. It was a misguided strategy, however, only effective against operators who bought stock on margin. If they held the stock too long, the interest charges would wipe out profits from the corner. Drew, though, owned the cash stock outright. But independent of the bears, Drew had a second, unavoidable problem common to all corner operators. After the corner ended, he somehow would have to unload the stock without crashing the price. Drew had paid on average about ninety dollars a share for the stock he held, and if he kept it off the market, the price would stay above that. But if he sold out, the price could easily fall far enough to turn the profit from the corner into a loss. For some weeks, neither side would budge. Then, on January 11, Drew began to sell. Erie had closed at 96 on the tenth, but on the eleventh, the price fell more than three dollars. The next day the price went to 89½, recovered briefly, then fell steadily for the rest of January. One financial journalist later estimated the December corner cost Drew half a million dollars.[17]

The market was hard on everybody that November and December, but Drew's failures hardly seemed like the work of a master speculator. He was playing a double game, though, and lost in one to win in the other. Despite his agreement with the clique, he had continued to speculate in Erie shares himself. The clique agreement gave him a captive bull pool that he could trade *against*. He used the pool to run up the price of Erie stock while he simultaneously shorted it for his own account. During the late standoff with the bears, he had shorted Erie with delivery dates after January 11, the day he started to sell. A bull pool was a doomed enterprise during a protracted market decline, but Drew could profit when the clique could not. He could pick the time and know in advance the exact moment when the price of Erie shares would turn. And since he traded off-exchange through multiple brokers and kept no records, his own trades and clique trades were indistinguishable, when they could be traced to him at all. He could set down losses to the clique account and profits to his own.[18]

This shell game could not continue forever, though. Drew was collecting more and more Erie shares and had no good way to unload them. He still owned stock he had bought in November and December, when the market price was much higher. He knew, better than anyone, that the price would not rise to that level again anytime soon. Meanwhile, the whole market was getting worse. The easy money had been gone for some time. Now many long-term investors were switching out of railroad stocks and into government bonds, which were more stable and paid regular interest. The shares they sold went into brokers' inventories and stayed there. Increasingly, stocks were held in large blocks that could only be sold at a loss. Every major railroad stock had a clique behind it, trying to trap unwary buyers, but there were too few of them to go around. Recent corners in the New York & Harlem and the Milwaukee & Prairie du Chien railroads were at first successful, but afterward, the cliques could not unload their shares.[19]

Conditions were worsening and were dangerous even for experienced operators. Bulls earned meager profits, scooped up during fleeting and minute price changes. Bears fared little better. Competition was increasingly harsh, and the attrition was not random: the cleverest and most resourceful players won more often than they lost. When capital inflows to the market are small or even negative, the game forces out weaker players. Each elimination round makes the competition stiffer and the purse smaller. Drew's strategy had profited him thus far, but he was amassing more and more unsalable stock. A day of reckoning would come.[20]

Not everything Drew did was part of some grand strategy; he also took opportunistic detours. In early January, he approached Edward Harriman, uncle of the future railroad tycoon Edward H. Harriman and a partner in the investment firm of Hancock & Harriman. Drew proposed to Harriman that the two of them work together to tighten the corner on Erie stock. This would be easy, Drew said, because only forty-five hundred shares of cash stock remained in circulation on the Street. The two struck a deal and agreed not to sell any Erie stock themselves while they worked the corner. On January 10 Drew sent Harriman to a broker who had Erie stock, and Harriman bought seventeen hundred shares at 96. (Drew was still supporting the price.) However, when the shares arrived the next day, Harriman discovered that Drew was the seller. This was the day Drew abandoned the December corner, and after opening at 95½, Erie's share price dropped like a stone. Harriman, who had just written a check for $160,000, rushed to the bank to close the account before the check cleared. It was close, but he made it; the check bounced when Drew's broker presented it.[21]

Thwarted, Drew threatened Hancock and Harriman with arrest for nonpayment; they retorted that they would have Drew arrested for swindling. But Drew had the advantage: word had spread that Hancock & Harriman was bankrupt and had defaulted. The firm received some sympathy as the backstory came out, but the fact remained that Hancock & Harriman had bought stock and not paid for it. Regardless of the circumstances, continued nonpayment would irretrievably damage the firm's reputation. Drew, meanwhile, refused to take the shares back, since they were now worth less than he had sold them for. He eventually accepted them after Hancock & Harriman, trapped, agreed to give him a twelve-month note for $50,000. Hancock & Harriman signed the note and then immediately sued to recover the money. The suit stalled, however. Drew's attorney, the distinguished jurist David Dudley Field II, argued that the original agreement was a conspiracy to defraud the public and thus illegal and unenforceable. The plaintiffs, therefore, could not compel performance from Drew. The matter dragged on for months, with extravagant accusations on both sides. The next year, Harriman married a Mellon daughter and retired from business, and nothing more was heard of the suit.[22]

By now, many readers will have had enough of the greatest stock operator in Wall Street or at least of his commercial ethics. From a modern perspective, Drew's behavior is appalling. Under twenty-first-century rules, his handling of the clique account alone violated at least three U.S. securities regulations. But the standard is unfair. Before 1909, privileged information could be used in the stock market without restriction. From the earliest days of the U.S. stock market, speculators did most of the trading, and "stock-jobbing" had a bad reputation since the earliest days of the business in the U.S. Clique members often double-crossed their coconspirators, too, a situation known as "a leak in the pool." Other speculators sometimes criticized Drew, but like Hancock & Harriman, were themselves men who spent their days scheming to trick others. And while the newspapers routinely pilloried Drew, on the Street he mirrored the culture of his time and place. Criticism of him there was mild and short-lived. The losers in Drew's sharp transactions were doubtless angry for a while, but there was always another hand to play.[23]

After Drew abandoned the December corner, the most pressing issue he faced was the expiration of the clique agreement. Drew's dealings with the clique bore some likeness to a Ponzi scheme, in that he misused a fiduciary account to enrich himself. He also faced the typical Ponzi problem, namely, that as his own account grew, so did the shortfall in the fiduciary account. But Drew had a deadline: on January 29, less than three weeks off, he would have to settle. He could lay off some losses to the clique, but it would be hard to claim that the pool lost more money than was in it. So instead he told the clique that the pool had earned large profits and proposed to extend the agreement. He gave no details and distributed no money. Still, the clique took him at his word and extended the agreement another two months, to March 29. Drew supposedly would contribute more Erie stock, bringing the pool total to twenty-eight thousand shares. The group might have wondered how bulling the stock earned large profits over three months when the share price declined 12 percent, from 92 to 81. If they had read the financial news, too, they would have learned that market reporters thought Drew's recent speculations had been failures. The clique members were surprisingly naïve, given the duplicitous game they had chosen to play.[24]

Drew next sought to corner Erie's cash stock. In a cash corner, an operator would quietly buy all the available cash stock of some issue. Then, the bears could only settle their trades if they bought the stock from the operator, at the operator's price. In December, enough cash stock remained in circulation for the bears to break Drew's corner. This time, though, Drew would target the cash stock only. Superficially, early February seemed like a good time to try; Erie stock was cheap then. After Drew ended his fight with the bears in January, Erie dropped through the eighties for the rest of the month. But a cash corner in Erie would be harder than it would have been six months earlier. Long-term investors continued to desert the market, and increasing numbers of unsalable shares—Erie's included—swelled brokers' inventories. British investors had once held about 40 percent of the company's stock. Now, though, they were selling out and returning the shares to New York.[25]

Erie was down to 76½ by February 6, when Drew began to buy up the available cash stock. The price started to rise and continued to move up, with few interruptions, for the rest of the month. On Thursday, March 1, Erie closed at 86¾, up 13 percent in just over three weeks. As before, Drew's brokers continued to loan out the stock, and trading was brisk—too brisk, in fact. For unknown reasons, Erie's turnover was abnormally high compared to recent weeks, and abnormal behavior in a stock usually meant that a clique was at work. On March 7 Drew's brokers recalled the loaned stock; but the crowd was expecting the move, and the price rose only moderately. Then, the next day, to the surprise of everyone, the squeeze suddenly ended, and large quantities of cash stock were again available. The price immediately fell over three dollars, to 83½. It turned out that the month before, Drew had sold a call for ten thousand Erie shares at 85. When the price reached 87, the option holder bought the stock from Drew and immediately resold it. This was not an act of disinterested generosity; the operator earned a tidy profit. Once again, enough Erie stock circulated to make a cash corner impossible. By Friday the ninth, it was over.[26]

This account is largely a one-man show, because the supporting cast members have left few records of their passing. But more important than the characters' personal histories is what their actions show about their workplace. Every strategy described thus far involved deception, including what the Erie clique hoped to carry out. Every seasoned speculator, not only Drew, made use of the full repertoire. The pump-and-dump is a hoax that aims to create a phony price movement. In a corner, the operator secretly buys up all available shares of a stock while decoying bear speculators into making short contracts. Deception is also the common theme in lower-level, tactical moves such as wash sales, false rumors, and planted news stories. Other common maneuvers that do not figure in this account, such as bear raids and lockups, also rely on deception. All these strategies seek to tilt the playing field. A successful result would be for a price or interest rate to move to some artificial, preset value, which only the operator knows will occur. The central role of deception points to another important feature of the internal economy of the marketplace in 1866: asymmetric information. The efficient market hypothesis has come in for much criticism, most famously by Robert Shiller. But the hypothesis still commands qualified support. At its most basic, the hypothesis states that an asset's price reflects all available knowledge about the asset. But in the post–Civil War era, the goal of every strategy for stock speculation was to learn—or create—a secret about an asset, known only to a few.[27]

The game wasn't unfair for everyone. The short-term price movements produced by these means did not affect long-term investors, who traded rarely. At the other end of the spectrum, inner-ring insiders could take care of themselves. Within that group, a certain equal opportunity prevailed, since everyone had the same bag of tricks. The targets of the various deceptions were the two middle groups, stags and outer-ring insiders—preferably stags, since they had more money. No one at the time would have used the term "asymmetric information," which would not come into use for another century. In language the men of 1866 would have understood, stags and outer-ring insiders were playing a brace game—meaning rigged. Market reporters understood this well enough. Voicing a common sentiment, in early 1866, the financial columnist for the *New York Tribune*, Horace Greeley's paper, wrote, "Dealings in stocks have come to be gambling, and, in most cases, with loaded dice."[28]

After the cash corner ended, Drew was quiet for a time, but he was busy behind the scenes. Several problems loomed that could combine into a full-on crisis. On March 29 the extended pool agreement would expire, and Drew owned more Erie shares than ever. He had bought most of the recent lot in the low eighties, and by the last week in March, the price had dropped into the seventies. As matters stood, he would have to dig deep into his own pockets to settle with the clique. Erie itself was in trouble for reasons unrelated to Drew, but that could seriously damage his position. The company had no cash and was deeply in arrears of wages, bills, and charges of all sorts. Erie's creditors and the capital markets were out of patience with the company. In late 1865, Erie had sold a million-pound bond issue to English investors, supposedly to extinguish the company's short-term debt. The directors instead used the money as working capital, though they publicly announced they had paid down the debt (which included the money owed to Drew). The annual report was due out at that very time—in mid-March—and would have to give some account of the company's many embarrassments. Whitewash would only cover so much.[29]

The consequences could have been bad indeed for Drew, if the financial statements appeared right when the clique agreement expired. The year had been bad for railroads, but Erie had done worst of all. Railroad directors had a poor reputation anyway—"a disgrace to the name of American capitalists," as the *New York Commercial Advertiser* put it. But Erie was in a class by itself. The road earned good profits when the company was honestly and competently run, which was almost never. An accurate account of Erie's condition could prompt the state legislature to appoint a trustee to run the company. Then the stock price would crash, as would the value of Drew's shares. The trustee would probably fire the directors, and Drew would lose the lucrative position he had held so long. And he would still have to settle with the clique.[30]

So Drew withheld the annual report while he arranged matters with the clique. The pool had cleared nearly a quarter of a million dollars, he said, a 27 percent profit since the clique had formed (even though the share price had dropped 17 percent). He proposed another extension, once again without giving any details or distributing any profits. The clique believed him, since Drew was the greatest stock operator in Wall Street. They extended the agreement to May 29, giving Drew another two months to disentangle himself. Still Drew postponed the annual report for another month, while he leaked bad news out piecemeal. In late April he finally released a shortened earnings statement and the annual report soon after. Even by the lax financial reporting standards of the day, both documents were evasive, misleading, and incomplete, though still damning enough. But the stock scarcely moved. By then, the report revealed little information not already reflected in the share price. Over

the six weeks Drew had delayed the report, Erie's share price had declined almost 15 percent, from 83¼ to 71, while other railroad stocks
had risen slightly. It was a narrow escape. The legislature took no action,
and the directors kept their jobs. But all this maneuvering would seem
merely to postpone a smash-up that would be even worse when it finally
came.[31]

Erie still desperately needed cash. And as it had so many times before, Erie's incompetence handed Drew an advantage, one that he used
to escape his own predicament. Erie's directors knew only one remedy
for trouble, which was to borrow more money from Drew. In late March
Erie's president, Robert Berdell, asked Drew to increase his loan to the
company. Drew agreed to bail out the company yet again in return for
Erie bonds, deeply discounted, as collateral. (After the company lied to
the English investors, the bonds were unsalable.) On May 16, shortly
after the annual report came out, Drew and Berdell settled on terms.
Drew would lend Erie a further $1.5 million and take as collateral $3
million in company bonds, valued at par. On Saturday, May 26, the board
formally accepted the agreement, which increased Drew's outstanding
loan to $3.5 million, and approved the new bond issue on the spot. The
entire transaction—Erie's desperate cash-flow problem, Drew's loan, and
the bond issue—was kept secret.[32]

Meanwhile, about the time Drew and Berdell reached their initial
agreement in mid-May, the market for Erie shares began to act strangely.
The larger operators started to avoid the stock, but on-exchange turnover in Erie shares rose sharply. The week of the sixteenth, when Drew
and Berdell met, on-exchange volume was more than triple that of the
previous week. Also, after trading in the midseventies for over a month,
the price started to drop again. On May 23 the price touched 67, the
lowest level in over a year, though volume continued to rise. The week
the Erie board formalized the loan agreement, volume was almost five
times that of two weeks before. On Saturday, May 26, the stock closed at
67½, off nearly six dollars in a week. Financial journalists groped for ex-
planations but had none. For once, there were no rumors about Erie or
anything that pointed to clique machinations. Something was afoot, but
no one would say what.[33]

All was revealed Monday afternoon, the twenty-eighth. Without
warning, thousands of new Erie shares hit the market—cash stock, bright,
crisp, uncirculated certificates. The day began uneventfully. On the exchanges that morning, Erie opened at 66⅞, down ⅝ from Saturday's

close. The price dropped some during the early sessions on heavy volume, the same pattern as on the previous few days. Then, around 2 p.m., when the exchanges were between sessions and closed, great blocks of new shares appeared curbside and in other informal trading locations. The news spread fast, and enough new shares made their way to the exchanges to throw trading into confusion. When the Old Board ended its second session of the day at 2 p.m., Erie was at 65¼. Half an hour later, when the exchange reopened for its last session, the price had dropped a dollar. From there, it went straight down. At 3:30, when the Open Board began its last session of the day, the price was 62½. By the close, nearly fifty thousand shares traded on-exchange, the highest one-day volume in months and more than twice the volume of the previous Friday. In after-hours trading, the price fell to 61½. The stock had dropped 5⅜ from the open—the biggest one-day loss since the previous year.[34]

No one knew where the new certificates had come from or if they were even real. The simplest explanation was that the stock had come from London, where investors were furious with the company. But that did not explain why the shares were new. One rumor had it that Erie had violated its charter to overissue stock, but that seemed unlikely. New York state law scarcely touched the secondary market but had strict penalties for charter violations. Clearly, though, Drew was behind it all. Fisk & Belden was the selling broker for the new shares, and if it had other clients besides Drew, no one knew who they were. Estimates of the total number of new shares that day ranged from fourteen to forty thousand.[35]

As the story emerged later, the stock was new indeed—days or even hours old. The New York State railroad law of 1850 barred the issue of new stock without prior approval by the company's shareholders. The law was unclear, however, whether shareholders had to approve new bond issues or whether the company's board of directors could act on its own authority. Either way, section 28.10 of the law allowed company directors to make any bonds convertible into common stock. The intent of the clause was to make the bonds a more attractive investment and thus easier for railroads to raise new capital. On this occasion, the Erie board chose to interpret the law to authorize them to act alone. All in a single day, the board approved the bonds and handed them over to Drew, who then converted them to common stock. The idea for this maneuver probably did not come from Drew. By 1866, the law had been in force for sixteen years, and Drew had been on Erie's board for twelve. Throughout that time, no one—including Drew, who was illiterate besides—had spotted this possible use for section 28.10 of the law. The insight probably came from Frederick A. Lane, a railroad lawyer who specialized in bond issues of distressed properties. Later that year, Lane joined Erie's board.[36]

The next day, Tuesday the twenty-ninth, the new shares were the talk of the Street. At ten o'clock, the stock opened down on the two exchanges from the previous night's close, at 61½ on the Old Board and at 60⅜ on the Open Board. The disparity—the two exchanges were next door to each other—reflected the overall confusion. No one knew what the market price was. Trading remained feverish—unsettled and without clear direction—in the earlier part of the day. Then, in the mid-afternoon, Fisk & Belden dumped thousands more new Erie shares on the market. These shares, too, first sold curbside and then on the Open Board via resale. Trading normally wound down later in the day, but afternoon volume on the two exchanges was double that of the morning sessions. The disorder spread to other railroad stocks and started to pull the whole list down. Toward the end of the day, trading in other stocks almost stopped. At the close, Erie was 57½, off four dollars, its lowest point in over a year. On-exchange trading volume in Erie exceeded fifty-eight thousand shares, the heaviest in recent memory. Still, the price had fallen less than the preceding day, and in after-hours trading, outside orders started to arrive. Compared to other railroads, the stock now seemed oversold; that is, the price was too low. A few brave souls started to buy, and the price gradually turned. By 5 p.m., the curb price was up over a dollar from the close at the Open Board, to 58¾.[37]

This same day, in the middle of this engineered chaos, the pool that Drew had managed expired for good. There was no way to know whether the pool had been successful or not. Drew kept no records, and as it suited him, he variously claimed that the pool earned huge profits or suffered a loss. No one complained later, so Drew probably paid the clique members enough to keep them quiet. The clique disbanded, and its members went their separate ways. Three of the seven went on to middling careers and obscure ends. Two went bankrupt. One, the bank president Leonard Huyck, went to jail for embezzling the money he put in the pool. The seventh, H. Henry Baxter, became president of the New York Central Railroad.[38]

The next day, Wednesday the thirtieth, Erie opened higher still, at 60¼ and 59⅞ on the Old Board and the Open Board, respectively. The stock reached 62 in the early afternoon, but then thousands more new shares arrived and pushed the price back down. The stock closed almost flat, at 59½. Volume was still high but lower than the day before. The price held steady in after-hours trading. The next day, Thursday, the crowd was tense, but no more new shares appeared. Nor did they on the succeeding days. The mood gradually settled into a watchful calm. Still, the new stock had spooked everyone and was the talk of the Street for days. Railroad shares declined overall, and volume was low, except Erie: the stock remained turbulent through the end of the week but trended higher. The new shares clearly diluted the ownership interest of existing shareholders, though no one knew how much. Even so, the prevailing view was that the price had dropped too far.[39]

Neither Drew nor Erie commented publicly on the new shares, but the *New York Times* and *The Nation* pieced together what happened. Drew had set the stage for the new stock weeks before it existed. Since early April, he had gone heavily short in Erie, while the stock traded in the middle seventies. On May 15 when Drew and Berdell agreed on the terms of the new loan, Erie had sold at 76. On Saturday the twenty-sixth, Drew had received the bonds and converted them into thirty thousand shares of common stock, at a cost to him of fifty dollars a share. Then, starting Monday, May 28, he started closing out his short positions with the new shares. While Fisk & Belden was selling the new certificates, Drew's other brokers dumped the rest of his Erie holdings. On the exchanges alone between May 28 and 30, the number of Erie shares traded was nearly four times the normal volume.[40]

Drew lost heavily on the Erie shares he was carrying from previous months, but they pushed the price down even more and increased his short-sale profits. In a grace note to the larger plan, Drew himself had started the rumor that circulated on Monday that Erie had illegally overissued the new stock. The next day, acting as Erie's official spokesman, he emphatically denied that the company had done any such thing. His likely motive was to create even more confusion about the stock and push the price down further still, to benefit his short position. As it was, the price had dropped from 68 on Saturday the twenty-sixth to 57½ on Tuesday the twenty-ninth, when Drew started to buy again. By mid-June the price was back in the low sixties, giving Drew a handsome profit for the shares he had bought when the price bottomed out. Drew had, in the language of the day, milked the Street—that is, made money on both sides of a transaction. There was a contemporary Street saying that you can lose ten thousand dollars to make twenty thousand. And so he had.[41]

The financial press worked up a fine rage over the matter. The Erie board had increased the company's outstanding stock by more than one-third, thus diluting the value of existing shares by more than one-quarter. The speculative director—Drew—had damaged the Erie Railway Company, its shareholders and customers, the market, and the public interest. The board of directors should expel him. The exchanges should sanction Drew and delist the company. Investors should boycott the stock. The *New York Times* published the Erie directors' names to shame them into action. (It didn't work.) The tone was more strident than before, but the papers had long held Drew responsible for Erie's never-ending troubles. Regarding the company's finances, the charge was just. Even before Drew diluted the stock, he had wrecked the company's credit in the capital markets. But nothing came of the newspapers' efforts to stir up public indignation over the share dump. Drew remained in his post, and the story died. The last articles on the subject appeared June 9, ten days after Fisk & Belden finished selling the new shares.[42]

The call to action failed because the papers were writing for a readership that no longer existed, namely, long-term investors who held Erie stock. Such investors would have every right to be angry. Over the preceding seven months, during which the pool had existed, Erie's share price had declined 34 percent. During the same period, the other six railroads that, with Erie, accounted for most on-exchange trading volume in New York, had declined an average of 5 percent. But long-term investors had sold out, and Erie was now street property, meaning the stock traded only within the market crowd. And the crowd did not shun Erie after Drew's bond stunt, as the newspapers urged. Instead, the stock sold better than ever. Erie's on-exchange trading volume in June nearly doubled its earlier level, reaching almost a third of all shares traded. In late June, the *New York Daily Tribune* reported that Erie was "still a leading favorite with speculators." Erie traded actively not because the company was sound but because the price moved "with fluctuations rapid enough to satisfy the most ardent gambler," as *The Nation* put it. The share price never came close to reflecting the dilution. By July the stock was back in its pre–May 28 range.[43]

The market crowd, for its part, ignored the newspapers. The crowd got its news personally and on location, in the market itself. And the crowd did not talk about, and had no interest in, investment securities. Instead, the crowd focused on what were then called "fancy stocks" or "fancies." These were the stocks of fraudulent or near-worthless corporations set up by shady financiers to cheat the public. Fancies, according to Armstrong's commentary, "never paid a dividend, and are never expected to. ... The more worthless and uncertain in value any Stock may be, it is proportionately a favorite among Stock Gamblers." For the gamblers, aka the market crowd, dividends meant nothing except a brief uptick in the stock price before the record date. Instead, the crowd looked for volatility, and fancies were volatile because they had little connection with any real enterprise. Also, they were usually small issues, which made them easy to manipulate. Erie was an unusual fancy, as a large, going concern with over 160,000 shares outstanding even before the new issue. But Drew took care of the volatility, which suited the crowd. A man could do well with shares that went from 85 to 45 and back to 95 within six months, as Erie had in 1865.[44]

For the crowd, shares were only counters in a gambling game and could be backed by seawater for all anyone cared. The big money came from taking large positions, which for most players meant margin loans. Even in 1866, Wall Street mainly ran on borrowed money, and a change in the call rate immediately affected share prices and carrying costs and set off a flurry of trading. Holding periods for securities were short; planning horizons for pools, corners, and other maneuvers lasted a few months at most. Most clique alliances were temporary, and allies one month could be rivals the next. Losers in rigged transactions were less likely to plot revenge than to recoup losses by tricking others. A thing is only worth what someone will pay for it, and a grudge about what a price *should have been* is worth nothing. It wasn't quite a zero-history environment, but it was close. Making a living in the market is like riding a spirited, unfamiliar horse. The rider concentrates on what is happening *right now* and on what will happen in the next few seconds. Financial speculation is fast work, and the money is always ahead—never behind.[45]

The preference for volatile stocks did not develop overnight but was already in place when Drew came to Wall Street in 1839. In 1811, New York State had passed an innovative law to streamline the incorporation of manufacturing concerns. The law included a clause that, for the first time anywhere, limited shareholders' liability to the value of their shares. Previously, only quasi-public corporations, those that directly benefited the general welfare, were routinely granted limited liability. Private, for-profit corporations were only allowed limited liability on a case-by-case basis. The provision caused a fair amount of controversy. The law's supporters argued that it would protect investors and promote capital formation; detractors countered that every swindler in the country would come to New York to set up bogus corporations. Both sides were right.[46]

As so often happens, the Street found its own use for an important financial innovation. The law of 1811 succeeded in its intended purpose and was of immediate help to the state's burgeoning manufacturing sector. But swindlers also abused the law, as its critics predicted. No one foresaw, though, that many investors would prefer the swindlers' stock issues, the fancies. The fancy stocks were more visible as well. In a stock market corollary to Gresham's Law, the better stocks didn't trade much, because long-term investors held onto them. The first significant stock corner in the New York market, in 1834, was in a fancy, the Morris Canal and Banking Company. Manipulation didn't bother the gamblers either, which was another way they differed from long-term investors. A manipulated stock moved according to a plan, and plans can become known, one way or another. And while the law further strengthened the already dominant position of New York's stock market, it also broadened the playing field for gamblers high and low—another unintended result.[47]

Even in this short-term world, the memory of Drew's bond conversion endured for many years. In the memoirs of Wall Street operators, they recalled the convertible bonds as a grand trick, a worthy piece of market history. To outfox a whole casino full of crooked gamblers was no mean feat, if unlikely to win a public service award. The convertible bond trick was the first great stock manipulation of the postwar period. Drew, making use of the convertible bonds as he did, once again provided a bridge from the old Wall Street to the Gilded Age. Years before, he had fallen victim to a similar maneuver. In about 1854, Jacob Little, the greatest operator of his generation, had gone heavily short in Erie stock to Drew's business partner, Nelson Robinson. Robinson thought he had cornered Little, but Little filled his contracts with new stock created from convertible warrants that Erie had issued in 1844 during a cash crisis. Little had bought up the warrants years before for next to nothing, and by 1854, everyone but Little had forgotten them. The episode was a Wall Street legend in its day, though by 1866, only long-serving insiders, such as Drew, would have remembered it. Drew would have remembered, too, what it had cost Drew & Robinson. More recently, in 1863, Henry Keep had defeated Addison Jerome the same way, when the latter tried to corner the stock of the Michigan Southern and Northern Indiana Railroad (the "Old Southern"). That episode garnered less attention; the contest was essentially a duel between two inner-ring insiders that caused little collateral damage. Also, the railroad was an out-of-state corporation, and Keep's move depended on a loophole in the Southern's charter.[48]

But the real significance of Drew's 1866 bond conversion was that it pioneered the strategy that won the Erie War, one of the defining episodes of the Gilded Age. In that famous financial brawl, Jay Gould and Jim Fisk used article 28.10 of New York's railroad law to thwart a hostile takeover of the Erie Railway by Cornelius Vanderbilt. Vanderbilt could not buy enough of the outstanding shares to gain control because Fisk and Gould, aided by the lawyer Frederick A. Lane, kept issuing new stock. Article 28.10 became a means to an early version of the modern-day poison pill used to defend against hostile takeovers. Later, as Erie's president, Gould continued to create new Erie stock as a miracle cure for any problem. During the three and a half years that he headed the company—until March 1872, when insurgent shareholders ousted him— he more than tripled the outstanding shares. Showing how slowly a democracy can move, the New York State legislature only closed the bond loophole in 1887, after years of public agitation to limit the power of corporate directors.[49]

Drew was an heir to a long stock market tradition in one last sense: that of public scapegoat. In the United States, the first publicly excoriated stock market villain was William Duer, following the country's first-ever stock market crash, in 1792. Duer had attempted a corner (another first in the U.S.), and the press roundly abused him as an "arch impostor," "infamous swindler," and "robber and miscreant," among other things. The title then fell into disuse for some years, and the stock market operators of the antebellum period, Drew included, received little press coverage. At the end of the Civil War, though, the New York newspapers fixated on Drew as the master villain of all Wall Street. In his later career, he received more bad press than all other stock operators combined. Drew's prominence made him a natural target, but his success made him an outlier, not his business ethics or methods. In his other enterprises, steamboats and cattle, Drew was known as a sharp businessman, not as a swindler. His biographer Clifford Browder writes, "Whenever [Drew] ventured into the street, fresh tales of his deceit and treachery proliferated; they stuck to him like burrs." But Vanderbilt, the Jerome brothers, Henry Keep, and other prominent speculators of the day behaved no better.[50]

What truly distinguished Drew on Wall Street was not his commercial ethics but his virtuosity in plotting. At his peak, no one could outdo him at keeping multiple schemes in motion simultaneously, nested one within another like matryoshka dolls. Drew was Wall Street's champion conniver for years, until Jay Gould bested him in the Erie War. In 1868, Drew lost his seat on Erie's board after a tenure of nearly fifteen years. He was almost seventy-one then and past his prime. His later speculations turned out badly. He went bankrupt in 1876 and spent his last years living with his son, dying in 1879 at the age of eighty-two. He bore his reverses with his trademark good humor. After Drew's star had set, Gould became financial Public Enemy Number One. Near the end of his life, Drew famously said of Gould, "His touch is death." The word of such a famous operator has counted as proof of Gould's wickedness ever since. But everyone played the same game, and some people lost. That was all.[51]

CHAPTER TWO

Chicago, 1888
Off-Color Man from the East

He was willing to play fair when fair was the game. When it was not, the reach of his cunning was not easily measured.

—THEODORE DREISER, *The Financier*

THIS CASE DOES NOT focus on a single individual but instead follows a high-stakes struggle between two rival cliques. Probably unintentionally, the two sides wound up in a lurid market shoot-out that was nationwide front-page news for days. The trading venue here, the Chicago Board of Trade, was far more bounded and organized than the marketplace in 1866 New York. The behaviors first shown in 1866 are also in evidence here, as are other typical patterns that did not figure in Daniel Drew's scheming. Also, probably because the CBOT trading floor was a restricted, members-only space, the crowd itself was more tightly knit than in 1866 New York. The crowd's acceptance—or not—of individual members was a potent force in this hothouse atmosphere. Both competing factions tried to weaponize the crowd's opinion against their rivals.

On a Friday morning in late September 1888, hundreds of Chicagoans gathered outside the Board of Trade building, hoping to get inside. In its hometown, the Board of Trade wasn't just a financial institution; it was entertainment. The exchange was a volatile gambling environment, full of social drama, ritual, and layers of connivance. When the market was hot, a man could get rich and go bankrupt all in the same day. The place overwhelmed some people, and newspapers often described floor scenes as pandemonium. Others fell in love at first sight and never wanted to leave. It was a boys' club without parallel, and the whole neighborhood bore its stamp. Thirty saloons stood within a block of the building.[1]

Behind the day's excitement was a seemingly mundane event, a poor wheat harvest in the season just past. A rational observer might suppose the price of wheat would therefore rise, and investors who anticipated the rise would profit at the expense of those who guessed wrong. But in 1888, the short crop sparked a brawl on the Board of Trade to *control* the price, a fight that rattled agricultural markets around the country for days. The struggle received nationwide press coverage that launched a speculative mania among the public and widespread demands for market reform. Congress, which until then had ignored the subject, has concerned itself with the conduct of markets ever since.

This Friday, September 28, the crowd of people seeking visitors' passes overflowed the intersection of Jackson and LaSalle Streets. People wanted some excitement; in Chicago, the most noteworthy event so far that year had been the Republican Party convention in June. Tension had been growing within the Board of Trade for a while, but the previous day the conflict had literally spilled out into the street. Brokers and clerks had poured out of the building, yelling and carrying on. The story made front-page, above-the-fold headlines in leading newspapers coast to coast and in small-town papers belonging to the Associated Press. The *New York Times* headline read, "The Wheat Pit's Master: B. P. Hutchinson in Full Control in Chicago." On the other side of the country, the front page of the *San Francisco Chronicle* read, "Shorts Cinched—Old Hutch's Corner in Wheat—He Makes Chicago Bears Squeal." Closer to home, the *Chicago Herald* was more flippant: "All the Bears Danced—and Old Hutch Did the Piping."[2]

"Old Hutch" was Benjamin Peters Hutchinson, who had once been branded a swindler and a thief in his native Massachusetts and had come to Chicago one step ahead of outraged creditors. Many a man reinvented himself on the Board of Trade in those days; and by 1888, Hutchinson was mostly honest, though in a tricky and legalistic way that reassured no one. His rehabilitation was not entirely successful, however; now he was viewed as a crank and a drunk. Now he was showing that he had other qualities as well. And despite his character defects, he was getting some

Fig. 5. Benjamin P. Hutchinson, "Old Hutch,"
1890 ("B. P. Hutchinson, 'Old Hutch,' the Great
Chicago Wheat Operator during a Trading
Session," *Harper's Weekly*, May 10, 1890, 1).
(Scan by the author)

sympathy in the present conflict, on the exchange and off. "Mr. Hutchinson," as members now called him, was at war with a powerful and arrogant clique that had dominated the exchange for years: the Big Four. Of all the members who would be on the floor that day, these were the five who mattered.[3]

More was at stake than the fortunes of a few grain gamblers, as the press called them. After a shaky start as a chamber of commerce in 1848, the Board of Trade by the 1880s was the second most important exchange in the country, after the New York Stock Exchange. The Board of Trade priced and marketed the products of one of the world's great agricultural regions, the U.S. Midwest, drawing on a hinterland of seven hundred thousand square miles and a population of fifteen million people. The Board of Trade had more influence on grain prices than any other institution anywhere. On this day, produce markets around the country would do little business, as they waited for news from Chicago. The result of this fight later drove the head of a prominent New York brokerage firm to suicide.[4]

Three other corners were in progress on the Board of Trade, but nobody thought about them today. Philip D. Armour, the meatpacking king, had October pork and ribs in his clutches. There were corners in lard and barley as well, though the latter was a shadowy affair. The *Chicago Daily News* reported that "Joe Watte [the principal broker] is the fat woman and boa constrictor of the barley corner, but it is not known who the unfortunate individual is the boa has nailed to the cross." (That month, *Harper's New Monthly Magazine* had called Chicago journalism "one of the wonders of the times.") But the wheat corner had outrun the fat woman and the boa constrictor.[5]

As soon as the massive doors opened, everyone—spectators, members, clerks, telegraph operators, newspapermen, messenger boys—charged inside. Many who came were turned away, but still the visitors overwhelmed the doorkeepers and spilled onto the trading floor. Inside, the galleries were so full that people hung precariously over the railings. Most spectators were men, but enough women came to draw surprised comments from journalists. No one thought a respectable woman should watch, or want to watch, a trading session. They were "women of the town," according to one paper. More than anything, people wanted to see Hutchinson. But for that, they had to wait, even though he had been in the building for hours. He routinely came in at 6 a.m., before anyone except the settlement clerks.[6]

The crowd on the floor was especially large too. In 1888, the Board of Trade had over nineteen hundred members, and hundreds of them showed up even on slow days. And today would not be slow. Members who came just to watch waited calmly; those with money at risk conferred anxiously about what the day might bring. Those on the wrong side of the market looked so beaten that one journalist compared them to the doomed French aristocrats in a popular nineteenth-century print, *The Last Roll-Call of the Condemned*. But no one felt safe. Members were still recovering from a disastrous speculation mounted by Edward L. Harper, a Cincinnati banker, in the previous year. Harper had looted his bank to fund the scheme and received a well-deserved prison sentence. The chaos that followed Harper's failure had cost members millions of dollars and ended many careers. For months, the exchange was a financial morgue.[7]

Few in the overflow crowd would trade today; the safest course would be to stand back and watch. There would be subtlety in the contest, for those who knew what to look for. Though the present struggle had become something of a death match, it was still broadly typical of business on the Board of Trade. Every man on the floor made his living from the market, one way or another. They were in the same club, and they spoke the same language. Everyone knew by name the handful of inner-ring insiders who ran the show—wealthy, well-connected, long-term members of the exchange. Most Board of Trade members were none of these things.

The session would open at 9:30. Minutes before the bell rang, Hutchinson strode in. In the market jargon of the day, he was the man in the air, meaning the man in control, the wire-puller. He was Lincoln-esque in stature and build, well over six feet tall and lean and muscular. He was covered almost head to foot in a long overcoat with the collar turned up and a battered slouch hat pulled low over his face. The lower buttons of the coat were undone, and the ends flapped as he walked, showing old-fashioned, square-cut clothes of a dull, dingy-looking brown or faded black. A reporter once wrote that Hutchinson's clothes looked like they had come out of an old trunk. Between the coat collar and the hat, little showed except a great prow of a nose and a pair of bright, steel-blue eyes.[8]

The conflict, now entering its second day, had started with an incident that almost killed Hutchinson. Ten weeks earlier, on July 10, he had spent a convivial evening with equally profane companions at the Century Club. The club was a drinking and gambling den that Hutchinson had founded and where he now lived, having left his wife some time before. Sometime after midnight, when everyone else had left, he walked through the wrong door and fell down a flight of iron stairs. Severely injured and semiconscious, he lay sprawled on the floor until a club employee discovered him shortly after dawn. At first people doubted he would recover. He had a dislocated shoulder blade and what his doctor termed a concussion of the spine.[9]

Hutchinson was lucky to be alive and would be confined for weeks to the Century Club, lying on the couch where he normally slept. Being away from the trading floor probably pained him as much as his injuries. After a long and varied business career in Chicago, of late he had taken to spending all his time at the Board of Trade. He was one of the grandees of the place and had unmatched staying power. In 1888, he had been a member for thirty years. After his inauspicious arrival in Chicago, he had become a prominent industrialist and financier with interests in meat-packing, banking, real estate, and carpets. The Corn Exchange Bank, which he had founded and controlled, was thriving. His son, Charles L. Hutchinson—known as "Young Hutch"—now led the bank and in 1888 was also president of the Board of Trade. The elder Hutchinson's other businesses now needed little attention, but speculation was a hands-on affair. On the floor, he could tell when he "got right" with the market. Now he would have to trade through his brokers (known on the exchange as the "pirate band"). It wasn't the same.[10]

Hutchinson was now fifty-nine years old. Much had changed since he had been "off color" in the East, as an 1888 *Harper's* article called men who went west for such reasons as he had. Dun's credit service called him a "worthless scamp" then, noted that he sometimes used an alias, and counseled its subscribers to beware of him. But he had long ago settled his debts back in Boston. To be doubly sure that he had appeased his former creditors, he gave their wives silver tea sets. Still, Hutchinson's past occasionally caught up with him. In Massachusetts before the Civil War, he had once engaged the legal services of Benjamin Butler, who afterward became a controversial Union general. Years later in Chicago, Hutchinson attended a reception for Butler, by then a U.S. senator. As soon as Butler saw Hutchinson, Butler flew into a rage and threatened to cane him, going so far as to menace Hutchinson with his stick. Neither would speak of the incident later, but people assumed that Butler had cause.[11]

Though Hutchinson had almost no education, he was an omnivorous reader. He consumed great quantities of fiction, poetry, and drama and could quote long passages by memory. For business, he daily read four or five newspapers from Chicago, Minneapolis, and Duluth down to the last advertisement. Of Chicago's five mass-circulation dailies, he favored the *Chicago Tribune*, walking to the printing plant every day before dawn to get one of the first copies. Now, stranded in the Century Club, he read even more. As he did, he saw ominous signs about the prospects for the coming wheat crop. It was still early in the growing season, but by late July scattered signs of trouble were appearing. Chinch bugs plagued some counties in Wisconsin, Iowa, and Nebraska. Elsewhere localized droughts, torrential rains, blight, rust, and army worms worked their malice. These were local issues, however, and official crop forecasts through July reported better prospects for spring wheat than in 1887.

But Hutchinson sensed a larger pattern and kept reading. Finally, on August 13, a month after his accident, he walked across the pedestrian bridge that linked the Rialto Building, which housed the Century Club, with the Board of Trade. When he came onto the floor, looking pale and thin, the crowd greeted him with a cheer and carried in a chair for him.[12]

It was a fine place. Like Chicago itself, the Board of Trade had come from nothing to great power and influence in a few years, and its members took pride in the success of their club. In 1858, when Hutchinson joined, the Board of Trade had under three hundred members, and it cost $5 to join. Now, in 1888, there were nineteen hundred members, and the entrance fee had risen to $10,000, equivalent to more than $300,000 in 2022. In 1885, the association had built a grand new headquarters occupying half a block fronting on Jackson Street at the foot of LaSalle. This location would be the Board of Trade's permanent address for another 120 years. The Board of Trade had an image to keep up: its main trading partner, the New York Produce Exchange, had the year before opened the most imposing exchange building ever erected in the United States. At 265 feet, the new Chicago exchange was the second-tallest man-made structure in the country, after the Washington Monument, and the first public building in Chicago wired for electricity.[13]

Like all great buildings, the new exchange building was an expression of economic power and a public statement about its sponsors. The architects' original conception mainly addressed the special needs of the organization and had relatively spare ornamentation, by the standards of the day. But the Board of Trade was a populist, democratic organization, and its members had their own ideas about how to show they had arrived. The completed building cost almost twice the original estimate, most of the excess going to decoration. The result, the *Chicago Tribune* proclaimed, was "the boldest, most picturesque building in the country," and there was something to that. The outside of the building sported two large griffin figures and nine large and many lesser statues, representing different types of commerce and industry. In the main trading room, there were fifty-nine frescoes, stained-glass windows, and ceiling panels decorated with representations of the continents, the ages of humankind, the arts and sciences, Greek and Latin gods, the months and seasons of the year, the four elements, national and international coats of arms (whatever these might have been), signs of the zodiac, and various inspirational and allegorical scenes such as old age and death, Bacchus and his harvest, and a foxhunt. Groping for words, the architects called the style "modern Gothic."[14]

Fig. 6. The main trading floor, Chicago Board of Trade, 1886, facing north, toward Jackson and LaSalle Streets (*Frank Leslie's Illustrated Newspaper*, March 27, 1886, 85). (Scan by the author)

Hutchinson's chair and particular spot were in the northeastern section of the floor, near the wheat pit. The earliest trading pits had been round, but these proved unsatisfactory; the members had upended them and rolled them around the trading floor, crashing them into each other. By 1888, the pits had assumed their modern form: octagonal, stepped amphitheaters, designed so every person inside was visible to every other. From Hutchinson's seat (beneath murals representing Europe, gymnastics, Australia, and the landing of Columbus), he traded in all three of the main markets: wheat, corn, and provisions (dressed pork). As he had from the Century Club, he kept the pirate band running from one trading pit to another. Meanwhile, he himself held court while friends and acquaintances stopped by, hangers-on pumped him for tips, reporters tried to interview him, and his brokers yelled their trades at him. Between answering questions and conducting several conversations at once, he shouted instructions to his brokers and watched the quotation clocks. Hutchinson kept no books and kept track of everything in his head. He traded in the cash market, meaning the actual foodstuffs, but he chiefly speculated in futures contracts, near ancestors to the futures contracts traded today.[15]

The details of futures trading are complex, but the business of the exchange was and still is simple in concept: members bet against one another on the future price of some item. In the 1880s, the bets were on the prices of a few agricultural commodities, but the list is much longer today. To simplify trading, the exchange had created standardized units, called contracts, of a set quantity, grade, and fixed date of delivery. In 1888, a trader who bought a contract for September wheat—"Sep wheat"—got five thousand bushels of number-one- or number-two-grade wheat, deliverable by September 30. Also, such contracts were (and are) contracts in the usual sense, that is, legally enforceable agreements. Contracts that specify a date of performance in the future go back at least to Babylonian times and are known as "forward contracts." But forward contracts are not standardized at all; each one must be valued individually. A futures contract, though, is as standardized as a dollar bill or an ounce of gold and is just as easy to price or to transfer.

The Board of Trade had invented futures contracts during the Civil War to supply the Union army. But like many other military inventions, futures contracts had peacetime uses. After the war, bakers, millers, brewers, distillers, and meatpackers continued the practice to lock in future supplies and sales at known prices. This revolutionary market model, exchange-traded futures contracts, allowed buyers and sellers of agricultural commodities to do something new: avoid the risk of future price changes. The idea caught on quickly. By 1888, Chicago-style futures trading had spread to locations throughout the U.S. and to Toronto, London, and Liverpool. By the early 1890s, futures contracts traded in Hamburg, Bremen, Berlin, and Paris as well. Collectively, the members of the Board of Trade were a fine example of Adam Smith's invisible hand. The system transferred risk from parties who wished to avoid it to parties who wished to bear it, namely, the market crowd. Each member followed his own self-interest, and together they advanced the good of all.[16]

Not everyone approved of this application of the invisible hand. For the crowd, a futures contract was simply a wager, rather than a transaction in physical goods. Speculators in futures contracts had no more interest in owning wheat, say, than bettors did in owning a racehorse. Speculative trades typically settled by check, and no real wheat, corn, or pork changed hands. Over 90 percent of the volume on the Board of Trade was speculative, and nearly every jurisdiction in the republic outlawed gambling in 1888. Futures trading survived legal challenges because speculative and commercial transactions were often inseparably intertwined. The behavior of some of the members didn't help the institution's reputation. Off and on throughout the existence of the Board of Trade, it was under a cloud of scandal. In 1867, the *Chicago Daily Tribune* wrote, "There are few branches of business that afford so many opportunities for the commission of legal frauds as the grain trade." Some of the earliest national press coverage the Board of Trade got, that same year, was to report mass arrests on the floor of the exchange. Hutchinson got one of his own first press notices on that occasion. But then and now, if the check clears, no one cares about the drawer's character. The crowd is like the Foreign Legion that way.[17]

Coincidentally, the same day Hutchinson returned to the exchange, the *Chicago Tribune* published the first thoroughly bad forecast for the coming wheat crop. From then on, the crop news steadily worsened—first for the United States and Canada and then for the Atlantic world's other main wheat-producing regions, France and Russia. Hutchinson's suspicion was becoming a certainty: a serious wheat shortage loomed. Prices on the Board of Trade took time to catch up, however. Hutchinson spotted the inconsistency, and for the balance of August and through September, he told everyone in his wide acquaintance that wheat prices would rise. No one listened. The bears, the dominant faction on the exchange, continued to bet on a future *decline* in prices.[18]

The terms "bear" and "bull" carried the same meanings on CBOT as they did on the New York exchanges. These and other terms had spread to the Board of Trade in the middle 1850s from the New York Corn Exchange. That institution had in turn adopted the terminology of the New York Stock Exchange and Board, which then stood a few blocks distant. As in New York, in Chicago the terms "bull" and "bear" applied strictly to speculators, men who risked sizable sums of money and followed an investment strategy. Most exchange members did neither and were instead either "scalpers" or "tailers." A scalper looked for a quick profit, however small, and bought and sold many times a day. Tailers followed the trades of prominent speculators. Scalpers and tailers were usually men of limited means, glad to finish the day a few dollars ahead. A "short," though, was not the same as a bear. Bears followed a consistent strategy, and scalpers and tailers went wherever the wind blew them. Speculators viewed both groups as scavengers and inferior castes.[19]

Though Hutchinson's predictions about wheat went unheeded, he was nothing if not an independent thinker. He bought more and more wheat, both the real thing stored in Chicago's grain elevators—cash wheat—and the speculative, nonexistent variety that existed on paper only, so-called wind wheat. Of the latter, he chiefly bought contracts for Sep wheat, that is, with a delivery deadline of September 30. Hutchinson was normally a scalper, though a rich one, so buying wheat and holding it marked a radical change from his usual practice. Now, he was behaving like a bull speculator. In all the market crowd, he alone realized that the bears were putting themselves in a dangerous position. And if the bears were willing to sell contracts to deliver wheat, Hutchinson was willing to buy them.

Speculators and scalpers were no more likely to come into conflict than were ships and seagulls. But Hutchinson's altered trading strategy put him on a collision course with the most powerful bear clique on the exchange, the Big Four. This group had formed in 1883 after the spectacular collapse of an attempted corner in lard by Peter McGeoch, a Milwaukee speculator. Though McGeoch and many others went bankrupt, each of the Big Four—Norman Ream, Jack Cudahy, Charlie Singer, and Nat Jones—managed to come out ahead. As a team, they were so successful that they became a proto–hedge fund, attracting outside investment capital from New York, Liverpool, and London. And like a successful fund, the Big Four had a reputation for financial wizardry that gave them further leverage: other members watched what they did and copied them.

Fig. 7. Norman B. Ream, 1880s.
(Public domain, Ancestry.com)

Since most speculators on the exchange were bears (bulls needed more money to play), the Big Four at their peak wielded great influence.[20]

Even small groups have leaders, and Norman Ream and Jack Cudahy led the Big Four. Ream was the most reflective and a close student of the market. Ream was a fine figure of a man, over six feet tall, sleek, and a sharp dresser even by the flashy standards of the crowd. A newspaper reporter, interviewing him, wrote admiringly of Ream's glove-textured French kid boots and purple linen suit. Jack Cudahy led through charisma and force of character. Born in County Kilkenny, Ireland, Cudahy had come to the U.S. as a child on one of the famine boats. When scarcely into his teens, he worked as a blood-tub boy in a Milwaukee slaughterhouse. But a succession of wealthy entrepreneurs recognized Cudahy's ability and went out of their way to help him. He came to Chicago in 1876 as a protégé of Philip D. Armour, who would become the largest meatpacker in the country. The remaining two members of the group, Singer and Jones, were clever and successful but usually stayed in the background. In their day, they came to public attention

Fig. 8. Jack Cudahy, 1880s.
(Public domain, Ancestry.com)

chiefly for making money and spending it. By 1888, all four had been Board of Trade members over ten years.[21]

The Big Four, being bears, had sold contracts for millions of bushels of September-delivery wheat that they did not own. Trading in the contract would end on Saturday, September 29. Then, if they had not settled earlier, they had until Sunday, September 30, to do so. On that day, they either could deliver real wheat or else write a check for an equivalent amount of wheat at the September 29 closing price. But as inner-ring insiders, they would not simply wait and hope the price went down; they would *put* the price down. As the deadline approached, the Big Four and a posse of allies mounted a series of bear raids to drive down the price of September wheat. A bear raid was a ruse to trick stags and outer-ring insiders into thinking the price of the traded commodity was about to drop significantly. Working behind the scenes, the bear raiders would create a flurry of wash sales at progressively lower prices. Hopefully, then, the smaller operators would take fright and sell out, bidding the price lower still. Once the raiders thought the price had bottomed out, they would start to buy anonymously, through brokers, to avoid alerting the crowd. A bear raid was a performance to make the crowd believe that a price was about to drop, the opposite of the pump-and-dump strategy described in chapter 1. In 1888, on the Board of Trade, any such feint or bluff to move a price was called a "gallery play."[22]

But the raids did not live up to expectations. A few members responded as hoped and bid the price of Sep wheat down some. But after thirty years on 'change, Hutchinson had seen too many gallery plays to be taken in by another one, and he continued to buy when no one else would. He was a famously sharp trader, and the tailers watched him closely. Because he was buying Sep wheat, they bought too. Each of the raids fizzled out, and the Sep wheat price bobbed back to its original level or higher. Most of the market crowd were small fry and simply copied what they saw inner-ring insiders and their hangers-on do. Now, though, the inner-ring insiders were sending conflicting signals. To the chagrin of the Big Four, the crowd chose to copy Hutchinson.[23]

At this point, the Big Four apparently were still willing to settle with Hutchinson, if they had to. Since Hutchinson by now owned almost all the actual wheat stored in Chicago, the Big Four and their friends thought to bring wheat from out-of-town markets to fill their contracts. By Board of Trade rules, cash grain traded on the exchange had to be stored in the city. But a canvass of grain dealers and elevator operators within shipping distance of Chicago confirmed what Hutchinson had been saying for weeks: there was no wheat. The 1888 crop was terrible, and granaries throughout the Midwest were empty. At last, the Big Four realized the fix they were in. They had sold Hutchinson vast quantities of Sep wheat, and now he owned nearly all of it—cash and wind alike. The only way they could fill their contracts to Hutchinson was to first buy the wheat from the man himself, at any price he set. They were cornered.[24]

This was an unusual situation and probably not anticipated by anybody, including Hutchinson. In Chicago in 1888, inner-ring insiders took greater pains to avoid conflicts with one another than they had in New York in 1866 and to settle any difficulties privately. It wasn't professional courtesy but a recognition that nothing would be gained by fighting among themselves. As in the Hancock & Harriman case, lawsuits accomplished little. All litigants could—and did—bribe judges and hire first-rate lawyers. And in 1888, the Board of Trade and the surrounding curb market were big enough that elite members could avoid collisions. They could not and did not try to deceive one another and exchanged comparatively minor sums of money in routine trading. Like professional gamblers, ordinary business was to target the weaker players, outer-ring insiders and stags. Those groups played a different game; they tried to pick the right tip and discern which rumor was true. Usually, of course, they picked wrong. Corners were so common on the Board of Trade then that only the grandest attempts—such as Harper's—received much notice in the news. The heaviest losers were the transient players, and nobody cared about them. Outer-ring insiders usually only lasted two or three years on the exchange, except for the few who became inner-ring insiders. The rest quietly moved on, poorer than before.

This time was different: Hutchinson had deviated from the usual arrangement. A fundamental rule of survival for any elite is for its members to avoid attacking one another. Why Hutchinson crossed the Big Four is unknown, but he may not have realized how much of his profit would come out of their pockets. As in New York in 1866, inner-ring insiders hid their real trading strategies. By 1888, the transatlantic telegraph made even more elaborate concealment possible. A common strategy was to telegraph orders first to brokers in Liverpool, who then passed them to correspondent brokers in New York. The New Yorkers would then send the orders to Chicago, where they had originated, for execution. In August and September 1888, the Big Four may have covered their tracks too well.[25]

To be cornered would be bad news for anybody but especially so for the Big Four. As the dominant clique on the exchange, financial wizards, nobody bested them—nobody. A public beating from a scalper, for God's sake, would humiliate them in the eyes of everybody. Money wasn't the issue; the Big Four could easily pay off Hutchinson. The real cost would be to the clique's reputation. Their wealthy backers in New York and England might rethink their investment strategies, even move their money over to Hutchinson.

The clique's next move, in mid-September, was to apply social pressure with a smear campaign against Hutchinson. As such cliques do, the Big Four had a sizable collection of allies, admirers, and hangers-on. This was the faction that made the most noise, and they told everyone that Hutchinson was an evil, flinty-hearted old man who would mercilessly bankrupt everyone. In normal times, Hutchinson was reasonably well liked, if cautiously so; over the years, he had quietly helped many members out of financial scrapes. But whatever other members thought, they kept it to themselves. Publicly, at least, Hutchinson became the most reviled man on the exchange.[26]

The point of all this was to browbeat Hutchinson into selling his wheat. Character assassination was well outside the bounds of what counted as fair play on the exchange and shows how seriously the Big Four took the threat Hutchinson posed. The tactic was seldom used, but there had been times when a corner operator had given up and sold out, rather than face the collective fury of the members. Outsiders' opinions didn't matter, but reputation within the crowd was all-important, ethically challenged though they all were. A man who went too far could find himself shut out of the business. But once again the Big Four failed. Hutchinson gave no public sign that he so much as noticed, and he continued to strengthen and consolidate his position.[27]

At this point, the Big Four decided to floor Hutchinson—that is, drive him off the exchange. They would launch the mother of all bear raids and scare everyone that another Harper disaster was about to happen. Fifteen months earlier, the Big Four and their allies had shipped so much cash wheat to Chicago that Harper's clique couldn't buy it all. The oversupply sent cash wheat from $92\frac{1}{8}$ to 73 in twenty-four hours, taking down not only Harper's gang but much of the crowd. Memories of that debacle were all too fresh, and fear of a similar crisis would provoke panic selling. Then, the price would indeed crash, as would the value of Hutchinson's holdings. They would crush him.[28]

The show would focus on Dec wheat, wheat to be delivered at the end of December. The market for Sep wheat was nearly dead, since Hutchinson owned it all. The success of the scheme would depend on the banks; in Chicago as in New York, most speculation ran on borrowed money. To trade on margin, a speculator would borrow money to buy some financial asset: stocks, bonds, or contracts to receive wheat. The asset purchased served as collateral for the loan. If the value of the asset rose, the speculator would sell it, repay the loan, and keep the profit. If the value dropped, the lender would ask the investor for a payment, called a "margin payment," to keep the loan and the collateral roughly equal in value. If the speculator failed to make the margin payment, the lender would force the sale of the collateral to collect the loan.

The Big Four knew that Hutchinson held contracts for large quantities of Dec wheat, as well as Sep wheat. The more the price of Dec wheat fell, the higher the margin calls on Hutchinson would be and at some point would exceed his ability to pay. The banks then would force the sale of his wheat—Sep wheat included—to collect their loans. Then the bluff would become reality; millions of bushels of wheat would flood the market. The price would drop further still. Then, the Big Four and their friends could buy the wheat and close out their September contracts with great profit. They could do even better: they could buy more wheat, at these fire-sale prices, both cash wheat and for delivery in later months; then they could sell out when the market recovered and make yet more money. In Chicago in 1888, to make money on both sides of a transaction like this was called "pressing the deal." The Big Four could dispose of a troublesome rival, burnish their reputation for market invincibility, and profit all at once.[29]

On Wednesday, September 26, four days before the September contract deadline, Hutchinson met with a group of September shorts and advised them to settle their contracts with him. They should do so, he said, because tomorrow he would raise the price. Sep wheat closed that day at 104, a two-cent advance over the previous day. The Wednesday price, a six-year high for number-two wheat on that day, was itself proof of the price rise that Hutchinson had predicted. The day he had returned to the exchange, August 13, Sep wheat had closed at 82. About twenty shorts took the deal at the price Hutchinson offered, 105. Then they immediately had to resell the wheat to him at the much lower price in their contracts. The *Chicago Times* estimated that between three and four million bushels settled, at an average loss of ten to twelve cents per bushel to the shorts. If the *Times* was correct, Hutchinson's profit was between $300,000 and $500,000, equivalent to between $9.5 million and $15.9 million in 2022. The shorts may not have thought so, but Hutchinson had treated them generously. He had his own informants, and he knew what the Big Four intended. His quarrel was with them, not with the crowd. The newspapers reported that the Big Four had settled on Wednesday. But they had not, nor had the larger group of bear speculators who followed them.[30]

Instead, the Big Four were busy with their plans to floor Hutchinson the following day, Thursday. With many other preparations, they would bring all the real wheat they could find to Chicago and dump it on the market. By late Wednesday, they had arranged with St. Louis brokers to ship a hundred thousand bushels of wheat to Chicago. St. Louis was the largest nearby market, but the bears also had their brokers search in the smaller cities and towns. It wouldn't be enough wheat to make a real difference, and it wouldn't arrive by Thursday. But that was all right. News of the shipments would give substance to the rumor of vast quantities of wheat coming to Chicago. Tomorrow's fight would be about appearances.[31]

Next, the Big Four telegraphed their friends in New York, Liverpool, and London to ask them to stage bear raids of their own. The Big Four also sent market advisories to their contacts in distant cities. September contracts had all settled, they said. This was a patent lie; they themselves and scores of other members were short millions of bushels. The Big Four also reported that everyone in Chicago expected a sharp price break tomorrow, because December wheat was too high and a reaction was due. In Chicago, they sent their brokers and clerks to prowl through the offices, saloons, and other places the market crowd gathered. Something big would happen on Thursday, the bear agents confided. Hutchinson had overextended himself and was broke. The banks were calling their loans and would force him to sell out. He would dump millions of bushels of wheat on the market, and the price would crash.[32]

To finish their day's work, the bears sent a broker to the curb exchange on Wednesday evening. The curb exchange was an informal group that met outside the Board of Trade building to buy and sell small quantities of wheat, corn, and pork. It was an unofficial, nickel-and-dime game; unlike the securities markets, agricultural futures mainly traded on-exchange. Still, the crowd viewed after-hours curb prices as a leading indicator of what would happen the following day. On Wednesday evening, the broker waited quietly with the curb traders until the group gradually dispersed. Then he walked around the empty street, loudly offering a hundred thousand bushels of Dec wheat at 97, three-quarters of a cent under the Board of Trade's official closing price earlier that day. This was more "proof" that wheat prices were falling. The more convinced everyone was of this, the more likely it would happen.[33]

On Thursday, September 27, the bears set about fulfilling their prophesied drop in the price of Dec wheat. Everything was ready. Their friends in New York and England had obliged with cables full of dire news from their home markets. Before the opening bell rang, everyone in the wheat pit expected a major price decline. The bulls were gloomy; the bears were in fine fettle and counting their money already. The Big Four and their allies could outspend Hutchinson many times over, and they had used every resource at their command—real and psychological— against him. Hutchinson was on the floor too and had been for hours. Now, he sat in his chair facing the wheat pit and waited for the open, calm and poker-faced. He had heard the bears' rumors that he was broke and would unload his wheat; he had heard, as well, every scrap of gossip and foul name the bears' agents had circulated about him. His counter-move was a show of complete unconcern.[34]

When Board of Trade Secretary George F. Stone rang the opening bell at 9:30 a.m., the Big Four and their friends had their brokers standing ready in the wheat pit. These were young men, junior partners and employees of their various firms. They did the physical work of elbowing, shoving, and shouting while their bosses watched. The brokers tag-teamed, buying and selling hundreds of thousands of bushels of Dec wheat at progressively lower prices. But this raid, like the others, quickly went awry. Other than the bears' own brokers, few members bought; instead, they waited for the price to drop further. Dec wheat had opened at 97⅛, five-eighths below Wednesday's official close. In the first half hour, Dec dropped below 97 and continued to fall. But the price decline was too slow. For a panic, such as the Big Four wanted, they needed a sudden, sharp break.[35]

Also, the crowd in the pit had not forgotten about Sep wheat, as the bears had hoped. The idea had been to divert attention from Sep wheat long enough to break Hutchinson with Dec wheat. But Sep wheat had gone rogue. While Dec fell slowly, Sep was rising fast. Sep had closed Wednesday at 104; this morning a few early trades carried the price to 107½. A gain that large was alarming; the trading session had just begun. Hutchinson had no part in it, either. The pirates stood silently in the pit, their hands at their sides. The push was coming from the smaller operators who were short Sep wheat. They were increasingly anxious to cover their positions, and they were bidding against one another. The tension was rising but not over Dec wheat.[36]

Then suddenly the game changed. The bears' brokers had been offering Dec wheat for sale in hundred-thousand-bushel lots and getting few takers. Then at 10 a.m., the price fell to 96⅝ and hung there. Hutchinson waited a beat and then signaled the pirates from his chair. Their hands shot up, and they started taking the bids. Too late, the bears realized that the banks would make no margin calls on Hutchinson, because they hadn't loaned him anything. *He had bought the wheat with his own money.* It was a critical error. The margin-call strategy would have worked perfectly if, as the bears had assumed, Hutchinson had bought the wheat on margin. But the bears knew Hutchinson as a scalper, and they had underestimated him. Worst of all, he clearly still had cash reserves.

The bears conferred agitatedly about what to do. There was a brief confusion while the pirates wrote on their trading cards. The bears' brokers looked to their leaders for direction but got none; the offers dwindled down, and the pit went almost silent. For a moment, the market stopped.[37] Then suddenly the bears lost the initiative. The pirate Sandy Eggleston raised his hand and shouted, "Buy Sep at eleven!" No one took his bid, but it was a shock and a wakeup call. Prices usually moved by eighths, quarters, and halves, but Eggleston had just raised the bid three and a half cents. The bidding started again, and the whole market began to turn. Dec began to rise too, undoing the bears' hard work. Over the next half hour, Sep and Dec wheat first rose slowly and then faster and faster, and the noise level increased. The crowd was starting to panic but not like the bears wanted. The crowd was pushing the price up, not down.[38]

Hutchinson, meanwhile, remained seated by the pillar at the foot of the gallery stairs. He looked as calm as he had when the bears were pounding the market and trying to force him out at eighty cents a bushel. As usual, a group stood around him, and a favorite pirate, Johnny Brine, waited nearby to take orders. The more excited the crowd in the pit became, the more Hutchinson relaxed. Until now, he had remained largely silent, but now he began to talk. And talk. "—Well, as I was saying, you may have your views on religion, but I'll stick to mine. These Baptists and Presbyterians are all right. But you see, I've read Tom Payne a good deal myself.—Well, if he was an infidel, he had some brains. He wouldn't have come on 'change this morning and sold wheat that he didn't have to deliver.—I got the utmost respect for religion.—It's a damned lie if anyone says he had a million bushels in store. The crops are bad, very bad—that is, the crop of wheat. There's a big crop of suckers and the harvest is just beginning."[39] He went on like this for a good half hour, while the racket in the wheat pit steadily increased. The crowd around Hutchinson grew. Men strained to hear what he said over the noise, hoping to catch a hint of his plans. Now and then some anxious short approached, hoping to buy Sep wheat. Hutchinson heard each of them out and nodded if the bid suited him. If not, he shook his head and resumed his monologue. Bargaining was useless; anyone who tried wound up paying more. "What's the market?" Hutchinson asked one nervous short who had approached him. "It was 110 when I left the pit," said the short. "Well, it'll be 115 before you can get back." Just then the pirate Ed Ryder shouted above the roar in the pit, "Buy Sep at fifteen!"[40]

With that, Hutchinson got up and left the floor, crossing the pedestrian bridge to the Rialto Building and the Century Club. There, he tossed down a couple of glasses of the vile club whiskey—Jersey lightning and fuel oil, according to one journalist. Hutchinson stocked the bar, and he was cheap in certain ways. Using a telescope, he peered through the windows of the brokers' offices in the Board of Trade building, across Van Buren Street from the Century Club. Then he returned to the floor.[41]

By then, the wheat pit was like an oven, packed with agitated, perspiring men shouting bids at one another. Dec wheat held for a bit at 99, but Sep wheat kept rising. The shorts bid wildly against one another, but no one was selling. Clearly there were more shorts, and more open contracts, than anyone had thought. Sep wheat went to 116, dropped back, and then moved to 118. The market had entered uncharted territory. On the wall, the exchange's up-to-date electric sign, the wheat dial, showed the most recent price. The marker hand went round and round, and at every advance, the crowd yelled. Traders shouted themselves hoarse. From 118, September wheat suddenly jumped four cents to 122. Everyone wanted to buy; no one wanted to sell.[42]

At noon, everything happened at once. The panic in Sep wheat spread to Dec, and from 99, Dec jumped a full cent. Then, at twelve sharp, Sandy Eggleston bid 125 for September, and seconds later, every wheat contract—September through December and May—stood at a dollar or more. A great whoop went up from the pit, rattling the inspirational stained-glass windows eighty-five feet up. The wheat dial showed everyone in the room what had happened. Everyone yelled: the shorts howled, the longs cheered. The lucky ones embraced and shook hands; they flung their hats and trading cards into the air. Men ran shouting through the corridors of the building. A crowd of hatless, coatless men and boys poured out the doors into Jackson and LaSalle Streets, yelling, "Wheat's a dollar!" People blocks away heard them.[43]

Hutchinson remained in his chair, impassively watching the explosion on the floor. Still the Sep price rose: one lot of five thousand bushels sold at 128. The shorts could stand it no longer. They swarmed out of the pit and surrounded Hutchinson, begging him to sell. Hutchinson looked them up and down for a moment and then turned to Johnny Brine. The crowd quieted instantly. "Sell them all they want, Johnny, at one twenty-five," he said. Hearing that, the group pushed and scrambled over to Brine and began shouting their orders at him. For the next twenty minutes, Brine scribbled furiously on his trading cards, eventually selling 350,000 bushels in 5,000-, 10,000-, and 25,000-bushel lots. Hutchinson watched a while and then yawned and stretched. He signaled to Brine, and the crowd went silent immediately. "Johnny, I've got to go over to the club," he said. "Sell all they will take at one twenty-five; buy all they will sell at one twenty-four."[44]

With that, he stood and pushed through the crowd around the wheat pit. The rest of the floor was semideserted; many corn and provisions traders had left their pits to watch the wheat spectacle. At the Century Club, Hutchinson drank more whiskey and spied on the brokers' offices with his telescope. He returned to the floor at 12:30, with forty-five minutes left in the session. As he entered, a messenger handed him a telegram from a Duluth grain broker, one of Hutchinson's regular correspondents. It was good news. The elevators in Duluth were empty and could send the bears no wheat.[45]

Back in his chair, the author of this mayhem surveyed the total rout of his enemies, who that morning had expected to drive him off the exchange. His face flushed with the Century Club's whiskey, Hutchinson spent the last half hour of the session quoting romantic poetry. He recited lengthy passages from authors on all sorts of topics. He had much to say about religion; he had been raised Universalist and delighted in exposing the fallacies of Unitarianism. Nowadays he was an agnostic, he said, but he still had opinions on theology. "Let the boys settle up their deals, and all futures will take care of themselves." And so on. Religion somehow intertwined with the wheat crop. "You see, the farmers have not been getting enough for their wheat of late years and I have really felt sorry for them. I have said for months I thought they ought to have better returns for their work, and now most of the men on the Board of Trade are getting into my turn of thinking. . . . That Golden Rule is getting in its work and the boys are doing more for the farmer that all the laws Congress can pass."[46]

The trading day was winding down, but the market was roaring. The shorts who had settled at 125 straggled off the floor dazed, unsure whether they had suffered a catastrophe or narrowly escaped one. Some had no doubt. One short who settled twenty thousand bushels at 125 had lost thirty-five cents a bushel—$7,000 on an investment of $18,000. Those who remained around the wheat pit were breaking into different groups. Men long on wheat raised toasts with hip flasks. There was no further doubt about Sep wheat; the price was whatever Hutchinson said it was. Occasionally he "predicted" that wheat would be two dollars by Saturday, adding that tomorrow, Friday, he would sell wheat for 150. Anyone who bought wheat today should be happy, he said, since they were getting off easily.[47]

No one worried now about another Harper fiasco. The crowd now feared other disasters or a whole string of them. Beyond the immediate plight of the September shorts—stuck with contracts to deliver millions of bushels of wheat—there was Hutchinson's next move to think about. He could easily corner wheat in the succeeding months, since he already owned nearly three-quarters of the cash wheat in Chicago. All he had to do was to hang onto it. This was not some hysterical fancy. That day, Hutchinson had been the largest single buyer of wheat contracts for more extended delivery, October through May. Worried that Hutchinson would corner October next, shorts in that month scrambled to close out their positions. The bidding pushed up the October price, which in turn pulled up December.[48]

At 1:15 p.m., Secretary Stone rang the bell to end the session. Sep wheat closed at 125, having ranged twenty-four cents during the day. The advance was the largest one-day increase in the wheat price in the Board's history, though the next two days would break the record twice more. The price had not been this high since the Civil War. Overall, the price for Sep wheat had increased more than 30 percent since Monday's open, four trading days earlier. The price increases in other contracts were nearly as large. When the session started, nearly everyone except Hutchinson and the pirates thought prices would fall.[49]

After the close, many members stayed on the floor talking, desperate for information. No one wanted to believe what Hutchinson had said, that tomorrow he would sell for 150 and on Saturday for two dollars. If he did, there would be mass bankruptcies on the exchange. The *Chicago Tribune* reported that a million bushels remained unsettled; the *Milwaukee Sentinel* reported three million. But no one knew who held these contracts. Many believed that most Chicago shorts had settled already, and those who remained were New Yorkers and English, friends of the Big Four. The Chicago brokers for these clients were all at grave risk. Late in the day, a prominent New York speculator wired a Chicago crony to ask if the bears had floored Hutchinson yet. The Chicagoan replied, "Hutch has bought all the cash wheat in Chicago and paid for it with his own money. He is lending the bears money to margin their trades with him for all the wheat they can sell him for future delivery, knowing that by no possibility can they get the wheat to deliver. If you think you can make Old Hutch let go his grip under such circumstances before he gets ready, try it." The New Yorker's reply is not recorded.[50]

The bears were confounded: they had lost control of the market. They still had fight, though, and some followers. The more credulous of these believed that special trains laden with wheat were speeding to Chicago to save the day. Others pointed to an Illinois law against market corners in the necessities of life. But better-informed members knew the law was vague and for the fourteen years since its passage had been unenforceable. Hutchinson knew the law too and had been careful to keep the pretense of a free market. He was now more entrenched than ever because his cash position was stronger. Before today, he had most of his liquid capital tied up in cash wheat or in futures contracts. But by the Thursday close, the trapped shorts had bought over half a million bushels of wheat from Hutchinson at 125. Then, they had to sell it back to him for whatever they had contracted, between 85 and 97. Hutchinson cleared $675,000 in cash that day, about $200,000 in profit—equivalent to $6.3 million in 2022. It made a fine payday, and others like it were coming.[51]

This, then, was the situation that led up to the Friday morning crowd at Jackson and LaSalle Streets and newspaper stories all over the country. It would be a long night for many people. For hours after the close, anxious groups of men loitered outside the LaSalle Street entrance to rehash the day's events. Every conversation revolved around Hutchinson. After dark, the neighborhood presented an unusual sight, with office buildings lit from top to bottom. Even casual observers sensed that something was wrong. Inside, men worked over their books until long after midnight.[52]

Now that readers have seen the crowd at work in two different settings, some of the group's defining features can be pointed out. Both the 1866 and 1888 groups are indifferent, at best, to the welfare of outsiders, and members routinely do business in ways most people would consider unethical. In both 1866 and 1888, powerful competing cliques dominate the scene. These similarities, and others that will be pointed out later, are noteworthy, given the differences between the two cases in time, space, and type of market.[53]

That modern-day workers in geographically distant financial centers behave in similar ways is not surprising. The markets are electronically linked twenty-four hours a day, and the big international banks routinely transfer their personnel around different foreign locations. But for most of the history of finance, geographically separated marketplaces had little contact with one another. Financial centers in countries with strong political or economic ties, such as Britain and the U.S., did some business with one another, and new exchanges cribbed rules from older, more settled institutions. Terminology spread through the financial pages of newspapers.[54] But the real breakthrough came with electronic telecommunications: commercial telegraphy in the 1830s and the transatlantic (telegraph) cable in 1867. From that time on, connections among geographically separate financial markets have grown progressively tighter.

But the similarity of the 1888 CBOT crowd to its Wall Street counterpart twenty-two years before suggests that something more is going on. The Board of Trade was an institution of a new type, the world's first derivatives exchange. In its early years, members had to figure out the business and invent the rules for it as they went. In 1888, CBOT had almost no contact with securities markets in New York or anywhere else, nor any reason for contact. Few members had any prior financial experience (Norman Ream worked briefly as a livestock broker). For an identical evolution to occur in different locations and circumstances suggests an emergent process at work.[55]

Emergence, the self-organization of individual actors into more complex forms, is an old concept in Western thought. Aristotle, writing in the fourth century B.C.E., noted the phenomenon in *The Metaphysics*. Ants self-organize into anthills, and bees make beehives without any conscious thought as humans understand it. The role of emergence in the capitalist market has been a topic of study since the late eighteenth century. Adam Smith's invisible hand is a famous instance of this spontaneous order, as it is now called. The most influential modern work on the topic is by F. A. von Hayek, corecipient of the 1974 Nobel Prize in economics. And so with the market crowd: without conscious intent, two groups in different locations that had no contact with each other self-organized in the same way. Each of the two groups made up a *standing* crowd rather than a transitory one, such as attendees at sporting events or people caught in a rush-hour scrum. Transitory crowds form, dissolve, and reform differently every time. Standing-crowd members take up the same positions relative to one another day after day.[56]

Before the end of September 1888, Hutchinson was almost unknown outside Chicago. He preferred anonymity, possibly to avoid encounters such as he had with Benjamin Butler. As he rose to prominence, would-be interviewers sometimes approached him, with little success. He refused most such requests, often with a barrage of profanity. Now he was under a media spotlight, and newspapers published whatever they could find on him, including stories years old.

One such story was from before the Great Chicago Fire in 1871, when neither Hutchinson nor the Board of Trade yet amounted to much. Hutchinson, then in his early forties, was walking one day down State Street with a friend named Boggs. Chicago was growing explosively then, and the city was one big construction site. The two came to a loose cobblestone that partly blocked their way. Hutchinson kicked the stone aside and jokingly suggested that he and Boggs bet on its weight. Boggs agreed, and they wagered ten dollars, no mean sum then. They weighed the stone in the scale of a nearby grocer, and Hutchinson won. Boggs paid up and forgot the matter. Sometime later, at a chance meeting in a saloon, Hutchinson handed Boggs a ten-dollar bill. He reminded Boggs of the wager and confessed he had weighed the stone earlier. Then Hutchinson had placed the stone where they would pass it and so had won the bet. As Boggs told the story, they both laughed, and Boggs broke the ten dollars over the bar buying drinks for himself, Hutchinson, and the rest of the saloon crowd. One might wonder about a man who would deceive a friend in this way. But such a stunt would have been commonplace on the Board of Trade, where members routinely set complicated traps for one another. Boggs was not a member, and Hutchinson may have returned the money because he regretted taking advantage of a naïf. Boggs made light of the incident, but he never forgot it, either. He might have been less forgiving if Hutchinson had kept quiet and Boggs had discovered the ruse himself.[57]

This was the sort of thing newspaper readers were now learning about the man who controlled the wheat price in the world's largest grain market. Hutchinson was now a public figure and would remain so for the rest of his life. Readers of the *New York Times* knew who he was, as did readers of the *Bismarck (Dakota Territory) Weekly Tribune*. For the most part, the Chicago papers treated Hutchinson like a favorite son, a hometown hero, possibly raising suspicions elsewhere about the character of Chicagoans. (Coverage of the Big Four was markedly less sympathetic.) The socialists applauded Hutchinson, because in September 1888, it looked as if he would single-handedly incinerate the Board of Trade and everyone in it. Some midwestern newspapers recalled that the

Big Four and their friends had depressed grain prices for years, at great cost to farmers. Regardless of Hutchinson's motives, these editors argued, his corner benefited producers. But most of the media coverage was unflattering. The *New York Graphic* portrayed him as a monstrous spirit that stole bread from poor families. In 1892, during congressional hearings on "fictitious dealings in agricultural products," Hutchinson was named repeatedly as a notorious offender. Nationwide, the majority attitude toward Hutchinson and his place of business was succinctly expressed by one irate critic, who damned the Board of Trade as "that hell-hole ruled by 'Old Hutch.' "[58]

Friday at 9:30 a.m., when Secretary Stone rang the bell, everyone in the vast room—members, clerks, visitors, and journalists—watched the wheat pit. But the opening was subdued. There were scattered trades in the more extended contracts but none in Sep wheat, the great issue of the day. The shorts were afraid to touch it. Then, shortly after 10 a.m., the pirate Abe Poole raised his hand and yelled, "Buy Sep at twenty-five!" This was no more than Thursday's official closing price, but the shorts howled with despair. No one took the bid. Poole bid 130, 135, and 137½ with no better luck. Then Billy McHenry, a fellow pirate, bid 140 and got ten thousand bushels. The Sep wheat price was now 140, up fifteen cents—12 percent— on a single trade thirty minutes into the session.[59]

Still, the shorts held back, refusing to aid in their own destruction. But it was no use. After a brief standoff, Hutchinson ordered the pirates to buy and sell his own wheat in wash sales. In 1888, wash sales were legal, and Hutchinson used them now to avoid violating the state's anticorner law. The official record would show that the market, not Hutchinson, had set the price, even though everyone on the floor knew otherwise. By 11:30, the pirates had raised Sep wheat to 150, the price Hutchinson had "predicted" on Thursday. The crowd jeered; the "free market" was a fraud.[60]

Then Hutchinson briefly let his control slip. While the crowd was still hooting at the 150 price, a broker jokingly offered Hutchinson 175 for Sep wheat. Hutchinson looked at him silently for a moment and then replied, "Clear in the cool September morn." He turned to Johnny Brine, who stood beside him. "That's Whittier, Johnny—'Barbara Frietchie.' Whittier had the 'meadows rich with corn.' He didn't say anything about wheat, Johnny. But wheat's lookin' pretty rich on this September morn, Johnny."[61] He gassed on like this to Brine for some minutes, during which several of the shorts in the pit forgot their earlier resolve and started bidding on Sep wheat. The price started rising fast, to the consternation of the pirates; Hutchinson had not told them what to do if the price passed 150. When Hutchinson next looked at the wheat dial, Sep wheat was 180 and still rising. Hutchinson grabbed Brine and shoved him toward the pit, saying, "Now you run over, and don't you let 'em pay a damned cent more than fifty for wheat. You see, those eight carloads I bought for forty-nine and a half fix it up for those fellers that want to squeal. I ain't a'goin' to pay no more than that, Johnny, so don't you let 'em pay no more." Translated, Hutchinson told Brine that he bought cash (actual) wheat to keep it from the shorts and that he wanted the price held at 150. "Those fellers that want to squeal" were shorts who would try to renege on their contracts. Brine charged into the pit, yelling, "Sell thirty thousand Sep at fifty!" meanwhile signaling to Abe Poole. Poole took Brine's bid, and between them, they reset Sep wheat to 150 from 180, a price drop of 17 percent in a single transaction. Seeing this charade, the crowd began to jeer again. "Give the gentleman your watch, Abe!" someone yelled. Everyone laughed except Poole and Brine.[62]

This pas de deux killed the September trade for the rest of the day. Everyone knew that Hutchinson had his price and wouldn't move from it. Trade continued in the extended contracts, October through May, but the crowd was spooked. Whenever a price looked shaky, traders stampeded to sell; a minute later, they tried to buy when nothing was for sale. The September contract would expire in little more than twenty-four hours, and everyone, in his own way, imagined the worst. Some feared Hutchinson might corner wheat in the succeeding months. If so, the smart move was to buy. Alternatively, after September closed, Hutchinson might sell his millions of bushels of cash wheat and crash the price. If so, anyone holding wheat should sell immediately, take any loss now, rather than wait. And anyone not holding wheat should short it. Hutchinson would corner or he would unload, and the price would skyrocket or crash. The wrong guess would be ruinous.[63]

The man himself remained mostly idle today, again with a show of imperturbable calm. The pirates knew what to do, and the bears were powerless. Shadowed by Johnny Brine, Hutchinson occasionally got up and prowled around the floor. He went to the Century Club several times for whiskey and espionage. He returned each time murmuring, "Clear in the cool September morn," and in a whisper asked Brine what was happening. Whenever he spoke, members for twenty feet around went quiet and strained to hear him. Veteran traders who had known him for decades stared at him as if seeing him for the first time. Spectators leaned over the gallery railings and craned their necks to see him. He had clearly stated his plans for Friday and Saturday but said nothing about what he would do afterward.[64]

He had much to say on other topics, though, including the state of the wheat market. "They accuse me of running a corner," he said in the early afternoon.

> Some parties who have sold [wheat] to me for delivery this month, and who can't turn over the goods, say they won't settle at one-fifty. . . . Others had the same privilege of buying September wheat that I had. It was free to everybody, and if they did not avail themselves of the opportunity it is not my fault. I bought the wheat, paid my money for it, and I know of no law compelling me to sell it until I get ready and at such a price that suits me. The same opportunity will exist to make money in December and other options that has been in September. I am buying futures because I believe they are very cheap. Others can do as I am doing if they like. But by and by, when every option traded in on the floor has crossed one-fifty, it will not be said that the price has been put up by me or any speculative ring. It will go up on a natural demand.[65]

As printed, Hutchinson's remarks were probably extensively redacted. Despite his intelligence and wide reading, Hutchinson's speech was by all accounts rambling, vulgar, and ungrammatical and so laced with exchange jargon and profanity as to be both unintelligible and unprintable. "That feller Shakespeare—there's more'n a hundred thousand short in that chap," he once remarked cryptically, though he could quote Shakespeare by the yard. He may have spoken as he did so people would underestimate him. But if the editor retained Hutchinson's meaning, he made a reasonable argument. He had based his trades on publicly available information, and the shorts had chosen a different strategy, namely, to follow the big bears. If they lost, that was a risk they had willingly accepted. Without saying so directly, Hutchinson made an argument for a free market. The market *was* free, too—more so than it is today. The exchange rule book was thin in 1888, and government oversight of secondary markets was still decades off. But on the Board of Trade that day, few members wanted a free market, not like this. Instead, they wanted a *fair* market, meaning fair for themselves. No one in the market crowd expressed any concern about a fair market for the public.[66]

For Hutchinson, the situation was fraught with irony. He had violated no law or exchange rule, of his day or of our own, except for the wash sales. Despite his shady history, he met a higher standard of marketplace ethics than his enemies did. Unlike the Big Four, on this occasion Hutchinson had not deceived anyone. On the contrary, the shorts were counting on the Big Four to pull off a successful deception and push down the price of Sep wheat. If Hutchinson had been less resourceful, the Big Four would have taken his money and run him off the exchange, and no one would have stopped them. Regardless of his character, it is hard to fault Hutchinson for fighting back.

Few trades were made that day, and those only in the extended contracts. The market was toxic. Corn and provisions traders abandoned their pits and came to watch the wheat melodrama. A certain jocularity prevailed among the idle members and clerks. One wag suggested charging spectators for admission and using the money to help indigent shorts. Another offered to sell a kernel of wheat for fifty cents and throw in a portrait of Hutchinson. His profits, he claimed, would easily cover his market losses. One member suggested that Hutchinson hire himself out as a freak at Kohl & Middleton's Dime Museum. The light mood spread to the New York Produce Exchange, where Hutchinson's corner was the talk of the day. The New York traders largely suspended business and stood around waiting for telegrams of news from Chicago, often responding with flippant telegrams of their own. One prominent broker, Henry Clews, wired, "Ask 'Hutch' what he will charge me for enough cash wheat for tomorrow's breakfast. Put it on the ground of a personal matter." The Chicago reply read, "Can't get enough for breakfast at any price."[67]

It was a disappointing time for the visitors, who had come hoping for blood sport. (That would come tomorrow.) The exchange floor, normally a charged, electric place, today was unusually quiet. The big bears and their allies stood back and watched with suppressed fury, while their brokers stood idle. Other members lounged about. Boos, catcalls, and bursts of raucous laughter alternated with periods of near silence. Normally the exchange was a kind of theater where inner-ring insiders and their brokers and hangers-on performed for the crowd. Today, though, Hutchinson controlled the market, and everyone knew it. No gallery play would change that.[68]

Hutchinson, however, put on a show of his own in the early afternoon. After a long period of near stasis, the shorts were at the end of
their endurance. At first a few and then increasing numbers of them left
the pit to beg Hutchinson for easier terms. They lined up in front of
him, each one waiting for a brief audience. *And Hutchinson let them all off.*
He either scratched their trades outright or else let them settle at a lower
price. No one on the floor had ever seen the like. Successful corner operators or cliques invariably squeezed the last dollar from their victims. But
not this time.[69]

This was a performance indeed, though not the usual sort; Hutchinson
was sending a clear message rather than a deceptive one. As when he fixed
the price of Sep wheat at 150, he was showing that he alone controlled the
market. The money he allowed the shorts to keep was the price he paid to
make a statement about turf, reputation, power, and payback. Any street-
corner gangster would have understood the stakes. The gesture raised his
standing, too. Remarkably, in a market that the Big Four and their allies manipulated unceasingly, they had convinced many people that Hutchinson
had taken unfair advantage. The Big Four had done their utmost to turn the
members against Hutchinson, and Hutchinson's show of leniency was his
answer. A reporter asked him what he was doing, and he replied, "I want the
boys to see what I can do for them."[70]

This play and counterplay—the Big Four's smear campaign and
Hutchinson's generosity—shows an important feature of insider thinking
that did not figure in the 1866 case. Here, both Hutchinson and the Big
Four weaponized their social capital, backed by their money, in the corner fight. In the closed-off world of an exchange, acceptance—at least—
by the group was essential to do business at all. Modern terms sometimes
used for etiquette at CBOT and the Merc were "floor rules" and "pit discipline." Nearly a century after the events recounted here, I was present
on one side of a furious and obscene telephone argument over a disputed
trade. The call ended when Roger, the fed funds trader, drop-kicked the
phone with such force that it snapped back on its cord and almost hit his
trading assistant. *"Take him off my list!"* Roger yelled, with much impolite
language. Too many run-ins like that and you're off everybody's list.[71]

Hutchinson was not granting a general amnesty, however. The Big
Four and their friends did not line up in front of him; they knew
Hutchinson would never scratch their trades. He wanted their blood—
their money—for attacking him. But he would humiliate them as well.
Friday was even worse than Thursday. The corner was the talk of Chi-

cago, where the Big Four lived and worked. In the days following, newspaper readers throughout the country would learn of their defeat. So too
would the wealthy New York and English investors who banked on their
supposed expertise. On the floor, the clique still had followers, whose
loyalty had profited them until now. Several now stood before Hutchinson and shook their fists at him, shouting, "Robber!" and "Highway-
man!" and the like. One yelled, "You damned old hog!" This last taunt
got to him. "Damned old hog, hey?" Hutchinson shot back. "Well, I
guess wheat's worth ten cents a bushel more for that." But such demon-
strations gave the bear high command little comfort. They could fume
and threaten all they wanted, but nothing would change.[72]

The men who taunted Hutchinson were not ordinary shorts. If they
had been, they would have joined the others to ask him for clemency.
Hutchinson had made it clear that he was only gunning for the Big Four.
The men who baited him were allies of the clique, and their behavior is
an example of insider clout at work. The network of market crowd members exists to traffic in money, but the money moves according to information. Inner-ring insiders are the best connected of all market actors
and learn new information first. They can use their information advantage to profit themselves, to help family members and friends, and to
create patronage relationships. A posse of loyal agents scattered throughout the crowd can spy, spread rumors, plant news stories, support gallery
plays, or help in unforeseen ways—such as to harass Hutchinson.

Finally, the bell ended the session, after a day of trench warfare
rather than battle joined. Trading volume in Sep wheat was only 240,000
bushels, while between one and three million bushels remained unsettled. Extended contracts closed slightly off, near the one-dollar mark,
after a desperate bear assault. But Hutchinson had moved Sep wheat up
twenty-five cents a bushel to 150—a 20 percent increase in a single day,
exceeding even Thursday's gain. Few people paid that price, though.
Hutchinson had released many smaller shorts, and the big bears were
still desperately searching for a way out.[73]

Many members stayed on the floor to talk about the day's events, as
they had the day before. The bears had much to say about what they
would and wouldn't do; some of them muttered that Hutchinson would
get himself shot. Others declared they would go to court. The place
swirled with rumors. People said that Hutchinson originally either
owned outright or had contracts for four million bushels of wheat for
September delivery. Also, he supposedly had sold three million bushels to

the trapped shorts by Friday evening, and the defaults thus far totaled eight hundred thousand bushels at 150 a bushel. Others had heard that on Saturday, Hutchinson would sell wheat for 200 until noon and for 250 afterward. Many prominent men were said to be broke.[74]

The bears had two remaining hopes. The first was that the Illinois law on corners would void their contracts with Hutchinson. But over its lifetime, the law had never helped anyone. Second, enough out-of-town wheat might arrive in time to break the corner. The more knowledgeable bears knew there wasn't enough wheat for that, but even a smaller amount, properly handled, might stampede the crowd into panic selling. To wring as much drama as possible from the situation, the bears would dump their wheat on the market all at once on Saturday. By exchange rule, cash wheat could only be sold after 11:30 a.m. in a set location near the wheat pit. That would be the bears' big moment. Again, the bears sent out agents to talk up the vast quantities of wheat that would soon arrive.[75]

And the wheat came. After the Friday close, 125,000 bushels arrived from Saint Paul, Detroit, and St. Louis. This was a negligible amount compared to the millions of bushels still outstanding in open contracts. To disguise how little wheat the bear leaders had, they bribed the railroad freight agents to keep the shipments out of the official record of daily receipts. The wheat would then fail to appear in the Saturday morning report of the total grain supply in the city. But the wheat had to be inspected and graded before it could be sold, and it had to be logged before it could be inspected. Withholding the wheat gave the inspectors too little time to do their work. To keep them working throughout the night, the bears offered bonuses and sent cases of iced champagne to the railroad yards.[76]

Like everyone else on the exchange, Hutchinson knew about the bears' wheat. But he had his own sources of information, and he knew the wheat posed no real threat. After the Friday close, he spoke to a reporter for the *Chicago Tribune*. "It was never my intention to put the price above one-ten," he said.

> But the boys wouldn't settle. There was every reason to believe that wheat was worth at least that price on its merits. The demand for millers now proves it. I warned the boys the prices are going up, but they refused to come in. They let things run along up to the last three days of the month and I still had no idea of

crowding them until I found that they were chartering special trains and secretly bringing in wheat from St. Louis, Milwaukee, and Joliet. That was more than I had bargained for, and when they began emptying the private elevators on me I got tired, then got ready to protect myself. I had given them fair warning at one-oh-five Wednesday and they hadn't come in. So now I concluded to let things take their course.[77]

Saturday morning came, the last trading day of the month and of the September contract. At the end of the trading session, all remaining open contracts for Sep wheat would have to settle at that day's closing price. Defaulters would lose their trading privileges. For professional speculators, the stakes could not be higher. Now, before the session opened, strong winds buffeted the market. The corner had created a gold rush in Chicago's near hinterland, and anyone with wheat to sell, however little, was shipping it to the city. Also, the newspapers reported that many dealers believed that the U.S. crop was too small to support further exports and that a worldwide shortage loomed. Early cables from New York brokers brought large buy orders from abroad. Hutchinson had set in motion forces that were far greater than himself and that were now pushing prices higher.[78]

Chicago's major newspapers all carried front-page stories about the corner, as did many other papers around the country. The *New York Times* called it one of the most complete corners the Board had ever seen. Three thousand miles away, readers of the *Los Angeles Times* saw "Grain Gamblers: 'Old Hutch' Still Booming the Markets in Chicago." For anyone with a connection to wheat, Chicago was the only place that mattered that day. In the morning, the crowd of visitors seeking admission to the exchange was larger than ever. People filled the intersection of Jackson and LaSalle and both streets for a block and more. As soon as the doors opened, the galleries filled and members occupied the trading floor wall to wall. Every member who was in town and able to walk was there, including ones who hadn't come in years.[79]

When the bell sounded at 9:30, Sep wheat started at 160, the curb price from the night before. But there were no September trades at first; the shorts would not bid against one another. After a brief wait, Hutchinson ordered his brokers to move the price with wash sales, which provoked a countermove. Led by Nat Jones of the Big Four, the bears launched a raid on the December contract, with some early success. For the first half hour, there was a spate of selling, as many believed that prices would break after the September contract expired. Hutchinson sold Dec wheat as well. By 10 a.m., half an hour into the session, Sep wheat had advanced only to 165.[80]

Then Hutchinson suddenly changed course and started to buy all the Dec wheat the bears offered, throwing the pit into confusion. Then the whole market swung around. Dec wheat went wild, setting the bears' efforts to naught. Quotes traveled up faster than they ever had for an un-cornered future. Shorts bought everything they could at any price, but bids far outnumbered offers. At times, the market advanced a full cent without fifty thousand bushels changing hands. Brokers with New York correspondents were overwhelmed with buy orders they could not fill. Telegraph messengers pushed frantically through the crush of men, but messages arrived faster than they could be delivered.[81]

For the rest of the day, everything rose. Most speculators on the Board of Trade were bears, and it was a terrible day to be a bear. At 11 a.m., after Sep wheat had remained at 165 for an hour, the pirates raised the price ten cents. This brought a great roar from the pit, and for a moment, everyone paused to see what would happen next with September. But the pirates did nothing further, and attention quickly shifted back to the later months. Prices for these contracts moved up chaotically, while the pirates raised Sep wheat in small, timed increments. At every price increase, the crowd grew louder and more agitated.[82]

The pirates were the only ones in the pit who knew where they stood that day. The tension was killing for other members, many of whom were deeply in debt for margin loans. Hutchinson controlled Sep wheat, and the other contracts were haywire, with prices varying by half a cent in different parts of the pit. At times, prices of the months' different contracts pulled apart and moved independently, which was almost unheard of. The provisions and corn pits might as well not have existed; everyone was jammed into the northeastern corner of the floor around the wheat pit. For the rest of the day, the pit was a frenzied mass of yelling, shoving, perspiring men, packed together so tightly that they could scarcely breathe. Traders shouted until they lost their voices. They flung cards and pencils and hats at would-be sellers to attract attention. The crowd was so dense that men on the upper steps sometimes fell onto the heads of those below. Occasionally a man broke free and ran to a saloon to gulp a glass of whiskey before charging back inside.[83]

The bears' last best chance was the out-of-town wheat, for the past three days the subject of the tallest rumors the bears could invent. The inspectors had cleared the wheat for sale by 11:30 a.m., when the cash market opened. But when the time came, the gallery play fell flat. The receiving houses that held the wheat deserted the bears and refused to throw the wheat on the market all at once, as they had earlier agreed. Instead the dealers released the wheat piecemeal, knowing the price would rise toward the close. Sold thus, the new wheat did not cause the price to even wobble. And Hutchinson was ready for the wheat too. Earlier in the day, he had sent Tom Seymour, a trusted man, to wait with the cash wheat crowd and buy whatever came up for sale. Seymour managed to buy almost everything on offer.[84]

The failure of this last desperate shift further inflamed the rage and sense of injury harbored by the remaining bears. While they had some hope—however faint—that they would escape whole, that anger remained in check. Now they were finished, and they knew it. Throughout the day and with increasing frequency, Big Four loyalists had confronted Hutchinson and shouted abuse at him. Hutchinson managed to remain calm, but he stayed away from his usual seat a good deal. Instead he stalked about the floor, his slouch hat pulled down over his face, his collar turned up, and his fists rammed into his overcoat pockets. Many of these walks took him to the Century Club. During these absences, Johnny Brine saved Hutchinson's chair for him and became the target of the increasingly unruly crowd that surrounded the spot. Brine was well liked, but today he was taunted and pelted with pencils, wadded-up trading cards, and trash. "Johnny, get your gun," someone yelled. "I need some protection, sure," Brine shouted back.[85]

The noon hour came, and Sep wheat still stood at 175. Only an hour and a quarter remained in the session, and everyone knew Hutchinson would raise the price. The crowd around him grew, and the shouting became continuous. At 1 p.m., fifteen minutes before the close, the pirates moved Sep wheat to 180. As loud as the scene already was, a new roar rose from the pit, a short distance from where Hutchinson sat. The mob surrounding him, now hundreds strong, took up the cry. They surged forward and crowded against him. Clerks and runners howled and barked, and some climbed on steps, chairs, and tables to watch. Hutchinson stood and tried to leave but was pushed back. At that, he lost his temper and shouted at those surrounding him and menaced them with his fists. This provoked the crowd further. Finally, several pirates shoved their way through and rescued him. "See, the conquering hero comes!" a bear yelled, as Hutchinson, shaken and half fainting, was dragged to safety.[86]

Many experienced market reporters witnessed the attack on Hutchinson, and all accounts agree the danger to him was real. With a single rash or ill-timed move, he could have been seriously injured or killed. The exchange was a rowdy place, but members usually behaved civilly to one another, according to their lights, despite the seriousness of the game they played. Members went broke all the time, and suicides were not uncommon. But a mob attack on a member, however unpopular, was extraordinary. Only one faction on the exchange was angry enough at Hutchinson to wish him serious harm—the Big Four, their allies and supporters, and their brokers and clerks. The small-fry shorts would not benefit by injuring Hutchinson. They needed him alive and in good temper. The attack was another round in the hardball game played since the Big Four realized they were cornered, and it showed how vicious things could get when inner-ring insider money was at stake. Competition on the floor could be rough indeed, but character assassination, attempting to bankrupt a rival, and mob violence were not everyday business practice. Hutchinson, in his way, had responded no less furiously. Between them, the combatants created such an almighty ruction that it entered exchange folklore.[87]

Meanwhile, the clock was ticking down fast. It was 1:10, five minutes before the session ended and the close for the day and for the month. Hutchinson, surrounded by his brokers, made his way to the cash wheat group. The pirates got him through the dense knot of yelling men to where Tom Seymour was bidding 185. Hutchinson, who towered over Seymour, reached out a long arm and with one finger touched him on the shoulder. "I want you!" he said. The two turned aside for a moment. When Seymour faced around again, he yelled out, "Give two dollars for cash wheat!" Simultaneously in the wheat pit, the pirates Billy McHenry and P. B. Weare both bellowed, "I'll give two dollars for Sep wheat!" "Give two dollars for Sep or cash wheat, ten million bushels or any part!"[88]

With that, the crowd let out a new shout, and from then on, everyone yelled flat out until the bell sounded at 1:15. The fight was on now to set the closing price for the day. Ten feet away from McHenry and Weare, Billy Linn, an important ally of the Big Four, was frantically signaling and shouting. "Sell five thousand cash or Sep wheat at one-fifteen! Ten thousand at one-fifteen! Twenty thousand! Fifty thousand at one-fifteen! Sell one hundred thousand cash or Sep at one-fifteen!" At almost the last possible moment, Seymour got two carloads of cash wheat, making the two-dollar price official. The mob was so densely packed that Seymour, a large and heavyset man, was swept off his feet and lifted into the air. Still, he kept his hand up, gamely shouting, "Give two dollars for cash wheat! Two dollars!" Only seconds remained in the trading day, the September contract, and the corner. But the din was such that men standing side by side couldn't understand each other. When the bell ending the session struck a few moments later, the *Chicago Herald* reported that there arose "an unearthly shriek from hundreds of brass-lined throats."[89]

The session, now officially ended, degenerated into a riot. Fights and shoving matches broke out in various places on the floor. The leading actors shouted at one another, angrily disputing the closing price. The bear speculators Henry Parker and Leopold Bloom got into a row with the pirate P. B. Weare, with Bloom charging that Hutchinson's profits were plain robbery. Weare retorted with an insult to Bloom's ethnicity and said that every penny in Bloom's pocket was stolen anyway. Friends intervened before things got worse. Others immediately forgot about Sep wheat. October was now cash wheat, which moments before had sold for two dollars a bushel. Ignoring the exchange rule that banned postsession trading, members kept shouting bids at one another. In less than a minute after the bell, October wheat sold at 102½, the greatest one-day drop in the wheat price in the Board's history—and this after a price rise of almost a dollar a bushel over a span of three days, a sight never seen on the exchange.[90]

Gradually the floor emptied. Reporting the events of the day, the *Chicago Herald* wrote, "in some respects it is the most remarkable corner that has ever been run." And so it was. Hutchinson had raised the price of the September contract to an unprecedented level, both in absolute and in percentage terms. September wheat closed at 104 on Wednesday the twenty-sixth and at 200 on Saturday the twenty-ninth—more than a 90 percent increase in three business days. Other successful corners raised prices between 10 percent and 40 percent. The failed Harper corner of 1887, measured at its high point, raised the price of June wheat about 18 percent. And Hutchinson had taken on the most powerful clique on the exchange and brought them low for all to see.[91]

A full list of the shorts was never disclosed. In Chicago, most believed the remaining shorts were out-of-towners, probably New Yorkers. The *Tribune* estimated that five hundred thousand bushels remained unsettled after the Saturday close. The *New York Times* reported that up to one million bushels remained unsettled and that many of the shorts would hold out for arbitration. If so, the shorts were fooling themselves. There was no law or exchange rule that required parties to accept binding arbitration. The September contracts all settled eventually, though at different prices. In an interview with a reporter, Hutchinson stated that he would let off members who were broke but would pursue those who could pay and would not. He never revealed how much he made on the deal. The *Boston Globe* estimated his profits at between $1.5 and $2 million, equivalent to between $47.6 million and $63.5 million in 2022. The more serious newspapers inclined to these figures or a little more. But no one knew for sure. The New York correspondent of a Kansas paper reported that Hutchinson had made $4 million and his followers—presumably the pirates—between $5 million and $6 million. The latter figures might be high, but several pirates did well. Ed Ryder later said that he came out $200,000 ahead. Whatever the total, the money came mainly from the big operators since Hutchinson had released the lesser shorts. To save face, none of the bear clique would admit they had lost money. However, on Friday Jack Cudahy wrote a clearing-house check for $325,000 and then stayed home sick on Saturday.[92]

The markets took a while to recover. Hutchinson's prediction of continuing high prices for the 1888 wheat crop proved correct, but for a different reason. Prices stayed high for months because the corner sparked a rage for wheat speculation among the public. Even before the corner ended, get-rich-quick stories spread like an epidemic. People repeated stories of profits ranging from $5,000 to $500,000, earned within minutes. One man supposedly bought a hundred thousand bushels of Sep wheat and resold it for ten cents a bushel more two minutes later, making $10,000. Another netted $1,500 on a five-thousand-bushel deal, a nearly 200 percent return on his investment. Someone else earned twelve cents a bushel on a quarter million bushels, and so on.[93]

Stories of instant riches always circulate during a bull run in the market, whether for tulip bulbs, wheat, dot-com stocks, or anything else. The people who come into the market with such inflated expectations are a bonanza for insiders. At such times, even the least experienced outer-ring insider can make money. On the upturn in business after Hutchinson's corner, one veteran speculator commented, "Let one innocent lamb jump the fence, and every <blank-blank> old ewe and buck in the crowd goes <blank-blank> scoot right after it." Statements like these did not help the Board of Trade's image, but for many, the lure of easy money trumped all else. The new customers ignored advice such as that given by the *Saint Paul Pioneer Press*, which warned its readers not to "look upon the wheat when it is amber, when it stirreth itself aright in the pit, for in the end it stingeth like a yellow jacket and biteth like a Mississippi sand fly."[94]

The speculator who commented on "lambs," though, was a typical market crowd member of his time and place. Disparaging epithets for customers are a constant in the crowd's vocabulary, as is the underlying attitude. When Armstrong wrote *Stocks and Stock-Jobbing on Wall-Street*, customers were "flunkies"; by Drew and Hutchinson's time, they were "lambs." Another such term for customers used on CBOT in those days was "granger," meaning a bumpkin or hayseed.[95] Today, the terms are different, but the sentiment is not. The implication for how customers are to be treated is obvious: lambs are herded, shorn, slaughtered, and eaten. It is hard to find positive or even neutral references to customers in the crowd's unguarded speech, even now.

Some financial journalists had predicted that Hutchinson's corner would kill the business, since no one would trade in such a market. These commentators misread the public mood and addressed the wrong audience, as had the New York financial journalists after Drew's 1866 bond conversion. Long-term investors didn't speculate anyway and already knew to avoid a market dominated by the likes of Hutchinson and the Big Four. For those attracted to the game, even a rigged market offered a chance to get rich that ordinary employment did not. And the market was open to the common man. Few Board of Trade members in the 1880s even had middle-class backgrounds. Most came from far more modest circumstances. Hutchinson, Ream, and Jones had joined the exchange trailing debts and failure. Many, like Hutchinson and Cudahy, had been truly poor: Hutchinson's father was a farmhand who abandoned his family, and his mother was a washerwoman. And for market regulars, insider control had advantages over anarchy. Control meant human agency and a plan, and whoever knew the plan could profit. External events affected the market randomly and without warning and could wipe a man out.[96]

What they all wanted—newcomers, stags, and outer-ring insiders— was a connection with an inner-ring insider. A market runs on talk, information, and rumors both true and false. Not until the early twentieth century was there any ban on the use of privileged information, and a man who knew which rumors were true could prosper. Someone acting on a good tip cannot lose, and the counterparties to his trades cannot win.

Such tips could only come from an inner-ring insider—a Hutchinson, a Cudahy, or some other mighty man of renown. Everyone else got market advice such as the Big Four put about on Wednesday: bald-faced lies.

The papers did tap into a substantial backlash, though. Even before the corner, many people viewed the Board of Trade as a degenerate gambling hell that should be shut down to prove that crime didn't pay. That the commodities traded were agricultural gave the issue immediacy. Besides objecting to gambling, many people found it offensive that a gang of speculators controlled food prices. Some states had laws against so-called grain gambling, but as with the Illinois law, enforcement was problematic. At the federal level, except for a short-lived 1864 law to curb gold speculation, the government had largely ignored market abuses. Between 1864 and the 1888 wheat corner, Congress considered only two bills to regulate commodities and derivatives trading. Neither measure passed.[97]

Times were changing, though. In 1887, Congress passed, and President Cleveland signed, the Interstate Commerce Act—the first federal law to regulate private industry in the United States. The Sherman Antitrust Act followed in 1890. The publicity that Hutchinson's corner received focused public attention on abuses in commodities markets, and by 1892, Congress had received thousands of petitions calling for a law to restrict grain speculation. From 1890 and for the next thirty-five years, Congress considered over two hundred bills to regulate or abolish futures trading and launched thirty different investigations into trading practices in commodities markets. The first durable federal law to regulate commodities trading (Congress repealed the 1864 law after two weeks) was the Cotton Futures Act of 1914. Five years earlier, the Supreme Court decision *Strong v. Repide* had become the first federal regulation of U.S. securities markets. On paper, a new era had arrived.[98]

After the corner, the world of grain gambling remained seriously disturbed for a time. Fear ruled the marketplace, and it was fear of Hutchinson. He had a famously bad temper and was furious about the treatment he had received on Saturday. Over the weekend, a story circulated that he would raise December wheat to 125. Many feared that if he did, so many bankruptcies would follow that the exchange would go under. The September corner was all but forgotten—except by the remaining unsettled shorts and about two dozen newly insolvent members. Many brokerage firms were in trouble; New York and Liverpool customers were not paying their margin calls, which left their brokers liable.

Badly frightened by the events of the past days, banks and brokers de-
manded huge margins for trades.[99]

When the Board of Trade reopened on Monday, October 1, once
again crowds jammed the galleries and the floor. When the bell rang, all
was chaos. Wheat prices jumped around erratically for no clear reason, at
times moving five cents either way within five minutes. Bids and offers
came so fast that many went unrecorded. At 10 a.m., Secretary Stone announced that two firms had failed. After that, Dec wheat started to rise
so fast that members could scarcely bid on it. Within five minutes, the
price went from 104 to 108. But then Hutchinson surprised everybody
by ordering the pirates to sell huge quantities of wheat to lower the
price. Since he owned all the wheat, such an action was directly contrary
to his interests. The pirates sold half a million bushels of Dec wheat and
then paused and waited for further orders. The price immediately began
to rise again. Hutchinson signaled to the pirates to resume selling, and
they kept on until the price held steady.[100]

For the rest of the week, Hutchinson single-handedly stabilized
prices, until the mood calmed. Instead of wrecking the exchange, as he
could have, Hutchinson put the welfare of the institution and its members before his own. So far as anyone could recall, no other corner operator had ever done such a thing. It later came out that on Monday
morning, Hutchinson's son Charles, Young Hutch, had talked his father
around. Charles reportedly told him that if he kept to his present course,
he would destroy the exchange and ruin scores of members, including
many of their friends. After some histrionics, the elder Hutchinson re-
lented.[101]

Late in the trading day on Monday, the market reporter for the *Chicago Herald* spoke to Hutchinson as he sat watching his brokers sell wheat
in hundred-thousand-bushel lots. Amid his usual blather (he praised the
philosophy of Henry David Thoreau extravagantly and at length),
Hutchinson belittled the crowd outlook of wheat speculators, bears especially. "The boys have all gone crazy," he said. "They don't know what
they are doing. Wheat is going to be very high on this crop on its mer-
its." "Here you are," said the reporter, "bulling the market and at the
same time selling wheat." "That's all right," Hutchinson replied. "I want
to break up all these crazy boys and teach them to be decent."[102]

That was a tall order, but he taught them to be decent to him. After it
was all over, the *Chicago Tribune* wrote that the corner contained a lesson,
namely, "*Boys, don't fool with the buzz-saw*"—meaning Hutchinson. No one

did, either, for the rest of the time that the buzz-saw was on the Board of Trade. He also broke up the Big Four. They continued to trade individually but never worked together again. Their later fortunes ran to extremes. Cudahy and Singer remained wealthy men but left little to remember them by. Nat Jones died penniless in 1895 at the age of fifty-four, broken in health and spirit. Norman Ream lived another twenty-six years and died one of the richest men in the United States. In 1903, he moved to New York, where the *Wall Street Journal* described him as "one of the great powers of Wall Street, although not much in the public eye."[103]

The grand Board of Trade building, which became the setting for Frank Norris's 1902 novel *The Pit*, lasted until 1928. The new Board of Trade building, opened in 1930, is itself a famous landmark. In this book, the 1885 building gives the first glimpse of what has become an identifying feature of the market crowd: competitive consumption. Nineteenth-century journalists sometimes sniped at vulgar, nouveau-riche stock operators, but the latter were more often portrayed as shabby, sinister, and frequently Jewish. Perhaps to give the business a more respectable front, palatial exchange buildings began to appear in the early nineteenth century. Improbably, the Russians were first, when the government of Czar Alexander I paid for a fine Greek Revival building for the Saint Petersburg Stock Exchange, completed in 1810. The Paris Stock Exchange building, which easily topped Saint Petersburg, followed in 1826. The British waited to enter the game. The first London stock exchange building, built 1802, had been small and dark; the new 1854 building made up for it. New York, flush with Gilded Age money, followed suit in 1871. The exchanges' own members often referred to these edifices as "temples of mammon." Exchange buildings, grand and otherwise, are now obsolete, but over-the-top consumption and display remain marked features of the business.[104]

The collective memory of the 1888 corner endured for decades, despite the crowd's short attention span. But Hutchinson himself had little time left; within three years, he had lost his mental acuity and could no longer trade. He died in a sanitarium in 1899, at the age of seventy. A wealth aristocracy is the most unstable kind, and the great men of 1888 left few traces of their lives and labors.[105] But the market is eternal.

The preceding account may at first appear remote from the experience of modern readers. Then, as now, the market crowd kept its business close, and the past, as has been said, is a foreign country. The corner itself took an unusual course. Most such undertakings failed, and when

Fig. 9. The newspapers' "temple of mammon": New York Stock Exchange trading floor, as remodeled in 1871 (Engraving, "Interior of the New York Stock Exchange," in "The New York Stock Exchange," *Harper's New Monthly Magazine*, November 1885, 829–853, 837). (Scan by the author)

successful, they mainly caught minor players. But viewed as a generic account of group conflict, the fight could have occurred in any middle school or high school. A powerful clique, for whatever reason, attempts to make someone a social outcast. When that effort fails, the clique tries to expel the person from the group entirely. Finally, the clique resorts to violence.[106] The contests in these two very different settings develop along similar lines because both groups self-organize the same way, a topic taken up in chapter 3.

Hutchinson was a true original. But despite his peculiarities, he pointed toward the future and not the more conventional Big Four. From a modern perspective, Hutchinson's victory in the corner is not surprising. He saw something others had missed in publicly available information and came by his profits fairly. But nineteenth-century financial speculation was even more inwardly focused than it is now. Historically, this orientation made sense, since news from distant markets was out of date, fragmentary, and often just plain wrong. But by the 1880s, the

Board of Trade had connections to U.S. and European markets via tele-graph, ticker tape, telephone, and the transatlantic cable. Out-of-town newspapers, agricultural journals, and government reports arrived in Chicago within a few days of their publication. More and better market information was available than ever before, but in late 1888, Hutchinson was the only one on the exchange who put it to good use. And critically, Hutchinson had the money to push back against the Big Four. If he had not, his information advantage would have availed him nothing. By 1888, the outside world mattered more than it had before, but it still took money to win.

Lastly, the time was still decades off, but a day would come when campaigns of social ostracism in the market crowd would lose much of their effectiveness. In 1888, the social pressure that the Big Four put on Hutchinson would have stopped a lesser member. Hutchinson, though, was himself a formidable inner-ring insider; he had his own supporters, and during the corner, he skillfully handled the lesser shorts. But times were changing. Paradoxically, the ever-closer links between geographi-cally distant marketplaces would weaken the participants' personal con-nections. The face-to-face network organization of the market crowd, which had endured so long, would give way to something new.

CHAPTER THREE

The Chicago Board of Trade,

1910–1940
Longitudinal Network Analysis

THE TWO CASE STUDIES in chapters 1 and 2 introduced readers to the ways and attitudes of the market crowd. The perspective was as personal as could be, one case focusing on the actions of a single individual and the other on the rivalry of two small groups. The present chapter leaves the case study method and employs a different research approach altogether, with different objectives. Here, the object of study is an entire crowd, inner- and outer-ring insiders alike, over an extended period. This study explores how the network connections that linked members of the crowd stratified them into more- and less-favored groups and traces the effects of that division. A principal argument of this book is that attitudes and practices of the crowd have remained remarkably consistent over the long term. The CBOT member network was itself very stable during the time period of this study and would have supported this cultural persistence better than a shakier environment.[1]

This book explores the culture of financial insiders, both the inner- and outer-ring groups, known here as the "market crowd." The case studies have focused on inner-ring actors because they set the pace and deserve special attention. The behaviors identified, though, are common to all: the pervasive deception, baroque scheming, short-term thinking, and the rest. The cases in this book were chosen because the moves and counter-moves of the different players were more visible than usual. But the main actors were hardly typical. Drew, Hutchinson, and the Big Four were exceptional men, Hutchinson most of all. Hutchinson's eccentric engagement with the market worked for him, but you would search a long time to find another Hutchinson. Even with more representative actors, sample sizes in case studies are too small to draw broad conclusions. This chapter employs a different research approach, a longitudinal network analysis of the membership of an entire exchange, the Chicago Board of Trade from 1910 to 1940.

Networks have long interested mathematicians and natural philosophers, but detailed study was impossible until computers could process massive amounts of complex data. Network theory is grounded in mathematics, but network *analysis* is not itself a formal, unified theory—at least not yet. Rather, it is a broad strategy—"a loose federation of approaches"—to examine connections among entities, human and otherwise. Linton C. Freeman characterizes social network analysis as an approach with four defining properties. First, its foundational premise is that links among social actors are important. Second, the fundamental research approach is to collect and analyze data that record social relations. Third, analysis makes extensive use of graphic imagery to show patterns among links. Fourth, it develops mathematical and computational models to describe and explain those patterns.[2]

Inner- and outer-ring insiders are different, as anyone who works in the market knows, but the boundary between the groups is fuzzy. Viewed from the outside, though, the inner ring has two distinguishing traits: its members earn more, and they survive longer, in a high-attrition industry. People routinely hide their wealth, the more so the wealthier they are. But survival in the marketplace, defined here as long-term exchange membership, is in the open. In this chapter, long-term survival will serve to identify likely members of the inner ring. The measure is imperfect because external events (e.g., death) can shorten careers, and risk-averse, reasonably lucky small players can survive a long time. Still, a long-term survivor group should have a high concentration of inner-ring members.

The network graph in figure 10 gives an idea of what this chapter will cover. The 1888 case study should still be fresh in readers' minds, though 1888 is outside the study period. Figure 10 shows The CBOT members' affiliation network on December 31 of that year, three months after Hutchinson's wheat corner ended.

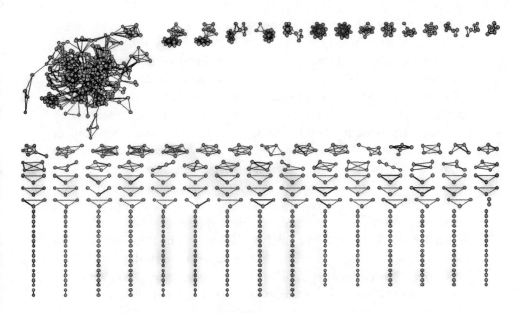

Fig. 10. 1888 CBOT affiliation network graph—entire.

An *affiliation network*, like this one, shows institutional connections among network participants. Here, the connections are firms, shared office space, seats on exchange governance committees, and obvious kinship connections. Such a network is bipartite, meaning a network with two classes of nodes: N actors each belong to one or more of M groups. The illustration shows just over half of CBOT's 1931 members at year-end 1888. The rest were isolates, meaning not connected to other members, and are omitted for clarity. Only thirty years ago, detailed investigation of a network this large would have been impossible. Even small networks are dauntingly complex, let alone ones with nearly two thousand nodes. Before the spread of online social media, the upper limit of a manageable personal network for an average adult was estimated to be about 150 people. Presuming that you cannot link to yourself, a 150-person network has 22,350 (150 × 149) total possible links among members, but 2^{150} possible *configurations*. Two to the 150th power equals 1.4E45, meaning 1.4 with the decimal point moved forty-five places to the right. By comparison, a common estimate for the number of stars in the Milky Way is 1.0E11.[3]

The affiliation network is one of three networks that connect participants in the marketplace. Another is the transaction network, the business of the market, which consists of impersonal exchanges between unrelated parties—in theory. In Wayne Baker's work on the Chicago Board Options Exchange (CBOE), he found the transaction network to be partly socially structured. Pit trading is noisy, literally and figuratively, and the more noise, the more risk of error. On the CBOE, members traded within micronetworks of more manageable size. Inclusion, or not, in these smaller groupings depended partly on personal considerations such friendship, ill will, or sycophancy. We can assume that things worked the same way on the Board of Trade sixty and seventy years earlier. The setting was the same—a too-loud, too-large crowd, face-to-face trading, and zero technology. Still, the affiliation network and the transaction network (mostly) are rational-legal constructs, designed to achieve specific organizational objectives: efficiency, control, accountability, and so on. The third network, the members' social network, is different, and the term needs disambiguation. In general, a "social network" is a set of relations that apply to a set of actors, plus accompanying information on those actors and relations. But the term has two uses. "Social network" may mean any network of people rather than things, for example, electronic circuits or airline routes. But the term also refers to informal, unofficial connections shared by a group of people. This study uses the term in the second sense. The second part of the chapter focuses on the CBOT members' social network.[4]

Photogenic though the affiliation network is, it is not the target of the present inquiry but a means to it. Nobody passes you valuable information because you both sat on the Wheat Inspection Committee last year. By themselves, neither the affiliation network nor the transaction network identifies members of the inner ring. Floor trading is a face-to-face business, but a crowd of men shouting at one another in an all-against-all competition allows only for schematic and limited public communication. The inner ring depends on the third network: the social network. There, relationships entail privileged access between people and trust—a little or a lot—and special treatment. The noneconomic features of the transaction network are not separate from the larger, exchange-wide social network but rather a subset of it.[5]

But CBOT's affiliation network is still useful. Personal connections between members existed throughout the exchange, but these are beyond recovery for a period so long past. Nor would a random sample of members in a study population this large all know one another. Members of committees and employees of the same firm, though, would have had frequent face-to-face contact. Many studies show that simple propinquity—

being in the same place at the same time—is one of the strongest influences on friendship formation. Circumstances as random and trivial as seating charts and dormitory-floor assignments can be the start of life-long connections. Beyond that, in the network graph shown in figure 10, the different clumps of members each represent some focus of activity. That is, for each of the five affiliation types charted here, the members are *doing* something together; they aren't simply thrown together by chance. To have a focus of activity further increases the likelihood that a social connection will form. The affiliation network, therefore, should identify clusters of members with an unusually high *density* of personal relationships. Social network researchers often compare an "official" formal network to an "unofficial" network of personal connections, and so we shall here. We will use the official affiliation network to make inferences about the unofficial social network. Research on the affiliation network is like lidar photography: a minute and detailed aerial survey of surface irregularities to discover underground structures.[6]

This analysis avoids three problems common in network studies: biased sources, a single period, and incomplete data. Survey questionnaires, the most common method used to research social networks, are unsuitable for a deceased study population. But even in ideal circumstances, many types of bias can skew survey data. Bias can be acute in an industry as close-mouthed as finance and where an unguarded answer could land the respondent in trouble. (For example, a researcher who asks respondents if they cheat on their income taxes should not expect honest answers.) This analysis is an archival study of primary-source data, a type of observation study. Properly designed observation studies can uncover unimpeachable facts, not what a survey respondent wants you to think. Second, social networks continually evolve, and to know *how* they evolve gives a much deeper understanding of the network than a single take. The present study tracks changes to the CBOT affiliation network at three contiguous ten-year intervals, so a random effect in one interval cannot be mistaken for a long-term trend. Third, because social networks can be so large, for example, online social media applications, analyses often rely on sampling. But the CBOT data allow for a detailed reconstruction of the members' entire affiliation network. A study of this sort is known as "general network inference," or a "network census," and is the gold standard in network data.[7]

The Chicago Board of Trade, now merged into CME Group, left behind complete, well-documented membership lists and is a good study subject for other reasons besides. First, it was a leading U.S. exchange for over a century. Second, the members made up a "sociocentric network," in formal terminology, meaning a closed, bounded set, which included few or no outsiders. By 1910, the exchange did a specialized business, and the entry fee alone would have discouraged casual interest: $25,000 in 1919—over $400,000 in 2022. The turnover rate also showed that members took their work seriously. The 1940 list gave the year each member joined the exchange: the median join year was 1930, and the mean was 1925. The longest-serving member, William Dunn, had joined in 1879—sixty-one years before. Overall, average ten-year member turnover for the period studied was around 50 percent, or 6.5 percent yearly.[8]

During this time, market forces buffeted the members, as they always do, but not much else did; the exchange's internal and external environments changed comparatively little. The period 1910 to 1940 is close to our own era; communications were by radio, telephone, and telegraph, and transport was by water, rail, and truck throughout. Market regulation remained unchanged (there hardly was any). The U.S. started trying to regulate grain futures in 1921, but enforcement was weak. With the notable exception of the Great Depression, there had been no major national upheavals. The U.S.'s nineteen-month involvement in World War I came and went in 1917–1918 but had limited impact on the civilian economy. Finally, exchange governance and the members' self-organization were stable as well. Figure 10 showed CBOT's affiliation network in 1888. The overall configuration of the members' affiliation network in 1940, shown in figure 11, is unchanged.[9]

To summarize, this section of the chapter examines how CBOT members' network positions correlated to their chances of long-term survival on the exchange. "Long-term survival" means ten years or more. The analysis will use the CBOT membership lists at year-end 1910, 1920, 1930, and 1940. Ten-year survival will be measured using the three paired data sets 1910–1920, 1920–1930, and 1930–1940. Unless otherwise stated, the study population will only include members on the exchange ten years or less, for example, members on the 1920 list who were not on the 1910 list.

The following discussion uses a minimum of formal network analysis terminology, but five terms are essential. A network diagram, such as those of 1888 and 1940 shown here, is a *graph*. Second, *nodes* are the points in a network that connect to one another, in this case CBOT members. Third, *edges* are the lines connecting the nodes if traffic is two-way and symmetrical, as assumed here. Fourth, one of the most common

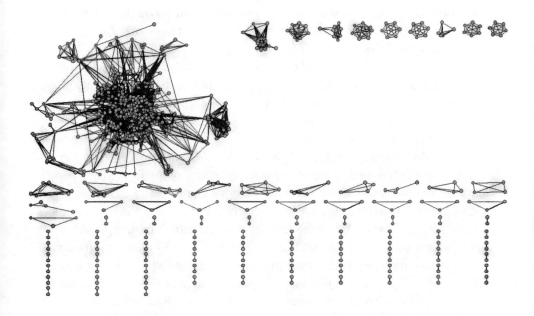

Fig. 11. 1940 CBOT affiliation network graph—entire.

measures in network analysis is *degree centrality*, meaning the number of connections a node has to other nodes. A member with connections to five other members has a degree centrality of five. Fifth, this member could have more than five edges. If two members have more than a single tie, for example, both are employees of the same firm and share an office, they have a *multiplex* relationship.[10]

Readers familiar with network analysis will probably find this one fairly basic. The available data would support a deeper and more thorough analysis of CBOT's member affiliation network, but that would add little to the larger study. As important as CBOT was, it was one exchange of many, and this book aims for a more general picture of the insider group. To calculate, for example, the exact year-on-year attrition rate for isolate members would be fitting for a study focused on CBOT alone. It would be a step too far, however, to generalize from those findings. Also, many of the more complex network measures cannot be calculated for a disconnected graph, meaning a network of two or more components without connecting paths. Key higher-order measures calculated for core components only showed no correlation with members' long-term survival, at least at ten-year intervals.[11]

Before moving on, I want to reference two recent books that relate, in different ways, to the subject matter of this study. The first is *Out of the Pits: Trading and Technology from Chicago to London*, by Caitlin Zaloom. The second is *Gentlemen Bankers: The World of J. P. Morgan*, by Susie J. Pak. Turning first to Zaloom, she and I share a research subject, FICC traders, in her case, CBOT members circa 1998–2000, during the switch to electronic trading. Zaloom's study is qualitative rather than quantitative, but her work comes closest to mine is in her discussion of the social construction of the traders' workplace personalities. Zaloom argues that the change in the "abstract space of the marketplace" profoundly affected the traders themselves, not just the mechanics of the job. She describes at length and in colorful detail the fraternity-boy behavior she witnessed during her fieldwork. With the transition to electronic trading, most of this behavior went away, as did many of the traders, who found it difficult to adapt to the new screen-based work. Their replacements were usually better educated and of a higher social class—and much quieter. But the book has little to say about money. Money flows are a foundational theme of *Floor Rules*, which only makes passing mention of the traders' often flamboyant social presentation. Zaloom's *Out of the Pits* is an ethnographic study that focuses on physical space and gender identity; *Floor Rules* is about a behavior pattern that affects markets, prices, and customers. Zaloom and I look at the same group, but we focus on different things.

Quantitative network analysis is not a commonly used approach—at least not yet—for study of participants in financial markets. Readers who wish to see another application of this methodology can look to *Gentlemen Bankers: The World of J. P. Morgan*. Pak conducts a detailed analysis of the Morgan family and the many people and firms connected to them. This is an illuminating study of one of the most influential U.S. families of its day, and Pak and I both argue that social connections play an important role in the business of our respective subjects. But the Morgans were exceptional men by any standard and not a good basis for broad conclusions about investment banking at the time. (Pak makes no such claims.) The network analysis in *Floor Rules* is less granular but lends itself better to generalizations, as it traces the shifting fortunes of nearly four thousand CBOT members over a thirty-year period. A second problem in comparing study findings of *Gentlemen Bankers* and *Floor Rules* is that one book is about investment bankers and the other is about traders. Investment banking, as I state in my introduction, is a branch of finance different enough from FICC to require separate study. Investment bankers' business relationships are fundamentally different from those of traders, fiduciary and long-term rather than transactional and brief. The nature of the work is entirely different as well. Conditions specific to FICC push the traders toward certain kinds of behavior, conditions absent in investment banking.

To begin, the two most obvious features of the CBOT members' affiliation network illustrations show the importance of visual imagery in network analysis. All four of the 1910–1940 data sets in this study are disconnected graphs, like the 1888 and 1940 illustrations. Second, the 1910–1940 networks all show core-periphery patterns, that is, a large, dominant component surrounded by smaller ones. Core-periphery patterns are widespread in social life; we have all seen them on primary-school playgrounds and just about everywhere else since then. The smaller components show members with four types of connections: family, firm, shared office space, and a seat on an exchange governance committee the previous year. The members in the "core component," as it is called, in the upper left have the same connections, plus one. There, each smaller cluster had at least one member on a current-year governance committee. Some members sat on more than one. Only a handful of members had all five affiliations.[12]

The disconnected graph and the core-periphery pattern split CBOT members into three distinct classes. Members were either (1) *isolates* with no affiliation connections, (2) in the *core*, or (3) in a smaller disconnected component, from now on called the *connected noncore* member class— CNC for short. In all four 1910–1940 data sets, the CNC member class was the smallest. In 1910 and 1920, the core and the isolates classes were equal in size; in 1930 and 1940, the isolates class was larger. In 1888, Hutchinson, the Big Four, and other important speculators of the day were all in the core. In all three paired comparison sets, 1910–1920, 1920–1930, and 1930–1940, core members survived at the highest rates; CNC members came second, and isolates did worst of all. In all years, core members had an over 50 percent better chance of surviving ten years than isolates did. After that, the core members' advantage eroded vis-à-vis CNC members, possibly because the CNC members who survived past the ten-year mark were a tougher bunch than those who left. This is a robust finding, consistent across all three comparison sets. These, however, are *average* survival rates for member classes. More than other members, core-component members varied widely in their node characteristics (and the members' likely importance on the exchange).[13]

The 1910 and 1940 network graphs show one final significant feature: some edges are thicker than others, marking a multiplex relationship. The percentage of nonisolate members with multiplex relationships in the four data sets varied between 36 and 57 percent. Such relationships correlate strongly to long-term survival: in all three ten-year comparison sets, members with multiplex relationships survived at higher rates than members without did. In all four data sets, a lower percentage of CNC members had multiplex relationships than did core-component members, and CNC members had lower survival rates as well. Even though these are affiliations and not social connections, it is easy to see why multiplexity matters. To see the same member in different settings—say, in a shared office and on a governance committee—would increase personal contact. And more contact would make a social connection more likely to form. Separately, many studies have shown that multiplex relationships are critical to the formation of trust between parties.[14]

The core component figures prominently in this discussion and warrants a closer look. In the four data sets, about a third of all members were in the core, but in all years, they had over 80 percent of all edges (network connections). Note that the core is not the inner ring; the core is part of the members' affiliation network, not the all-important social network. Significantly, membership in the core was unstable. CBOT had a tiny administrative staff, but the governance committees were all drawn from the members at large. The committees held the core together, and terms were for one to three years. Annual turnover of committee members ranged from one-quarter to just under half. Once a committee member's term expired, he and members connected to him would move from the core to the CNC member class. Being on a governance committee does not correlate with higher likelihood of long-term survival; committee members fared no better than other members with similar node characteristics. In general, committees were administrative rather than executive, and members wielded little power. CBOT was consensus governed to a fault, though doubtless only the consensus of members who counted.[15]

As described, core-component members had consistently higher average ten-year survival rates than members of the other two classes did, despite the revolving-door core membership. An easy assumption to make, but a false one, would be that simply being in the core made the difference. Instead, node characteristics found more often among core members are what matter. An analogy would be a party thrown by the ambitious and social-climbing Dr. Dash Riprock for the university's most famous boffins. An outsider unfamiliar with university politics might suppose that the party made the luminaries luminous. But the party is a marker, not a cause, and so is the core component. Both are collection points for a certain population.

The graph of the 1910 core in figure 12 shows some members well connected indeed and others hardly at all. James C. Murray of the Quaker Oats Company led the pack with forty-two connections, but thirty 1910 core members had only one connection apiece. One would expect members like Murray to be better off, somehow, than these thirty; forty-two connections seem better than one. So they are, and for much narrower differences in degree. In both the core and CNC member classes, members with above-average degree centrality or (separately) edges for that class survived at higher rates than below-average members did. The core and CNC classes differ, however, in survival rates. In all comparison sets, CNC members survived at lower rates than core members did, probably because the former had fewer connections on average. In the 1910 CNC member class, two members had twelve connections, the highest number for that group. In the 1910 core, nearly half the members had twelve or more connections.[16]

Above-average degree centrality and edges for the membership class unambiguously correlate with higher long-term survival rates. Members with even a single connection to another member survived at higher rates than isolates did. Multiplexity also unambiguously correlates with higher survival rates within the member class. The relationship between member class, by itself, and long-term survival is less straightforward. To be an isolate was clearly *dis*advantageous. But some core and CNC members overlap in measures of degree centrality and multiplexity, and these factors can be held constant. Then, there is no clear pattern of survival advantage for either class. It was still to a member's advantage to be in the core, because higher levels of degree centrality and multiplexity were possible there than in the CNC class. The three factors, therefore, are additive: members with all three characteristics—core-component membership, above-average degree centrality for that class, and multiplex relationships—had the best ten- and twenty-year survival rates of all CBOT member splits. From 1930 to 1940, for example, 78 percent of "trifecta" members survived, compared to 59 percent for other core members and 42 percent for isolates.[17]

A natural question to ask at this point, but a difficult question to answer, is, How many inner-ring insiders were there? The group would not

Fig. 12. 1910 CBOT affiliation network core component graph.

have had a clear boundary, and we cannot ask the members themselves. We can, however, make rough estimates of lower and higher limits. At the low end, we can assume that trifecta members were inner-ring insiders. In the three 1910–1930 member lists, on average 12 percent were trifecta members. For an upper limit, we can look to twenty-year survivors on the exchange. In the two comparison sets 1910–1930 and 1920–1940, on average 30 percent of members survived twenty years. We can be confident about the lower limit, well connected and placed as the trifecta members were. The upper limit is too high. Little people—scalpers, tailers, and small-time speculators—could and did survive long term, though the odds were against them. At a guess, and it is no more than that, between 15 and 20 percent of members would have been inner-ring insiders. Rank-and-file members in those years would have known who counted and who did not, but we cannot ask them.[18]

But even the best-connected members eventually left the exchange, and positions would become vacant—including within the inner ring. The exchange itself would seem a logical place for the remaining inner-ring insiders to find replacements. Inner-ring insiders were not the only members with staying power; the more adept small players hung on as well. The Membership Committee would have vetted and approved them, and they had all paid a stiff entrance fee. All had survived years of punishing elimination rounds in a Hobbesian environment, no small thing. They honored their debts, or they would have been off the exchange; and everybody knew them. But the Board of Trade did not work that way. The core component would have had the most inner-ring insiders, but when core members left, new members usually replaced them—not long-term CNC or isolate members.

Not only was there little upward mobility from the noncore member classes, but there was little movement between classes at all. In all three member classes and for all three ten-year comparison sets, members who survived ten years mostly remained where they started. All three member classes were far more likely to leave the exchange or remain in their original class than to move to another. The CNC member class was the most volatile (or unstable) of the three and was the source of more movement than the other two. Even so, only about a third of CNC members changed member classes ten years on. Looking backward, all three member classes had far more new members than they had long-term members from other classes. Even the core, the most desirable network location, got far more newcomers with no visible history on the exchange than it got transfers from other classes. Who, exactly, were these mystery men?[19]

A detailed examination of members' social connections could go a long way to answering that question, but the people to ask, the members themselves, are long gone. We can still explore the most important social connection of all: family. Certain names recur in the thirty-year time span of this study, and not Smith and Jones, either. Julian Rumsey was a founding member of the Board of Trade in 1848 and was president of the exchange in 1858 and 1859. By 1888, when Hutchinson ran his wheat corner, Julian was gone, but four new Rumseys were on the floor. Rumseys are present in every data set used here, including 1940, ninety-two years after the exchange opened. The surname alone makes it a good bet the Rumsey members, from Julian in 1848 to Henry in 1940, were kin. They belonged to the same specialized organization, and the name was rare: The 1920 Chicago census lists only eight adult white male Rumseys. The Rumseys were not an anomaly; extended family connections are common in the markets. Writing about the New York Stock Exchange in the 1980s and 1990s, Michel Abolafia describes specialist positions as routinely passed from father to son and from more distant generations. Caitlin Zaloom in *Out of the Pits* writes that multigenerational extended families were common on the floor of CBOT at the end of the twenty-first century.[20]

The Rumsey family line suggests a way to use surnames to look at nepotism on the exchange. Many other CBOT members had uncommon surnames as well. Out of almost 850,000 adult white males in Chicago in 1920, only five were surnamed Badenoch, but the name appears in every member list cited in this study, including 1888. Even if the Badenochs did not all work for the same firm (they did), chances that they were not kin would be vanishingly small. Using uncommon surnames, we can compare new members who probably had a family member already on the exchange to new members who did not. First, though, common surnames must go. We can safely assume that the Badenochs are related, but we can make no such assumption about members surnamed Smith, Jones, or Johnson. Johnson was the most common surname for adult white men in Chicago in 1920, with over seven thousand census entries. The four CBOT membership lists used here contain thirteen different Johnsons, with twenty-four separate entries between them. And this is a single surname, of over six thousand entries on the combined lists. Detailed genealogical investigation could resolve questions like these, but the data set is too large. A researcher who took such an approach might never be seen again.[21]

But nepotism is important and worth exploring, even if we cannot come up with precise answers. The member lists are long enough to exclude the most common surnames and still leave a large data set. Using the 1920 Chicago census as the benchmark for surname frequency of adult white males, we can exclude members with the top 995 most-common surnames before sample sizes get too small. For example, of CBOT's 1,602 members in 1920, 764 had joined recently—that is, after 1910. Removing members with the top 995 most-common surnames shrinks the data set to 452. Of the 452, 117 had surnames found on the 1910 list; the remaining 335 did not. The 1920 sections of the different surname tests cited in the following paragraphs use various splits of these two groups.[22]

This approach will produce some false positives—mistakenly identifying a family connection where none exists—but probably not too many of them. The 117 new members with "old" surnames include only members who (1) joined after 1910, (2) had an uncommon surname, and (3) had the same surname as a different member in 1910. After the exclusions, the most common surname among the 117 was Rowan, with 84 census entries. We can be confident about the kinship of members named Rumsey or Badenoch, less so about members named Rowan. But false positives should occur randomly and not be a source of systematic error, that is, bias. Counterbalancing that, the study will miss family connections: grandsons, stepsons, nephews, cousins, and in-laws with different surnames. These relationships will also occur randomly throughout the data set and should well outweigh the number of false positives. Finally, calculations on the 1910–1920 comparison set, say, can be repeated using 1920–1930 and 1930–1940. The three-way comparison will help flag random variations in results, whether because of false positives, missing data, or any other reason. Findings of the surname study just outlined will be conservative and identify trends, rather than exact measures.[23]

In the three comparison sets, then, the matching-surname test just described shows a family connection on average for 21 percent of new members. The real number would be higher. The 21 percent—call them family connected—occupied better network locations than did new members without a matching surname. When family-connected new members first appear on a membership list, they are overrepresented in the core, the best location for long-term survival. For example, in 1920, 26 percent of uncommon-surname new members had surnames that appeared on the 1910 list but were 38 percent of new core members. Old-surname new members were also disproportionately represented among new trifecta members. For isolates, the member class with the lowest long-term survival rates, the reverse was true. There, old-surname new members were underrepresented, compared to new-surname new members. In 1920, 26 percent of all new members had old surnames but were 8 percent of all new isolate members.[24]

So it was that new members with a relative already on the exchange started out in better network locations than other members did. But the data show that the family advantage only extended to the members' network locations. As described earlier, three nodal measures correlate with higher likelihood of ten-year survival: above-average edges per member for the member class, above-average degree centrality per member for the member class, and multiplex relationships. In the first two of these measures, new core members with old surnames have *lower* averages than do members with new surnames. In the third measure, multiplexity, old-surname core members have a small advantage. And in the acid test, ten-year survival, new core members with old surnames did worse than members with new surnames did. The same was true of the isolates member class: old-surname new members did worse. In the CNC member class, results are mixed. Separately, ten years on, newly joined core members with old surnames left the core at higher rates than did new-surname members, either by leaving the exchange or by moving to a less desirable member class. To sum up, though younger family members were disproportionately represented in advantageous network locations, they survived at lower rates than nonconnected members who were similarly situated. Over the long term, one would expect the two groups to become more similar, as competition forced weaker players to exit the game. But this was not the case; the new-surname correlation to higher survival rates persists in years eleven through twenty.[25]

The most obvious interpretation of these findings is that the younger family members were less competent and without the family connection would not have been where they were. But the survival rates are averages for the entire group, within which there is one major exception. In the core component, the "trifecta" members—core members with above-average degree centrality and multiplex relationships—are an elite bunch. Trifecta members survive at the highest rates of all member subgroups. The group is small—only forty-one in 1920 and thirty-seven in 1930. Breaking down the trifecta members further into old- and new-surname splits, old-surname members survive at higher rates still. Not only did old-surname members have an entry-level advantage in landing in the best member class, the core. They were also overrepresented among trifecta members, the most successful subgroup of all for long-term survival. These few "four-fecta" members, who had the highest survival rates of any subgroup tested, were evidently thoroughly competent and perfectly suited for the Board of Trade. Removing these members from the larger group of family-connected members makes the average survival rate of the remaining group even worse.[26]

This finishes the affiliation network analysis. The central question addressed here has been, What network characteristics distinguish CBOT members who survived ten years or more from members who did not? We have focused on inner-ring insiders, the most influential group in the marketplace and started with three propositions. First, viewed from the outside, inner-ring insiders have two key distinguishing traits: they earn more and survive longer in the market than others do. Second, they do better because they belong to a social network that shares information known only to a few. Third, the members' affiliation network contains clues to the informal social network, which is otherwise lost. And as we have seen, certain affiliation network positions and node characteristics do correlate with better or worse chances for long-term survival.

Findings are summarized in the following list. Unless otherwise stated, findings refer to "new" members, rather than long-term members or the entire membership of the exchange. "Survival" means ten-year survival, unless otherwise stated.

I. Exploratory/descriptive
  1. The Board of Trade affiliation network is a disconnected graph that forms a core-periphery pattern. All members regardless of joining date divide into three classes: core-component members, connected noncore (CNC) members, and isolates. This network configuration was already present in 1888 and is consistent in all four 1910–1940 data sets.[27]
  2. Core-component members have a higher average number of edges, higher degree centrality, and a higher percentage of multiplex relationships than do CNC members. Isolates have no other connections at all.[28]
  3. Core-component members have the highest ten-year survival rates, then CNC members, then isolates.[29]
II. Node characteristics and survival
  1. Within their respective classes, core and CNC members with above-average degree centrality and/or edges have higher average survival rates than do below-average members.[30]
  2. Even a single connection to another member correlates to a higher likelihood of survival, compared to having no connections.[31]
  3. Within their respective classes, core and CNC members with multiplex relationships have higher average survival rates than do members without.[32]
  4. "Trifecta" members who (1) are in the core component, (2) have above-average degree centrality, and (3) have multiplex relationships have higher average survival rates than do members missing one of these traits. The three factors are additive.[33]

5. Core membership is important because the highest degree centrality network locations and most of the multiplex relationships are in the core, not the CNC member class. When those factors are held constant, core and CNC members survive at equal rates.[34]

III. Mobility

1. Throughout the 1910–1940 study period, ten-year turnover for new members is about 50 percent.[35]

2. In descending order, after ten years, new members are most likely to (1) leave the exchange, (2) remain in their original member class, and (3) move to another member class. Even members who survive twenty years are most likely to remain in their original member class.[36]

3. Chances of noncore new members moving to the core ten years later are low but are better for CNC members than for isolates.[37]

IV.a. Kinship: Family dominance

1. Using the surname test, a little over a fifth of new members have relatives already on the exchange.[38]

2. Total old-surname members (members already on the exchange ten years before plus new members with old surnames) dominate the core component numerically, with between 70 and 78 percent of all core members in the three test sets.[39]

3. Together, long-term members and their recently joined younger relatives make up over three-fifths of total exchange membership.[40]

IV.b. Kinship: Network position

1. Old-surname new members are more likely to occupy network positions that correlate with high survival rates than are new members with new surnames. Old-surname new members are overrepresented in the core and among trifecta members and underrepresented among isolates.[41]

2. Node characteristics give a mixed picture. Old-surname new core members have fewer average edges and lower average degree centrality than do new-surname members. However, old-surname new core members have a higher proportion of multiplex relationships.[42]

IV.c. Kinship and Survival

    1. In all three member classes—core, CNC, and isolates—
old-surname new members survive at lower rates than do
new-surname members.[43]

    2. Old-surname new core members leave the core component—
either by leaving the exchange or by changing member
class—at higher rates than do new-surname members.[44]

    3. Old-surname trifecta members ("four-fecta" members)
survive at a higher average rate than do new-surname
trifecta members. The four-fecta members have the highest
ten-year survival rates of any test group.[45]

The second part of the study, the surname analysis, gives some insight into one of the main drivers of the social network: family connections and nepotism. The data show over 20 percent of new members related to long-term members, but the real number is higher. The surname test allows for both false positives and false negatives, probably many more of the latter. The test identifies likely same-surname family members but misses those with different surnames. In 1930, one-third of the core members had joined after 1920. Of these, over half—18 percent of the total core—had no known family connection to another member. Two things seem likely about this group: many had family connections that the surname test missed, and many others joined the exchange with useful social relationships already in place.[46]

Even at the surname-test figure of 20 percent, long-term members and their younger relatives were a formidable force on the exchange. Each such relationship was a miniature power center. These relationships and the alliances they represented would have been common knowledge among members and of real operational value during trading sessions. As a group, family-connected new members and long-term members dominated the exchange numerically, including the core. There, through the governing committees, they approved new members, set trading rules, and controlled arbitration, appeals, the clearing house, inspection, and relations with banks, railroads, and elevators. Like a country club in a small city, the kinship connections weighed in the balance for organizational control and would have given the exchange a conservative tilt. The younger relatives would have been compliant and team spirited; no one sponsors a family maverick for membership when an unpredictable move could bring disaster.[47]

The family-connected new members had a problem, though. The desirable network locations in which they started could scarcely have been evidence of anything but favoritism. Still, except for the best of them, the four-fecta members, they had *worse* average ten- and twenty-year survival rates than their nonconnected peers did. Looking at node characteristics, the family-connected new members' lower average degree centrality and fewer average edges are conditions consistent with lower survival rates. The group's higher percentage of multiplex relationships would correlate with improved chances for survival but clearly did not offset the group's other weaknesses. The real disparity in survival between family and nonfamily new members is greater than the surname test shows. The test misclassifies family members with different surnames as non-family-connected, which makes the two groups' survival averages appear closer together than they really are.[48]

The surname study shows a possible success strategy open to new members without family connections. It could go like the following. The affiliation network would have meant nothing to the members themselves, save in one respect: everyone wanted a connection to a big operator. Little people everywhere hope to attract the notice of the great, and an ancient strategy is to get physically close to them. Thousands of members passed through CBOT, and a few perceptive and enterprising types would have seen possibilities in the trifecta factors. There was little upward mobility from other member classes into the core, the best network location, but there was some. A new member might join as an isolate and form as many ties with other members as possible. A committee seat would be an obvious way to gain visibility, and the Arbitration and Appeals Committees were open to nondirectors. There, one would meet other core members, including rich and influential ones. And that could lead to better things. The whole point of CBOT was to make money, of course, and the perceptive and enterprising member would trade with the younger sons whenever possible. Their lower survival rates suggest that they were mediocre traders, and a close student of the market, a Norman Ream, say, would notice that. Professional gamblers (and inner-ring CBOT members were exactly that) do the same: they target weak players.

This route to upward network mobility was theoretically possible; whether it was actually so is another matter. At best, odds were poor. In 1930, 37 percent of isolate new members in 1920 survived; but only 1 percent of the original 1920 group—two members—were in the 1930 core. CNC members did better: 50 percent survived from 1920 to 1930, and 25 percent—seventeen members—of the original 1920 group were in the 1930 core. We have no way of knowing how many, if any, of these nineteen members followed a deliberate strategy. However they got there, their changed-up network locations would not have affected CBOT's power structure. The core was the place to be, but the dominant groups there would have overwhelmed the nineteen: in 1930, the 1920 core holdovers (two hundred members), family-connected members (174 members), and members new to the exchange (174 members).[49]

Yet, despite the importance of family, the exchange was not a closed, hereditary aristocracy. The younger family members' lower survival rate didn't help, and as best we can tell, in each ten-year cohort new members without family connections significantly outnumbered the family con-nected. With occasional exceptions such as the Rumseys, family lines did not last long enough to become dynasties. In 1920, two-thirds of CBOT members had surnames found on the 1910 list—those who themselves had been members in 1910, plus same-surnamed relatives who joined later. By 1930, this group was down by a third and by 1940 by a third again, to 25 percent of the uncommon-surnamed members. Family co-horts eventually disappeared, and other families took their places; but it took a while. In 1940, 8 percent of members had surnames found on the 1888 list. Only two were themselves members in 1888; the others had joined since. Also in 1940, besides Henry Rumsey, four other members were descendants of the eighty-two men who signed the original charter in 1848. There are police and military families; the Board of Trade had exchange families. CBOT's early members were a mongrel lot, and the organization's purposes were diffuse and ill-defined. But by 1910, CBOT had sixty-two years to find its way, and to a large extent, it had become a family affair.[50]

Present-day readers of financial news automatically assume that nep-otism is bad. So it could be viewed here, given the weaker performance of the younger family members. Not everyone would agree, though. A family business exists to support the family, and to bring in better-qualified outsiders is not necessarily a good idea. Also, if CBOT had been more straightforwardly meritocratic, competition among members would have been more intense. But given the crowd's business practices and outlook, more intense competition would have meant even more elaborate plotting, bluffs, double- and triple-crosses. Except for pious Chamber of Commerce speeches by the exchange president, ideas of public service and responsibility to customers were mostly unfamiliar concepts then. From 1921 on, commodities trading was subject to some regulatory oversight, but it was so lightly exercised that it scarcely mattered. And there was little pressure to change. The exchange got along comfortably in its hometown. Floor fights could be highly entertaining, and the newspapers covered them like sporting events. To judge by the local press, Chicagoans mostly viewed the place with amused tolerance and some civic pride. It's a shark tank, but it's *our* shark tank.

A question often asked about network analysis is whether less exotic methods would achieve the same results. The answer here is no. The only way to learn about inner-ring insiders' shared connections is through quantitative analysis of a large data set. The foundational premise of network analysis is that structure matters, and so it does here. Certainty is out of reach, but the findings have face validity. Members with high degree centrality, multiplex relationships, and ties to exchange government probably were not small fry. Within the limits of the study, it is robust: findings come from observation rather than survey, and the three ten-year comparison sets allow for repeat testing. We might expect to find similar relationships in other face-to-face financial markets, but it would be a mistake to overgeneralize. CBOT's committee structure made the network's core-periphery pattern, and exchange administrations vary widely. The Chicago Mercantile Exchange, CBOT's crosstown rival, had a more centralized administration, and the Merc's affiliation network would reflect that. The NYSE, long organized around specialist stations, would be different yet again.

The discussion of family ties is a useful transition to the final topic of this chapter: the social network itself. The older CBOT members were a natural bridge for their younger relatives into a wider range of personal relationships. Trading sessions offered few chances for socializing, but over the years, long-term members gradually would have formed personal connections. Except for newspaper reporters and visitors holding guest passes, the exchange floor was a members-only space, and the regulars assembled there every day, year in and year out. Many sources note the importance of nonfamily personal connections in the markets. As recounted in chapter 1, Jubilee Jim Fisk started on Wall Street because he knew Daniel Drew. In Theodore Dreiser's *The Financier*, Frank Cowperwood gets into the business through a personal reference. More recent accounts show the same pattern. Michael Lewis recounts in *Liar's Poker* how Salomon Brothers hired him after he made a good impression on the wife of a managing director at a fund-raiser. Lewis had earlier applied for jobs up and down Wall Street without success, sometimes getting laughed at. After his conversation with the managing director's wife, Salomon invited him to walk through an open door.[51] I got my own start on Wall Street through a personal connection. And a CBOT trader once told me, "I landed the trading job through an old friend of my dad."

Social networks are always invisible and transitory and, for this time and place, mostly untraceable as well. But we have hints and scattered anecdotes, such as a story from 1888 in the *Chicago Inter-Ocean*. In mid-September Hutchinson advised an acquaintance, a small-time speculator, to buy wheat. The tinhorn, as such individuals were called then, bought the wheat and then watched in horror as the price quickly dropped. His little capital wiped out and in debt now besides, the tinhorn went in a panic to find Hutchinson, whom he located at the Century Club. "I took your advice, Mr. Hutch—" he stammered. "Buy more" was the abrupt reply. "But—but I am broke!" the tinhorn wailed. "Borrow and buy more," said the great man, walking off. Screwing up his courage, the tinhorn borrowed every cent he could to buy wheat. After several sleepless nights, he sold out and netted $150,000—about $4.8 million in 2022. The tinhorn "fairly worshiped" Hutchinson after that. The point is, they knew each other.[52]

This story shows the essential character of the social network: unfair, irrational, and discriminatory. If the tinhorn had beat Hutchinson at poker the night before, Hutchinson might have said nothing. Unlike the transaction network and the affiliation network, the social network is not deliberately organized or rule based. Instead, social networks are emergent, meaning they spontaneously self-organize, with connections based on friendship, homophily, and propinquity. Network traffic, or its lack, depend on trust, obligations, and sanctions. Structurally, all such networks are of the small-world network type.[53]

The idea of the small-world network is of recent origin, popularized in a 1967 article by the sociologist Stanley Milgram as "six degrees of separation." But the real foundational work only dates from 1997 and 1998, when Duncan Watts and Stephen Strogatz at Cornell University published their findings. The illustration in figure 13 is an example of a simple small-world network.[54] Watts and Strogatz originally applied the term "small-world network" to human social organization. But such networks are common in nonhuman settings as well, including electric power grids, highway and commercial airline maps, nematode neurons, and the internet. The illustration comes from an article on the spread of childhood scabies; the second choice was a graph of mentoring relationships among Brazilian salesmen. Small-world networks all share the same overall pattern of low density, a high level of clustering, and short average path length. While they may contain many nodes, each one can reach every other through a few intermediary links. In the densest clusters, every node has links to every other, which in social networks may signal the presence of a clique. Also, some nodes are more "popular" than others, in that they have more links to other nodes, near and far. These "hubs," so called, serve as shortcuts between distant nodes. In commercial air travel, for instance, a passenger who starts at a small airport can reach any other small airport anywhere with a few transfers, by passing through hubs. In finance, a Kuala Lumpur banker who seeks an introduction to a New York counterpart would go to the best-connected inner-ring insider he knows. Even if the insider did not know the New Yorker, he might know another New York banker who could bring the two parties much closer together.[55]

Social networks, like all small-world networks, are simple in concept, but they can be hard to research. "Unofficial" as they are, social networks are undocumented and normally discovered via interview and survey. But bias is an ever-present problem with surveys, and survey results give only a snapshot of a continuing evolutionary process. Small-world networks are so common because they need only two simple preconditions to form. First, if two nodes A and B are connected and B is connected to C, then C is more likely to connect to A than to a randomly selected node. Second, connections form with some degree of randomness. That is, any network node A may link to any other, say Q, which has no relation to A's other connections. A may have good reason to connect with Q, but that reason will have nothing to do with B or C. From their viewpoint, A's connection to Q is random. Depending on the network, the random factor can be almost anything: sexual attraction, frequent travel, or an unusual hobby. As a result, small-world social networks are not static but dynamic on two levels: because individual nodes can act independently of other nodes, the network itself continually evolves in unpredictable ways. A configuration can change while it is being described.[56]

We cannot look directly at the Board of Trade members' social network, but rather, we can look through the affiliation network to learn what we can. Some general observations about the character of the social network are possible because social networks all share certain features.

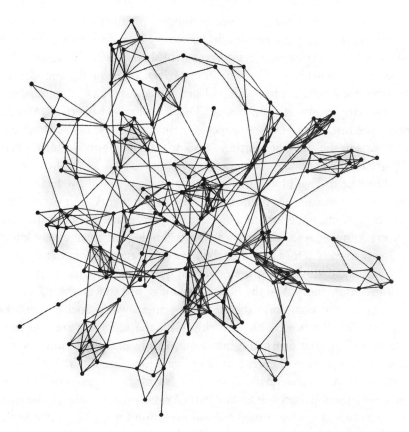

Fig. 13. A small-world network. (Illustration from Gilmore, "Control Strategies for Endemic Childhood Scabies")

There is little to be gained, however, from pointing out that, socially, the CBOT members formed a network of this type. My undergraduate alumni association also is a small-world network, and so is the Mafia. The point is, small-world social networks are value-neutral: the network does not set the course of its members' behavior. However, features of small-world network architecture do contribute to one of the most notable features of financial insider culture: its persistence. Small-world social networks are well suited to preserve and pass on cultural and behavioral norms, whatever they are.

In a generic small-world social network, it seems obvious that social power, or capital, will be concentrated in the clusters, not the outlying nodes. This is true even in a different sort of network, the CBOT affiliation network. There, the best-connected members have the longest average survival, and the isolates do far worse. In a small-world network, the network structure will reinforce established power. Nodes can become hubs for many reasons, including trivial ones, or flat-out chance. But once established, a hub will add new links faster than nonhubs, and the disparity grows as time passes. The sociologist Robert K. Merton coined the term "the Matthew effect" for this process, after the parable of the talents in the Book of Matthew. Also, while such networks form easily, they are hard to break up. A hierarchical network such as a military command can be disabled by destroying or taking control of the head, but a small-world network has no head. Small-world networks can survive and rebuild even after the loss of a significant percentage of nodes. Regulatory crackdowns, scandals, crashes, and technological change may knock out many market actors and alter the network configuration, but the network itself will survive, with enough long-term participants to preserve institutional memory. And the hubs, once hubs, will stay that way.[57]

Despite the common architecture of small-world social networks, they will differ in how dense and close-knit the members are. On face-to-face trading platforms, the business and physical environments will push the actors toward certain types of relationships. As far back as we know anything about financial markets, inside a larger population of more occasional participants, a nucleus of regulars assembles in the marketplace every day. Over time, multiplex relationships, a key factor in the establishment of trust, inevitably form. On the Board of Trade, members often belonged to the same fraternal lodges, frequented the same bars and restaurants, and, as noted, were often related. At different times, Hutchinson had a brother, both sons, a brother-in-law, and two nephews on the Board of Trade. Such a network, a closed-off group of actors meeting daily, would have had many Simmelian triads, meaning groups of three members, A, B, and C, with strong ties to one another. On the floor, all this togetherness has practical consequences. At CBOE, Wayne Baker found that experienced traders typically dealt with only two or three trusted counterparties.[58]

In a network like this, social pressure is an ever-present force field. The network would have a high degree of closeness centrality, meaning any network member could reach any other member through a few links. Information spreads quickly under these conditions, reaching the best-connected insiders fastest of all, with implications for control and cultural continuity. When a group norm or the interests of a powerful clique are crossed, it can go hard for the offending party. At CBOE, different financial instruments had regular traders and occasional influxes of outsiders when profit opportunities were especially good. At the highly profitable times, regulars used a range of social control tactics, legal and otherwise, to exclude the newcomers. From the regulars' viewpoint, the problem with the newcomers was that nobody knew them. James Coleman gives a famous example of social control and enforcement of market norms among the diamond merchants of New York, Tel Aviv, and Amsterdam. Besides their commercial relationships, the merchants have religious (Hasidic Jewish), family, and social ties with one another. The physical, institutional, and knowledge barriers to entry serve to exclude outsiders and strengthen the network further through its very isolation. To stay in business, a rule violator must make amends that satisfy the network's cultural arbiters; there is no place else to go. In extreme cases, the diamond merchants will expel a deviant member altogether. On the Board of Trade, the Big Four's vilification campaign against Hutchinson wasn't to make him feel bad but to get other members to shun him. If successful, the strategy would have forced Hutchinson to abandon his corner or ended his career on the exchange.[59]

This chapter has explored how the market *crowd* behaves, rather than individual operators. The self-organization shown in the analysis was entirely of the members' own choosing, as the study period preceded any meaningful market regulation. That is, the network was not torqued to accommodate regulators or to avoid their scrutiny but was made and maintained by the members without any outside influence. The analysis shows a clear stratification of members, one group of whom have a denser network of business and family connections, control of exchange governance, and longer membership on the exchange. Whatever they may have called themselves, the stratification matches the inner- and outer-ring split of the crowd outlined in the introduction to this book.

Since the time frame of this study, though, the nature of the crowd's network has markedly changed. From the earliest meetings in front of the Ter Beurse Inn in Bruges until quite recently, financial markets have been in fixed locations. Anyone who wanted to participate directly had to be physically present. But like CBOT itself, the physical marketplace is gone, and a virtual crowd has now replaced the actual one. For all the immediacy of modern electronic communication, it lacks the personal engagement of the old system. Nonetheless, chapter 4 shows the crowd alive and well and adapted to its new, distributed environment.[60]

CHAPTER FOUR
London, 2005–2012
"It's a Cartel Now in London"

THE SETTINGS OF THE first two cases and the network study were typical of financial markets for nearly their entire history: in an actual crowd, with business done face-to-face. This case takes place during the changeover to the present era of electronic markets, when physical locations were becoming irrelevant. As exchange floors and the curb market have gradually lost importance and often disappeared altogether, the big banks have become the crowd's main workplace. Now, the "crowd" is a virtual one, with members spread worldwide and linked through electronic media. The new network is larger, shallower, less dense, with fewer multiplex relationships and Simmelian triads. Floor rules, the traditional social controls enforced through personal observation, are weaker in the new distributed environment. But many of the old ways of doing business persist, notably cliques and pervasive deception. Critically, insider culture has now spread to the crowd's employers, the banks.[1]

The first widespread public notice of what would become the largest financial scandal in history up to that time attracted little attention. On April 16, 2008, the *Wall Street Journal* carried a front-page article by the paper's staff reporter Carrick Mollenkamp titled "LIBOR Fog: Bankers Cast Doubt on Key Rate amid Crisis." The *Journal* takes care to explain complex technical issues to its readers and did so this time. Even many financially literate readers were unfamiliar with LIBOR—the London

Interbank Offered Rate. The article was somewhat daunting, running past the jump to a second page and stuffed with details. Readers who took the effort learned that LIBOR is a key benchmark rate, that is, a rate used to set other rates. Mollenkamp asserted that the banks that set LIBOR were deliberately distorting it, so the prices of trillions of dollars' worth of financial assets held around the world were wrong.[2]

The article was a model of investigative journalism, supported with data, analysis, and statements by prominent financial economists. The trouble Mollenkamp took over his article was ironic in a way, since the thinking that went into setting the LIBOR rates was of a very different order. In the following chat transcript, two brokers discuss that day's three-month and six-month yen LIBOR fix:

> DERIVATIVES BROKER 1: Make 6m go lower! They r going up. [Senior Yen Trader] will buy you a ferrari next yr if you move 3m up and no change 6m
> CASH BROKER 1: Not bad I suppose 9625 against 01625[3]

Here, two London-based Rabobank traders discuss that day's one- and three-month Eurodollar LIBOR fix:[4]

> U.S. DOLLAR TRADER: IF THE AMBASS DOESNT HV ANY PREFERENCES, CAN I HAVE LOW 1S AND 3S THE NEXT FEW DAYS PLS MATEY . . . CHEERS HOPE U R GOOD[5]
> PRIMARY SUBMITTER: His exact word's are .. "i don't give a f*ck"..[6]

Despite the flippant tone, the stakes were high as could be. The LIBOR fix set interest rates for an estimated $350 trillion worth of loans and financial instruments held on every continent except Antarctica. In general, an interest-rate benchmark, such as LIBOR, is a moving index calculated periodically on some financial instrument or transaction. The result then sets the interest rate for some other floating-rate security. There are many benchmarks, most of them industry specific. In real estate finance, for instance, the Investment Property Databank calculates benchmark indices based on property values in thirty national markets.[7]

As of mid-2023, LIBOR is being phased out, to be replaced by SOFR—the Secured Overnight Financing Rate. But for over forty years, LIBOR was the king benchmark of them all, used to set short-term interest rates on a wide range of securities. LIBOR is actually a family of rates calculated daily for each of the world's major currencies. For money invested in a money-market- or short-term-bond fund or borrowed for a mortgage or a small-business loan, the rate was often based on LIBOR. In the U.S., the products affected most directly include private student loans, adjustable-rate mortgages (ARMs), money market funds, and bank loan funds. Th U.S.'s top four mortgage lenders—Bank of America, JPMorgan Chase, Wells Fargo, and U.S. Bancorp—all used LIBOR to set ARM interest payments. When Mollenkamp's article appeared, around 75 percent of U.S. incorporated cities and towns had some contracts, such as bonds, tied to LIBOR. It was the reference rate for about 70 percent of the U.S. futures market, including two-thirds of the swaps market, where businesses hedge against interest-rate risk. Analysts, central banks, regulators, and institutional investors used LIBOR to gauge the overall mood and direction of the market.[8]

The LIBOR fraud, for so it turned out to be, diverted far more money from its rightful owners than Bernard Madoff ever did or than any other financial fraud had up to that time. By mid-2012, regulatory agencies on four continents were investigating or prosecuting about twenty global banks that together dominate world finance. Now, more than a decade on, the LIBOR affair has faded even from the memories of readers of financial news, while Madoff still has worldwide name recognition. Madoff gave villainy a human face, and LIBOR was too complex and abstract for that. Both the Madoff and LIBOR frauds were found out during the global financial crisis of 2007–2008, which is a common pattern. When financial booms end, particularly when they do so abruptly, the receding wave exposes objects previously hidden from view.

LIBOR originated in London in 1969, near the end of the Bretton Woods era of international finance. By then, Bretton Woods had been in trouble for a while. Since the late 1950s, the U.S. economy had run persistent and large (for the time) balance of payments deficits, later enlarged further by the Vietnam War. In 1961, President John F. Kennedy tried to stem the outflow by placing controls on capital exports, which he strengthened several times during his administration. Kennedy's successor, Lyndon Johnson, imposed stricter measures still, but the policy was a failure. After President Richard M. Nixon's inauguration in January 1969 and over the course of his administration, he removed most U.S. controls over international capital movements.[9]

End to end, the U.S. experiment with capital controls lasted eight years. The controls did not affect capital movements but killed off foreign bond origination in the U.S., which previously had been a lively business. The policy had a more important and lasting result, though, in that it gave London an opportunity to recover its former position in international finance. The city had been the undisputed center of international banking until the First World War but had languished since 1945. As the U.S. withdrew from the marketplace, London once again had a role to play. The City's banking infrastructure was anachronistic and quaint, but it was comprehensive and global in reach, and it still worked. English, the imperial language, was an unbeatable advantage, spoken in capital cities everywhere.[10]

Regulatory arbitrage also played a key role in routing international banking back to London, instead of elsewhere. The Bank of England quietly discriminated in favor of cross-border transactions in foreign currencies, which made doing business in London easier and cheaper. The Bank taxed and otherwise regulated transactions and deposits denominated in pounds sterling, but not in other currencies. Other central banks, those of countries with cities that might have challenged London as a financial center, did the opposite. Worried about the disruptive effects of hot money, other large European countries actively discouraged foreign currency deposits (and foreigners who held them) within their borders. France and Germany, for instance, barred interest payments to foreigners. France and Italy banned exchanges of Eurodollars into local currency. During the later 1960s, big non-U.K. banks rediscovered the comparative advantages of London and went through a flurry of paper expansion, chartering merchant-banking subsidiaries there. U.S. banks did as well, through arm's-length offshore subsidiaries, so-called Edge Act corporations.[11]

The lax regulatory environment also drew foreign currency deposits to London banks from the mid-1950s on. European banks had held small amounts of expat money off and on since before World War I. But after World War II, much larger sums, mainly dollars, wound up in European banks. Some of the money came from Marshall Plan aid, U.S. military outlays in Europe, and U.S. balance of payments deficits. Most, though, came from bookkeeping entries that arose from international trade and investment. *The Economist* first mentioned foreign currency deposits in London banks in July 1959, estimating the total at $500 million. "Eurocurrency," though the term did not exist then, means money held outside its country of issue, whether European in origin or not. And the total was growing fast. By 1964, five years after the first mention in *The*

Economist, London Eurocurrency deposits had grown eighteen-fold, to
$9 billion.[12]

But large as the pool was, for the first fifteen or so years, there was
little loan demand for the money. Unlike domestic currency, Eurocurrency was unstable, in that interest rates changed continuously and un-
predictably. Central banks and regulators work to stabilize interest rates,
but only for their own national currencies. Eurocurrency was not regulated at all. Supply and demand, and nothing else, moved Eurocurrency
rates. Dollars, yen, Swiss francs, and so forth held in London banks had
no reserve requirements, interest-rate ceilings, limits on borrowing or
lending, depositor protection, or lender of last resort. Almost all loans
were fixed rate then, and no one wanted to commit to a long-term Eurocurrency loan because the future cost of funds could not be forecast. For
very short-term loans—270 days or less, the Eurocurrency market had
an edge: unregulated banking is cheap, like a car without safety equipment. Dollar deposits in London earned more than in New York, and
loans cost less. Central banks were active in the Eurocurrency market
from the start, and as the pool of money grew, the commercial paper
business increasingly migrated to London. But with that, the Eurocurrency market seemed to have reached the limits of its usefulness.[13]

That situation changed in 1969, when the banker Minos Zombanakis invented LIBOR. Born in an impossibly picturesque region of Crete,
Zombanakis had come a long way. Now, he headed the brand-new London merchant-banking subsidiary of Manufacturers Hanover Trust. The
title, though, was more impressive than the reality. London was full of
paper banks in those days, and Manufacturers Hanover Limited had less
reason to exist than most. The parent bank was the fourth largest in the
U.S. but was second tier even so and was less than that in London. The
bank had no international experience, reputation, or connections. If
Zombanakis didn't establish some credibility soon, the place would dis-
appear and take his job with it. Manufacturers Hanover Limited formed
in February 1969. By then, the London Eurocurrency pool stood at $44
billion, up from $9 billion five years before.[14]

In August 1969 Zombanakis made both his and the bank's reputation
with an innovative loan package. The loan was to Bank Markazi, the
Central Bank of Iran, to fund development projects in that country, and
contracted on better terms for both sides than a conventional loan. Zombanakis did better than that. He found a way to sell into a high-demand
market for large, medium-term loans that until then had gone com-

pletely unserved. He also found a way to make better use of the Eurocurrency pool. LIBOR made this and much else possible and, in time, transformed financial markets.[15]

Bank Markazi wanted $80 million for five years, and the whole request was fraught with problems. No one bank wanted to lend that much, so Zombanakis put together a syndicate of nineteen British, U.S., and Continental banks to make up the total. Even though the deal crossed many international borders, since the loan was in Eurodollars, neither side of the transaction was subject to exchange controls and taxation. Then, there was the question of the term of the loan. Odd as it sounds now, banks rarely made medium-term loans for large sums then, for reasons beyond the scope of this monograph to explain. Zombanakis solved that problem by packaging the loan as a series of short-term loans with an interest rate that reset every renewal period. Finally, the syndicate banks needed to agree on an interest rate. Zombanakis proposed, and the banks agreed, to reset the rate each loan period according to a formula that Zombanakis devised. Shortly before the rollover date, Manufacturers Hanover (the "agent bank") polled each syndicate bank for its estimated borrowing cost for a six-month Eurodollar loan in London. The weighted average, rounded to the nearest one-eighth percent plus a markup for profit, then became the interest rate that Bank Markazi paid in the next period. Zombanakis named the calculated rate the "London Interbank Offered Rate"—LIBOR. The fundamental calculation has remained the same ever since.[16]

Like photocopying and FedEx, LIBOR was such a good idea that it seemed obvious in hindsight. But no one had thought of LIBOR or anything like it until Zombanakis did. The invention of the Euroloan, as loans of this type came to be called, was itself a landmark. LIBOR-priced Euroloans transformed the Eurocurrency pool from a money market into a capital market—that is, for loans with maturities greater than one year. As with many other transformative products, the Euroloan made use of several recent innovations, each important in its own right. Banks within a single national market had formed underwriting syndicates to sell stock and bond issues for over a century, but cross-border syndicates dated only from 1963. Syndicated loans were newer still; New York banks made the first such loans in 1967. Floating-rate loans dated only from mid-1968. Euroloans filled a huge gap in the kinds of cross-border financing that banks offered. Before, the banks' international customers could only get short-term credit similar to overdraft protection and

Fig. 14. The inventor of LIBOR: Minos Zombanakis (standing),
with Khodadad Mirza Farman Farmaian, governor of the Central
Bank of Iran, 1971. (Personal papers of Andreas Zombanakis)

long-term financing through Eurobonds, both for smaller sums than the
Bank Markazi loan. The model caught on quickly. A few months later,
Iran got another, larger loan on the same terms, and other country loans
followed.[17]

The first Bank Markazi loan ushered in a new era of global finance.
Financial markets, until then essentially national, began to draw together
into a single, unified whole with its own interest rates and rules, independent of central banks. After World War II ended, the European and Japanese colonial empires broke up, and by 1969, the world was full of new
nations. All of them, even the resource-rich ones, were capital poor and
needed cash for infrastructure projects. Using LIBOR, London banks
could offer a full range of funding at attractive rates. And the money was

there: by 1970, total Eurodollar deposits exceeded all gold and dollar reserves held by governments. London once again became the world's
money mart, with a much longer customer list than before. Côte d'Ivoire
didn't need a country loan in 1910 because Côte d'Ivoire didn't exist.
Within five years, LIBOR was important enough that banks far from
London kept track of it. During my brief stint at the Bank of America in
the middle 1970s, one of my duties was to record the daily LIBOR fix,
which came to the bank every morning via the now-defunct wire service
Telerate. I then sent the updated rates to the bank's other departments,
five thousand miles and eight time zones from London.[18]

Even with LIBOR, many potential customers still found the Eurocurrency market too unstable. A floating interest rate that reset every few
months made capital budgeting, long-range planning, and projections of
revenue, income, and dividends uncertain as well. The solution was a
swap, a form of financial derivative. In a swap, two parties exchange
a stream of payments based on a fixed interest rate for a stream based on
a floating rate. Each term payment in a swap amounts to a separate futures contract, the whole packaged together as a single transaction.
Swaps involving relatively small sums of money originated sometime in
the 1970s, but the first deal of note was in 1981. On that occasion, Salomon Brothers put together a $290 million foreign-currency swap be-
tween IBM and the World Bank. A trade journal called this transaction
the "deal of the year," the first time two major institutions covered their
future needs in a given foreign currency all at once. Other banks copied
the Salomon deal, and swaps became wildly popular.[19]

LIBOR was not yet the center of everything, though, because for a
long time, the calculation was not uniform. For the early years of its existence, LIBOR mainly served its original purpose, to set interest rates for
syndicated Euroloans and later for Eurobonds. Each banking syndicate
calculated LIBOR as it chose, though differences between calculations
were usually small. But as time passed, traders increasingly used LIBOR
to price financial derivatives, which made the daily LIBOR fix critical.
Then, varying interpretations could move the rate up or down a few
basis points and make the difference between huge profits or disastrous
losses. To simplify matters and avoid ruinous infighting in the market,
the British Bankers' Association, a trade body, standardized the calculation. The result, BBA LIBOR, went live January 1, 1986, eleven months
before the Big Bang agreement restructured London's financial markets
to compete more effectively internationally.[20]

These, then, have been the twin pillars of international finance since the late 1990s: a huge, stateless pool of money, chiefly U.S. dollars, and financial derivatives. And LIBOR was the lynchpin of it all. New uses multiplied after the BBA standardized LIBOR and the derivatives markets adopted it, and the calculation spread worldwide. Today the total notional value of the derivatives market is several times the world gross domestic product. From the mid-1990s, U.S. banks started to price in LIBOR because the money market was already doing so. Banks and other financial institutions, including central banks and regulators, watched LIBOR because it moved daily and gave a real-time read on credit conditions in the international marketplace. Government policy drives many other important interest rates, such as the fed funds transfer rate (FFTR) and the prime rates of U.S. banks, but not LIBOR. All this business led back to London, which by the turn of the twenty-first century had regained its place as the world's premier financial center. New York, big as it is, mainly does a domestic business and was in second place until recently. Owing to the unsettled state of British politics, New York is now number one.[21]

The return of international banking to London was a rational development, in the classical economic sense. Eurocurrency accumulated in London and banks set up subsidiaries there because costs were lower and profits higher than in other possible locations. But much of this positive trade-off came from the permissive attitude of British regulators. Life was more complicated in New York. Legal limits on insider trading in the U.S. began in 1909 and were strengthened and elaborated in the Securities Act of 1933 and the Securities Exchange Act of 1934. For many years, U.S. prohibitions on insider trading were only lightly enforced, but the U.K. only made insider trading a criminal offense in 1980. One of many weaknesses in British market governance was that no rule, anywhere, required the banks to give accurate LIBOR quotes. No one pressed for any meaningful reforms as international banking revived in London from the 1960s on, and no reforms were made. When banking came back, traditional business methods came back as well. The 1986 Big Bang created a new financial regulatory agency, the Financial Services Authority (FSA), but it did little. The growth of London's banking business did have significant trickle-down benefits for the rest of the British economy. By mid-2007, City of London financial firms employed over 350,000 people. But later events would show that doing business this way has substantial costs.[22]

The system was at its apogee in 2007, right before the global financial crisis hit. The four largest City banks (RBS, Lloyds, Barclays, and HSBC) employed nearly eight hundred thousand people worldwide. The British Bankers' Association continued to oversee the daily LIBOR fix, which over the years had expanded well beyond Eurodollar rates. The fix came to include ten of the world's principal currencies in fifteen different maturities ("tenors"), ranging from overnight to one year—150 rates in all. For each currency, the BBA selected a panel of between eight and sixteen banks, based on the banks' reputation for expertise and London market share of transactions in various maturities for the currency. Eighteen big London banks covered all ten currencies between them. Every business day shortly before 11:00 a.m. London time, each panel bank answered the following question for its assigned currency:[23] "At what rate could you borrow funds, were you to do so by asking for and then accepting interbank offers in a reasonable market size just prior to 11am?"[24]

Traders in the panel banks who worked directly with the money market in that currency gave the daily quotes. The banks sent their quotes to Thomson Reuters, which had replaced Telerate as agent for the BBA. For each tenor, the calculation excluded the highest and lowest quartiles of submissions and averaged the remaining ones. The results then became the official daily BBA LIBOR fix, or fixing. Thomson Reuters and other BBA licensees then broadcast the fix to their subscribers, including the individual submissions of each panel bank. The LIBOR model had spread as well, and other major banking centers created similar benchmark rates. The European Banking Federation in Brussels oversaw EBF-EURIBOR for fifteen different tenors of the euro currency, and Singapore banks calculated SIBOR, for Singapore Interbank Offered Rate. There were also TIBOR (Tokyo), HIBOR (Hong Kong), MIBOR (Mumbai), and others. Rates trading became the banks' single-biggest revenue source, accounting for about 37 percent of fixed-income trading. In June 2007 the total notional amount outstanding for swaps of all kinds exceeded $500 trillion worldwide. Money flew around the world at ferocious speed and in ever greater volume.[25]

By 2007, London's banking business had burst the boundaries of the traditional financial district, the Square Mile, and powered the growth of the fabulous new Canary Wharf development. Neither the bankers nor the developers would have cared, but the location was emblematic of London's restored fortunes. Canary Wharf stood in the middle of what a few years earlier had been a miserable industrial slum, the Docklands.

Fig. 15. Canary Wharf, London, 1986. Aerial view of Docklands & West
India Dock before Canary Wharf development in East London—June 1986.
(Alamy stock photo, D2TENT)

The site once had been the Port of London, one of the greatest shipping
centers in the world, but containerization had made the docks obsolete.
The last docks closed in 1980. For years, the area spiraled downward
into ever-worsening blight, a fearsome portent of a possible future for
London and for once-mighty Britain itself. But now this. Some of the
world's largest banks moved their world and European headquarters to
Canary Wharf, including Barclays, HSBC, and RBS, all banks that later
would get into deep trouble over LIBOR. The London property market
peaked in June 2007, when HSBC's Canary Wharf building sold for a record £1.1 billion (US$2.2 billion). The architecture critic Deyan Sudjic
has labeled the impulse to this kind of building "the edifice complex."[26]

The glitz of Canary Wharf continued the trend that began in the
early nineteenth century of excessively gaudy exchange buildings. If such
displays started as an effort to dress up the business, the results are
mixed. The overall impression is often more beggar-on-horseback than
respectable, which says something about the taste of the market crowd
and its origins—"the lower walks of rural life." Then, from the early
1980s on, stories of outrageous individual excess began to circulate, at

Fig. 16. Canary Wharf, London, 2005. (Photo by Krisztian Miklosy,
depositphotos.com, license #100302246)

first occasionally and then with increasing frequency. Some of the accounts are doubtless exaggerated, but it is a common pattern and widely
known in the business. Writing of the LIBOR years, the journalist David
Enrich describes private jets to San Tropez, Monaco, and other luxury
locations and much bad behavior with prostitutes. The 2013 film *The
Wolf of Wall Street* dwells at length on the characters' full-spectrum glut-
tony. As in the film, such expenditures are often kickbacks written off
as "client entertainment," but the result is the same. Nowadays, a top-
earning inner-ring insider will spend money—or have money spent on
him or her—like a bad Roman emperor. Speaking anonymously, a New
York sommelier recalled a group of Wall Street diners asking him,
"What's your best wine over ten thousand dollars?" Consumption of this
sort is competitive, a means of displaying superior status. Michel Abolafia
quotes a young bond trader: "It's about how much you made this year or
what you bought with it. How many cars, where you go on vacation,
where your apartment is or how big."[27]

The crowd is wise enough, however, to put up a more decorous front most of the time. Nowadays, the middle office includes mathematics PhDs, and they work very hard inside the fancy buildings. But Canary Wharf and the Square Mile were not a modern version of the Dutch Golden Age or of Renaissance Florence, when commercial success joined with intellectual brilliance. In setting the LIBOR rates, the thinking was of this order:

> YEN DESK HEAD: what does [Senior Yen Trader] want with libors?
> DERIVATIVES BROKER I: . . . KEEP IMTH AS LOW AS POSSIBLE PLEASE
> YEN DESK HEAD: no probs. marking 1m down at 62
> DERIVATIVES BROKER I: HE'LL SUCK YOUR OLD FELLA[28]

On another occasion, regarding six-month yen LIBOR:

> UBS TRADER A: I need you to keep it as low as possible. If you do that . . . I'll pay you, you know, $50,000, $100,000 . . . whatever you want . . . I'm a man of my word[29]

And during a particularly sensitive deal:

> UNNAMED TRADER: Mess this up and sleep with one eye open at night[30]

Conspiracy, bribery, and intimidation are not market forces normally considered in econometric models, which suggests limits to the accuracy of the models. Yet here these behaviors are, in the biggest banks in the world's leading financial center. This was how things ran when the crowd had its way. Even a bright high school student would probably find the traders' messages disturbing, a sign of something seriously wrong—and not because of the language. At the least, rates set like this do not answer the question that supposedly underlies the LIBOR quotes. But a student only slightly older, in accounting or prelaw, could immediately name two major problems. First, traders control both assets (they buy and sell) and the record keeping for them (they set LIBOR). Second, the traders' duties create a conflict of interest. The profitability of the traders' books, and thus of their own compensation, depends on their LIBOR quotes.

The formal labels—segregation of duties and conflict of interest—may give the impression that these are merely theoretical concerns. But that is hardly true. To spell out the conflict of interest just noted, the banks employ the traders to advance the banks' interests. The traders' compensation plans, however, give them an incentive to advance their own interests instead, using the banks' assets. The more serious problem of the two is the conflict of interest, which gives traders the incentive to act wrongly. Improper segregation of duties then gives traders the ability to act and to avoid detection.

Neither of these issues is complex or obscure; both are standard features of an organization's system of internal control. Since the early 1800s, a large body of Anglo-American case law on conflicts of interest in commercial relations has accumulated, and much money has changed hands in court judgments. Conflicts of interest can result in asset loss or wastage, or the firm can blunder into civil or criminal wrongdoing. Even a cursory investigation of the LIBOR fix would have uncovered the control failures and resulting exposure. But government regulators, independent auditors, and the banks' internal auditors and compliance departments all failed. Multiple watchdog organizations had decades to identify these issues and insist on changes—and did not. The 1984 Gower Report, on which much of the London Big Bang was based, proposed limited objectives for the new regulatory agency, the FSA. Supervision should not, Professor Laurence Gower wrote, "seek to achieve the impossible task of protecting fools from their own folly. . . . [It should] be no greater than is necessary to protect reasonable people from being made fools of." But the FSA protected no one.[31]

The world financial system, backstage LIBOR rigging included, ran with few obvious problems in the years leading up to 2007. In retrospect, all the people who could have made a difference—policy makers, regulators, and senior bankers—were dangerously oblivious to the emergence of global systemic risk. When regulatory barriers insulated national capital markets, a crisis in one location was less likely to spread. The 1997 Asian financial crisis showed that times had changed. The crisis began in Thailand and spread through East Asia, and it contributed to the 1998 Russian sovereign debt default and the resulting collapse of Long-Term Capital Management in the U.S. Ten years later, when the global financial crisis struck, the lessons of 1997 had been forgotten, while market linkages had grown tighter still.

The earliest sign of what would become the global financial crisis of 2007–2008 came at the end of February 2007. On the twenty-seventh, the U.S. Federal Home Loan Mortgage Corporation (Freddie Mac) announced that it would no longer buy the riskiest subprime mortgages and mortgage-related securities. No one paid much attention at the time, but the markets were dangerously top-heavy with these instruments. By 2007, financial firms owned more than $1 trillion in securities backed by subprime mortgages. But after Freddie Mac's February announcement, more and more signs of trouble appeared. Only by the second half of the year did the firms and their minders realize that something was seriously wrong, and not just with individual banks.[32]

Interest rates generally, and LIBOR in particular, are an important gauge of the overall mood of the market—market "color," in trader jargon. Higher rates mean fear, and by the second half of 2007, fear was crowding out every other sentiment. By August and September, hedge funds had gone bankrupt or suspended withdrawals, and major financial institutions were on emergency government life support. The phrase "Shanghai, Mumbai, Dubai, or Goodbye" made the rounds, as bankers frantically cast about for places where they might remain employed. These locations are financial Siberia compared to London and show how desperate the bankers were.[33]

Then LIBOR began to act strangely. The rates had risen steadily as the crisis intensified and by the end of July stood at levels not seen in years. Then, in early August, the banks started to quote rates far too low to bear any relation to their true borrowing costs. Securities analysts and financial journalists spotted the discrepancy immediately. There are other important rates besides LIBOR, and they have known mathematical relationships to one another. To judge by such indices as the overnight index swap (OIS) rate and the fed funds transfer rate (FFTR), August LIBORs were wrong. In early September articles in the trade press drew attention to the problem, but no one yet suggested any wrongdoing. Conditions were so dire that freaks of nature seemed to be the order of the day. An unnamed Barclays Bank employee, though, had a story to tell about the odd rates. In mid-August the source told the Bank of England and the New York Fed that Barclays was deliberately submitting unrealistically low LIBORs, and the source supplied internal Barclays correspondence as proof.[34]

Over the following months, the whistleblower passed more information to the Fed, the Bank of England, and a widening range of other contacts. Meanwhile, as terrible as the markets were, they were getting worse. The regulatory agencies did not exactly ignore the LIBOR anomalies, but there were more urgent priorities. Besides, by then, LIBOR was practically a fiction; the market was so toxic that banks would scarcely lend to one another at all. Finally, in December, the New York Fed assigned several analysts to examine the LIBOR issue. On December 17 the anonymous Barclays contact told one of the Fed analysts that Barclays reported unrealistically low rates to "fit in with the rest of the crowd [the other panel banks]." The Fed analyst reported the conversation to her managers, but there the matter rested. U.S. jurisdiction over LIBOR was unclear, since it mainly concerned what foreign banks did outside U.S. borders. Also, the problem seemed mainly to be in the over-the counter (OTC) swap market, which was viewed as outside the regulatory net.[35]

The turning point came in April and May 2008, when the *Wall Street Journal* published two articles by the financial reporter Carrick Mollenkamp. The first of the two, which appeared April 16, presented evidence that LIBOR rates were wrong, as market analysts had been saying for months. But Mollenkamp for the first time accused the banks of *deliberately* quoting bad rates to make their institutions appear more solvent. A front-page article in the *Journal* gave the issue its broadest exposure yet. The Fed, the Bank of England, and the British Bankers' Association held more meetings. On the seventeenth, the day after Mollenkamp's first article appeared, the BBA announced that it would review LIBOR-fixing procedures.[36]

Six weeks later, on May 29, Mollenkamp's second article came out. Here he identified the most suspicious LIBOR tenors and banks and once again provided supporting data. Mollenkamp named Citigroup, WestLB, HBOS, JPMorgan Chase, and UBS as having the oddest submissions of the sixteen banks on the LIBOR Eurodollar panel. Coincidentally, on the thirtieth, the day after the second article appeared, the British Bankers' Association announced the results of its LIBOR review. The LIBOR fix procedures were sound, the BBA proclaimed, and needed only minor changes. By then, though, between the market conditions and the fishy rates, the big banks were reluctant to use LIBOR for anything.[37]

The *Journal*'s exposé made little impression on the most important regulators. But the articles made the critical difference nonetheless, improbably by spurring the United States Commodity Futures Trading Commission to act. The CFTC was the smallest and weakest of the U.S. financial regulators and had no clear jurisdiction over anything LIBOR related. The CFTC's writ then ran only to exchange-traded derivatives, and LIBOR chiefly affected OTC products. But Mollenkamp's articles caught the interest of two CFTC investigators, Vincent McGonagle and Gretchen Lowe. A couple of weeks later, the two alerted Stephen Obie, the acting head of the CFTC's enforcement division. Obie was then finishing a long-running and successful prosecution of several energy companies for manipulating oil prices. The CFTC had argued that the altered prices in turn distorted the prices of exchange-traded energy futures contracts. The agency's foundational law, the Commodity Exchange Act of 1936, bars acts to manipulate or falsely report information to affect prices of exchange-traded commodities. As Obie saw the LIBOR issue, if Mollenkamp was correct, then the banks had committed the same violation as the energy companies. Bad LIBOR quotes would change the prices of Eurodollar and other futures contracts traded on U.S. exchanges. The CFTC, therefore, had jurisdiction.[38]

Obie launched a formal investigation in early May 2008, but almost eighteen months passed before the agency could provide much support. Remarkably, the financial crisis was still worsening, and many of the CFTC staff were helping other agencies in rescue operations. Looking back on that time, a hedge fund manager compared the 2007 crash to a thunderstorm and the 2008 crash to an earthquake followed by a tsunami. Over the summer and fall of 2008, Countrywide, IndyMac, HBOS, and Wachovia met various ends; in the U.S., three out of the five major independent investment banks disappeared. On May 27 the Dow closed at 11,346.51, down over 20 percent from its 2007 peak. The U.S. and U.K. governments saved Royal Bank of Scotland, Fannie, Freddie, and AIG from collapse with massive infusions of cash. On September 29, 2008, the Dow dropped a record-breaking 778 points in a single day— almost 7 percent—to close at 10,365.45. In October the Bank of England estimated the total cost of the crisis to the world's taxpayers stood at £4,473 billion—US$7,808 billion—or 14 percent of 2008 global GDP.[39]

As seen from the Street, by spring 2009, every major financial institution was on the brink. On March 6, 2009, the Dow hit 6,443.27, down 54 percent since the 2007 high. But that was as bad as it got. After March 6 the Dow and other indices started to turn around. Bad as the crisis was, it would have been even worse without the vigorous defensive measures taken by the major central banks. In 2008 and 2009, the U.S. Federal Reserve Bank extended swap lines to fourteen foreign central banks to create dollar liquidity for foreign firms. As conditions gradually eased, regulators could look beyond basic survival.[40]

On May 26, 2009, Gary Gensler took over as President Barak Obama's appointee to head the CFTC. Shortly after starting his new job, Gensler learned of Obie's work on LIBOR and made the investigation a priority. Later, Gensler recalled that it took twenty months to collect enough evidence against the banks to take the cases to court. But the ball was rolling. In 2010 and 2011, the U.S. Department of Justice, the U.S. Securities and Exchange Commission (SEC), and Britain's FSA launched investigations of their own. When the agencies did file their cases, they had the banks cold.[41]

What had happened, it turned out, was the banks had panicked when the financial crisis was ramping up in 2007. Among LIBOR's many uses, it serves as a public gauge of the stability and creditworthiness of the panel banks. For the first part of 2007, the banks submitted LIBOR quotes that reflected actual market conditions. Over the summer, market conditions worsened, and the rates climbed higher and higher, as the banks' doubts about one another's solvency grew. High quotes from a bank meant that a bank was at risk, and other banks were charging it a premium to borrow money. The market routinely overreacts to news or rumors, and during a panic, any hint of a problem can easily become the real thing. By the second half of 2007, all the big banks were in trouble, Bear Stearns and Lehman Brothers terminally so. In August the banks' nerve broke, and they began to submit low LIBOR quotes to put up a false front of financial strength. The September 3, 2007, issue of the *Wrightson ICAP Newsletter*, a weekly market report, first drew attention to the problem. Other market watchers followed soon after.[42]

If that was all the banks had done, their actions would have been defensible. In 2007 and 2008, nobody, including the regulators, wanted to put further pressure on banks already struggling to survive. But the regulators' investigations found that the banks did not begin to manipulate LIBOR in August 2007. Rather, they began to manipulate it more egregiously. The lowball figures the panel banks submitted during the worst months of the crisis were a *second* conspiracy to falsify quotes. There was an earlier, underlying conspiracy that was more extensive, international in scope, and had gone undetected for decades. As market conditions eased in 2009, the banks gradually returned to their original level of rate manipulation. This original conspiracy, Conspiracy One, continued until regulators and the courts shut it down in 2012–2014. Conspiracy Two, which started in August 2007, left a trail that drew in the dreaded U.S. regulators, starting with the CFTC. But Conspiracy One was a near-perfect crime and could have continued indefinitely if Conspiracy Two hadn't blown its cover. Conspiracy Two, by itself, would have been page-three news. It was Conspiracy One that gave the LIBOR story legs, once the facts started coming out. In neither Conspiracy One nor Conspiracy Two had the banks given truthful answers to the LIBOR question about their borrowing costs, but the motives were different. In Conspiracy Two, the bankers had feared that their institutions would suffer a fatal loss of confidence and collapse if their true borrowing costs were known. In Conspiracy One, the banks had given bad LIBOR quotes to increase the profitability of their trading books.[43]

Conspiracy One began at some undefined but early point in the history of BBA LIBOR. The panel banks were already manipulating LIBOR as far back as prosecutors chose to look, which was to 2005. While the trials were in progress, a former banker wrote to the *Financial Times* that LIBOR manipulation was already routine when he started working in 1991. The manipulation could have started earlier still. At no time since the 1986 launch of BBA LIBOR had any internal control or monitoring procedure existed that would have caught such tampering. Before that, to manipulate LIBOR in its earliest, syndicated loan period would have served no purpose. Conspiracy One rigging was a version of penny shaving, accumulating fractional pennies from interest calculations in a separate account. The traders only moved their quotes by a basis point or two or three, but the banks' huge trading volume translated these changes into big money. Tom Hayes, a former UBS and Citigroup trader who became a scapegoat for an industry-wide problem, testified that a one-basis point move could make a $2 million difference in his trading book. But the rate changes were too small to measurably affect end-user prices. The only way to detect Conspiracy One tampering would have been to review the banks' internal procedures for submitting quotes. But no such review took place before the CFTC investigation started in May 2008.[44]

The full extent of Conspiracy One will remain unknown, since most of the banks prudently agreed early on to settle the cases against them. After that, prosecutors could no longer compel the banks to surrender evidentiary material. Even so, prosecutors pieced together a complex picture of many individual actors, institutions, and products, and that spanned regulatory jurisdictions around the globe. Prosecutors found evidence of wrongdoing by sixteen banks, mainly through their offices in London, Tokyo, Singapore, Zürich, and New York. Most of the tampering occurred in the shorter-term tenors, especially one- and three-month LIBOR for yen, pounds sterling, dollars, and euros. Besides LIBOR, manipulation extended to related benchmarks such as EURIBOR, TIBOR, and SIBOR. The products involved were mainly swaps—interest-rate swaps, cross-currency swaps, overnight index swaps, and others. Traders at the different banks had loosely grouped themselves into two "cartels" (their own term), though some overlap existed.[45]

Remarkably, as close-knit as the crowd is and as long as Conspiracy One ran, it was still spreading at least until 2005. Jay Merchant, formerly of Barclays and one of the most senior people charged, testified that in that year, his bosses sent him to New York to show traders there how to work LIBOR. Even then there were traders in the market who didn't get it and thus more dumb money for the taking. In the following 2007 chat, an RBS trader confers with a colleague at Deutsche Bank.[46]

> RBS TRADER: It's just amazing how Libor fixing can make you that much money or lose if opposite. It's a cartel now in London.
> DEUTSCHE BANK TRADER: Must be damn difficult to trade man. Especially you not in the loop.[47]

Court documents in the various trials published transcripts of the traders' messages, which were first-rate journalistic fodder. In this book, the messages are a unique source: they give a glass-walled view of insider cliques at work. Primary sources for the 1866 and 1888 cases show the market from the outside only. In the nineteenth century, nobody hid from market regulators because there weren't any, but there are no comparable transcripts of insider conversations. Instead we have journalists' reports of statements by Drew, Hutchinson, and others of their set, usually made to influence prices. The journalists understood the quality of the information they received and sometimes commented tartly on it. The LIBOR transcripts, though, are different. The traders were performing indeed but only for one another, or so they thought. Investors learned that their portfolio returns depended on exchanges like the following.[48]

> YEN TRADER: can we lower our fixings today please
> PRIMARY SUBMITTER: make your mind up[,] haha, yes no probs
> YEN TRADER: im like a whores drawers [that is, going up and down rapidly].[49]

And:

> U.S. DOLLAR TRADER: HI MATE, LOW IS HIGH 3S LIBOR PLS !!!
>   DONT TELL THE AMBASS HAA HAAAAAAA. SOLD THE MARKET TO-
>   DAY DOOOOOOHHHH!
> SENIOR MANAGER 1: OK MATE, WILL DO MY BEST . . . SPEAK LATER
> U.S. DOLLAR TRADER: CHEERS GEEZ, BANG ON THE MONEY!
> SENIOR MANAGER 1: NO WORRIES, I HAD TO WORK MY WAY OUT OF
>   AN AMBASS HEADLOCK TO GET THOSE IN![50]

And to encourage a novice:

> UNNAMED TRADER: If you aint cheating, you aint trying.[51]

These exchanges are revealing. Aside from the financial arcana ("can u put 6m swiss libor in low pls?"), the traders speak in one of the universal dialects of half of humanity—the male half. Not all men speak like this—hardly—though many did once and outgrew it. But all men, everywhere, will recognize the tone of horseplay, profane amusement, and phony-tough posturing. Women scarcely figure at all, except as props for lewd sniggering. A visitor to a grammar-school playground will hear this talk in its formative stages and see the boys'-club society from which it springs. From there, both language and society move on to fraternities, locker rooms, bars, and trading rooms. While the LIBOR traders engaged in the largest and longest-running criminal conspiracy in history, they conversed in fraternity-house banter. It makes a curious impression, coming from high-functioning adults earning six- and seven-figure incomes. But the market crowd has a deep-rooted cult of "toughness," perhaps stemming from the centuries of face-to-face trading, often in rough venues and between rough characters. It is hard, though, to act tough while seated at a desk. The job is all talk, all day, so that is where the macho displays come out. This speech is so widespread in the market crowd and otherwise so uncommon in their socioeconomic bracket that it is a reliable marker of membership, like gang colors.[52]

During the court trials, the accused parties had two different defenses. Not surprisingly, the traders and the executives accused one another. The traders insisted that they had followed their managers' orders. The former Barclays trader Jay Merchant testified, "Everybody knew the banks set LIBOR to their own commercial interests." The managers and senior executives, as they always do, asserted that the fraud was the work of a few rogue traders. They had been too trusting, the executives claimed. What had happened was an aberration in an otherwise blameless system. One CEO testified that he didn't know how LIBOR was calculated. To great public disappointment, there was never enough evidence to send the CEOs, directors, and executive committee members to jail. But even if they had not known specifics, the executives could hardly have been ignorant of how the traders worked. This was the business as it had always been, in the industry where the executives had apprenticed and spent their careers.[53]

It took a while, but prosecutors in one jurisdiction after another prevailed against the banks. Then came the fines and penalties. The Japanese acted first, sanctioning UBS and Citi in December 2011. The Irish followed in June 2012, also against UBS. But the list quickly grew. Between 2012 and 2014, regulators in every major world financial center fined and otherwise penalized the banks, as did the European Union. Often the fines were the largest the agencies had ever imposed. The guilty parties were a who's-who roster of the global banks, including Barclays, Citigroup, Deutsche Bank, HSBC, JPMorgan Chase, Lloyds, Rabobank, RBS, UBS, and various lesser players. British and U.S. judgments and penalties were the steepest, and the first of these were against Barclays. In 2012, the bank paid fines of $453 million to Britain's FSA, the U.S. Department of Justice, and the CFTC. Barclays cooperated with investigators and got off comparatively lightly; other banks paid more. Deutsche Bank paid the record fine, $2.5 billion. As of mid-2023, Libor-rigging penalties and civil-suit penalties are close to $10 billion.[54]

The industry itself reacted with much anger to the LIBOR revelations. Financial commentators expressed disgust over the comparatively light penalties and called instead for jail and breakup. Fund managers, industry spokespeople, and senior figures like Lloyd Blankfein, Sandy Weill, and Minos Zombanakis were unanimously harsh in their judgments. Zombanakis, retired to the citrus and olive groves of his native Crete, condemned the new bankers as lesser, coarser, and worse men than his old colleagues.[55]

But there were good reasons not to punish the banks further. As big as LIBOR was, it quickly metastasized. The investigation started with Barclays but quickly led to other banks and evidence of similar problems elsewhere. Other indices and markets for foreign exchange, energy, and metals came under investigation as well. The problems with LIBOR cast doubt on the integrity of hundreds of financial benchmarks around the world. Fearing exposure to further litigation, many banks withdrew from benchmark-setting panels, including ones untouched by scandal. So many problems emerged that the whole system began to shake, while the recovery was still fragile and incomplete.[56]

Even the U.S. regulators, usually ready to impose much heavier penalties than their foreign counterparts, worried that collateral damage could get out of hand—and with good reason. In 2002, the accounting firm Arthur Andersen was convicted on felony charges for the role of the firm's Houston office in the Enron scandal. In 2005, the Supreme Court reversed Andersen's conviction, but by then, the firm was effectively dead. In 2007, Andersen had two hundred employees, down from a 2002 total of eighty-five thousand worldwide. During the crisis, the rescue of Bear Stearns in March 2008 was costly; the collapse of Lehman Brothers six months later was much more so. Lehman Brothers had been the fourth-largest U.S. investment bank and at year-end 2007 had twenty-eight thousand employees and total assets of $691 million ($974 million in 2022 dollars). Lehman's bankruptcy was the largest in U.S. history and at the time made the financial crisis even worse than it already was. And as large as the banks were in 2008, the forced mergers during the crisis made them larger still. By year-end 2012, Bank of America Merrill Lynch, Citigroup, and JPMorgan Chase had, between them, nearly eight hundred thousand employees and $6.5 trillion in assets. Bad as Lehman's failure was, the collapse of one of the remaining banks would have been worse.[57]

Despite the scale of the fraud, LIBOR failed to create much of a public stir except in Britain. On balance, the banks' LIBOR manipulation benefited more retail customers than it hurt. Conspiracy One had negligible or anyway unprovable effects on outside customers, individual or institutional. During Conspiracy Two, retail debtors such as mortgagors benefited from the artificially low rates. Conspiracy Two mostly injured other financial institutions, and it is hard to feel sorry for a hedge fund.

In Britain, the reaction was sharper. The British economy depended heavily on the financial sector, and the LIBOR affair caused much upheaval inside the banks. In October 2012 UBS alone announced that it would cut its London-based staff by one-third. By January 2013 employment in the City was down 18 percent from a year previously. Banks closed business units, exited some countries, and subcontracted back-office work. National pride suffered as well. With the decline of British manufacturing, the banks had become the new champions. Now, they stood exposed as thieves, and the government regulators as incompetents and lackeys. Many board chairmen, CEOs, and executive committee members were forced out. The head of Britain's Financial Conduct Authority (FCA), Martin Wheatley, and deputy Bank of England head Paul Tucker both resigned.[58]

In terms of news reporting and time spent by the people involved, the LIBOR affair peaked in 2012 and then gradually wound down. By 2018, most of the bankers directly involved had different jobs or had taken early retirement to spend more time with their families. Traders, the ground troops, suffered the highest casualties. At UBS alone, by the end of 2012, fallout from LIBOR had cost thirty to forty people their jobs. A fair number found work in friendly venues; Swiss hedge funds were especially welcoming. The two main LIBOR scapegoats, ex-Barclays CEO Bob Diamond and ex-UBS and Citigroup trader Tom Hayes, had afterlives emblematic of their respective classes. Diamond resigned from Barclays in disgrace in July 2012 and was quiet for a while. Then, in December 2013 came news reports that he had raised $325 million to create a new African banking network. Hayes received a fourteen-year prison sentence.[59]

Meanwhile, business has continued as before. The LIBOR manipulation, huge as it was, was not a one-off, and no one seriously expects the banks to act differently in the future. In November 2015, six months after Barclays agreed to pay fines of $2.4 billion for foreign exchange (Forex) manipulation, the bank had to pay another $150 million for *more* Forex manipulation. This time, Barclays had set its electronic execution system to block Forex trades disadvantageous to the bank. Barclays got off lightly, again, but the failures of Bear Stearns and Lehman Brothers are experiences no one wants to repeat. By year-end 2018, the four largest of the top twelve banks each employed over two hundred thousand people and had more than $2 trillion in assets—each bank far larger than Bear Stearns or Lehman Brothers ever were.[60]

As of mid-2023, LIBOR itself is almost gone, and it has been a complex process. In 2017, the U.K. Financial Conduct Authority (FCA) announced that it would phase out LIBOR by 2022. At the time of the 2017 announcement, LIBOR and other related interbank offer rates (IBORs) set prices for financial instruments with a total notional value of $370 trillion worldwide. In April 2018, the Federal Reserve Bank of New

York began to publish the Secured Overnight Financing Rate (SOFR) to replace LIBOR. In November 2020 the Fed announced that financial institutions should not make new U.S.-dollar LIBOR-based contracts after December 31, 2021. In March 2022 President Joe Biden signed the Adjustable Interest Rate Act (LIBOR Act), which set SOFR as the default rate to transition legacy transactions priced using LIBOR. On June 30, 2023, the five remaining U.S.-dollar LIBOR settings were published for the last time. Some other IBORs remain in use; Canadian CDOR will be discontinued in 2024.[61]

In retrospect, the human dimension of the LIBOR fraud was the easy part. Conspiracy One did not stay hidden for years because the participants were fiercely loyal to one another. The main obstacles to investigation were institutional. Penny shaving is always difficult to detect, and the regulators knew almost nothing about LIBOR when they received the first evidence that something was amiss. Jurisdiction was unclear, and calculating damages and identifying specific victims and culprits have all been maddeningly difficult. But when the authorities were finally able to bring charges, the accused readily gave evidence against their colleagues in return for lighter punishment. Fifty years earlier, the trader network would probably have been harder to penetrate. Then, an insider who spoke against his fellows would end his career in finance and lose many friends besides. Social pressure in any small, close-knit network is a powerful force for conformity; to investigate crime among the diamond dealers, for instance, is all but impossible. But by the early 2000s, the changes to the financial marketplace had changed the market crowd as well, and social pressure counted for less.

For most of the history of finance, it has been a business conducted in separate, largely independent enclaves. In each location, the business was as personal as could be: every day, the same men assembled in the same small space to play the same game, one-on-one, face-to-face. Close relations were unavoidable and were essential to the business besides. A trading floor was a small, isolated village, with its own language and whose citizens worked in a specialized, little-known industry. Into the early 1970s, it could not be otherwise. Long-distance communications links could not support a high volume of real-time messaging, and regulators barred the banks' access to many markets. It is hard to imagine now, but until 1956, transatlantic voice traffic was by radio telephone. The next few years saw some improvements, but the real breakthrough came in 1965 with the launch of the first commercial communications satellite, Intelsat I. By the early 1990s, long-distance telecommunications were so fast and cheap that people took it for granted. Banks quickly put the new technology to use. They had been early adopters of Telex (tele-printer exchange) and in the early 1960s had pioneered private messaging networks. In 1977, a proprietary network, the Society for Worldwide Interbank Financial Telecommunication (SWIFT), went live, linking 239 member banks in fifteen countries. In its first twelve months, SWIFT processed about twenty-seven thousand messages daily. By 2007, SWIFT connected eighty-three hundred financial institutions of many different kinds and carried 9.6 million messages daily.[62]

Telecommunications advances would have mattered little if 1970s-era banking rules—national and international—had remained unchanged. But by the early 1970s, U.S. policy makers were losing patience with the intellectual torpor and perceived backwardness of the nation's securities industry. Firms were also near the limits of their competence. In 1968, Wall Street almost choked on a daily NYSE volume of twelve million shares, up from five million three years before. (In 2018, average daily NYSE volume ranged between two and six billion shares.) A full discussion of the legal and regulatory changes that transformed the securities industry in the U.S. and eventually the world is beyond the scope of this book. Briefly, though, U.S. regulatory changes increased transparency and competition and allowed firms to conduct a wider range of business. Many changes were controversial, with the industry or the public or both, but the business changed dramatically. Throughout the 1980s, the number of U.S. securities and commodities firms and their total labor force grew quickly.[63]

Changes in the U.S. industry had knock-on effects in foreign markets. To keep London competitive with New York, the British government imposed a host of reforms in 1986—the so-called Big Bang. All at once, brokers' commissions were negotiable, foreigners could join the stock exchange, and electronic trading was on a timetable to replace open outcry. In 1992, Japan followed with even more radical reforms to the country's securities industry. Around the same time, after the emerging markets debt crisis of the early 1980s, the World Bank and the International Monetary Fund (IMF) (both U.S.-dominated institutions) adopted a market-based strategy to promote economic development in poor nations. Briefly, the idea was that financial markets open to foreign participation would channel investment capital to the most promising projects. Responding to First World pressure and money, more and more countries opened their capital markets to foreign investors, sometimes having to first create the markets. In 1980, 59 countries had stock exchanges. By 2005, the number had grown to 117, including such unlikely places as Swaziland, Bhutan, and Cape Verde. And the money flowed. The World Bank reported that in 1986, there were nineteen emerging market country funds and nine regional or global market funds. By 1995, there were over five hundred country funds and nearly eight hundred regional and global funds.[64]

The global integration of finance was a years-long process, but today the boundaries between different financial centers seem more notional than real. Trading networks for financial instruments extend worldwide, and even the best-connected inner-ring insiders have never met many of their counterparties. Absent face-to-face contact, relations among trading partners are shallower and weaker, and business connections are less likely to become personal. Traders' relationships now more closely resemble a network of social media users than a high school student body: larger, more diffuse, and with weaker ties among members.[65]

The differences between the old- and new-style trading networks are not theoretical; people comfortable in one may not be in the other. Different kinds of people will excel or, alternatively, fail. And indeed, the people on Wall Street changed noticeably toward the end of the twentieth century. In *Flash Boys*, Michael Lewis quotes a market regular: " 'There used to be this guy called Vinny who worked on the floor of the stock exchange,' said one big investor who had observed the market for a long time. 'After the markets closed Vinny would get into his Cadillac and drive out to his big house in Long Island. Now there is the guy called Vladimir who gets into his jet and flies to his estate in Aspen for the weekend. I used to worry a little about Vinny. Now I worry a lot about Vladimir.' "[66]

The big investor is not the only one who noticed the change. My own Wall Street experience spanned the years when the Vinnys still ruled, but Vladimirs were showing up in increasing numbers. They were different types indeed. Vinny is a familiar character: a working-class borough New Yorker. In his day, Vinny's coworkers would have been relatives and even neighbors, large as New York is. Vladimir is a *hergelaufener Mensch*—literally, a "run-to-here man"—a stranger to all, whose past life is whatever he chooses to tell people. A basic lesson of migration studies is that people who leave are different from people who stay, and Vinny stayed home while Vladimir left. If they switched places, Vladimir's network would probably strike Vinny as unstable and impersonal. Vinny's network would probably lock Vladimir out completely.

As the big investor characterized Vinny, it would be easy to patronize him. But that would be a mistake. In his time and place, Vinny was the right man for the job. You don't cheat your cousin, not if you work with him every day and see him regularly at family events. Instead, you will probably help him when you can and expect help in return. But local, face-to-face networks of personal connections lost much of their value as the marketplace expanded. Then, an employer with a position to fill would look for other qualities.

Ethically challenged though it is, the crowd is tolerated because it does an important job: it sets prices. That, though, is as far as the crowd's influence has reached for most of its long history. With some exceptions, the crowd's individual members have typically been little people, in both capital and influence, off to one side of the main action of high finance. Since the Gramm-Leach-Bliley Act of 1999 ended the legal separation of commercial and investment banking, FICC has become one of the banks' most important profit centers. Once many levels down from the executive offices, the crowd now has an important say in how the banks are run. When the banks became the crowd's main employers, the crowd brought its culture with it, which has now spread to other parts of the banks.

The LIBOR case shows that, despite the radical change in the physical setting and medium of the crowd's member network, the group still behaves as it always has. From a public policy standpoint, one possible upside to the new, distributed network is that the weakened personal connections may make conspiracies easier to crack. The LIBOR case contains two important lessons: first, that insider culture has taken root in the big banks; and second, that the crowd is now independent of the members' physical location. The case in chapter 5 shows the crowd moving toward a working environment that places even fewer constraints on the crowd's activities, with implications for the group's role in high finance.

CHAPTER FIVE

New York, 2015–2022
"What Is Said on Chat,
Stays on Chat"

THIS LAST CASE CONSIDERS the use of private, unmonitored messaging platforms by the banks and the market crowd. The case shows, as do the others, crowd members ignoring external norms (in this case, regulatory standards) to survive in the marketplace. The time frame of the case runs from a few years before the COVID pandemic to mid-2023. Public emergencies often leave a society permanently changed after the initial danger has passed, and so it has been with COVID. The extended lockdown made work from home (WFH) a major public policy issue; in financial services, WFH trading seriously weakened the ties that connect the market crowd to the banks. The messaging apps made WFH trading possible during the lockdown; without the apps, the business would have been crippled. The success of this forced field experiment showed that the crowd needed much less from the banks than was once true. The banks and the crowd were already parting ways before the pandemic; the separation will now probably speed up. The crowd is gradually retiring to private practice, but the banks will remain critical institutions at the center of financial capitalism, now doing business using the crowd's methods.

Banking scandals and fines are common enough that even readers of financial news often skip over them. Such was the case in September

2022 when the largest SEC and CFTC actions in recent years attracted little notice. Then, those agencies levied fines totaling $1.8 billion against eight of the world's twelve largest banks: Bank of America, Barclays, Citicorp, Credit Suisse, Deutsche Bank, Goldman Sachs, Morgan Stanley, and UBS. Three smaller firms—Cantor Fitzgerald, Jeffries, and Nomura—paid lesser amounts. The issue was the use by the banks' front-office employees of private, unmonitored messaging apps for business purposes. Bankers at all levels had used their personal phones to message clients, counterparties, and colleagues using such apps as WhatsApp, Telegram, Signal, iMessage, and WeChat. The SEC, the CFTC, the Financial Industry Regulatory Authority (FINRA), and the banks themselves all ban these programs unless the messages are recorded and archived, which was not done. Also, as part of the regulatory settlements, the banks had to admit to wrongdoing, which was unusual. Typically in such cases, the penalized banks neither admit nor deny. But there was more than that. Several banks went on to admit that they knew their staff used unapproved messaging apps and had done nothing about it.[1]

To the contrary. Everywhere investigators looked, they found virtually everyone in the banks' front offices using messaging apps, including the compliance officers themselves.[2] In the period covered by their investigations, regulators found tens of thousands of messages sent over these channels. All this traffic should have gone through the banks' approved communications channels, such as Bloomberg Chat, Symphony, and company-issued phones. The company platforms record and archive all messages, which the banks' compliance departments (in theory) later review. The private messaging apps have no controls at all. They neither save nor forward messages, and they have end-to-end encryption so third parties cannot read them. The Signal app will automatically delete messages after a set time or once the recipient has read it. The SEC fined each bank $125 million; the CFTC fined Bank of America $100 million and each of the other banks $75 million. Since there was no way to tell if some banks were worse offenders than others, the fines levied on the banks were uniform. Bank of America paid more because one trading desk head had told his team to delete messages from their personal devices, after he learned about the CFTC investigation. They should, he said, use Signal instead and set messages to automatically delete.[3]

The cases against the eight banks originated with a 2021 SEC and CFTC investigation of a ninth, JPMorgan, by capitalization the biggest bank of all. The regulators had asked for documentation on a job the bank had done for its client WeWork in 2018 and 2019. The materials the bank turned over were incomplete, because much of the communication between the bank and WeWork had gone through private messaging apps. Investigators estimated that the two parties had exchanged at least twenty-one thousand messages in this fashion, messages that were now unrecoverable. The SEC argued that not only had JPMorgan flouted both the agency's and the bank's own rules, but the deleted messages impeded other, unrelated investigations. To judge by what was missing from the available documentation, the deleted messages contained extensive discussions between senior JPMorgan bankers, WeWork, and third-party advisers about debt and equity underwriting. JPMorgan paid a $125 million fine to the SEC and $75 million to the CFTC.[4]

These are by far the largest fines ever levied against the banks for record-keeping lapses. Fines of $200 million usually come only in cases of fraud or harm to customers, which was not the case here. The fines were as large as they were because the messaging apps can cover illegal or reckless behavior. They may have done so on this occasion; there was no way to tell. The LIBOR case showed regulators how useful (to them) electronic messaging could be for policing the markets. After LIBOR, electronic messaging records provided key evidence in all the big financial scandals of the time, including Forex, tax evasion, money laundering, and mortgage debt manipulation. For a good ten years before encrypted messaging apps were available, traders had messaged one another over Bloomberg terminals, which recorded their conversations. There was no reason to think bankers were behaving worse than usual during this time, but it was a period of unique transparency. For the first time, outsiders could read traders' conversations, complete with attitude and patois. Witnessing the fate of their unfortunate colleagues—some of whom went out of trading rooms in cuffs—bankers learned the obvious lesson.[5]

WhatsApp was founded in 2009 and did well from the start; within five years, it had about six hundred million users and was the most widely used messaging app in the world. Toward the end of 2014, the company's founders contracted with Open Whisper Systems to encrypt WhatsApp messaging; rollout was completed in 2016. The encryption feature was key. WhatsApp was ideal for bankers who wanted to escape the over-transparency of their employers' sanctioned communications channels. Users could get around compliance departments, regulators, bosses, journalists, and everybody else. Starting in the Asian markets in 2015, WhatsApp use spread rapidly and by 2017 was on its way to becoming the worldwide standard in finance and just about everywhere else. Nowadays WhatsApp has about two billion users and remains the most widely used messaging platform. WhatsApp started with text chats and has since added encrypted voice messaging and video recordings.[6]

Bankers did not migrate to WhatsApp and similar programs just to avoid scrutiny. The apps are faster than email, and the industry rewards speed. Critically, too, the bankers want to accommodate their clients. Client preferences, more than anything else, put the bankers—and the banks themselves—in a difficult position. Regulatory standards for many clients, especially international ones, are not as strict as for the bankers. A banker is not going to refuse to accept a client's message because it comes over an unauthorized channel. The problem is especially acute in investment banking, which is a relationship business. Bankers spend years developing ties with clients, which inevitably result in informal communications. Bankers do not want to ask a prospective client to switch phones in the middle of a conversation. Common practice on Wall Street nowadays is for traders, brokers, and bankers to exchange messages with many different counterparties, colleagues, and customers all at once. Depending on the client's preference, these chats may take place on different platforms as well: WhatsApp for one conversation, Telegram for another, WeChat for Chinese customers.[7]

The revolution in mobile communication has left departments and government regulators permanently behind, with no clear way to catch up. In 2017, the U.S. Department of Justice and the U.K.'s Financial Conduct Authority warned about the dangers of off-system messaging. In 2018, FINRA and the SEC issued statements that encouraged firms to stay abreast of the evolving technology. Later in 2018, the SEC issued guidelines that forbade the business use of private encrypted messaging platforms, but the policy was too strict. The agency relaxed the rule the following year to allow limited, supervised use of the messaging apps. The banks also groped for a response. At first, they banned personal phones on the trading floor, but the policy was unrealistic. In the last half of the decade mobile phones were everywhere, and people used them indiscriminately for business and personal messages. The banks then tried issuing separate company-owned phones for business communications, but nobody wanted to carry two phones. The banks eventually settled on a one-phone policy—the employee's own—and looked for information technology (IT) solutions to solve the message-capture problem. Results have been mixed.[8]

While the banks were willing to spend money on IT, they paid less attention to the more difficult problem of creating an effective enforcement regime. The banks' compliance departments focused instead on areas where penalties are harsher, such as money laundering and tax evasion. Historically, record-keeping cases have been rare and the fines small. Before the 2021 JPMorgan case, the largest record-keeping fine had been a $15 million charge against Morgan Stanley in 2006. FINRA, not the SEC or the CFTC, usually policed record keeping, and FINRA's fines were smaller still. In late 2020, FINRA fined Deutsche Bank $2.5 million for not having a proper system to enforce the SEC's record-keeping rule. Typically a bank would write up a policy forbidding the business use of the messaging apps and then forget about it—which was good in its way, because the policies were in equal measures strict and unrealistic. Even virtual whiteboards presented in online meetings were sometimes to be retained and archived. Phone conversations and text messages with business content were all to be recorded and sent to the compliance department. Given how fast the market moves and the daily volume of messages even a single banker might send or receive, the requirement was impossible to meet. Bankers reacted as people do when faced with unrealistic rules; they ignored the rules but tried not to be too obvious about it. Occasionally the banks would fire somebody for using the messaging apps but too seldom to be taken seriously.[9]

So matters stood at year-end 2019, before COVID changed everything. The COVID pandemic is recent history, but it is still surprising to look back and see how quickly it happened. On December 31, 2019, the government of Wuhan, China, reported a mass outbreak of pneumonia, cause unknown. Three weeks later, on January 20, the United States and other countries confirmed cases. On January 30 the World Health Organization declared a global health emergency, and the following day, the Trump administration restricted travel to and from China. By then, worldwide infections stood at nearly ten thousand, and over two hundred people had died. By early March the news was full of horror stories, and for all anyone knew, the end of humanity had come. There was no cure or vaccine, and there might never be. By March 26 the U.S. led the world in number of infections.[10]

At the beginning of March, staff still crowded the banks' trading rooms, and the scene looked relatively normal. That would soon change. *Insider* called the days that followed the most volatile trading days in history. The CBOE Volatility Index, the VIX, shot up on February 24 and after that swung about wildly. Stocks, bonds, currencies, and commodities all made records in how far and how fast they dropped. Investors stampeded to safer assets, mostly U.S. treasuries and German bunds, and yields plunged. On March 9 the yield on benchmark U.S. ten-year treasuries dropped to a record low of 0.31 percent in the worst sell-off since the global financial crisis. U.K. bond yields tumbled below zero for the first time. Saudi Arabia and Russia chose this moment to engage in an oil price war, after talks among OPEC members to support prices collapsed. Both countries flooded the market with cheap crude, just as COVID was causing the first drop in demand since 2009. On Monday, March 9, oil closed down 25 percent in New York, the biggest one-day drop since 1991. The same day, the S&P 500 plunged almost 8 percent, the biggest one-day drop since 2008. On March 16 the VIX closed at a record high of 82.69, surpassing the record set in November 2008. The same day, the Dow Jones Industrial Average dropped nearly three thousand points, the worst day since the Black Monday market crash of 1987. From the S&P 500's all-time high in late February, by the end of March it lost 34 percent of its value.[11]

The banks sometimes try to present themselves as technology companies, perhaps to persuade people they aren't really banks. But they are and always have been people organizations, with low fixed capital except for real estate. Their fortunes rise or fall on the creativity and efforts of their employees. Such organizations can move fast when they have to, and so the banks did now. The big technology firms took a decade to figure out WFH. The banks did it in a couple of weeks, during the worst public health emergency in a century.[12]

Banks depend on their people, and it was precisely the people who were at risk. The banks quickly understood how dire the health emergency was and by early February were already canceling investment conferences, sales meetings, and employee business travel of every kind. The trading rooms were the bigger problem. They were an ideal environment for the spread of a contagious disease, and there was a real possibility that half a bank's FICC staff could get sick all at once. Starting in early March, the banks started sending traders home and scrambled to get them the necessary hardware and software, without knowing if trading from home was even possible. Cybersecurity, compliance oversight, and communications speed and reliability all became secondary considerations at best. The SEC, FINRA, and the CFTC all relaxed many rules. As during the global financial crisis, the regulators did not want to put pressure on the banks when they were already struggling to cope. By the first of April, when the U.S. led the world in confirmed COVID cases, most of the banks' New York FICC staff were working remotely.[13]

WFH trading was a gamble and would have been reckless if the banks had had any choice, but they did not. But the traders were up to the job. The market crowd might fall short of some standards of polite society, but its members are smart, fast, and nervy—good qualities to have in a crisis. Plus, they knew crises. Anyone who has survived any length of time in the markets has gone through periods of enormous stress. And trading from home proved more doable than originally supposed. Trade in options worked less well, for reasons that were unclear. But most FICC lines of business did fine. It helped that the traders' own compensation hinged on their performance. In the early stages of WFH, traders improvised with whatever tools they could find, stringing together laptops, phones, and big-box electronics, often in fanciful and even humorous ways—"rona rigs," they came to be called.[14]

In this anything-goes environment, messaging traffic exploded. Pre-COVID, the banks would not have considered letting their employees use applications like Zoom and WhatsApp. Now they were essential. If the apps had not existed, trading from home might not have been possible. The apps were the fastest communication lines the traders could use right away, without waiting for the specialized hardware and software the banks would provide. WhatsApp message traffic nearly tripled from March through May, compared to the previous three months. At the end of April, Zoom reported that the rate of installations on Windows devices in financial services firms had almost doubled over the previous four weeks. By April 2020 Zoom had three hundred million users, up from ten million the previous December. Based on traffic volume, messaging applications, customer relationship management software, and email were the most popular workplace tools, in that order. The apps were especially useful for traders who transacted across asset classes, and they even helped with market color. Traders could get a sense of the whole market by keeping multiple message threads running at once.[15]

The COVID lockdown forced the banks' managers to take measures they previously would have considered unacceptable, but things went better than anybody expected. Forced to work from home, many bankers—not only traders—found that they could do their jobs just as well and sometimes better. Wealth managers worked with confidential client data and had to work privately anyway. Investment bankers did fine as well.

Some jobs saw a productivity jump. Many traditional business practices, once thought indispensable, proved not to be. Bankers found that meeting clients in person was less important than they thought. In February, when Morgan Stanley canceled its annual investor summit in Hong Kong and moved it online, registrations jumped 50 percent from the previous year. The number of companies taking part topped early estimates four-fold, and for the first time, some conference registrants came from outside Asia, including several from Qatar, Canada, and France. With business travel restricted, the time spent on airplanes, client entertainment, and co-ordinating meetings among many participants all went away. Bankers could arrange Zoom meetings in minutes and instead spent more time working with clients. Business moved faster than ever, which surprised everybody. The business of financial markets has always run through a crowd of buyers and sellers jammed together. Many, especially senior executives who had grown up in the business, could scarcely imagine otherwise.[16]

And now was the time to run the business flat out. The havoc in the marketplace caused by the pandemic opened up risks for huge losses but also opportunities for huge profits. Trading spiked as investors rushed to protect their portfolios from declines. Four of JPMorgan's all-time top ten volume days in foreign exchange trading came in the two-week period around the end of February and the beginning of March. On March 9 the bank traded a record number of shares in the U.S. On March 16 Barclays brought in $250 million in trading revenue in a single day, with profits all across the trading franchise. Citigroup reported in early March that it had brought in $500 million more in revenue in 2020 than the same period the previous year.[17]

Investment banking did well too. Corporate bonds are the single most important source of financing for U.S. corporations, and they needed cash—lots of it—to get through the crash in demand. Investment bankers who worked in origination and restructuring could scarcely keep up with the business. By the end of April, U.S. debt capital market volumes topped $1.5 trillion, up 39 percent from the same time the previous year. Mergers and acquisitions, though, suffered badly. M&A depends on good prospects for future earnings, and conditions were so unsettled that earnings were impossible to predict. The money from trading and investment banking came at a good time, because it offset heavy losses stemming from loan defaults, decreased consumer spending, and near-zero interest rates. Most of the banks lost money in 2020, but it was not a disastrous year.[18]

After several false starts, the banks reopened their offices for good in spring 2022, but there was no consensus on how many staff should return or for what percentage of the time. Some banks, mainly U.S. ones, wanted everyone in the office full time. Other banks, mainly European ones, allowed many staff to continue WFH, if they so wished. Many employees had discovered that they preferred WFH and resisted the calls to return to the office. The banks that took the hardest anti-WFH line had the most trouble. Already in mid-2020, when COVID was still raging, Bloomberg surveyed eighty-five traders, and four-fifths of them said they wanted to work remotely at least part time, when the lockdown ended. Over 50 percent said they wanted to work from home at least half time. Not everyone felt this way, but many did. The clash of wills between employees who want to continue WFH and bosses who want otherwise is ongoing; positions are far apart and with little give on either side.[19]

Messaging app use had ramped way up during the COVID lockdown, and it stayed up. Whether the bankers were in the office or not, by 2022, WhatsApp, Signal, and the rest had become the information highway in financial markets for both bankers and clients. As the pandemic wound down in 2021 and 2022, the banks once again made private messaging apps off-limits, but enforcement remained lax. In a mid-2022 survey, only 15 percent of senior compliance officials in financial services firms reported that their firms monitored WhatsApp at all, and only 3 percent monitored Signal. Even approved channels got little attention. Only 40 percent of firms monitored Bloomberg Chat, and the same for Microsoft Teams. As before the pandemic, in 2021 and 2022, a bank would occasionally fire somebody who was caught out. But these disciplinary actions were so widely spaced that the only lesson they taught was, Don't be stupid.[20]

But regulation had changed, even if the banks had not. Under the Biden administration, the SEC and CFTC penalties of 2021 and 2022 showed that the U.S. government once again took white-collar crime seriously. Having found nine large and three smaller banks in flagrant violation of the messaging rules, the SEC is looking for more of the same and will doubtless find it. To prosecute such cases is an easy, cost-effective choice for the agencies, and their legal right to demand that bankers archive and preserve their electronic communications is beyond dispute. The SEC's foundational law, the Securities Exchange Act of 1934, required broker-dealers to preserve business records but did not specify the medium. Also, these are offenses of the firms rather than individual employees, which could get messy. They are strict liability cases, so wrongful intent is not an issue. Such cases are easy to prove, so investigations are not long and costly; either the bank has complete records, or it does not. Nor must the agency go to court if the offending bank is willing to settle. In 1990, Congress gave the SEC power to set penalties in its own administrative proceedings. A bank could contest a penalty in court, but firms would rather avoid a fight with their regulatory agency, with which they will have to get along in the future. Also, court fights bring publicity, and nobody likes the banks anyway. Most firms would rather settle in advance rather than fight a battle with significant political and reputational risks.[21]

Finally, investigations of messaging violations are almost certain to succeed because regulatory standards and the banks' own policies, as they now stand, are almost impossible *not* to violate. In early 2023, the SEC issued a multipoint description of best practices for compliance. These included a risk assessment, setting strict policies and supporting procedures, providing training, displaying leadership by example, and much more. The SEC also advised banks to prepare for anticipated guidelines, before knowing what those guidelines might be. There is little chance of all these things being done so thoroughly that a regulator could not find something wrong. And even the most detailed and rigorously enforced compliance regime will not stop private messaging, not where it counts. Employees have no right to privacy in the workplace, and the banks can watch their employees' workplace activities as closely as they like. But while employees have any personal lives at all, they will have private conversations beyond the reach of compliance departments and regulators, short of a search warrant. The business of financial markets rests on relationships that are at least partly personal. U.S. employers have no clear legal basis on which they can inspect employees' personal communications, and the Supreme Court has held that the public has a reasonable right to personal privacy. Companies that cross that line risk lawsuits.[22]

Owing to the sizable penalties that the banks have recently paid, they will probably try harder to police messaging app use. But the banks are in an impossible position, trying to enforce an unenforceable policy. The enforcers and their targets will probably settle into an imperfect but mutually acceptable equilibrium, which could last a long time. The banks will make a credible effort to comply with the agencies' messaging policies, but there will inevitably be breaches. The agencies will penalize the breaches with large fines, but compared to the banks' overall revenue and profitability, the fines will be small. Bank of America Merrill Lynch paid the biggest fine in 2022, $225 million, which was less than 1 percent of the bank's after-tax profits that year. As a percentage of profitability, Morgan Stanley fared the worst of the eight banks, paying just over 5 percent of the bank's after-tax profits. Much of the profit came from the banks' FICC operations, which consistently earn the most revenue of the three front-office divisions. If the FICC business costs a bank an extra couple of hundred million dollars a year, the bank will pay it. As noted earlier, an 1860s Wall Street saying was that you can lose ten thousand dollars to make twenty thousand, and the thinking has not changed.[23]

The market crowd, for its part, will fiercely resist any interference with the crowd's app usage, which would strike at the heart of how the crowd does business. In these days of a single, geographically dispersed marketplace, the apps carry the communications traffic that connects the crowd's social network. The network makes the crowd; without it, they are stags and outer-ring insiders, far from the action, without access and too slow. Also, traders share tips, information, and rumors with one another all the time. No one is going to use official channels to send a message that might set off an alarm. Using the apps, the market crowd can do business in the old style, through efficient use of its social capital and instant response to any valuable insight or piece of information. Freed from the banks, crowd members will once again do business as individual operators and in small partnerships and cliques. With the apps, the crowd can continue business without interruption—and without the banks.

One of many unexpected results of the COVID pandemic was to free the crowd to leave the banks and return to its roots. For nearly thirty years the banks and the crowd have been partners and fellow travelers, but with different and often antithetical interests. The forced switch to WFH during the pandemic showed that modern-day trading is movable. The technical kit can go anywhere, and the universal use of messaging apps for market communications makes the company-sponsored platforms unnecessary. The banks have less and less to offer crowd members, other than the money to back their trades. Post-COVID studies show that experienced, senior staff can work well remotely, can be more productive than in the office, and are more likely to choose WFH than are junior staff. The latter want to be in the office; they learn their jobs more quickly there, and they get more opportunities for professional advancement. But inner-ring insiders do not need training; they do not care about promotions or professional advancement unless they afford an opportunity to make more money. And WFH comes with a benefit beyond price: *You never see the boss.*[24]

To conclude, the scofflaw attitude, as outsiders could view it, that the crowd displayed with the messaging apps is consistent with the crowd's behavior in the earlier case studies. The broader significance of this case is what it shows about the *banks*. It is odd to recall that until recently, people viewed banks as stodgy—low-paying, low-energy places to work, without much of a career path. Industry news was dull, page-three stuff. In recent years, though, the banks have been embroiled in one scandal after another. The LIBOR and Forex schemes required the collusion or at least complicity of many people and use of the banks' money, infrastructure, and specialized expertise. Nor were LIBOR and Forex the end of it. Time after time in recent years, the banks have grabbed profits earned in questionable or flat-out illegal ways. The market crowd's trademark practices now are standard operating procedure for the central institutions of financial capitalism. It was not always so.

The market crowd will leave its mark on the banks, as the two slowly part company. But for some time to come, the crowd and the banks will remain together, and they understand each other. With the messaging apps, the best that the banks can ever do is to *show* that they did their best to enforce the rules. The banks' compliance departments do important work, but the job here will be mainly performative. No one will ever say so aloud, but the unspoken directive from the banks' management to their FICC employees might go like this: *Make your numbers. We don't care how, and we don't want to know. We have a compliance regime we will follow and enforce, even though we know it is unrealistic. If something goes wrong, we will mount a credible investigation, but we hope we don't find anything. If we do, we will throw you to the SEC. Make your numbers.*

Conclusion

FINANCIAL COMMENTATORS HAVE HAD much to say about how the market crowd treats investors and how well, or poorly, the industry serves the public interest. This book has focused on a topic that has received less attention, on how members of the crowd behave toward one another and what sets the group apart from the business and cultural mainstream. The case studies show that the crowd's ways have changed little as far back as archival sources allow for detailed examination, to the middle nineteenth century. Scattered evidence suggests that the group had similar customs all the way back, in the first stock market of all in seventeenth-century Amsterdam. The crowd itself has reorganized over the past thirty or so years, but the culture endures. In the case studies presented here, the crowd's key features are the following:

1. Division between outer-ring and inner-ring insiders
2. Small-world network self-organization
3. Strong group identification and inward focus (entitativity)
4. Contempt for customers
5. Leading role of cliques
6. Pervasiveness of deception (opportunism), in both external and internal dealings
7. Patronage relationships
8. Very short-term planning horizon and memory
9. Constant search for an edge[1]

Superficial distinguishing behaviors of the present-day crowd include competitive consumption, excessively profane language, and much conversation about and preoccupation with money.

This cultural persistence stands out since everything else about the marketplace has changed multiple times even within the past century. Continued change is a given, and the ground is shifting now. The crowd will benefit by leaving the banks, but the banks will benefit too. The extended COVID lockdown showed that many jobs, including banking jobs, can be done from home as well as in the office, and sometimes better. The biggest costs to businesses are real estate and people, and firms continually look for ways to use less of both to do the same work. The front office is an expensive labor force, and the top four financial centers—New York, London, Singapore, and Hong Kong—have some of the highest real estate prices anywhere.[2]

The banks have worked for years to reduce their front-office headcount anyway, and post-COVID staff preferences for WFH will probably speed the process. Total front-office headcount in the top twelve banks peaked in 2012, and since then, the group has steadily shrunk. By year-end 2022, head count was down 25 percent, to forty-nine thousand, from the 2012 peak. FICC head count dropped even more over the same period—from twenty-five thousand in first quarter 2012 to sixteen thousand at year end 2022—a drop of 36 percent. In 2019, FICC revenue was $4.3 million per FTE; in 2022, it was $5.9 million, a 37 percent increase. Over the same period, FICC head count dropped 2 percent.[3]

The rate at which the banks can automate trading sets the pace of staff shrinkage. Robots are not only cheaper but often better. A McKinsey study found that digital trade execution increased front-office revenues per producer eightfold, and automated posttrade processing quadrupled back-office productivity. Another study found that algorithmic trading outperformed humans for the entire period from 1992 to 2015. The artificial intelligence models did five times better than humans in the 2000 dot-com collapse and seven times better during the worst of the global financial crisis. Put another way, the study showed that neither crisis would have been as severe if robots had been trading. According to Deutsche Bank, in 2019 in the U.S., algorithms completed 90 percent of equity-futures trades and 80 percent of cash-equity trades without any human input. In a related development, high-frequency trading (HFT) continues to grow as a percentage of total volume and now accounts for half the trades in the U.S. stock market. For some classes of derivatives, the percentage is higher.[4]

The crowd will not entirely depart from the banks but mostly will, probably to the relief of the banks. As the case studies show, the market crowd is not an ideal labor force. Worse, rogue traders pop up disturbingly often, and they can cost a bank far more than any fine. A famous case, but not the largest, was the "London Whale," Bruno Iksil, a London-based derivatives trader for JPMorgan Chase. In 2012, Iksil cost his bank over six billion dollars in trading losses and more than a billion dollars in fines for regulatory violations. There are many other examples. The present record holder for the greatest loss is Jérôme Kerviel, formerly a junior derivatives trader at Société Générale who in his last full year at the bank earned $66,000. In January 2008 Kerviel's supervisors finally noticed that he had made almost eleven hundred un-authorized trades in stock index futures. He had accumulated a position of $73 billion, just under two and a half times the bank's total sharehold-ers' equity. When everything settled, Kerviel's trades had cost the bank $9.8 billion, 73 percent of the firm's 2007 operating income. Kerviel went to jail, probably small comfort for the bank's employees and share-holders. More recently, in 2019, a rogue oil trader cost Mitsubishi $320 million in unauthorized transactions disguised as legitimate hedges for customers.[5]

That the crowd and the banks are moving apart does not mean the crowd will become extinct, just that it will become less visible. The crowd will once again be an inward-focused subculture on the edge of the economic mainstream, as it has been for most of its history. Inner-ring insiders can still earn a princely living, and profits will come as they always have, from efficient use of social capital. Trading in financial in-struments will continue to be a major profit center for the banks, but the crowd will have little to do with it. The banks' new hires into FICC will probably have degrees in mathematics and be skilled in coding and artifi-cial intelligence. And as the crowd moves away from the banks, the num-ber of Harvard and Princeton graduates in the group will drop sharply. In the banks' Ivy League recruiting, they promoted themselves as "the next Harvard" and "the next Princeton." According to the banks, the lucky few they hired would be the elite of the elite, astride the world. But no one will mistake the future, postbank market crowd for the next Har-vard. For most of the crowd's long history, it has been all but invisible to the larger world, and so it will be again. The crowd itself will gradually move away from the market center, but it will leave behind an important legacy: the spread of insider culture to the big banks.[6]

It has been said that when commercial banking and investment banking get together, investment banking wins. So it seems, and more than that; within investment banking, trading wins: that is, the bank's focus shifts from fiduciary relationships to transactional relationships. Investment bankers try to develop fiduciary relationships, ideally putting clients' interests first and forming long-term connections with them. A transactional relationship, as in trading, is straight-out competitive and ends when the money changes hands. The banks' relations with their clients increasingly are of the latter sort. In money terms, it makes sense that trading would dominate the front office and, through it, the rest of the bank: trading is more profitable. Now, across business lines, in recent years the banks have repeatedly shown that when money is on the table, they will pick it up, regardless of its source. In the future, with the move to electronic trading, the pervasive deception, backchannel information sharing, price manipulation, and all the rest will probably be embedded in computer code. Already there have been problems with algorithmic and HFT strategies that shade into illegality.[7]

Until now, this book has focused on *how* market insiders behave, rather than *why* they behave as they do, in particular, why the group has such a high incidence of opportunistic behavior. On this topic and on reasons for the group's surprising long-term cultural persistence, more remains to be said.

The persistently high rate of opportunistic behavior is one aspect of the broader long-term cultural persistence of the group. Turning first to persistence in general, the longitudinal analysis of CBOT members showed a network structure where group norms and folkways, however they originated, could survive unchanged for a long time. Many barriers, including physical ones, separated the CBOT market crowd from the public. The family ties would have bound members together even more tightly. And the floor was hardly a democracy; an elite dominated the group, and elites tend to be conservative. They benefit from the status quo, and they want to preserve it. Isolates were clearly an inferior caste, counted for little, and didn't last long. The inner-ring insiders, who would have been in the larger group of long-term members, were the men who counted on the exchange. Inner-ring insiders had the advantage of their shared social network, and they ran the exchange's governance committees. Because they outlasted other exchange members, they had the time to form more personal connections, which would have strengthened their position further. They were also the keepers of institutional memory and the arbiters of what passed for fair play on the exchange.

But public attitudes also help preserve the ways of the crowd. Just as the crowd's customs have remained unchanged for a long time, so has the crowd's reputation. Commentary in British newspapers and broadsides shows that public disapproval of financial speculation preceded the South Sea Bubble of 1720 and has changed little since. The U.S. stock market began in 1791 with the issue of two corporate charters, for the Bank of the United States and the Bank of New York. Almost immediately, a speculative bubble began to build in the two stocks and collapsed as bubbles always do. Journalists and politicians deplored the excesses of the market in terms that could have come from British newspapers seventy years before—or two hundred years later. Deceit, sharp practices, and outright fraud were rife in the marketplace; and to get money through speculation was contemptible. Unlike agriculture, manufacturing, or trade, speculation produced nothing of value. Something must be done.[8]

Finance is not the only industry that is the target of unrelenting public hostility. The business falls into an occupational category that sociologists label "dirty work," and dirty work comes in three varieties. Physically dirty work entails contact with offensive material (garbage collection); socially dirty work brings workers into contact with objectionable people or conditions (addiction counseling). Neither category applies to finance, except in one important respect. The public typically views physically and socially dirty occupations as necessary evils, and this is true of finance. As disliked as the banks are, there are no serious calls to abolish them altogether. Big business has been markedly unpopular since it first emerged in the 1860s, some industries more than others. Finance is toward the low end of the list, with tobacco, oil, pharmaceuticals, and agribusiness: disliked and distrusted, grudgingly tolerated.[9]

But more than tobacco or pharmaceuticals, finance also falls into the third category of dirty work: morally dirty. While physically and socially dirty occupations are generally viewed as more necessary than evil, the opposite is true of morally dirty occupations. The sex trade, loan sharking, and professional gambling are examples. Such occupations are considered on or over the boundary of what is legally and socially acceptable. Unlike workers in the first two categories, workers in morally dirty occupations are at best presumed to be themselves of dubious virtue and probably not even that. The products of mass culture mirror public attitudes. In Anthony Trollope's 1875 novel *The Way We Live Now*, during a heated argument with her family, a highborn young woman threatens to go off and marry "some horrid creature from the stock exchange." So there. In 2015, *The Economist* noted that Hollywood villains either have British accents or work in finance. To my knowledge, no film has ever portrayed Wall Street even in a neutral light. Bank *robbers* receive more sympathetic treatment. People who have never been on the same continent as Wall Street know the place by name and don't like it.[10]

These attitudes are not abstractions. When my son was in elementary school, a teacher told him and his whole class that because I worked on Wall Street, I must be a crook. In those years, I sometimes deliberately avoided mentioning my job. I did not want to have to defend my industry, my firm, my work, and my character—again. Finance workers often have such experiences, but not workers in other legitimate but unpopular industries. Except for senior executives, employees of tobacco, oil, pharmaceutical, and agribusiness firms are not assumed at prima facie to be personally corrupt. Nor do companies in other industries face regular calls for their breakup, as do the banks. To work on Wall Street in some ways resembles being a member of a hard-done-by racial or ethnic minority. People always assume the worst.[11]

Workers in other occupations do not face these kinds of challenges to their self-esteem and place in society. Morally dirty workers must rely on one another for support and acceptance to a degree that most people would find unfamiliar. Stigmatized groups, the market crowd included, have a strong sense of "entitativity," being distinct and different. In finance, the instant connections made possible by modern telecommunications have strengthened the sense of a shared group identity. Meeting by chance, insiders from widely separated markets will often experience a feeling of species recognition. While a feeling of belonging may sound desirable, the crowd's thinking has a paranoid cast. Members are wary of outsiders, often for reasons of personal experience. Probably as an ego defense, a common feature of the thinking in morally dirty occupations is contempt for the customers. In finance, the older terms for customers, "flunkies," "lambs," and "grangers," are no longer used; the modern term is "dumb money," though variations exist. In one firm that I know of, some years ago absorbed by another, employees called customers "millet." An ex-Goldman banker recently charged that Goldman's London managing directors referred to clients as "Muppets." (Goldman denies this.) However the public hostility started, it is now both cause and effect.[12]

Moving on to opportunistic behavior, plenty of evidence shows that a real problem exists, not just prejudice and misperception. A broad-based study of equities options found evidence of "informed" trading in 25 percent of the sample. One study found that economics students are significantly more dishonest than others in matters of business ethics and money. Another study showed that attendance at top U.S. business schools weakens students' moral character. In a survey of five hundred senior financial executives in the U.S. and the U.K., nearly one-third said their compensation plans created pressure to compromise ethical standards or violate the law. One-quarter said they believed financial services professionals may need to engage in unethical or illegal conduct to be successful. Another recent study found that a higher percentage of banking employees behave dishonestly than do workers in other industries. But the banking employees were as honest as the others, *except at work*.[13]

While the banks and the market crowd are nowadays both carriers of insider culture, the ways of the crowd predate its employment by the banks. Small-world social networks are value-neutral; but cliques are a defining feature of such networks, and cliques are powerful influencers. Research shows that cliques commonly foster feelings of deindividuation, that is, loss of self-awareness and personal identity, and a weakened sense of personal accountability. The best-known study of deindividuation effects looked at conditions under which children would steal candy. The researchers divided thirteen hundred children into groups to measure effects of anonymity versus nonanonymity, alone versus group, and groups with or without someone "in charge." The researchers set out a bowl of candy, told the children to take one piece of candy each, and then left the room: 8 percent of lone children took extra candy when their names were recorded, and 21 percent did when they could act anonymously; but 57 percent of children in an anonymous *group* took extra candy.[14]

When corruption is widespread and long term in an industry, studies of white-collar crime note the existence of a *deviant subculture* that normalizes the behavior. As sociologists use the term, a culture is "deviant" because its thinking and values are well out of the mainstream, and "corruption" is "the misuse of authority for personal and/or organizational gain." While sharp practices on Wall Street are probably less common now than when William Armstrong wrote *Stocks and Stock-Jobbing in Wall-Street*, the culture remains one of complicity. The crowd tolerates bad behavior and covers for it. Since widespread and frequent financial crime is not considered mainstream, both the banks and the market crowd can be said to have a deviant subculture. Of the two, the banks are by far the most important, since they remain at the center of world finance and the market crowd is gradually returning to private practice. The crowd, I believe, is incorrigible; and the banks show no sign that their business ethics will improve anytime soon.

In business, deviant subcultures can be bottom-up, top-down, or both. The former is a grassroots affair, where rogue groups of junior employees use their positions for illegal, personal benefit. Alternatively, senior executives can misuse their authority to benefit the organization and thus themselves (e.g., Enron). Wall Street and City of London firms appear to have both problems, though senior executives have mostly stayed out of jail. Without directly ordering employees to break the law, firms have proven willing to profit from unethical or illegal behavior of employees. Rather than crime-coercive, financial firms are more likely to be crime-facilitative. In mature industries, such as finance, a deviant subculture can be the norm and endure indefinitely. No one thinks they are doing anything wrong since they are following industry practice, and companies that try to act differently risk bankruptcy. Jeffrey Sonnenfeld and Paul Lawrence quote a convicted executive in the folded paper carton industry: "Our ethics were not out of line with what was being done in this company and, in fact, in this industry for a long time." Deviant subcultures are typically conservative and change little over time, since they vet prospective members for conformity and loyalty. Deviant subcultures that have spread throughout a company are extremely hard to change, short of takeover or breakup. No one has yet found a way to reform an entire industry.[15]

Corruption in finance is even more intractable, though, because in finance, an additional factor is at work: corruption (bad) and innovation (good) are linked. Ironically, though it goes by a different name, deviance is a main reason the business exists. Long-term investors accept the market rate of return, but other market players do not. They want a higher return, alpha, and much of the business is about the pursuit of alpha. To beat the market requires some advantage, something not widely known—an edge, in industry jargon. An edge makes a critical difference, as popular investment guides will tell you. An edge can be a new product or trading strategy but can also be inside information or a trap for the unwary. An advantage must be seized quickly, though; news that something pays out above market travels fast. The goal in the business is always to make money *now*, any way that presents itself. The search for an edge will always push players to the boundaries of the game and beyond. Clients, firms, and the crowd itself all want the money—and all that matters is that the check clears.

The nature of the work also tilts the group toward opportunistic behavior. Broker-intermediated transactions in financial markets are anonymous; only the retail broker who makes the initial customer contact knows the customer's identity. Once in the market, both the money and the financial instruments purchased transfer repeatedly to different holders. The traders and institutional brokers at the market center do not know the identities of the beneficial owners, and the information is irrelevant. Nor do customers know where their money goes or who handles it. The market is a money-laundering machine in many ways, and one can easily forget that owners exist. The money is simply there, to be picked up.

That the market's anonymous clients hold the crowd in such low esteem—of which the crowd is well aware—does not encourage a sense of responsibility to them. It is hard to care much about the welfare of people who use your services while they hold you in contempt. One modern investment banker commented, "I remember that if I voiced an opinion based on moral considerations [when dealing with clients], I'd get looked at as if I were an alien." This sounds bleak, but I doubt the banker meant that his colleagues were amoral. Rather, they felt they owed nothing to *outsiders*. Insiders have rules of conduct but only for other insiders. And this attitude—of owing nothing to clients—makes behaving dishonestly with them a matter almost of indifference, and one encounters sharp practices in the marketplace all the time anyway. All these conditions weaken the moral floor under the crowd, and it is easy to fall into a gangster worldview: "They're all crooked, so *why not* take their money?" It is a common attitude, and there is nothing to pull you back from it. The nature of the business and human nature are, in a way, bad influences on each other.[16]

In this book, I have tried to present a fair picture of the market crowd. This has necessarily included commentary on aspects of the crowd's behavior and character that could be—improved. Despite all this and even though I left the scene myself long ago, I have much affection for the crowd, rowdy and profane as it is. The markets can be a pleasant place to work; the regulars share a sense of solidarity and even fair play: everyone knows the full range of tricks. Intragroup competition is intense but typically good-humored. Relations are collegial in many ways, including among members of different firms. A rival today may be a colleague tomorrow—and a useful contact always. The crowd tolerates and largely ignores checkered pasts and personal quirks, sometimes outrageous ones, and you never know when you might need some tolerance yourself. But it is, in its way, a dangerous work environment.

Years ago, I learned a little about another industry that posed similar risks for its workers, risks that also hinged on industry structure and job design. When I was at Wharton, the school hosted a celebrity speaker, Pehr Gyllenhammar, chairman and CEO of Volvo Group. Probably the whole graduate division came to hear him; Volvo was a leader in what was called "reinventing manufacturing," which was a hot topic at Wharton then. Volvo was investing heavily in training and job redesign, hoping to make better jobs as well as better cars. Gyllenhammar contrasted Volvo's programs to American methods, of which he was sharply critical. "In the U.S.," he said, "you have made jobs so poor, it's absolutely incredible. You are turning good people into trash." When he finished, we gave him a standing ovation. Gyllenhammar's judgment may be too harsh to apply to finance. But it is a dangerous, seductive occupation.[17]

Appendix 1: Industry Statistics

NAICS Classification

Since 1997, the U.S., Canada, and Mexico have classified industries using the North American Industry Classification System (NAICS). In 2021, NAICS Sector 52, Finance and Insurance, employed an average of 6.1 million people in the U.S., 5 percent of the total labor force. But Sector 52 covers thirty-nine separate industries. "Wall Street" in the sense that most people mean spans two industries of the thirty-nine: NAICS codes 523110 and 523130. The first covers firms chiefly engaged in investment banking and securities dealing, and the second is for firms engaged in commodity contracts dealing.[1]

NAICS Head Count

In human terms, these two industries composing high finance are not large. In the U.S., in the most recent figures available from the U.S. Bureau of the Census, in 2021, NAICS 523110 employed an average of 142,217 people; NAICS 523130 employed 13,885. Combined, the two industries accounted for 2.1 percent of total employment in Sector 52. By itself, Walmart, the biggest U.S. employer, has a domestic labor force more than ten times as large. Big employers dominate the two industries. In industry 523110, much the larger and better capitalized of the two, sixty-four firms, less than 1 percent of the total, had five hundred or more employees, but these sixty-four employed 44 percent of the workers. Not surprisingly, the largest concentrations of workers in industry 523110 are in the counties of New York (the borough of Manhattan),

Fairfield County, Connecticut, and Cook County, Illinois. But the NAICS counts firms and total employees, not occupations. Most employees of these firms have jobs that would be the same wherever they worked. Building maintenance and human resources staff perform the same duties in a big bank that they would anywhere else. Contrary to the stereotype, these employees receive the standard going wage for their services. In Wall Street jargon, these are middle- and back-office positions, there to support the revenue-producing part of the firm: the front office. It is this last group that draws all the fire and is the subject of this book. A big modern bank's front office has three divisions: investment banking, wealth management, and FICC, short for fixed income, currency, and commodities. FICC is the focus of this book.[2]

World Financial Centers Ranked

Other financial institutions have front-office staff or their equivalents: second-tier banks, hedge funds, private equity firms, boutique investment banks, and specialty firms. Since the industry is so top-heavy, the top twelve global banks probably account for half of total front-office employment. But many front-office workers are supporting players and extras for the main action. The Global Financial Centres Index (GFCI) ranks 119 world financial centers in order of importance, from New York, London, and Singapore down to Xi'an, Teheran, and Wuhan. A Barclays bond trader in London and a bond trader at a small firm in Wuhan are scarcely in the same business.[3]

Dominance of Big Banks

Employment figures for the world's top twelve multinational universal banks tracked by CRISIL Coalition, a data analytics company, give an idea of how small the front office is. In these banks, the largest divisions by head count are retail brokerage, branch banking, and operations. The front office has only distant connections with these groups. At year-end 2022, the twelve banks employed about 1.7 million people worldwide; 49,000 of these were front-office personnel, and only 16,000 of these were FICC staff, slightly less than one-third of the front office and less than 1 percent of the banks' total head count. As I stated earlier, the industry is top-heavy; with the top twelve global banks employing 16,000 FICC staff, FICC employment in the entire industry might be twice that. This, then, is the market crowd today or most of it: 30,000 to 35,000 people worldwide, about half of whom matter. Workers who hold other types of jobs in the industry classification are support personnel. A total of 16,000 to 17,000 people worldwide is not many, even compared to a medium-size professional association. The American Economic Association has 23,000 members. By way of comparison, the American Bar Association has over 400,000 members; FINRA, the U.S. Financial Industry Regulatory Authority, oversees 612,000 registered securities representatives.[4]

Appendix 2: Sources and Methods

This book aims to bring into clearer focus a subject that is necessarily indefinite: how a group thinks. Anyone who has ever worked in the market crowd will have experienced it as a different world. As important a role as financial markets play in the world, this topic has, I believe, received inadequate attention.

The nature of the research question dictated a limited approach. The case study method, like a focus group, is typically used to conduct exploratory research as a preliminary to more directed and detailed work. But the markets are too old, are too scattered, and have too many gaps in the data for a comprehensive study. More trading takes place in the OTC market than on exchanges, but the only reasonably complete data sets come from exchanges. Even so, "complete" is a relative term. Hundreds of exchanges have come and gone since the Amsterdam Stock Exchange opened in 1602. Some lasted for centuries, and others lasted only a few years. Most left no records at all. Today, according to the International Monetary Fund, there are over a hundred stock and derivatives exchanges worldwide. The World Federation of Exchanges (WFE) has sixty-four member institutions. In equities alone, in 2016, WFE exchanges processed an average of sixty-one million transactions a day, every day of the year. These figures do not include traffic on alternative trading platforms, which in the U.S. account for around 40 percent of total volume, or OTC transactions. Financial markets are big, muddy pools and always have been, and data are both massive in quantity and incomplete.[1]

As of mid-2023, in major markets such as New York and London, only about half of trading in financial instruments takes place on exchanges. The rest takes place on private networks run by banks, in broker-to-broker transactions, and in private sales between individuals. And so it has always been. Brokers have always traded directly, and the curb market, now largely extinct, was a complete free-for-all. Available data always set the limits of possible research, and for financial markets, exchanges are where the data are. Similarly, while there are accounts of individual financiers going back to the Renaissance, detailed accounts of the larger market setting in which they worked are of much more recent date. And that setting, the human part of it, is the focus of this book—the market crowd, a floating collection of largely anonymous operators, with whom the famous actors worked.

After reading this disclaimer, readers may wonder how case studies can tell us anything about this topic. But for the many trading sites and the millions of transactions completed daily, New York and London dominate. More than that, the Anglo-American stock market model dominates worldwide. To take part in any meaningful way in the world market, a financial hub must follow New York and London rules. At the far periphery, places like the Kyrgyz Stock Exchange may have different customs and etiquette. But it scarcely matters. The real power is in New York, London, and Chicago, and those are the places to study. Four cases were enough to show the consistency and important features of the culture. Given the inherent limitations of the method, a larger number of studies would have added redundant exposition without proving anything more definitively.[2]

If this book were about financial chicanery or bubbles and crashes, there would have been a profusion of material about which to write. But the topic I chose instead—business customs and patterns of thought—is difficult to uncover at best and especially so for this group. The crowd has always been reticent about its business dealings and understandably so. The unremitting public hostility directed at the crowd contributes to a *laager* mentality among group members. Since the 1980s, insiders have become even more reluctant to speak candidly about their business, as the regulatory net has progressively tightened. Wall Street memoirists mostly stick to safe topics: anecdotes of misogyny, sophomoric practical jokes, and outrageous excess. No one wants to admit to something that would lead to a lawsuit or prison time, and you cover for your work-mates. Success in the markets depends on reciprocity and relationships, and to get a colleague in trouble would be a career-ender. There are other obstacles as well. Concealment and deception are common trading strategies and can mislead researchers as well as the intended targets.

Finally, the market crowd is a crowd indeed, where everybody talks non-stop and the action is lightning fast. People quickly forget who said what, when, and to whom. Imagine the difficulty of trying to recall, in detail, who said what at a crowded party where everyone was talking at once. And the party never ends.

Case 1: New York, 1866. The events described in the first case immediately preceded the infamous Erie War. That titanic battle has received so much attention that it has obscured everything else happening in the stock market around that time. Many popular books of Wall Street anecdotes appeared in the late nineteenth century; most give a cursory account of Drew's bond conversion trick. But all these books, even those written by actual insiders like the broker and financier Henry Clews, get the details wrong. (To be fair to Clews, he wrote his books long after the events. *Twenty-Eight Years in Wall* Street appeared in 1886; *Fifty Years in Wall Street* in 1908.) Other books, such as *Men and Mysteries of Wall Street* and *Inside Life in Wall Street,* often merely copied from some earlier writer. Regrettably, some modern scholars have uncritically accepted these works as accurate sources.

There were four main primary sources for this case: (1) Trading data. In 1866, volume on the two main exchanges was small enough that the New York financial press printed details of every trade. The curb market collected no data; but it met in the street outside the Old Board, and prices would have been the same. For the exchanges, the newspapers printed price, number of shares traded, type of trade, settlement terms, sequence, and trading session. The illustration in figure 17 is an example of the raw data used in this case, the previous day's stock prices as reported in the April 28, 1866, *New York Times.* The entire column that day ran most of the length of the page, which was typical of weekday trading. Newspaper commentary on the day's affairs on 'change and at the curb were more complete in 1866 than ever before but were still quite brief. The share prices and trading volumes filled in the gaps left by the newspaper reporters. To cover the doings of the Erie pool, I located and transcribed trading data for Erie and other roads from the beginning of November 1865 through the end of June 1866. I then tabulated the data and graphed the fluctuations of the different stocks. (2) The New York State Supreme Court case *John B. Stewart v. Daniel Drew, Leonard Huyck, et al.* In 1867, Stewart, a creditor of the clique member Leonard Huyck, sued Drew, the clique, and Fisk & Belden. The court documents revealed

Fig. 17. Sample, trading activity on the Open
Board of Stock Brokers, New York, April 27,
1866 (*New York Times*, April 28, 1866, 2).

much about Drew's maneuvers and the clique during the period covered in the case. (3) The New York State *Senate Report No. 67*. By 1868, the Erie Railway Company had become such a spectacle (the Erie War) that the New York State Senate launched an investigation into the company's affairs. Market oversight before the twentieth century was left to the states, which mainly focused on shareholder rights and corporate governance. Through the end of the Civil War, New York had the most comprehensive statutes in these areas, but the law steered clear of regulating the secondary market. The exchanges exercised such oversight as there was, but they had few formal rules. (The curb market had none.) No punishment or sanctions resulted from the senate's investigation; the state had limited jurisdiction, and Jay Gould bribed the legislature. Still, the final report contained much useful information, including testimony from many of the principal actors. (4) *Between the Ocean and the Lakes: The Story of Erie*, by Edward H. Mott. Mott's history, published in 1901, reprinted many internal company documents that were previously unavailable.[3]

Case 2: Chicago, 1888. For this case, the two most important primary sources were (1) journalists' accounts of trading sessions and (2) trading data. In 1888, CBOT had a visitors' gallery and admitted nonmembers, including journalists, which the New York Stock Exchange and Board in 1866 did not. The major Chicago newspapers sent market reporters to the daily sessions, and the quality of the journalism was generally high. The floor action could be highly entertaining, and the newspapers' financial columns sometimes read like sports writing. The 1888 wheat corner was such a spectacle that major out-of-town newspapers such as the *New York Times* sent correspondents to cover the story. The floor scene, however, was so chaotic that observers in different locations sometimes gave conflicting accounts. Even traders on the floor got confused. During the most hysterical and panicky times of the corner, prices could vary in different parts of the trading pit. To discover what "really" happened became at times a *Rashomon*-like exercise. Trading data, though not as detailed as that published in New York in 1866, helped to clear up ambiguities. In 1888, the Board of Trade reported summary data, rather than individual trades—daily opening and closing prices, highs and lows, and volume estimates for the different contracts.

Network analysis: The Chicago Board of Trade, 1910–1940. All data for the network analysis came two sources: (1) the yearbooks of the Chicago Board of Trade, published every year from 1858, and (2) the 1920 U.S. census for the city of Chicago. Along with much else, the yearbooks contained complete lists of members as of December 31 of that year. The lists included some accompanying data about each member, data that varied somewhat from year to year but always included the member's firm, if any, and business address. The yearbooks also listed the exchange officers for that year and member lists for the different management committees. As with the railroad share prices, none of these data were digitized and so had to be transcribed. I used Pajek for the quantitative network analysis. The 1920 census data, thanks to the good work by the Minnesota Population Center, was digitized. It was easy to write a routine to record

LIST OF MEMBERS OF THE BOARD OF TRADE OF THE CITY OF CHICAGO.

	NAME.	FIRM.	BUSINESS.	LOCATION.
7770	Aaron, Harry J..........	Treas. The North American Prov. Co.	Provisions	73 Postal Tel. Bldg.
8574	Abbott, Harold A....... ....,..	The Albert Dickinson Co..............	Grain and Seed	Taylor Street and the River.
8071	Ackerman, Frederick S.............	....	....	220 So. La Salle St.
6	Adams, Cyrus H......	....	....	812 Postal Telegraph Building.
8434	Adams, Edward S. B...........	E. F. Hutton & Co......	Commission..............	36 New St., New York City.
3002	Adams. Edward S...........	Edward S. Adams & Co.	Commission..............	813 Postal Telegraph Building.
4130	Adams, John B...........	....	Grain Merchant..........	55 Board of Trade Building.
236	Adams, Samuel O...........	....	Commission..............	536 Postal Telegraph Building.
182	Adsit, Charles C...........	....	Stock Broker..........	218 So. La Salle St.
18	Affeld, Charles E...........	Witkowski & Affeld.......	Insurance	29 So. La Salle St.
6347	Agar, Woodbury Stearns...........	The Agar Packing Co...........	Pork Packers..........	519 North Green St.
6690	Akin, Thomas...........	....	Commission..............	202 Chamber of Commerce, St. Louis, Mo.
7225	Aldrich, Frank W...........	C. C. Aldrich & Son...........	Grain and Banking..........	McLean, Ill.
4063	Aldrich, Frederick C...........	With Finley Barrell & Co...........	Commission..............	5 Monadnock Block.
5402	Allen, John M...........	....	Commission Merchant.	Royal Ins. Bldg.
320	Allerton, Samuel W.... ..	....	....	737 First National Bank Bldg.
7308	Alstrin, Frank E...........	With Finley Barrell & Co	Commission..............	2 Monadnock Block.
4135	Alt, George E...........	With The Albert Dickinson Co......	Seeds..............	West Taylor St. and River.
4113	Anderson, John...........	....	....	1113 W. Taylor Street.
5705	Anderson, Lorenzo R.............	....	Stocks, Bonds and Grain......	710 Locust St., St. Louis, Mo.
95	Anderson, William H...........	....	Commission..............	544 Postal Telegraph Building.
6811	Anderson, Wm. Purdy...........	Pres't W. P. Anderson & Co...........	Commission..............	329 Sherman St.
6005	Anderson, William S..........	P., C. C. & St. L. R'y Co...........	Transportation..........	Commercial Nat. Bank Bldg.
5475	Andreae, Percy...........	Chi. Consolidated Brewing & Mall'g Co	Maltsters..............	1605 First Nat. Bank Bldg.
5053	Andrew, Edward...........	Nash-Wright Grain Co...........	Commission..............	715 Postal Telegraph Building.
7882	Andrews. Edward W...........	....	Commission..............	6 Board of Trade Building.
6453	Andrus, O. Walston...........	....	Commission..............	360 Produce Exchange, N. Y.
7196	Argile, Benjamin...........	Argile & Kirby...........	Grain	622 and La Salle Sts.
6514	Arxo, George R...........	....	....	Eastwood Hotel.
4011	Armour, Jonathan O...........	Pres't Armour & Company...........	Packers..............	127 So. La Salle St.
4084	Armstrong, Benjamin S...........	....	Commission..............	619 Postal Telegraph Building.
36	Armstrong, Chas. M...........	....	Commission..............	408-9-10 Postal Tel. Bldg.

Fig. 18. Sample, member list of the Chicago Board of Trade as of December 31, 1910 (CBOT, *Fifty-Third Annual Report* [1910], 220).

and count the last names of every adult white male within the limits of Chicago proper. The illustration in figure 18 is an example of the raw data used in the network study, taken from the 1910 CBOT member list.[4]

Case 3: London, 2005–2012. The three principal sources used for the LIBOR case were (1) court and regulatory agency filings, (2) reports by government commissions, and (3) articles in the financial press. Taken together, these sources give an incomplete picture of what the banks had been up to. The defendant banks had the sense to settle with prosecutors relatively early, after which investigation and discovery ended. Still, the various investigations and suits produced invaluable primary-source material for this study. The LIBOR case stands out in two ways: First, it pulls back the curtain from a key part of the OTC market—swaps. OTC trading is normally hidden since it is off-exchange and person-to-person. But the recordings and transcripts of the traders' messages give the most granular view of the market possible. Second, the messages are free of observer bias and effects. As far as the traders knew at the time, their messages were private and would remain so. They were not putting on a show for anyone. In the 1866 and 1888 cases, the OTC market is almost entirely hidden, and firsthand accounts come either from outsiders (journalists) or else insiders who hoped to influence the market. The LIBOR case has no such limitations. All the main primary sources for LIBOR were first rate, but the traders' messages were unique.

Case 4: Traders' messaging, 2015–2022. This final case made use of three sources: (1) newspaper and trade journal accounts, (2) SEC and CFTC filings and press releases, and (3) bank annual reports. Given the size and importance of the banks and their location—New York—there was no shortage of high-quality market reporting. The agency filings and press releases, besides describing the banks' offenses and the resulting fines, showed the regulators' shifting attitudes and policies concerning the messaging apps. The banks' financial statements in their annual reports helped to put the regulatory fines in context.

Notes

Epigraph: Smith, *An Inquiry into the Nature and Causes of the Wealth of Nations*, 1:200.

Introduction

1. At the time, the department was called Bank of America Department 6544, International Money Markets and Foreign Exchange, headed by Ray Peters.
2. Sometimes termed "industry culture": Baucus and Near, "Can Illegal Corporate Behavior be Predicted?," 9–36. Christensen and Gordon, "An Exploration of Industry, Culture, and Revenue Growth," 397–422. Also "industry recipe": Spender, *Industry Recipes*. Armstrong, *Stocks and Stock-Jobbing in Wall-Street*, 7, 13.
3. As of mid-2023, the most recent complete sets of figures are from 2021.
4. For further information on NAICS codes, see appendix 1. The earliest printed usage of the term "banksters" dates from 1893, as a humorous epithet. *Marion (IA) Sentinel*, May 25, 1893. The term acquired its strongly negative connotations during the Depression, first appearing in 1931. According to the *Alton (IL) Evening Telegraph* (December 22, 1931, 1), the term was a French import, expressing French disdain for American bankers. The term passed out of common use for many years, before being revived in the 1990s. "Spelling It Out," *Washington Post*, September 29, 1991, w10.
5. For the calculation of the estimated size of the market crowd, see appendix 1.
6. "Table One, GFCI 32 Top Ranks and Ratings," *Global Financial Centres Index 32: September 2022*, 4–5. H. Jones, "New York Still Top, Moscow Sinks in Finance Centre Ranking." In FY 2022, FICC earned $94 billion in revenue, versus $89.1 billion for equities and investment banking combined. Total headcount in FICC in FY 2022 was 15,900; for equities and

IBD, combined headcount totaled 33,000. Coalition Investment Banking Index—FY2022, 3, 7. In FY2019, FICC productivity was $4.3 million per FTE; and for the investment bank, $2.1 million per FTE. Coalition Investment Banking Index—FY2021, 9. In 2022, FICC revenue per FTE was $5.9 million; for investment banking, $1.9 million. Coalition Investment Banking Index—FY2022, 8.

7. According to CRISIL Coalition, a market intelligence firm, the top twelve global banks in 2022 are Bank of America Merrill Lynch, Barclays, BNP Paribas, Citigroup, Credit Suisse, Deutsche Bank, Goldman Sachs, HSBC, JPMorgan Chase, Morgan Stanley, Société Générale, and UBS. John C. (Jack) Bogle, founder of Vanguard, in 1976 created the first index mutual fund available to the general public: the First Index Investment Trust (a precursor to the Vanguard 500 Index Fund). Shen, "Updated: Vanguard Group Founder John C. Bogle '51 Passes Away at 89." Melamed, *Escape to the Futures*, 194; 167–199. Merton, "Theory of Rational Option Pricing," 141–183. MacKenzie, *An Engine, Not a Camera*, Kindle locations 554–991; 3481–3717. Fama and French, "Common Risk Factors in the Returns on Stocks and Bonds," 3–56. "March of the Machines—The Stockmarket Is Now Run by Computers, Algorithms and Passive Managers," *The Economist* (London), October 3, 2019. N. Ferguson, *High Financier*, 202–204. Thomas Landon Jr. "Robert F. Dall, 81, Innovator in Bonds," *New York Times*, November 20, 2015, B15. Tempkin, "1977: US$100m Deal for Bank of America." Mortgage-backed debentures, a financial instrument very similar to that created by Dall and Joseph, dated from the 1880s but had fallen out of use by 1900. Snowden, "Covered Farm Mortgage Bonds," 783–812; Snowden, *Mortgage Banking in the United States*, 18–22. E. Morris, *Wall Streeters*, 173–183.

8. Akerlof and Shiller, *Phishing for Phools*. "Self-interest seeking with guile," that is, self-serving criminal acts. Oliver Williamson, *The Economic Institutions of Capitalism*, 47. Abolafia, *Making Markets*, 19. Luke 19:46. Also Matthew 21:12–15; Mark 11:15–17; John 2:13–16. Armstrong, *Stocks and Stock-Jobbing in Wall-Street*, 24.

9. Sonnenfeld and Lawrence, "Why Do Companies Succumb to Price Fixing?"

10. De la Vega, *Confusion of Confusions*, 22.

11. Hamon, *New York Stock Exchange Manual*, 129.

12. Ho, *Liquidated*, 15, 223.

13. C. S. Lewis, "The Inner Ring."

14. *New York Herald*, January 8, 1866, 2; November 23, 1865, 2.

15. Social capital is the contextual complement to human capital. The social capital metaphor is that the people who do better are somehow better connected. Certain people or certain groups are connected to certain others, trusting certain others, obligated to support certain others, dependent on exchange with certain others. Holding a certain position in the structure of

these exchanges can be an asset in its own right. That asset is social capital, in essence, a concept of location effects in differentiated markets. Burt, "The Network Structure of Social Capital," 347. Adler and Kwon, "Social Capital," 7–40.

16. De la Vega, *Confusion of Confusions*, 9. Keynes, *General Theory*, 139–141. Graham and Dodd, *Security Analysis*, 23. Abolafia, *Making Markets*, 24 (original italics). Soros, *The Alchemy of Finance*, 15, 27–80. George Soros, "General Theory of Reflexivity," *Financial Times*, October 26, 2009, 3.

17. World Bank, "Market Capitalization of Listed Domestic Companies."

18. For example, Cohen, *The Great Bear*.

19. Wellman, "Structural Analysis," 32. Borgatti et al., "Network Analysis in the Social Sciences," 894, citing Burt, *Brokerage and Closure*. The affiliation network is a network of the subjects' memberships—in this case, shared offices, employers, seats on exchange governance committees, and obvious family connections.

20. There are still a few floor traders at the New York Stock Exchange, but as Eric Hunsader of Nanex puts it, they might as well be playing fantasy football. "This Is the Last Photo We'll Ever Run of the NYSE Trading Floor," *MarketWatch*, October 1, 2014.

21. Lo, "The Gordon Gekko Effect," 1–2.

Chapter One. New York, 1866

1. Davis, "William Duer, Entrepreneur," 178–190, 196–197, 286–287. Perkins, *American Public Finance*, 349–371.

2. Craigie Papers 2:214, cited in Davis, "William Duer, Entrepreneur," 200. Davis, "William Duer, Entrepreneur," 286. Richard Sylla, Jack Wilson, and Robert Wright collected data for nine active U.S. securities markets in the pre–Civil War period: Alexandria, Baltimore, Boston, Charleston, New Orleans, New York, Norfolk, Philadelphia, and Richmond. Sylla et al., "Price Quotations in Early United States Securities Markets." Armstrong, *Stocks and Stock-Jobbing in Wall-Street*, 8, 38. In the late 1840s, an English traveler who alighted in New York described the curb market on Wall Street between Hanover and Broad as "frequented by stock and real estate brokers. Here crowds of gentlemanly-looking men, dressed mostly in black, and of busy mien, crowded the thorough fare with scrip in hand." Benwell, *An Englishman's Travels in America*, 14. By 1820, membership had grown to forty. *Frank Leslie's Illustrated Newspaper*, October 21, 1871, 87. By 1848, the "Upper Board" (New York Stock Exchange and Board) had 112 members. In December 1865, the *New York Daily Tribune* noted that since 1861, two hundred new members had been added to the Stock Exchange and the Public Board established. *New York Daily Tribune*, December 18, 1865, 1. Medbery, *Men and Mysteries of Wall Street*, 288. *New York Times*, August 21, 1865, 1. Medbery gives the date of Lawton's Philadelphia trip as 1816, but

1817 is more likely. In September 1860, one of the last normal months the nation had before being plunged into crisis by the election of 1860, the New York Stock Exchange and Board averaged 159 trades per day. Calculations by the author. Daily means 10:30 a.m.–12 noon and 2:30–3:00 p.m. Hamon, *New York Stock Exchange Manual*, 16–17. For example, "Monetary Affairs," *New York Times*, October 20, 1860, 2.

3. In the Union, the consumer price index rose from 100 at the outset of the War to 175 by the end of 1865. Ransom, "The Economics of the Civil War." Stock prices rose even more. The index of U.S. railroad stock prices weighted by the number of shares outstanding rose from 15.49 in December 1860 to 31.65 in December 1865, an increase of 104 percent. Column 6 in table 10, "Short-Time Interest Rates, Bond Yields, and Stock Prices," in Macaulay, *Some Theoretical Problems*, A142–A144. The Erie Railway Company, the railway with which this chapter is concerned, had low to high prices in 1860 of 8½ to 43, average 25.75. In 1865, the corresponding low–high prices for the year were 45 and 97, average 71. Comparing the two average figures, the 1865 figure is an increase of 176 percent over 1860. Mott, *Between the Ocean and the Lakes*, 485. *New York Herald*, August 25, 1865, 2. Fowler, writing in 1880, makes the same point about the new speculators. Fowler, *Twenty Years of Inside Life in Wall Street*, 54–55, 53–57. Tomes, "The Fortunes of War," 229–230. New York Stock Exchange and Board trading sessions took place within a locked room closed to outsiders, and members were expected to keep quiet about what happened inside. Members could neither send nor receive outside communications during trading sessions. Hamon, *New York Stock Exchange Manual*, 8, 27. Clews, *Twenty-Eight Years in Wall Street*, 90. The new exchanges founded between 1862 and 1865 were the Gold Exchange, the Open Board of Stock Brokers, the Mining Exchange, the Evening Exchange, and two petroleum exchanges. The Gold Exchange was founded January 13, 1862. Cornwallis, *The Gold Room*, 3. The Open Board dates from the latter part of 1862. The Mining Exchange was founded December 21, 1863. The Evening Exchange was founded about March 1864. "Gambling in Stocks," *Harper's Weekly*, May 7, 1864, 299. The Petroleum Board was founded February 1, 1865; later that year, a second petroleum exchange was founded. Three of the four new exchanges specialized in either mining or oil stocks, but the fourth, the Open Board of Brokers, competed directly with the New York Stock Exchange and Board. "The New York Stock Exchange," *Harper's New Monthly Magazine*, November 1885, 829–853, 851. Priest, *Travels in the United States of America*, 132.

4. Davis, "William Duer, Entrepreneur," 201. *New York Times*, August 21, 1865, 1. The original records of the exchange were destroyed in the great fire of 1835. *New York Times*, September, 17, 1871, 6. "Financial Review," *The Nation*, March 29, 1866, 413.

5. Per the deposition of Joseph B. Stewart. Stewart gives the start of the clique as early November, but the three months' agreement expired and was re-

newed January 29, 1866. This latter date puts the date for the initial clique agreement at October 29, 1866. *New York Herald*, March 31, 1867, 10. On November 28, the approximate date of the first pool agreement, Erie opened at 92 and closed at 92½, trading that day at a high of 92⊠ and a low of 91½. Calculations by the author. Deposition of Joseph B. Stewart, printed in full in the *New York Herald*, March 31, 1867, 10. Leonard Huyck, banker (*New York Times*, May 14, 1866, 2); Andrew McKinley, attorney (Scharf, *History of Saint Louis City and County*, 1:751) and speculator (*Investigation into the Causes of the Gold Panic*, 307–308); George W. Wiley (Geo. [P.] Willey), broker (H. Wilson, *Trow's New York City Directory for the Year Ending May 1, 1868*, 1110); H. Henry Baxter, banker (*H. Henry Baxter*) and railroad financier ("Union Pacific Railroad," Executive Document No. 253, 1868, 7), later president of the New York Central Railroad; Henry Cohen, banker (*New York Commercial Advertiser*, February 2, 1866, 3; U.S. Census [manuscript], population schedule for the tenth census, 1880) and oil company promoter (*New York Herald*, March 24, 1865, 3); William C. Dornin, banker, Dornin & Boocock (H. Wilson, *Trow's New York City Directory for the Year Ending May 1, 1868*, 282); and Samuel W. Boocock, banker, Dornin & Boocock (H. Wilson, *Trow's New York City Directory for the Year Ending May 1, 1868*, 282). Daniel Drew, 53 Wall Street, broker (*Longworth's American Almanac* [1839], 226). The previous year's edition of Longworth showed Drew still at the Bull's Head Tavern. *New York Herald*, March 31, 1867, 10.

6. Jackson, *A Week in Wall Street*, 81. (The speculators were not, to my knowledge, ever called marks.) Sometime in the early 1850s, Drew and Vanderbilt had cooperated in putting up the price of Erie, but reports conflict as to exactly when and by how much. Stiles, *The First Tycoon*, 239, referencing R. G. Dun & Company entry for Nelson Robinson. Mott, however, shows a high for Erie stock in that month of 75½. In April 1853, Mott quotes Erie selling for a high of 92½, before commencing a long decline. Mott, *Between the Ocean and the Lakes*, 485. Blaine, "War Debts of the Loyal States," 2. During the Civil War, the national debt rose from $60 million to $2,675 million in the North. Homer and Sylla, *A History of Interest Rates*, 306. When the war ended, the U.S. Treasury, to restore the convertibility of greenbacks to gold (convertibility suspended December 30, 1861), immediately started to contract the money supply. Private-sector holdings of government currency fell by 15 percent a year from 1865 to 1868; wholesale prices dropped by 8 percent a year over that time. Timberlake, *Monetary Policy in the United States*, 90. *The Nation*, May 1, 1866, 557. By January 1866, railroad shares were down 8 percent from their level a year before. Prices continued to fall for the first several months of 1866 but started to rise again toward the end of the year. The index is calculated as the arithmetic average of all railroad corporation shares, weighted according to the number of shares of each company outstanding at the beginning of each year. At this time, nearly half the companies listed on the New York Stock Exchange and Board and the Open Board were

railroads. Between November 1865 and June 1866, seven railroads accounted for 74 percent of all shares traded on the two major exchanges, the Open Board of Brokers and the New York Stock Exchange and Board. The seven railroads were Erie, the New York Central, Reading, Michigan Southern, Cleveland & Pittsburg, Chicago & Northwestern, and Pittsburg & Ft. Wayne. Railroad shares continued to dominate U.S. securities markets into the twentieth century and only started to lose their prominence after about 1909. Column 3, table 16: "Four Index Numbers of the January Prices of American Railroad Common Stocks," in Macaulay, *Some Theoretical Problems*, 139, appendix A, A204. Calculations by the author. In a bull pool, the group tries to raise the stock price. A bear pool tries to push the price down.

7. "The New York Stock Exchange," *Harper's New Monthly Magazine*, November 1885, 829–853, 851. Browder, *The Money Game*, 22–30, 110. Daniel Drew, 53 Wall Street, broker (*Longworth's American Almanac*, 1839, 226). *New-York as It Is*, 111. "Try to Kill Book about Daniel Drew," *Carmel (NY) Putnam County Courier*, April 29, 1910. *New York Daily Tribune*, September 19, 1879, 5. M. Smith, *Twenty Years among the Bulls and Bears*, 131.

8. Drew and his business partner, Nelson Robinson, joined the Erie board of directors in October 1853. *Albany (NY) Evening Journal*, October 13, 1853, 2. *New York Times*, October 17, 1858. Drew became Erie's treasurer after Robinson resigned that post in March 1854. *New York Evening Post*, March 16, 1854, 1. Mott erroneously says he came onto the board in 1854. Mott, *Between the Ocean and the Lakes*, 115, 475–476. *New York Times*, April 15, 1866, 3. *Senate Report No. 67*, 24–25. *New York Herald*, November 13, 1865, 2. *New York Evening Post*, November 11, 1865, 3. *New York Herald*, November 13, 1865, 2. *New York Evening Post*, November 11, 1865, 3. Valuing Erie's stock at par, its total capitalization stood at around $50 million. *Annual Report of the State Engineer and Surveyor of the State of New York, 1866*, 253–254. Writing in June 1866, the *New York Commercial Advertiser* put Erie's total capitalization at $48 million. *New York Commercial Advertiser*, June 2, 1866, 3. In November 1865, there were 165,701 shares of Erie common stock outstanding. Adams, "A Chapter of Erie," 37. At the end of 1865, Erie owned, leased, or operated a little over eight hundred miles of track. *Annual Report of the State Engineer and Surveyor of the State of New York, 1865*, 318. Erie's connection with the Ohio and Mississippi Railroad went to St. Louis; its connection with the Atlantic & Great Western reached Cincinnati. Medbery, "The Great Erie Imbroglio," 111–121, 118. Calculations by the author.

9. A quote of 71 means seventy-one dollars. In this chapter, stock prices are quoted as they were in 1865–1866, in dollars and eighths. In November 1865, Erie common stock traded an average of 11,992 shares per day on the New York Stock Exchange and Board and the Open Board of Brokers. The average figure conceals wide variations in trading volume. The largest share volume traded that month was on Wednesday, November 7, 1865 (27,500 shares). *New York Times*, November 8, 1865, 2. The lowest volume was

Wednesday, November 22, when 3,400 shares traded. In May 1866, Erie common stock accounted for 21 percent of all shares traded on the New York Stock Exchange and the Open Board of Brokers. In June 1866, the figure was 32 percent. *New York Times*, November 23, 1865, 2. *Senate Report No. 67*, 24–25. *New York Herald*, November 13, 1865, 2; April 21, 1866, 4; May 2, 1866, 8. *New York Evening Post*, November 11, 1865, 3. *New York Commercial Advertiser*, December 1, 1865, 3; June 2, 1866, 3; July 2, 1866, 3. Adams, "A Chapter of Erie," 30–106, 33. Calculations by the author.

10. The *New York Herald* charges that speculators' "opinions" about stocks are valueless except as indicating their own course and ends on the market. *New York Herald*, January 29, 1866, 2. Securities and Exchange Commission, " 'Pump-and-Dumps' and Market Manipulations." Calculations by the author.

11. The curb market met at the intersection of William and Beaver Streets in lower Manhattan. Drew's trades, where known, almost never appeared in the official transaction records of the exchanges, which the newspapers published daily. *New York Commercial Advertiser*, December 1, 1865, 3. *New York Times*, November 8, 1865, 2; November 23, 1865, 2. *New York Herald*, January 29, 1866, 2. Fowler, *Twenty Years of Inside Life in Wall Street*, 55. Calculations by the author.

12. Merchants' Navigation and Transportation Company chartered in Connecticut, December 22, 1863. *Special Laws of the State of Connecticut* 6:927. On December 22, 1863 (date approx.), Drew sells the "Stonington Line" of steamships, formerly part of Drew's New Jersey Steamship Company—*Commonwealth*, *Commodore*, and *Plymouth Rock*—to the Merchants' Navigation and Transportation Company. *Hastings v. Drew*, in Howard, *Practice Reports in the Supreme Court and Court of Appeals*, 50:257. Chapter 5, "Long Island Sound. Providence and Stonington Lines," in Morrison, *History of American Steam Navigation*, 292. Drew sold the steamboat line to James Fisk Jr., who organized the Merchants Navigation and Transportation Company, composed almost wholly of Boston merchants with A. H. Fiske as president (probably source of confusion that J. Fisk Jr. was buyer), E. D. Jordan as treasurer, and Ira H. Palmer as secretary. "Twenty Years Ago: Reminiscences of a Few Famous Sound Steamers," *New London (CT) Day*, September 21, 1883, 2. "Fish [*sic*—James Fisk] & Wm. Belden, Bankers & Brokers, 37 Broad St.," R. G. Dun Mercantile Agency Credit Reports 416:91, R. G. Dun & Co. Credit Report Volumes, Baker Library, Harvard Business School. At that time, both the New York Stock Exchange and Board and the Open Board of Stock Brokers were trying to stamp out informal trading venues and to funnel all securities trading through their respective institutions. One measure the exchanges took was to prohibit their own members from off-exchange trading. Hamon, *New York Stock Exchange Manual*, 26, 31. The Open Board had no such rule, but in August 1865, both exchanges barred their members from attending Gallagher's Evening Exchange and from trading stocks, bonds, or gold uptown (above Twenty-Third Street)

after 6 p.m. *New York Herald*, August 28, 1865, 2. Clews, *Twenty-Eight Years in Wall Street*, 507. By one account, Drew had been doing business with Jay Gould since the Civil War, and it was through Drew that Gould first became interested in Erie stock. *New York Times*, December 3, 1892, 3. Gould at this time was a railroad executive on the smallest scale, being president of the thirty-two-mile Troy, Salem & Rutland Railroad (*Philadelphia Inquirer*, July 6, 1866, 51). The Troy, Salem &Rutland Railroad probably wasn't a full-time job, however, since the (somewhat). larger Rensselaer & Saratoga Railroad had leased the road since June 1865. *Reports and Decisions of the Interstate Commerce Commission*, 740–741. Gould meanwhile lived in New York and, in the judgment of his biographer Maury Klein, spent much of this period speculating in stocks in the various unorganized venues around the city. Klein, *The Life and Legend of Jay Gould*, 72–73.

13. Erie common had been trading at between $92 and $93. Around November 5 unknown parties, later widely assumed to be Drew, tried to force the price of the stock above its par value, $100. The price of Erie shares rose about $3 a share, to $96.25, compared to the November 4 close of $93. Then the rise faltered, the price afterward declining somewhat. Several sources state that time transactions (buyer's option and seller's option trades) almost invariably originated on the exchange, rather than in the larger investing public. Between November 1, 1865, and June 30, 1866, 877,360 shares out of a total of 2,602,971 traded, or 33.7 percent, were for either buyer's option or seller's option transactions (2,102 out of 5,066 trades). Each buyer's or seller's option transaction generated at least one additional transaction later, which would have been recorded as well. *New York Commercial Advertiser*, April 26, 1866, 3; March 3, 1866, 3. *New York Times*, November 8, 1865, 2. *New York Daily Tribune*, November 4, 1865, 8; December 18, 1865, 8; March 16, 1866, 6; July 2, 1866, 6. *New York Herald*, November 18, 1865, 2; February 18, 1866, 2. Calculations by the author.

14. *Strong v. Repide*. *New York Herald*, November 9, 1865, 2; November 13, 1865, 2; January 12, 1866, 2; January 20, 1866, 2; July 2, 1866, 2. "The Freight Monopoly," *Chicago Tribune*, December 15, 1865, 2. *New York Daily Tribune*, November 16, 1865, 8; November 23, 1865, 6; November 25, 1865, 8; December 18, 1865, 8; December 21, 1865, 8. De la Vega, *Confusion of Confusions*, 30–33. Armstrong, *Stocks and Stock-Jobbing in Wall-Street*, 7.

15. "What It Costs to Corner Wall Street," *Harper's Weekly*, April 14, 1866, 227. Hamon, *New York Stock Exchange Manual*, 55, 100; H. Smith, *Smith's Financial Dictionary*, 64. Calculations by the author.

16. "What It Costs to Corner Wall Street," *Harper's Weekly*, April 14, 1866, 227. *New York Daily Tribune*, December 15, 1865, 6; December 21, 1865, 8; April 20, 1866, 6. *New York Commercial Advertiser*, April 14, 1866, 3. *Milwaukee (WI) Daily Sentinel*, May 31, 1866, col. a. Calculations by the author.

17. Since Drew kept no books and did business with multiple brokers, it is unclear how *Harper's* arrived at this figure. Some estimates were more

sanguine. *New York Daily Tribune*, February 12, 1866, 6. "What It Costs to Corner Wall Street," *Harper's Weekly*, April 14, 1866, 227. *New York Evening Post*, December 26, 1865, 4. *New York Commercial Advertiser*, January 13, 1866, 3. *New York Herald*, January 14, 1866, 2. Calculations by the author.

18. Drew did most of his trading on January 8 and 9, before starting to unload toward the end of trading on the tenth. Between December 21, the day Drew called in the loaned Erie stock, and January 9, the day before he started to unload his own Erie shares, there were thirty-three short sales of Erie stock, totaling 7,200 shares in all. While the financial columns of the newspapers do not identify the authors of these trades, during this period Drew was the only Wall Street operator holding Erie stock and able to deliver on the short sales. Plus, he was overinvested in Erie at a high price and needed to unload. Finally, all thirty-three trades were profitable, with an average profit per trade of $1,143.94. Out of 1,125 total short trades in Erie stock made between November 1, 1865, and May 31, 1866 (which includes both informed and uninformed trades), 445 lost money, 629 made money, and 51 traded flat, for an average profit per trade of $436.50. Calculations by the author.

19. The principal railroads in 1866 were Erie, New York Central, Reading, Fort Wayne, Michigan Southern, Pittsburg, and Rock Island. "What It Costs to Corner Wall Street," *Harper's Weekly*, April 14, 1866, 227; *The Nation*, February 1, 1866, 156. *New York Daily Tribune*, November 30, 1865, 6; February 10, 1866, 10; April 2, 1866, 6; April 5, 1866, 6. *New York Evening Post*, November 13, 1865, 3; May 8, 1866, 3; May 10, 1866, 3; May 14, 1866, 3. *New York Herald*, July 2, 1866, 2. *New York Times*, April 5, 1866, 2.

20. *New York Herald*, January 8, 1866, 2. *New York Commercial Advertiser*, December 27, 1865, 3; December 30, 1865, 3.

21. Edward Harriman, broker, Harriman & Jerome, 20 Exchange Place and 63 Beaver. Hancock not found. H. Wilson, *Trow's New York City Directory for the Year Ending May 1, 1865*, 370, 376, 448. Neither Hancock nor Harriman was a member of the New York Stock Exchange and Board at the time. *New York Times*, February 4, 1866, 6. Hamon, *New York Stock Exchange Manual*, 114. Klein, *The Life and Legend of E. H. Harriman*, 34–35. *New York Commercial Advertiser*, January 13, 1866, 3. *New York Evening Post*, December 26, 1865, 4. *New York Herald*, January 14, 1866, 2. *New York Daily Tribune*, January 13, 1866, 6. *The Nation*, January 18, 1866, 92. Calculations by the author.

22. Hancock & Harriman claimed to have lost $134,000 on the operation, which is unlikely. January 10, Erie closed 96; January 12, Erie closed 89.50—loss of 6.50, or 6.7 percent. If Hancock & Harriman lost $134,000 on the deal, at 6.50/share, the loss would have been on 20,615 shares. Marriage notice, Edward Harriman to Clara, daughter of the late Thomas Mellon of Philadelphia, October 4, in New York City, *New York Evening Post*, October 6, 1866. *New York Commercial Advertiser*, January 13, 1866, 3. *New York*

Herald, January 14, 1866, 2. *New York Evening Post*, December 26, 1865, 4; October 6, 1866.

23. The three most obvious violations are parking (SEC Rule 10b-5), the Manning rule (FINRA Rule 5320), and best execution (FINRA rule 5310). Company directors profiting in this way from privileged information became the subject of the first lasting federal intervention into securities markets in the U.S., but that was still more than forty years off. The case *Strong v. Repide* (1909) spoke directly to the circumstances of Drew and Erie. The U.S. Supreme Court ruled that a director who expects to act in a way that affects the value of shares cannot use that knowledge to acquire shares from those who do not know of the expected action. Werner and Smith, *Wall Street*, 64–65. Davis, "William Duer, Entrepreneur," 201. *New York Herald*, May 30, 1866, 2.

24. *New York Herald*, March 31, 1867, 10. The stock contributed by the clique members to the shared account then stood at 9,300 shares, and under the new agreement, Drew would add a further 18,900 shares. Saturday, October 28, Erie closed at 91¾. *New York Times*, October 30, 1865, 2. On January 29, the day the agreement was extended, the stock closed at 80¾. *New York Times*, January 30, 1866, 8.

25. *New York Daily Tribune*, February 2, 1866, 6; April 11, 1866, 6; May 24, 1866, 6; June 13, 1866, 6. *New York Times*, November 13, 1865, 2; May 24, 1866, 3. *New York Evening Post*, November 17, 1865, 3. *New York Commercial Advertiser*, February 9, 1866, 3. *The Nation*, June 15, 1866, 765. Calculations by the author.

26. On March 8, Erie opened at 85.75, sold up to 86.63, and closed at 83.13. *New York Daily Tribune*, February 20, 1866, 6; March 1, 1866, 6; March 2, 1866, 6; March 3, 1866, 10; March 5, 1866, 6; March 8, 1866, 6. *New York Commercial Advertiser*, March 1, 1866, 3; March 2, 1866, 4; March 7, 1866, 3; March 9, 1866, 3. "What It Costs to Corner Wall Street," *Harper's Weekly*, April 14, 1866, 227. *New York Times*, February 5, 1866, 2; February 27, 1866, 2; March 9, 1866, 2. Calculations by the author.

27. *Wall Street Journal*, March 26. 2014. *The Economist* (London), May 27, 2017. Fama, "Efficient Capital Markets," 383–417.

28. De la Vega notes this as well. De la Vega, *Confusion of Confusions*, 5. The term "asymmetric information" first appeared in published sources in a 1967 article by Irving H. Lavalle, "A Bayesian Approach to an Individual Player's Choice of Bid in Competitive Sealed Auctions," 588. In 1978, the term gained much-wider currency in a famous article by George A. Akerlof, "The Market for 'Lemons': Quality Uncertainty and the Market Mechanism." According to Google Scholar, as of mid-2023 Akerlof's article has been cited nearly forty-three thousand times. *New York Daily Tribune*, April 9, 1866, 6.

29. Drew made a foray into Michigan Southern, though, which went badly. *New York Times*, April 5, 1866, 2. The *Evening Post* reported that one-half of

the original loan from Drew was repaid (hence the fourteen thousand shares returned), this the result of £1 million negotiated in London with J. S. Morgan & Co., Sterne Bros. & J. P. McKenna, on 7 percent convertible sterling bonds. The *Evening Post* anticipated that in a few days, Erie would pay off the outstanding balance to Drew and reclaim the remaining fourteen thousand shares. *New York Evening Post*, November 11, 1865, 3. *Senate Report No. 67*, 24. The company paid down no debt at all. Both bonded debt and floating (unsecured) debt increased between 1865 and 1866. Erie's bonded debt went from $18,285,900 to $22,368,834.94, an increase of $4,082,934.94. Floating debt went from $2,304,238.42 to $3,638,450.29, an increase of $1,334,211.87. Mott, *Between the Ocean and the Lakes*, 484. Calculations by the author.

30. *New York Commercial Advertiser*, November 27, 1865, 3.
31. On November 1, 1865, Erie closed at 92½. The ten thousand shares in the clique's pool would have been worth $925,000. A $250,000 profit would have been (250,000/925,000) *100 = 27 percent. On March 29, 1866, Erie closed at 77⅛. Erie's share price had declined [(92.5–77.125)/92.5]*100 = 16.6 percent. During the same six weeks, the average price rose 3 percent for the other six railroads that, with Erie, made up three-fourths of on-exchange trading volume. *New York Herald*, March 31, 1867, 10. *Philadelphia Evening Telegraph*, April 2, 1867, 1. *New York Times*, November 2, 1865, 2; March 30, 1866, 2; May 1, 1866, 2. *The Nation*, May 4, 1866, 573.
32. *Senate Report No. 67*, 25–26, 32.
33. In April 1865, the stock sold at a low of 51½. The week ending Saturday, May 12, Erie traded a total volume of 28,420 shares on the two exchanges. For the week following, ending Saturday the nineteenth, 98,395 shares; and for the week ending the twenty-sixth, 135,930 shares. Mott, *Between the Ocean and the Lakes*, 485. *New York Evening Post*, May 22, 1866, 3. *New York Commercial Advertiser*, May 23, 1866. *New York Times*, May 24, 1866, 3; May 25, 1866, 3; May 27, 1866, 6; May 29, 1866, 2. *New York Daily Tribune*, May 11, 1866, 6; May 28, 1866, 6. Calculations by the author.
34. The stock closed flat at noon. In morning trading, the two exchanges between them had fifteen trades, with a total of 13,370 shares. After scarcely moving a quarter in either direction in morning trading, an hour later, at 1 p.m., Erie opened at 65½, down 1⅜, but prices moved little. At the 1 p.m. session on the Old Board, Erie opened at 65½, and on the Open Board, at 65¼. (regular way). Prices held steady through the close. The Open Board began its last session for the day at 3:30, an hour later than the Old Board's third session. Erie opened at 62½ and closed at 62¼. Twenty-one thousand shares traded on the two exchanges during these sessions, almost half the day's total. The bulge in volume came through the Open Board, the upstart, more speculative-minded organization. On Saturdays, the exchanges were not open for a full day. On Friday, May 25, a total of 23,600 Erie shares traded on both exchanges. The stock closed at 62¼ and then broke down

further in after-hours street trading. This was the biggest one-day drop in the eight-month period, November 1865 to June 1866. *New York Daily Tribune*, May 29, 1866, 6. Calculations by the author.

35. *New York Daily Tribune*, May 29, 1866, 6. *New York Times*, May 29, 1866, 2. *New York Herald*, May 29, 1866, 8. *New York Commercial Advertiser*, May 29, 1866, 3.

36. The state's general incorporation law also passed over the question of bond issue but gave authority for a majority of the directors to act on behalf of the entire corporation. No known documentary evidence exists to show what connection, if any, Lane had with Drew or Erie in early 1866. But seemingly out of nowhere, Lane joined Erie's board five months later, in October. The following year, Lane helped get Jim Fisk and Jay Gould elected. Stiles, *The First Tycoon*, 671n33. According to the memoir of Morosini, Gould's bodyguard, Gould met Fisk when he and Lane came to solicit Erie proxies for the board of directors' election of October 1867. In July 1868, Gould, by then Erie's president, elevated Fisk and Lane to the Erie executive committee. Section 9, 214, in chapter 18, "Of Incorporations," in Edmonds, *Statutes at Large of the State of New York*, 557. Authority to issue convertible bonds given under New York State's General Railroad Act of 1850, that is, section 28, article 10, of "An Act to Authorize the Formation of Railroad Corporations, and to Regulate the Same." *New York Commercial Advertiser*, October 31, 1861, 3. Sibley, Private Journal, entry for February 26, 1864. Mott, *Between the Ocean and the Lakes*, 476. Klein, *Life and Legend of Jay Gould*, 79, 86, 97, 116, 199ff.

37. Regular way. Erie opened unchanged from Monday's close on the Old Board (at 61½) but down 1⅛ on the Open Board (60⅜). The latter's price was evidently more realistic. By the end of morning trading, the price on the two exchanges matched, with the Old Board having done most of the adjusting: the two sessions closed at 60¼ on the Old Board and 60½ on the Open Board. At 1 p.m., on the Open Board, Erie opened at 60¼, and on the Old Board, at 60⅞. In the morning sessions, 18,800 shares traded, with twenty-one trades; in the afternoon, 39,300 shares—twice as many—traded, with twenty-four trades. However, trading was more evenly distributed between the three sessions of the day: morning, early afternoon, and late afternoon—respectively, 18,800 shares, 16,800 shares, and 22,500 shares. In March 1865, Erie had sold down to 51½. Mott, *Between the Ocean and the Lakes*, 485. *New York Times*, May 30, 1866, 3; May 31, 1866, 3. *New York Evening Post*, May 29, 1866, 4. *New York Daily Tribune*, May 30, 1866, 6. Calculations by the author.

38. Andrew McKinley (Scharf, *History of Merchants' Magazine and Commercial Review*, June 1, 1866, 54; Scharf, *Saint Louis City and County*, 1:751), William C. Dornin (*New York Times*, February 3, 1916, 9), Samuel W. Boocock (*New York Times*, March 15, 1927, 15), George W. Wiley (Erie pool member) bankrupt (*New York Times*, July 23, 1868, 6; August 5, 1868, 6), Henry

Cohen, banker at 20 Wall Street, bankrupt (*New York Times*, October 7, 1877, 5; May 14, 1866, 2. *New York Herald*, June 5, 1866, 8; March 31, 1867, 10. *New York Times*, April 1, 1867, 2. *Philadelphia Evening Telegraph*, April 2, 1867, 1). *Annual Report of the State Engineer and Surveyor of the State of New York, 1868*, 338.

39. On Wednesday, May 30, 48,575 Erie shares were traded. *Merchants' Magazine and Commercial Review*, June 1, 1866, 54. *New York Herald*, May 31, 1866, 2; June 6, 1866, 2; June 7, 1866, 2. *New York Daily Tribune*, June 4, 1866, 6; June 6, 1866, 6. *New York Times*, June 1, 1866, 3; June 3, 1866, 6. *The Nation*, June 8, 1866, 734. *New York Commercial Advertiser*, June 2, 1866, 3; June 5, 1866, 3; June 6, 1866, 3. *New York Evening Post*, June 5, 1866, 3.

40. Smaller speculators tailed him. Over 165,000 Erie shares traded over the three days. For the month of May, to date, 14,076 shares average for nineteen trading days (Monday to Friday, not Saturday), May 1 through May 25, 1866, for a total of 267,450 shares. The *New York Times* estimated that between 80,000 and 100,000 shares of Erie sold, at cash and sellers' options, on Tuesday and Wednesday, May 29 and 30. On May 29 and 30, 58,100 and 46,875 shares traded on the Old Board and the Open Board. *The Nation*, June 1, 1866, 702. Stiles, *The First Tycoon*, 421–422. *New York Herald*, March 22, 1866, 2; March 30, 1866, 2; April 4, 1866, 2. *New York Times*, June 1, 1866, 3; June 4, 1866, 3; June 6, 1866, 3. Calculations by the author.

41. In mid-June Erie traded between $60 and $65 a share. *New York Daily Tribune*, May 30, 1866, 6. Calculations by the author.

42. Some papers did better. Drew's first loan to Erie was for $1,960,000 on January 6, 1865, for which he received 28,000 shares of treasury stock that remained unsold out of the $5 million (50,000 shares) authorized by the act of 1864. Before this, the company had $16,574,300 in common stock outstanding, valued at par, so 165,743 shares of stock. To this 28,000 shares, Drew added the 30,000 shares newly created by the bond conversion, and so 58,000 shares. Drew thus increased the amount of stock outstanding by 58,000/165,743 = 0.3499 = 35 percent. The addition of the 58,000 new shares brought the total number of shares outstanding to 223,743. For the original shareholders, every dollar of equity they had was now reduced to $0.741 (165,743/223.743). On Monday, May 21, 1866, the share price started to drop significantly, indicating that the more knowledgeable operators had some warning of what was coming and were selling out. Before that, from May 1 to May 19, 1866, the price had traded in a narrow range, averaging about 74. If the share price had dropped proportionately to the dilution, it would have gone to $54.81 (74 * 0.741), which did not happen. By December 1866, the stock was selling between 65 and 74 a share. The last news stories on Drew's convertible bond trick were published June 9. *New York Commercial Advertiser*, June 4, 1866, 3. Medbery, "The Great Erie Imbroglio," 111–121, 116. *Senate Report No. 67*, 24–25, 30. *New York Evening Post*, March 12, 1868, 2. Mott, *Between the Ocean and the Lakes*, 485. *New*

York Times, May 31, 1866, 3; June 3, 1866, 6; June 9, 1866, 3. *New York Herald,* June 9, 1866, 2; June 20, 1866, 2. Calculations by the author.

43. The seven railroads accounting for most on-exchange trading volume in New York were Erie, New York Central, Reading, Michigan Southern, Cleveland & Pittsburg, Chicago & Northwestern, Pittsburg & Fort Wayne. Erie's on-exchange trading volume was 18 percent of all shares traded on the Open Board and the Old Board in April 1866, the month before Drew dumped the new fifty-eight thousand shares on the market, and rose to 32 percent of total trading volume in June. For the rest of June, the stock traded between 65 and 58⅛. In July 1866, Erie common sold for a high of 77⅛ and a low of 66⅝; in August, for a high of 74¼ and a low of 68⅝. *The Nation,* April 26, 1866, 540; June 12, 1866, 750. Medbery, "The Great Erie Imbroglio," 111–121, 114. *New York Herald,* June 9, 1866, 2. *New York Daily Tribune,* June 23, 1866, 6. Mott, *Between the Ocean and the Lakes,* 485. Calculations by the author.

44. Of twenty identified fancy stocks in the period 1864–1868, Erie had much the largest number of shares outstanding, with 164,100 as of December 31, 1864. Next came the Chicago and Northwestern Railroad, with 119,905, and Mariposa Mining, with 107,400. Six of the companies had 20,000 shares outstanding. Excluding Erie, the remaining nineteen fancy stocks had on average 49,536 shares outstanding. In January 1865, Erie common reached 85½. In March, the stock touched 45 but traded as high as 95 again in July. Armstrong, *Stocks and Stock-Jobbing in Wall-Street,* 12–13, 30. *New York Herald,* January 8, 1866, 2; May 2, 1866, 8. Mott, *Between the Ocean and the Lakes,* 485. Calculations by the author.

45. In 1868, the comptroller of the currency estimated that half the funds of the national banks in New York went to finance trading in stocks and gold. *Report of the Comptroller of the Currency,* 23. *New York Herald,* January 8, 1866, 2; November 23, 1865, 2.

46. "For all debts which shall be due and owing by the company at the time of its dissolution, the persons then composing such company shall be individually responsible to the extent of their respective shares of stock in the said company and no further." Article 7 in chapter 67, "An Act Relative to Incorporations for Manufacturing," 111–114. "The Key to Industrial Capitalism: Limited Liability," *The Economist* (London), December 25, 1999. Angell and Ames, *The Law of Private Corporations Aggregate,* 362–363. Livermore, "Unlimited Liability in Early American Corporations," 674–676.

47. *Bankers Magazine* asserted that the Morris Canal was the first notable corner on the Street, not the first corner. The company had ten thousand shares outstanding and confined its business to northern New Jersey. Werner and Smith, *Wall Street,* 106–107. Hilt, "When Did Ownership Separate from Control?," 650. *New York Herald,* November 23, 1865, 2. Medbery, "The Great Erie Imbroglio," 111–121, 114. Hamon, *New York Stock Exchange Manual,* 128. Armstrong, *Stocks and Stock-Jobbing in Wall-Street,* 29–30.

Sobel, *The Big Board*, 43, 46n41. Also "The History of Wall-Street Corners," *Bankers Magazine and Statistical Register* 36 (October 1881): 309, referencing a history of principal stock corners since 1835 in the *New York World*. "An Act to Incorporate a Company to Form an Artificial Navigation between the Passaic and Delaware Rivers," 159.

48. The first press account of Jacob Little's maneuver to convert Erie warrants into shares appeared in September 1858. The most detailed account gives the year as 1855 (*New York Times*, February 23, 1882, 8). The circumstances described in that article, however, point to 1854, when serious discrepancies were discovered in the Erie financial records, causing the stock price to drop sharply. Erie's share price went from a high of 82⅞ in March 1854 to a low of 29 in September. Some accounts give 1857 as the year of Little's stunt with Erie warrants, but this is incorrect because Robinson died in early 1856. An 1858 *Harper's* article gives 1843 as the year, in error. Certificates of indebtedness convertible into common stock were authorized by the directors of the New York & Erie Railroad Company on November 8, 1844. Little himself had used the warrants in a similar fashion once before, in 1845, in a single-client transaction that resulted in a lawsuit. Clews, *Twenty-Eight Years in Wall Street*, 124. Adams, "A Chapter of Erie," 35. "Jacob Little, Esq.," *Harper's Weekly*, September 18, 1858, 1 Mott, *Between the Ocean and the Lakes*, 115, 485. *New York Daily Tribune*, March 26, 1856, 8. *New York Herald*, March 10, 1848, 5. *Wilson v. J. Little & Co.*, in Waterman, *Reports of Cases Argued and Determined in the Superior Court of the City of New York*, 1:350–360. *New York Times*, August 21, 1863, 3; September 28, 1863, 2. *New York Herald*, September 28, 1863, 8. *American Railroad Journal*, October 3, 1863, 943. Fowler, *Ten Years in Wall Street*, 259–261.

49. A poison pill is more formally known as a "shareholder rights plan." Erie's directors, led by Gould, successfully fended off Vanderbilt with new stock issued using the same feature of the state railroad law that Drew used in May 1866. The $10 million in bonds were first authorized at an Erie board meeting in February 1868 and then issued in two tranches of $5 million each in February and March. The company claimed authority to do so under the same provision of the state's general railroad law of 1850. At $100 par, the bonds were converted into 100,000 shares of common stock. In addition, on December 4, 1867, the Erie board authorized a stock issue in exchange for the shares of the Buffalo, Bradford, and Pittsburgh (BB&P) Railroad, which Erie had leased. The BB&P surrendered 18,910 shares of stock, or paper worth $1,891,000 at $100 par, and Erie issued the same number of shares of its own stock. Gould's biographer, Klein, gives an inaccurate account of the BB&P transaction, in *The Life and Legend of Jay Gould*, 81. Also Browder, *The Money Game*, 136–137, 154, 156. According to Mott, there were two of $5 million each. The first was on February 19, 1868, and the second on March 3. Mott, *Between the Ocean and the Lakes*, 148, 163, 484. The purpose of this bond conversion was not to short the stock but rather to stave off Vanderbilt,

who was trying to acquire the road or, in the opinion of Stiles, to revenge himself on Drew. Stiles, *The First Tycoon*, 456. During the three and a half years that Gould was Erie's president, the company's outstanding shares rose from 251,000 to 835,000. New York's 1881 penal code, section 607, "Railroad Company Contracting Excessive Debt," 191, closed the bond-conversion loophole that Drew and Gould had used. Other provisions of the 1887 penal code that addressed the abuses of Drew, Gould, Fisk, and others included section 603, which prohibited corporation officers from making false reports of the company's condition (190); section 602, which prohibited frauds in keeping corporate accounts (190); and section 594, which prohibited directors from paying dividends except from surplus profits (187). In *The Penal Code of the State of New York*. The convertible bond loophole was addressed directly in 1887, in section XI, "Fraudulent Insolvencies by Corporations, and Other Frauds in Their Management," of chap. 724, "An Act to Amend Chapter One Hundred and Forty of The Laws of Eighteen Hundred and Fifty, Entitled 'An Act to Authorize the Formation of Railroad Corporations and to Regulate the Same,'" *General Statutes of the State of New York for the Year 1887*, 284. Adams, "A Chapter of Erie," 30–106, 31. Browder, *The Money Game*, 155. *Senate Report No. 67*, 30. Authority to issue Erie stock in exchange for the BB&P shares came from a New York 1867 law, "An Act in Relation to Railroads Held under Lease," 444–445.

50. The Mercantile Agency gave Drew a generally favorable report. " 'Drew' is pretty well liked & not very grasping in his disposition but takes care that he gets his own." The correspondent added, however, that it would be better to get his contract in writing. Davis, "William Duer, Entrepreneur," 319. Entry for Daniel Drew, R. G. Dun Mercantile Agency Credit Reports 366:51, R. G. Dun & Co. Credit Report Volumes, Baker Library, Harvard Business School. Browder, *The Money Game*, 119.

51. More complete accounts of the Erie War can be found in Stiles, *The First Tycoon*, 449–465. Also Adams, "A Chapter of Erie," 30–106. A third account, including transcripts of some of the original documents, appears in Mott, *Between the Ocean and the Lakes*, 147–164, 475–476. Earlier details of Drew's tenure on the Erie board are described elsewhere in this chapter. Drew left the board in February 1868. He did, however, face a variety of legal problems: *Hancock and Others v. Drew*, New York Supreme Court, 1866, before Judge Ingraham (*New York Evening Post*, December 26, 1866, 4), *Joseph B. Stewart v. Daniel Drew, et al.* (*New York Times*, March 30, 1867, 2; April 3, 1867, 2, 3), *Marston v. Drew*, New York Superior Court, September 1867 (*New York Times*, September 13, 1867, 3, 4); The People, &c of the State of New York, by their Attorney General, Petitioners for the Removal of Daniel Drew, &c. (*New York Herald*, February 19, 1868, 6; June 11, 1884, 6. *New York Times*, February 18, 1868, 3; September 16, 1873, 5. *New York Daily Tribune*, September 19, 1879, 5. *Boston Evening Journal*, September 19, 1879, 2). Clews, *Twenty-Eight Years in Wall Street*, 119.

Chapter Two. Chicago, 1888

Epigraph: Dreiser, *The Financier*, 114.

1. *Chicago Daily Inter-Ocean*, September 29, 1888, 1. *Lakeside Annual Directory of the City of Chicago, 1885.*

2. *Chicago Daily Tribune*, June 19, 1888, 4; June 27, 1888, 2. *Chicago Herald*, September 28, 1888, 1. Three of Chicago's five mass-circulation daily newspapers reported the corner on the front page: the *Chicago Daily Tribune* (September 28, 1888, 1), the *Chicago Herald* (September 28, 1888, 1), and the *Chicago Times* (September 28, 1888, 1). The *Chicago Inter-Ocean* referenced the corner on page 1, but the main story was on page 6 (September 28, 1888, 6). The *Chicago Daily News* reported the corner on page 2 (September 28, 1888, 2). By the end of the day, Hutchinson's wheat corner and the man himself were the principal topics of conversation on exchanges from San Francisco to Liverpool. Prices in these markets did not react immediately, however, as would be the case now, even though the events in Chicago were the top news of the day. Reaction in other markets was mixed. The morning session at the New York Produce Exchange was quiet. The afternoon session was active, though, as cables from Chicago described the unfolding drama there. The mood of the speculators remained relatively calm, however, since few of them were short in the Chicago market, contrary to what the Chicagoans believed. Wheat prices on the St. Louis Mercantile Exchange briefly surged in reaction to the Chicago news but fell back to their earlier level. Markets in Duluth and San Francisco remained unchanged. The Toronto market was highly excited, though, suggesting that speculators there had a lot of money at stake in Chicago market, on the wrong side. *San Francisco Chronicle*, September 28, 1888, 1. *New York Times*, September 28, 1888, 1. *Chicago Herald*, September 28, 1888, 1, 6.

3. Entry for B. J. (*sic*) Hutchinson, dated July 15, 1859, R. G. Dun Mercantile Agency Credit Reports 27:303, R. G. Dun & Co. Credit Report Volumes, Baker Library, Harvard Business School. "The Man Who Makes the Market," *Chicago Times*, September 28, 1888, 1. *Saint Paul (MN) Daily Globe*, October 14, 1888, 23; July 1, 1890, 4; May 8, 1899, 7. *Chicago Daily Inter-Ocean*, January 28, 1888, 6. *Chicago Daily Tribune*, September 24, 1888, 10; October 20, 1889, 26. *Frank Leslie's Illustrated Newspaper*, December 22, 1888, 1. *Fort Worth (TX) Gazette*, February 15, 1889, 6.

4. *Saint Paul (MN) Daily Globe*, January 4, 1891, 11. *Boston Globe*, October 9, 1888, 2.

5. *Chicago Daily News*, September 28, 1888, 1. White, "Western Journalism," 687.

6. *Chicago Daily Inter-Ocean*, September 29, 1888, 1; September 30, 1888, a. *Saint Paul (MN) Daily Globe*, September 29, 1888, 1. *Milwaukee (WI) Sentinel*, September 30, 1888, c. *New York Times*, September 29, 1888, 1.

7. Nineteen hundred members: CBOT, *Thirty-First Annual Report*, 205–256. *Chicago Daily Inter-Ocean*, September 29, 1888, 1. *Chicago Herald*, September 30, 1888, 3. *Chicago Daily Tribune*, June 29, 1887, 9; September 30, 1888, 2. Cash wheat had gone from 92⅛ (bid) on June 13 to 73 on June 14 before dropping further, ending the month at 69¼. CBOT, *Thirtieth Annual Report*, 162.

8. "A Great Operator," *Harper's Weekly*, May 10, 1890, 367. *Omaha (NE) Daily Bee*, October 26, 1888, 8. *St. Paul (MN) Globe*, May 8, 1899, 7. *Milwaukee (WI) Sentinel*, September 29, 1888, 3. *Milwaukee (WI) Daily Journal*, September 28, 1888. *Chicago Daily Tribune*, September 24, 1888, 10. *Chicago Herald*, September 30, 1888, 1.

9. *Fort Worth (TX) Gazette*, February 15, 1889, 6. *Chicago Daily Inter-Ocean*, January 28, 1888, 6. *New York Times*, April 30, 1891, 1. *Chicago Daily Tribune*, July 12, 1888, 1. *New York Times*, July 12, 1888, 1. *New York Sun*, July 12, 1888, 2.

10. *Chicago Daily Inter-Ocean*, July 13, 1888, 7. *New York Times*, September 13, 1891, 11. "A Great Operator," *Harper's Weekly*, May 10, 1890, 367. CBOT, *Annual Statement (1858)*, 50. R. G. Dun Mercantile Agency Credit Reports, 42:150, 34:222, 39:319. R. G. Dun & Co. Credit Report Volumes, Baker Library, Harvard Business School. *Milwaukee (WI) Sentinel*, September 4, 1886, e. *Chicago Daily Tribune*, January 17, 1888, 3. *New York Times*, March 26, 1899, 13. *Chicago Tribune* March 17, 1899, 3. *Chicago Daily News*, September 21, 1888, 1.

11. Massachusetts, Town and Vital Records, 1620–1988. *Boston Globe*, April 30, 1891, 1; May 11, 1891, 1. White, "Western Journalism," 678. Entry for B. J. (*sic*) Hutchinson, dated July 15, 1859, R. G. Dun Mercantile Agency Credit Reports 27:303, R. G. Dun & Co. Credit Report Volumes, Baker Library, Harvard Business School. *Bismarck (Dakota Territory) Daily Tribune*, July 10, 1892, 4. *Pendleton (OR) East Oregonian*, October 10, 1888, 1. *Chicago Daily Tribune*, September 5, 1884, 4; September 5, 1884, 8. *Atchison (KS) Daily Globe*, September 22, 1884. *Washington Post*, May 3, 1891, 15. Hutchinson's bank had no connection to the Corn Exchange Bank of New York.

12. The five dailies were the *Chicago Daily Tribune, Herald, Inter-Ocean, Daily News*, and *Times. Boston Globe*, October 5, 1888, 1. *Fort Worth (TX) Gazette*, February 15, 1889, 6. *Lancaster (PA) Daily Intelligencer*, May 3, 1890, 3. *St. Paul (MN) Globe*, May 8, 1899, 7. *San Francisco Morning Call*, February 6, 1891, 6; July 19, 1891, 9. *Atchison (KS) Daily Globe*, October 6, 1888. *Bismarck (ND) Daily Tribune*, November 20, 1888. *Chicago Daily Tribune*, May 18, 1888, 10; August 6, 1888, 6; August 21, 1888, 1; September 30, 1888, 11. CBOT, *Thirty-First Annual Report*, xx–xxii; *Milwaukee (WI) Sentinel*, September 29, 1888, 3; March 17, 1899, 2. Taylor, *History of the Board of Trade*, 2:771. Leech, *Armour and His Times*, 261.

13. For the first twenty-one years of the Board's existence, new members paid an entry fee of $5. Beginning in 1869, the fee rose to $25, $100, $1,000, and finally to $10,000 in 1883. Alternatively, you could buy the membership of a

retiring member. The price hikes reflected the increasing value of member-ship and the institution's efforts to exclude riffraff. To convert to 2022 dol-lars, according to the data site MeasuringWorth, the CPI in 1888 was 9.22; and at year-end 2022, it was 292.66. (MeasuringWorth sets the CPI average 1982–1984 equal to 100.) The conversion factor from 1888 to 2022 is, therefore, 292.66/9.22 = 31.74 (rounded). The ten $10,000 (1888) entrance fee equals $10,000*31.74 = $317,419 (2022). MeasuringWorth, "The An-nual Consumer Price Index for the United States." Founded in 1861 as the New York Commercial Association, the New York Produce Exchange changed its name in 1867. From the street to the top of the building's flag-pole was 300 feet, and the flagpole was 35 feet high. The Washington Mon-ument, completed in 1884, stands 555 feet 5 1/8 inches high. *Boston Globe*, March 17, 1899, 4. *Annual Statement (1858)*, 46–55. CBOT, *Thirty-First An-nual Report (1888)*, 205–256. CBOT, *Act of Incorporation, 1869*, 20. CBOT, *Act of Incorporation, 1871*, 24. CBOT, *Act of Incorporation, 1875*, 37. CBOT, *Act of Incorporation, 1883*, 33. Chap. 30, "An Act to Amend an Act Entitled 'An Act to Incorporate the New York Commercial Association,' Passed April Nineteenth, Eighteen Hundred and Sixty-Two," passed February 13, 1867, in *Laws of the State of New York 1867*, 63. Christopher Gray, "A Brick Beauty Bites the Dust," *New York Times*, August 21, 2014. *Chicago Daily Tribune*, April 28, 1885, 9.

14. The new Board of Trade building was completed one year after the Home Insurance Company building, two and a half blocks north on LaSalle Street, considered to be the first skyscraper. The Home Insurance Com-pany building stood at 205 LaSalle Street, between Monroe and Adams Streets. *Lakeside Annual Directory of the City of Chicago, 1892*, 73. The Board of Trade building, however, lacked the distinguishing characteristics of a skyscraper, even though it was much taller than the Home Insurance build-ing. Seventeen stained-glass windows, twenty-six frescoes: *St. Louis Globe-Democrat*, April 29, 1885, 4. Sixteen ceiling panels: *Chicago Daily Tribune*, April 28, 1885, 9.

15. "A Great Operator," *Harper's Weekly*, May 10, 1890, 367. Falloon, *Market Maker*, 72. *San Francisco Chronicle*, October 8, 1888, 6. *Washington Post*, Sep-tember 23, 1888, 12.

16. Santos, "Grain Futures Markets," 4. Hieronymus, *Economics of Futures Trad-ing*, 74–76. Williams, "The Origin of Futures Markets," 306–316. Odle, "Entrepreneurial Cooperation on the Great Lakes," 439–455. United States Commodity Futures Commission website. *The Economist* (London), June 18, 1870, 773; July 19, 1873, 881; February 23, 1878, 220; September 27, 1890, 1233. *Fictitious Dealing in Agricultural Products*, 161.

17. In 1887, Albert C. Stevens estimated that the volume of wheat traded in fu-tures contracts was between fifteen and twenty times the actual amount of wheat in existence in that market. Stevens, " 'Futures' in the Wheat Mar-ket," 37–63. "The Tricks in the Grain Trade," *Chicago Tribune*, Jan 16, 1867,

2. "Members of the Chicago Board of Trade Arrested for Grain-Gambling," *New York Times*, August 11, 1867, 5.

18. *Chicago Daily Tribune*, August 13, 1888, 6; August 14, 1888, 6; August 15, 1888, 10; August 16, 1888, 1, 5; August 17, 1888, 3; August 29, 1888, 6; September 4, 1888, 10; September 7, 1888, 4; September 10, 1888, 10; September 15, 1888, 9. *Chicago Herald*, September 28, 1888, 6. *Chicago Times*, September 28, 1888, 1.

19. Originally incorporated 1853 as the New York Corn Exchange, predecessor of the New York Produce Exchange. Chapter 74, "An Act to Incorporate the New-York Corn Exchange," in *Laws of the State of New-York, 1853*, 103. The first known use of the terms "bull" and "bear" in Chicago was in a market letter and price circular of May 1855, in reference to the grain trade at the New York Corn Exchange, noted in Taylor, *History of the Board of Trade*, 1:206. New York Corn Exchange incorporated April 2, 1853. Chapter 74, "An Act to Incorporate the New-York Corn Exchange," in *Laws of the State of New-York, 1853*, 103. "Bears" in reference to corn trading in Chicago quoted from the *Chicago Democratic Press*, June 4, 1856, quoted in Taylor, *History of the Board of Trade*, 1:217. The Corn Exchange had itself adopted the terminology from the New York Stock Exchange and Board, which was at that time a five-minute walk from the Corn Exchange. The New York Corn Exchange met at 127 Broad Street (also 16 South Street, on the corner of Broad and South). New York Corn Exchange. 127 Broad St.: H. Wilson, *Trow's New York City Directory, 1857*, 616. Corn Exchange, 16 South St.: H. Wilson, *Trow's New York City Directory, 1856*, 185. New York Corn Exchange article and description: "The New York Grain Trade," *Farmer's Magazine* (London) 18, 3rd ser. (July–December 1860): 431. In 1853, the New York Stock Exchange and Board moved from the Merchants' Exchange building to a room in the Commercial Exchange Bank building, at the corner of Broad and William. Then, about 1857, it moved to Dan Lord's building, with entrances on William and Beaver. In December 1865, the New York Stock Exchange and Board occupied Dan Lord's Building, at 25 William Street. Clews, *Twenty-Eight Years in Wall Street*, 90. Broad and South Streets intersect southeast of Battery Park, right at the waterfront. In 1855, the New York Stock Exchange and Board was at Broad and William, so there were about five short blocks between the two, probably a five-minute walk. *Mitchell Map of New York City, 1860*. *Chicago Daily Tribune*, November 24, 1889, 25. The term "scalper" was in use on the New York Stock Exchange by 1888. "The New York Stock Exchange," *Harper's New Monthly Magazine*, November 1885, 839. The first documented instance of the term "tailer" there was in 1900. Nelson, *ABC of Wall Street*, 161.

20. *Chicago Daily Tribune*, September 26, 1886, 12. *San Francisco Chronicle*, September 28, 1888, 1.

21. *Chicago Daily Tribune*, March 21, 1886, 10; September 26, 1886, 12; September 23, 1888, 9; August 3, 1893, 1; May 28, 1899, 32; April 24, 1915, 1. *Chicago Press and Tribune* (former name of the *Chicago Tribune*), August 21, 1860,

2. CBOT, *Eighteenth Annual Report (1875)*, 192; CBOT, *Twentieth Annual Report (1877)*, 168, 181, 195, 199.

22. *Saint Paul (MN) Daily Globe*, September 20, 1888, 6.

23. "On 'change" is the nineteenth-century term for "on the exchange."

24. *Milwaukee (WI) Sentinel*, September 29, 1888, 3.

25. *Chicago Daily Tribune*, November 24, 1889, 25.

26. *Chicago Daily Tribune*, September 26, 1888, 12.

27. The Big Four would have looked to recent precedents, which are unknown. But in 1867, on an occasion still remembered on the exchange in 1888, the member Calvin B. Goodyear had cornered corn. The details have been lost, but something about how he did it so angered other members that Good- year gave up and sold out his position. "Corners of the Past," *Chicago Daily Tribune*, September 30, 1888, 2.

28. Cash wheat had gone from 92⅛ (bid) on June 13 to 73 on June 14 before dropping further, ending the month at 69¼. *Chicago Daily Tribune*, June 29, 1887, 9; October 6, 1888, 5. CBOT, *Thirtieth Annual Report (1887)*, 162. A price of 92⅛ equals ninety-two and one-eighth cents. In this chapter, prices are quoted as they were in 1888, in cents and eighths of a cent on the dollar.

29. Among New York stock speculators in 1866, the equivalent term for (1888 Chicago) "pressing the deal" was "to milk the street."

30. To convert to 2022 dollars, see note 13 above. A profit to Hutchinson of $300,000 (1888) equals $300,000*31.74 = 9,522,000 (2022). A profit to Hutchinson of $500,000 (1888) equals $500,000*31.74 = $15,870,000 (2022). *Chicago Daily Tribune*, September 29, 1888, 1. *Chicago Daily Inter-Ocean*, August 14, 1888, 8; September 27, 1888, 10. *Chicago Times*, September 28, 1888, 1. CBOT, *Twenty-Fifth Annual Report (1882)*, 71; CBOT, *Twenty-Sixth Annual Report (1883)*, 103; CBOT, *Twenty-Seventh Annual Report (1884)*, 91; CBOT, *Twenty-Eighth Annual Report (1885)*, 146; CBOT, *Twenty-Ninth An- nual Report (1886)*, 164; CBOT, *Thirtieth Annual Report (1887)*, 168; CBOT, *Thirty-First Annual Report (1888)*, 170.

31. *Washington Post*, September 29, 1888, 1.

32. *Saint Paul (MN) Daily Globe*, September 28, 1888, 6. *New York Tribune*, Sep- tember 28, 1888, 1. *Chicago Daily Tribune*, September 28, 1888, 1. *New York Tribune*, September 28, 1888, 1. *Chicago Herald*, September 28, 1888, 6.

33. *Chicago Herald*, September 28, 1888, 6. *Chicago Daily Inter-Ocean*, September 27, 1888, 2.

34. *Chicago Daily Tribune*, September 27, 1888, 10; September 28, 1888, 1. *New York Tribune*, September 28, 1888, 1. *Saint Paul (MN) Daily Globe*, Septem- ber 28, 1888, 6. *Chicago Herald*, September 28, 1888, 6. *New York Times*, Sep- tember 28, 1888, 1.

35. CBOT, *Thirty-First Annual Report (1888)*, 249. *Chicago Herald*, September 28, 1888, 6. *Omaha (NE) Daily Bee*, September 28, 1888, 3. *Chicago Daily Tribune*, September 28, 1888, 1. *New York Times*, September 28, 1888, 1.

Milwaukee (WI) Sentinel, September 28, 1888, e. To 96⅝ by 10 p.m.: *Saint Paul (MN) Daily Globe*, September 28, 1888, 6.

36. *Chicago Daily Inter-Ocean*, September 28, 1888, 1. *Chicago Daily Tribune*, September 28, 1888, 1.

37. *New York Tribune*, September 28, 1888, 1. *Chicago Daily News*, September 21, 1888, 1.

38. *Chicago Daily Tribune*, September 28, 1888, 1. CBOT, *Thirty-First Annual Report (1888)*, 218. Cohen, *The Great Bear*, 296. *Chicago Times*, September 28, 1888, 1. *New York Tribune*, September 28, 1888, 1. At 10:30: *New York Tribune*, September 28, 1888, 1. *Chicago Herald*, September 28, 1888, 6. *Chicago Daily Inter-Ocean*, September 28, 1888, 1. Eggleston's bid, "Buy Sep at eleven," is a bid for Sep wheat at $1.11 per bushel.

39. CBOT, *Thirty-First Annual Report (1888)*, 211. *Chicago Daily News*, September 27, 1888, 1. *Chicago Times*, September 28, 1888, 1.

40. *Chicago Herald*, September 28, 1888, 6. CBOT, *Thirty-First Annual Report (1888)*, 244. *Omaha (NE) Daily Bee*, September 28, 1888, 3.

41. *Chicago Daily Tribune*, May 2, 1888, 3; May 18, 1888, 10. *New York Tribune*, September 28, 1888, 1. *Chicago Daily News*, September 29, 1888, 1. *Frank Leslie's Illustrated Newspaper*, December 22, 1888, 1. Map of Chicago, in *Cram's Standard American Atlas of the World*. *Lakeside Annual Directory of the City of Chicago, 1892*, 86.

42. *Chicago Daily Tribune*, September 28, 1888, 1. *Omaha (NE) Daily Bee*, September 28, 1888, 3. *Milwaukee (WI) Sentinel*, September 28, 1888, e.

43. *Chicago Herald*, September 28, 1888, 6. *Milwaukee (WI) Sentinel*, September 28, 1888, e. *Chicago Times*, September 28, 1888, 1. *Omaha (NE) Daily Bee*, September 28, 1888, 3. *Chicago Daily Tribune*, April 28, 1885, 9; September 28, 1888, 1.

44. *Chicago Herald*, September 28, 1888, 6. *New York Times*, September 28, 1888, 1. *New York Tribune*, September 28, 1888, 1.

45. *Chicago Press and Tribune*, July 4, 1859, 2. *Chicago Daily Inter-Ocean*, September 28, 1888, 6.

46. *Chicago Times*, September 28, 1888, 1. *New York Times*, September 28, 1888, 1. *Chicago Daily Tribune*, March 20, 1899, 5. *St. Paul (MN) Globe*, May 8, 1899, 7. *Pendleton (OR) East Oregonian*, October 10, 1888, 1.

47. *New York Tribune*, September 28, 1888, 1. *Milwaukee (WI) Sentinel*, September 29, 1888, 3. *Chicago Times*, September 28, 1888, 1.

48. *Saint Paul (MN) Daily Globe*, September 28, 1888, 6. As of the preceding Saturday, Chicago's elevators held about 2.8 million bushels of contract-grade wheat. Hutchinson owned 2 million bushels, with the rest scattered among smaller holders. *New York Times*, September 28, 1888, 1. *Chicago Daily Tribune*, September 28, 1888, 1. *Saint Paul (MN) Daily Globe*, September 28, 1888, 6.

49. Sep wheat had opened at 104. Late in the session, one lot of five thousand bushels sold at 128. *Chicago Herald*, September 28, 1888, 6. *Chicago Daily*

Tribune, September 25, 1888, 10. *Chicago Daily Inter-Ocean*, September 28, 1888, 1. *New York Times*, September 28, 1888, 1.

50. *Chicago Daily Tribune*, September 28, 1888, 1. *Milwaukee (WI) Sentinel*, September 28, 1888, e. *San Francisco Chronicle*, September 28, 1888, 1. *Chicago Times*, September 28, 1888, 1.

51. The shorts who bought the 530,000 bushels from Hutchinson at $1.25 a bushel had to sell it back to him at their contract prices, which were between $0.85 and $0.97 a bushel, giving Hutchinson a profit between $148,400 and $212,000. To convert to 2022 dollars, see note 13 above. A profit to Hutchinson of $200,000 (1888) equals $200,000*31.74 = $6,348,000 (2022). *Chicago Daily Tribune*, September 28, 1888, 10. Taylor, *History of the Board of Trade*, 1:501–502. "Gambling in Grain, etc.," in Hurd, *Revised Statutes of the State of Illinois, 1874*, 372. CBOT, *Thirty-First Annual Report (1888)*, 245. *Chicago Times*, September 28, 1888, 1. *New York Times*, September 29, 1888, 1. *Chicago Daily News*, September 27, 1888, 1.

52. *Chicago Daily Tribune*, June 15, 1887, 1.

53. Traveling on the New York Central Railroad's Lake Shore Limited (opened 1897), the two cities are 959 rail miles apart. The two cities are about 730 air miles apart.

54. For example, in Chicago, the first recorded use of the term "corner," in the financial sense, was in an 1859 *Tribune* article. The *Tribune* reprinted a piece from the *Cincinnati Price Current*, in which that paper's New York correspondent commented on market practices there. *Chicago Daily Tribune*, December 9, 1859, 4. The term "corner" had been in use in New York at least since 1841. Jackson, *A Week in Wall Street*, 89.

55. *Chicago Daily Tribune*, March 21, 1886, 10.

56. "Whenever anything which has several parts is such that the whole is something over and above its parts, and not just the sum of them all, like a heap, then it always has some cause." Aristotle *Metaphysics*, 39 (book H 8-10). The idea was first developed fully by the Scottish moral philosopher Adam Ferguson, in his 1767 book *Essay on the History of Civil Society*, 183ff. Hayek, "The Trend of Economic Thinking," 121–137. Hayek, "The Use of Knowledge in Society," 519–530.

57. The Great Chicago Fire burned from Sunday, October 8, to Tuesday, October 10, 1871. From 1860 to 1870, the population of Chicago grew from 112,172 to 298,977, a rate of 10.3 percent per year. U.S. Census. *New York World*, August 27, 1890, 2. CBOT annual reports, 1858–1888.

58. For example, *Bismarck (Dakota Territory) Weekly Tribune*, October 5, 1888, 7; November 23, 1888, 3. Hutchinson died in 1899 after having been retired for over seven years. His passing was reported in papers around the country. Papers in major cities coast to coast published extended obituaries. *Chicago Daily Tribune*, January 13, 1890, 3. *Michigan Farmer*, October 6, 1888, 4. *Prairie Farmer*, October 6, 1888, 646. *Fort Worth (TX) Weekly Gazette*,

October 12, 1888, 2. *Chicago Daily Tribune*, October 4, 1888, 4. *Fictitious Dealing in Agricultural Products*, 53, 226, 261, 264, 276, 277, 309.

59. *Chicago Herald*, September 29, 1888, 1. CBOT, *Thirty-First Annual Report (1888)*, 233, 241. *Chicago Daily Inter-Ocean*, September 29, 1888, 1. Poole's bid, "Buy Sep at twenty-five," was to buy Sep wheat at $1.25 a bushel.

60. *Chicago Daily Inter-Ocean*, September 29, 1888, 1. Taylor, *History of the Board of Trade*, 1:501–502. "Gambling in Grain, etc.," in Hurd, *Revised Statutes of the State of Illinois, 1874*, 372. *Chicago Daily Tribune*, September 29, 1888, 1.

61. *Milwaukee (WI) Sentinel*, September 29, 1888, 3. *Chicago Times*, September 29, 1888, 1.

62. *Milwaukee (WI) Sentinel*, September 29, 1888, 3. *Chicago Times*, September 29, 1888, 1. *Atchison (KS) Daily Globe*, September 29, 1888, a. *Chicago Herald*, September 29, 1888, 1. *Chicago Daily Tribune*, September 29, 1888, 1.

63. *Chicago Daily Inter-Ocean*, September 29, 1888, 1. *Chicago Herald*, September 29, 1888, 1.

64. *Chicago Times*, September 29, 1888, 1. *Saint Paul (MN) Daily Globe*, September 29, 1888, 1.

65. *Chicago Herald*, September 29, 1888, 1.

66. *Pendleton (OR) East Oregonian*, October 18, 1888, 1. In 1888, the most recent rule book (1883) was 107 pages long, about a third of which was devoted to regulations for inspection of different agricultural products. CBOT, *Act of Incorporation, 1883*.

67. *Chicago Herald*, September 29, 1888, 1, 6. *Saint Paul (MN) Daily Globe*, September 29, 1888, 1. *Chicago Daily News*, September 28, 1888, 1. *New York Sun*, September 29, 1888, 2.

68. *Chicago Herald*, September 29, 1888, 1.

69. *Saint Paul (MN) Daily Globe*, September 29, 1888, 1.

70. *Chicago Daily Tribune*, September 30, 1888, 11.

71. The Big Four would have looked to recent precedents, which are unknown. An earlier instance involving the CBOT member Calvin B. Goodyear is noted earlier in this chapter.

72. *Chicago Times*, September 29, 1888, 1.

73. Taylor, *History of the Board of Trade*, 2:772. One million bushels, according to the estimate of the *Chicago Tribune*; three million bushels according to the *Milwaukee (WI) Sentinel*. On September 27, October closed at 100¾ and closed at 98¼ on September 28. On those dates, Dec closed at 98¼–98⅞ and at 98½. May closed at 101½–101⅝ and at 100¼. *Chicago Daily Tribune*, September 28, 1888, 10. *Milwaukee (WI) Sentinel*, September 28, 1888, e. *Chicago Daily News*, September 28, 1888, 2. *New York Times*, September 29, 1888, 1. *Chicago Daily Inter-Ocean*, September 29, 1888, 1.

74. *Chicago Daily Inter-Ocean*, September 30, 1888, a. *Chicago Daily News*, September 29, 1888, 1. *Wichita (KS) Daily Eagle*, September 30, 1888, 2. *Milwaukee (WI) Daily Journal*, October 1, 1888, g. *Milwaukee (WI) Sentinel*, September 30, 1888, c; October 1, 1888, 3.

75. The shorts had contracted with the railroads to divert passenger trains to make way for 230 carloads of wheat, emptying the warehouses in St. Louis. A smaller amount had been shipped from Milwaukee. According to exchange rules, before the wheat could be delivered to satisfy outstanding contracts, it first would have to be inspected, and then certificates of inspection and warehouse receipts issued. Hutchinson's own sources had advised him that only 80 of the 250 promised railroad cars of wheat would come from St. Louis and that only 50 more would arrive in time for delivery by Saturday. "Gambling in Grain, etc.," in Hurd, *Revised Statutes of the State of Illinois, 1874*, 372. *Chicago Daily Inter-Ocean*, September 29, 1888, 1. *New York Times*, September 29, 1888, 1. *Saint Paul (MN) Daily Globe*, September 29, 1888, 1; September 30, 1888, 1. *Chicago Herald*, September 29, 1888, 1.

76. That is, 250 cars at about 500 bushels/car. The shorts had hoped to get 100 cars of wheat from Saint Paul, 50 cars from Detroit, and another 100 cars from St. Louis. In fact, they got somewhat less than that: 90,000 bushels instead of 115,000 bushels from St. Louis, 25,000 bushels having been delayed at Joliet. Another 40,000 bushels arrived via the Illinois Central from points east. *Chicago Daily Inter-Ocean*, September 30, 1888, a. *San Francisco Chronicle*, September 30, 1888, 15.

77. Late during the Thursday trading session, Hutchinson received independent confirmation of the grain being shipped from St. Louis from the Grier Commission Company, a St. Louis brokerage firm with which Hutchinson did business. In his return telegram, Hutchinson advised Grier not to sell his wheat until it reached Chicago, where he could get 150 a bushel for it. *Chicago Daily Inter-Ocean*, September 28, 1888, 6. *Chicago Daily Tribune*, September 29, 1888, 1.

78. *San Francisco Chronicle*, September 30, 1888, 15. *Chicago Daily Inter-Ocean*, September 30, 1888, a.

79. *New York Times*, September 29, 1888, 1. *Los Angeles Times*, September 30, 1888, 4. *Milwaukee (WI) Sentinel*, September 30, 1888, c. *Chicago Herald*, September 30, 1888, 1.

80. *Chicago Herald*, September 30, 1888, 1. *Chicago Daily Inter-Ocean*, September 30, 1888, a. *Chicago Herald*, October 1, 1888, 6.

81. *Chicago Herald*, October 1, 1888, 6. *Chicago Daily Inter-Ocean*, September 30, 1888, a. *Boston Globe*, September 30, 1888, 2. *Saint Paul (MN) Daily Globe*, September 30, 1888, 14. *Chicago Daily Tribune*, September 30, 1888, 11.

82. *Chicago Herald*, September 30, 1888, 1.

83. *Chicago Daily Inter-Ocean*, September 30, 1888, a. *Milwaukee (WI) Sentinel*, September 30, 1888, c. *Chicago Daily Tribune*, June 16, 1887, 1; September 30, 1888, 11. *Chicago Herald*, September 30, 1888, 1.

84. *New York Times*, September 30, 1888, 1. *Chicago Daily News*, September 29, 1888, 1. CBOT, *Thirty-First Annual Report (1888)*, 245. *San Francisco Chronicle*, September 30, 1888, 15.

85. *Chicago Daily Inter-Ocean*, September 30, 1888, a. *Chicago Daily News*, September 29, 1888, 1. *San Francisco Chronicle*, September 30, 1888, 15.

86. *Chicago Herald*, September 30, 1888, 1. *New York Times*, September 30, 1888, 1. *Chicago Daily Inter-Ocean*, September 30, 1888, a. *New York Sun*, September 30, 1888, 2.

87. Two well-known operators from this period who committed suicide over their trading losses were Nelson Vankirk and Peter M'Geoch. *Chicago Daily Tribune* August 5, 1893, 8; November 28, 1895, 7.

88. *New York Times*, September 30, 1888, 1. *Chicago Daily Inter-Ocean*, September 30, 1888, a. *Chicago Herald*, September 30, 1888, 1. CBOT, *Thirty-First Annual Report (1888)*, 253. *Chicago Daily Tribune*, October 1, 1884, 9. *Chicago Daily News*, September 29, 1888, 1.

89. *New York Times*, September 30, 1888, 1. *Chicago Herald*, September 30, 1888, 1; October 1, 1888, 6. *San Francisco Chronicle*, September 30, 1888, 15. *Chicago Daily News*, September 29, 1888, 1. *Saint Paul (MN) Daily Globe*, September 30, 1888, 1.

90. Up until this time, the greatest one-day drop in the price of wheat following the end of a corner had been in August 1872, when the price dropped from 180 to 109. On this occasion, however, the "man in the air," as the corner operator was called, went down in disaster, and the corner was a spectacular failure. *New York Times*, September 30, 1888, 1. *San Francisco Chronicle*, September 30, 1888, 15. *Chicago Daily Tribune*, June 15, 1887, 1; September 30, 1888, 11. *Chicago Times*, September 30, 1888, 2.

91. The highest price quoted for June (1887) wheat during Harper's attempted corner was 94¼ cents a bushel. Early in March of that year, June wheat had sold at 80 cents a bushel. (14.75/80) = 0.184 = 18.4%. *Chicago Daily Tribune*, June 29, 1887, 9. *Chicago Herald*, October 1, 1888, 6.

92. To convert to 2022 dollars, see note 13 above. A profit to Hutchinson of $1.5 million (1888) equals $1,500,000*31.74 = $47,610,000 (2022). A profit to Hutchinson of $2 million (1888) equals $2,000,000*31.74 = 63,480,000 (2022). *Atchison (KS) Daily Globe*, November 15, 1888, a. *American Elevator and Grain Trade*, 38. *Chicago Herald*, October 1, 1888, 6. *Chicago Daily Tribune*, September 30, 1888, 11. *New York Times*, September 30, 1888, 1. *Boston Globe*, September 30, 1888, 2.

93. The highest price for October wheat (and for the rest of the year) was reached on October 6, when wheat reached 118⅝. On December 31, cash wheat closed at 101½ bid. Assuming the investor bought the wheat at 1.05 a bushel, five thousand bushels would have cost him $5,250. Purchased on margin, the wheat would have cost the investor 10 percent of that price, or $525. CBOT, *Act of Incorporation, 1883*, 43. The brokerage fee would have been one half of one cent per bushel (CBOT, *Act of Incorporation, 1883*, 38), or $25. The investor's total cash outlay, therefore, would have been $525+$25, or $550. The investor's profit on the deal would have been $1,500—$550, or $950. His return on investment would have been

$950/$550, or 172 percent. *Saint Paul (MN) Daily Globe*, September 29, 1888, 1. *Chicago Daily Tribune*, September 29, 1888, 1; September 30, 1888, 11; October 4, 1888, 2. *Chicago Daily Inter-Ocean*, September 29, 1888, 14; September 30, 1888, a. Taylor, *History of the Board of Trade*, 2:778.

94. *Chicago Daily Inter-Ocean*, September 27, 1888, 2. *Washington Post*, October 8, 1888, 4. *Saint Paul (MN) Pioneer Press*, October 3, 1888, 2.

95. *Chicago Tribune*, November 24, 1889, 25.

96. *Chicago Daily Tribune*, March 21, 1886, 10. *Chicago Daily Tribune*, April 25, 1895, 7. 1860 U.S. Census population schedule for Lynfield, Essex County, Massachusetts, 15. 1860 U.S. census population schedule for Fourth Ward, Salem, Essex County, Massachusetts, 330.

97. "An Act to Prohibit Certain Sales of Gold and Foreign Exchange." After the 1864 law, the next federal attempt to regulate commodities occurred in 1882, when during a congressional debate on a new federal bankruptcy law, Senator John Tyler Morgan of Alabama (*Biographical Directory of the United States Congress*) moved to insert wording into the bill that would bar bankrupts from trading in stocks, bonds, other securities, and a long list of commodities unless they owned the items traded. The Senate adopted Senator Morgan's wording, but the provision never made it into law. *Congressional Record: Forty-Seventh Congress, Second Session*, 1882, 14:114. The next attempt to enact a federal law regulating futures markets was in January 1888, in the aftermath of the Harper corner. Bill introduced January 23, 1888, by Rep. Benjamin Enloe, Eighth Congressional District of Tennessee, to punish dealing in futures in agricultural products, labeled H.R. 5689. *Congressional Record: Fiftieth Congress, First Session (House)*, 1888, 19:636.

98. Lurie, *The Chicago Board of Trade*, 109, referencing M. Wilson, "The Attack on Options and Futures, 1888–1894," 32–33. The Commodity Futures Trading Commission website states that from the 1880s and for the next forty years, some two hundred bills were introduced into Congress. There were, however, prior to 1890 only two bills introduced into Congress, cited earlier. United States Commodity Futures Trading Commission, "About the CFTC." Bakken, "Historical Evaluation, Theory and Legal Status," 19. "An Act to Repeal the Act of the Seventeenth of June, Eighteen Hundred and Sixty-Four, Prohibiting the Sales of Gold and Foreign Exchange." *Strong v. Repide*.

99. *Chicago Daily Inter-Ocean*, October 2, 1888, c. *Chicago Herald*, October 2, 1888, 2. *Chicago Daily Tribune*, October 2, 1888, 1.

100. The two firms that failed were Frank Clifton and S. C. Orr. *Chicago Daily Inter-Ocean*, October 2, 1888, c. *Chicago Herald*, October 2, 1888, 2. Dec wheat dropped and closed on Monday, October 1, at 105⅝. After the close, Hutchinson said that he had sold about six million bushels. *Chicago Daily Tribune*, October 2, 1888, 1.

101. *Chicago Herald*, October 2, 1888, 2; October 3, 1888, 5; October 5, 1888. *New York Times*, October 5, 1888, 2. *Chicago Daily Tribune*, October 2, 1888, 1; October 6, 1888, 5.

102. *Chicago Herald*, October 2, 1888, 2.
103. *Chicago Daily Tribune*, October 1, 1888, 4 (original italics); February 10, 1915, 4; April 24, 1915, 1; April 25, 1895, 7; June 18, 1914, 7. *Wall Street Journal*, January 19, 1903, 2.
104. While the new building was being completed, the Board met at 453 Clark Street. *Chicago Tribune*, December 8, 1928, 14. The Saint Petersburg Stock Exchange building was begun in 1804, completed 1810, opened 1816. Saint Petersburg, Russia, "Administrative and Government Buildings." Ayers, *The Architecture of Paris*, 61–62. *Illustrated London News*, March 25, 1854, 268– 269. "It is a plain building, with a stone front, except the attic, which is of brick": "The Stock Exchange," in Combe, *The Microcosm of London*, 104. *Illustrated London News*, March 25, 1854, 268–269. *New York Commercial Advertiser*, September 16, 1871, 3. *New York Evening Post*, September 16, 1871, 4. *New York Tribune*, September 16, 1871, 5. *New York Times*, September 3, 1871, 6; September 17, 1871, 6. *Frank Leslie's Illustrated Newspaper*, October 21, 1871, 87. Withers, "The London Stock Exchange," 105. The film *The Wolf of Wall Street* presents a fictionalized version of consumption culture in the market crowd. For real-life examples, see Enrich, *The Spider Network*, 50. Before and after images of the NYSE's makeover can be seen in figures 2 and 9.
105. In newspaper articles on later corners on the Board of Trade, Hutchinson's 1888 corner continued to be mentioned as a model corner through the 1900s. Payne, "The Chicago Board of Trade," 745. *New York Times*, April 30, 1891, 1; October 27, 1907, sm2; April 5, 1917, 20. *Chicago Daily Tribune*, March 17, 1899, 3.
106. Hartley, *The Go-Between*, 1.

Chapter Three. The Chicago Board of Trade, 1910–1940

1. All charts referenced as sources in the notes, as well as supporting data used to prepare the charts, can be found in appendix 3, available online at http://markwgeiger.com/.
2. Burt, "Models of Network Structure," 79. Homans, "Bringing Men Back In," 812. Freeman, "The Development of Social Network Analysis," 26.
3. CBOT, *Thirty-First Annual Report (1888)*, 205–256. Prell, *Social Network Analysis*, 16. Watts, "The 'New' Science of Networks," 248. The illustration shows 974 members out of 1931 total. CBOT, *Thirty-First Annual Report (1888)*, 205–256. The number 150 appears to be far too low for today's world. Using a different statistical method, Zheng et al. find that the average number of persons known by men is 650 and by women is 590. Zheng et al., "How Many People Do You Know in Prison?," 409–423.
4. Lazonick, *Business Organization and the Myth of the Market Economy*, 60. Baker, "The Social Structure of a National Securities Market," 775–811. Prell, *Social Network Analysis*, 8.

5. Rousseau et al., "Not So Different After All," 393–404. Kadushin, *Understanding Social Networks*, 101, 36.

6. Lidar is an acronym of (1) "light detection and ranging" or (2) "laser imaging, detection, and ranging." Lidar sometimes is called 3-D laser scanning. McPherson et al. "Birds of a Feather," 429–430. Feld, "The Focused Organization of Social Ties," 1016. Kadushin, *Understanding Social Networks*, 39.

7. Butts, "Social Network Analysis," 18.

8. Hawe et al. "A Glossary of Terms," 972. CBOT, *Sixty-Second Annual Report (1919)*, 29 (appendix). To convert to 2022 dollars, see note 13 in chapter 2. The $25,000 (1888) entrance fee equals $25,000*16.92 = $423,200 (2022). CBOT, *Eighty-Third Annual Report (1940)*, 161–200. Chart 1.1, "CBOT New Members 1910–1940: % of All Members." Out of 1,620 CBOT members in 1910, by 1920, 838 remained. Out of 1,602 CBOT members in 1920, by 1930, 798 remained. Out of 1,518 CBOT members in 1930, by 1940, 776 remained. Average ten-year attrition for the three periods equals: (838+798+776)/(1620+1602+1518) = 2412/4740 = 0.5089 = 51% (x^{10} =.51//x =.935, which computes to a 6.5 percent annual rate of decline). CBOT, *Fifty-Third Annual Report (1910)*, 220–269. CBOT, *Sixty-Third Annual Report (1920)*, 144–194. CBOT, *Seventy-Third Annual Report (1930)*, 195–232. CBOT, *Eighty-Third Annual Report (1940)*, 161–200.

9. Future Trading Act of 1921. CBOT, *Eighty-Third Annual Report (1940)*, 161–200.

10. An asymmetric connection, such as between an officer and an enlisted soldier, is known as an *arc*. In this analysis, all links between members are assumed to be edges. Prell, *Social Network Analysis*, 8–12, 78, 138. Brass et al. "Relationships and Unethical Behavior," 18.

11. For example, a more refined version of degree centrality, eigenvector centrality, measures the extent to which a focal actor's connections are themselves well connected. Prell, *Social Network Analysis*, 100–101, 154. For the core component member class only, measures for eigenvector centrality, closeness centrality, betweenness centrality, and cut vertices were calculated. A network with a single component is a connected graph.

12. Kadushin, *Understanding Social Networks*, 50. In each of the four data sets, years 1910–1940, ten or fewer members had connections of all five types: 1910, six; 1920, eight; 1930, ten; 1940, five. Calculations by the author.

13. Chart 1.2, "CBOT Members—All: Member Classes 1910–1940." Calculations by the author. Chart 2.1, "CBOT New Members: 10-Year Survival Rates by Member Class." Chart 2.2, "CBOT New Members: 20-Year Survival Rates by Member Class."

14. Chart 1.4, "CBOT New Members—Core versus CNC: % Multiplex Relationships." Chart 2.8, "CBOT New Members—Core: Multiplexity and 10-Year Survival." Chart 2.9, "CBOT New Members—CNC: Multiplexity and 10-Yr Survival." Uzzi, "The Sources and Consequences of Embeddedness

for the Economic Performance of Organizations," 681. Kadushin, *Understanding Social Networks*, 36.

15. Members in the core component made up one-third of all members of the exchange in that year, not just ten-year members. 1910, 601/1,620 = 37%; 1920, 600/1,602 = 37%; 1930, 496/1,518 = 33%; 1940, 435/1,484 = 29%. Chart 1.2, "CBOT Members—All: Member Classes 1910–1940." Calculations by the author. Chart 1.5, "CBOT Members—Core and CNC: % of Members and Edges 1910–1940." The exchange did not hire its first paid executive officer until 1948. Commons, *Institutional Economics*, 713. From 1910 to 1940, the number of committees ranged between twenty-three and twenty-eight. CBOT, *Fifty-Third Annual Report (1910)* x. CBOT, *Sixty-Third Annual Report*, xv. CBOT, *Seventy-Third Annual Report (1930)*, 15. CBOT, *Eighty-Second Annual Report (1939)*, 16. Seventy-six percent of 1909 directors and committee members were still in position in 1910; 77 percent from 1919 to 1920, 56 percent from 1929 to 1930, and 66 percent from 1939 to 1940. CBOT, *Fifty-Second Annual Report (1909)*, ix–x. CBOT, *Sixty-Second Annual Report (1919)*, xv–xvi. CBOT, *Seventy-Second Annual Report (1929)*, 15–16. CBOT, *Eighty-Second Annual Report (1939)*, 15–16. The number of directors and committee members varied, from a high of ninety-eight in 1930 to a low of fifty-three in 1940: sixty-eight in 1910, sixty-four in 1920, ninety-eight in 1930, and fifty-three in 1940. CBOT, *Fifty-Third Annual Report (1910)*, x. CBOT, *Sixty-Third Annual Report*, xv. CBOT, *Seventy-Third Annual Report (1930)*, 15. CBOT, *Eighty-Second Annual Report (1939)*, 16. Chart 2.12, "CBOT New Members—Core: Directors' Committees 10-Year Survival."

16. CBOT, *Fifty-Third Annual Report (1910)*, 250. Calculations by the author. CBOT, *Fifty-Third Annual Report (1910)*, 219–269. Chart 2.3, "CBOT New Members—Core: Average Edges and 10-Year Survival." Chart 2.4, "CBOT New Members—CNC: Average Edges and 10-Year Survival." Beyond the simple above/below-average split, there is no clear-cut relationship between number of connections and ten-year survival. Members in the top quartile of connections did not consistently survive in higher percentages than members in the second quartile did. Chart 2.5, "CBOT New Members—Core: Average Degree and 10-Year Survival." Chart 2.6, "CBOT New Members—CNC: Average Degree and 10-Year Survival." Chart 1.3, "CBOT New Members—Core vs. CNC: Average Degree." Calculations by the author. In 1910, 289 members out of 601 total in the core component, so 289/601 = 48 percent. Calculations by the author.

17. Chart 2.5, "CBOT New Members—Core: Average Degree and 10-Year Survival." Chart 2.6, "CBOT New Members—CNC: Average Degree and Ten-Year Survival." Chart 2.3, "CBOT New Members—Core: Average Edges and 10-Year Survival." Chart 2.4, "CBOT New Members—CNC: Average Edges and 10-Year Survival." Chart 2.7, "CBOT New Members: Zero vs. 1 Degree 10-Yr Survival." Chart 2.8, "CBOT New Members—Core:

Multiplexity and 10-Year Survival." Chart 2.9, "CBOT New Members—CNC: Multiplexity and 10-Yr Survival." In 1910, for example, about half of new CNC members and a quarter of new core-component members had comparable degree centrality and multiplexity. Chart 2.10, "CBOT New Members—Core and CNC: Survival with Constant Degree." A higher percentage of CNC members survived ten years than did core members in two out of three comparison sets (1910 to 1920, and 1920 to 1930). In the third comparison set, 1930 to 1940, the ranking is reversed. Chart 2.11, "CBOT New Members—Core: Trifecta 10-Year Survival." Chart 2.1, "CBOT New Members: 10-Year Survival Rates by Member Class."

18. Trifecta measures calculated for new members only. Chart 2.11, "CBOT New Members—Core: Trifecta 10-Year Survival." Chart 2.2, "CBOT New Members: 20-Year Survival Rates by Member Class."

19. Chart 3.1, "CBOT New Members—All: 10-Year Mobility." Ten years on, CNC members moved to the core component at only about one-half the rate that core members remained in the new core. Data show a higher level of back-and-forth between core and connected noncore than either group had with isolates, but core was still semiclosed to connected noncore. Chart 3.2, "CBOT New Members—Core: 10-Year Mobility." Chart 3.3, "CBOT New Members—CNC: 10-Year Mobility." Chart 3.4, "CBOT New Members—Isolates: 10-Year Mobility." Chart 3.5, "CBOT Members—Core: 10-Year Origins." Chart 3.6, "CBOT Members—CNC: 10-Year Origins." Chart 3.7, "CBOT Members—Isolates: 10-Year Origins."

20. CBOT, *Fifty-Third Annual Report (1910)*, viii–ix. CBOT, *Thirty-First Annual Report (1888)*, 244. CBOT, *Fifty-Third Annual Report (1910)*, 257. CBOT, *Sixty-Third Annual Report (1920)*, 181. CBOT, *Seventy-Third Annual Report (1930)*, 223. CBOT, *Eighty-Third Annual Report (1940)*, 191. CBOT, *Eighty-Third Annual Report (1940)*, 192. U.S. Census (manuscript) population schedule for the fourteenth census (1920), Cook County, City of Chicago, Ancestry.com. Abolafia, *Making Markets*, 103, 137. Zaloom, *Out of the Pits*, 63–66.

21. U.S. Census (manuscript) population schedule for the fourteenth census (1920), Cook County, City of Chicago, Ancestry.com. CBOT, *Thirty-First Annual Report (1888)*, 206. CBOT, *Fifty-Third Annual Report (1910)*, 221. CBOT, *Sixty-Third Annual Report (1920)*, 145. CBOT, *Seventy-Third Annual Report (1930)*, 197. CBOT, *Eighty-Third Annual Report (1940)*, 163. The 1920 Chicago census lists 7,018 white men aged eighteen and over surnamed Johnson. U.S. Census (manuscript), population schedule for the fourteenth census (1920), Cook County, City of Chicago, Ancestry.com. CBOT, *Fifty-Third Annual Report (1910)*, 241–242. CBOT, *Sixty-Third Annual Report (1920)*, 166. CBOT, *Seventy-Third Annual Report (1930)*, 212. CBOT, *Eighty-Third Annual Report (1940)*, 179. The four membership lists had a total of 6,244 entries, but that figure contains duplicates, i.e., holdovers from one list to the next. Counting each member once, 3,802 men

total were CBOT members at one time or another during this period; 13 of them were surnamed Johnson. Calculations by the author. As throughout this chapter, "new" members refer to members whose names did not appear on the membership list of ten years before.

22. In the 1920 census, the city of Chicago had a total population of 2,701,705, of whom 874,540 were adult white males. "Adult" is defined here as aged eighteen and over. U.S. Bureau of the Census, *Abstract of the Fourteenth Census of the United States*, 53. An even 1,000 were not excluded, as that would have put the cutoff in the middle of a group of fifteen surnames that all occurred eighty-four times. A cutoff at 995 excludes all surnames that occur eighty-five or more times. CBOT, *Forty-Third Annual Report (1900)*, 220–272. U.S. Census (manuscript), population schedule for the fourteenth census (1920), Cook County, City of Chicago, Ancestry.com. Calculations by the author. CBOT, *Fifty-Third Annual Report (1910)*, 219–269. CBOT, *Sixty-Third Annual Report (1920)*, 144–194. Calculations by the author.

23. James Rowan in 1910 and 1920; also James Joseph Rowan in 1920 only. Calculations by the author.

24. Chart 4.1, "CBOT Members—All: % Old versus New Surnames." Chart 4.2, "CBOT New Members—Core: % Old Surnames." Chart 4.12, "CBOT New Members—Core: New vs. Old Surname Trifecta Frequency." Chart 4.4, "CBOT New Members—Isolates: % Old Surnames."

25. Chart 4.5, "CBOT New Members—Core: Old vs. New Surname Edges/Member." Chart 4.6, "CBOT New Members—Core: Old vs. New Surname Average Degree." For example, in 1920, 54 percent of old-surname members have multiplex relationships, compared to 46 percent for new-surname members. Chart 4.7, "CBOT New Members—Core: Old vs. New Surname Pct. Multiplex Relationships." Chart 4.8, "CBOT New Members—Core: Old vs. New Surname 10-Year Survival." Chart 4.10, "CBOT New Members—Isolates: Old vs. New Surname 10-Year Survival." Chart 4.13, "CBOT New Members—Core: 4- vs. Trifecta 10-Year Survival." Chart 4.14, "CBOT New Members—Core: Old versus vs. Surname Attrition." Chart 4.11, "CBOT New Members: Old vs. New Surname 20-Year Survival."

26. As throughout, unless noted otherwise, counting "new" members only. Chart 4.13, "CBOT New Members—Core: 4-vs. Trifecta 10-Year Survival."

27. Chart 1.2, "CBOT Members—All: Member Classes 1888–1940."

28. Chart 2.3, "CBOT New Members—Core: Average Edges and 10-Year Survival." Chart 2.4, "CBOT New Members—CNC: Average Edges and 10-Year Survival." Chart 1.3, "CBOT New Members—Core vs. CNC: Average Degree." Chart 1.4, "CBOT New Members—Core vs. CNC: % Multiplex Relationships." Chart 1.5, "CBOT Members—Core and CNC: % of Members and Edges 1910–1940."

29. Chart 2.1, "CBOT New Members: 10-Year Survival Rates by Member Class."

30. Chart 2.5, "CBOT New Members—Core: Average Degree and 10-Year Survival." Chart 2.6, "CBOT New Members—CNC: Average Degree and 10-Year Survival."
31. Chart 2.7, "CBOT New Members: Zero vs. 1 Degree 10-Year Survival."
32. Chart 2.8, "CBOT New Members—Core: Multiplexity and 10-Year Survival." Chart 2.9, "CBOT New Members—CNC: Multiplexity and 10-Year Survival."
33. Chart 2.11, "CBOT New Members—Core: Trifecta 10-Year Survival."
34. Chart 2.10, "CBOT New Members—Core and CNC: Survival with Constant Degree." Chart 2.11, "CBOT New Members—Core: Trifecta 10-Year Survival."
35. Chart 1.1, "CBOT New Members 1910–1940: % of All Members."
36. Chart 3.1, "CBOT New Members—All: 10-Year Mobility."
37. Chart 3.8, "CBOT New Members—Non-Core: 10-Year Upward Mobility."
38. Chart 4.1, "CBOT Members—All: % Old vs. New Surnames."
39. Chart 4.3, "CBOT Members—Core: % Old Surnames."
40. Chart 4.1, "CBOT Members—All: % Old vs. New Surnames."
41. Chart 4.2, "CBOT New Members—Core: % Old Surnames." Chart 4.4, "CBOT New Members—Isolates: % Old Surnames." Chart 4.12, "CBOT New Members—Core: New vs. Old Surname Trifecta Frequency."
42. Chart 4.5, "CBOT New Members—Core: Old vs. New Surname Average Edges." Chart 4.6, "CBOT New Members—Core: Old vs. New Surname Average Degree." Chart 4.7, "CBOT New Members—Core: Old vs. New Surname Pct. Multiplex Relationships."
43. Except for one split out of six: in 1930–1940, old-surname new CNC members survive at a higher average than do new-surname new CNC members. Chart 4.8, "CBOT New Members—Core: Old vs. New Surname 10-Year Survival." Chart 4.9, "CBOT New Members—CNC: Old vs. New Surname 10-Year Survival." Chart 4.10, "CBOT New Members—Isolates: Old vs. New Surname 10-Year Survival."
44. Chart 4.14, "CBOT New Members—Core: Old vs. New Surname Attrition."
45. Chart 4.13, "CBOT New Members—Core: 4- vs. Trifecta 10-Year Survival."
46. Counting only core members with uncommon surnames, 314 members in all. Including the common-surname members, total core membership was 496.
47. Chart 4.3, "CBOT Members—Core: % Old Surnames."
48. Chart 4.11, "CBOT New Members: Old vs. New Surname 20-Year Survival." Chart 4.8, "CBOT New Members—Core: Old vs. New Surname 10-Year Survival." Chart 4.7, "CBOT New Members—Core: Old vs. New Surname Pct. Multiplex Relationships."
49. The 1930 core component had 496 total members. The figures cited will not add because of double counting. For example, a new member could also be a family-connected member.

50. Chart 4.8, "CBOT New Members—Core: Old vs. New Surname 10-Year Survival." Chart 4.9, "CBOT New Members—CNC: Old vs. New Surname 10-Year Survival." Chart 4.10, "CBOT New Members—Isolates: Old vs. New Surname 10-Year Survival." In 1920, 929 of 1,602 total members had uncommon surnames; 594 (64 percent) of the 929 had surnames that were on the 1910 list. In 1930, 879 members had uncommon surnames; 368 (42 percent) of these were on the 1910 list. In 1940, 877 members had uncommon surnames, of which 217 (25 percent) were names on the 1910 list. CBOT, *Fifty-Third Annual Report (1910)*, 220–269. CBOT, *Sixty-Third Annual Report (1920)*, 144–194. CBOT, *Seventy-Third Annual Report (1930)*, 195–232. CBOT, *Eighty-Third Annual Report (1940)*, 161–200. Calculations by the author. Besides Rumsey, Henry Gerstenberg and Edward J. Wynne shared uncommon surnames with founding members. In 1940, CBOT had 877 members with uncommon surnames; 66 (8 percent) had surnames on the 1888 list. CBOT, *Thirty-First Annual Report (1888)*, 205–256. CBOT, *Eighty-Third Annual Report (1940)*, 161–200. Calculations by the author. CBOT, *Eighty-Third Annual Report (1940)*, xiii.

51. Dreiser, *The Financier*, 14. M. Lewis, *Liar's Poker*, 18–23.

52. To convert to 2022 dollars, see note 13 in chapter 2. A profit of $150,000 (1888) equals $150,000*31.74 = $4,761,000 (2022).

53. Kadushin, *Understanding Social Networks*, 91, citing Weber, *From Max Weber*, 78–79.

54. Milgram, "The Small-World Problem," 61–67. Watts and Strogatz, "Collective Dynamics of 'Small-World Networks," 440–442.

55. Milgram, "The Small-World Problem," 61–67. "Mathematicians Prove That It's a Small World," *New York Times*, June 16, 1998, F3. Robins et al. "Small and Other Worlds," 894–936. Watts, "Networks, Dynamics and the Small World Phenomenon," 493–527. Watts, *Six Degrees*, 96. Watts, "The 'New' Science of Networks," 250. Gilmore, "Control Strategies for Endemic Childhood Scabies." Claro and Neto, "Sales Managers' Performance and Social Capital," 325. Prell, *Social Network Analysis*, 173, citing Watts, "The 'New' Science of Networks."

56. Watts, *Six Degrees*, 98–99, 83. Yellen, "Interconnectedness and Systemic Risk," 5. Watts, *Six Degrees*, 54.

57. Watts, *Six Degrees*, 108, citing Barabási and Albert, "Emergence of Scaling in Random Networks," 509–512. Sageman, *Understanding Terror Networks*, 140. Watts, *Six Degrees*, 108. "For unto every one that hath shall be given, and he shall have abundance: but from him that hath not shall be taken away even that which he hath." Matthew 25:29 and Luke 19:26 (KJV). Merton, "The Matthew Effect in Science," 56–63. Mizruchi, "Social Network Analysis," 340.

58. William J. Ingalls (brother-in-law), joined 1859. Augustus L. Hutchinson (brother), joined 1874. Charles L. Hutchinson (son), joined 1875. George A. Hutchinson (nephew, son of Augustus), joined 1888. Fred A. Ingalls

(nephew, son of William J. Ingalls), joined 1890. William I. Hutchinson (son), joined 1899. CBOT, *Second Annual Statement (1859)*, 18. CBOT, *Seventeenth Annual Report (1874)*, 168. CBOT, *Eighteenth Annual Report (1875)*, 191. CBOT, *Thirty-First Annual Report (1888)*, 227. CBOT, *Thirty-Third Annual Report (1890)*, 244. CBOT, *Forty-Second Annual Report (1899)*, 249. A Simmelian triad exists when all three parties are connected by strong ties. Krackhardt, "Simmelian Ties," 22–24. Baker, "Floor Trading and Crowd Dynamics," 122.

59. Brass et al., "Relationships and Unethical Behavior," 21. Stephenson and Zelen, "Rethinking Centrality," 3. Baker, "Floor Trading and Crowd Dynamics," 120. Sherwood, "The Unseen Elephant," 2–6, 15. Coleman, "Social Capital in the Creation of Human Capital," S98–S99. Brass, et al., "Relationships and Unethical Behavior," 21.

60. Dieleman and Sachs, "Oscillating between a Relationship-Based and a Market-Based Model," 521–536.

Chapter Four. London, 2005–2012

1. Baker, "The Structure of a National Securities Market," 782. Abolafia, *Making Markets*, 189–190.
2. Carrick Mollenkamp, "LIBOR Fog: Bankers Cast Doubt on Key Rate amid Crisis," *Wall Street Journal*, April 16, 2008, A1.
3. Exchange dated February 29, 2008, in United States Commodity Futures Trading Commission, "Order Instituting Proceedings, In the matter of: ICAP Europe Limited," September 25, 2013.
4. Officially, Coöperatieve Rabobank U.A., a Dutch international bank.
5. "Ambass" is "the ambassador," Rabobank's senior dollar Eurodollar trader in London.
6. Exchange dated August 15, 2006, in United States Commodity Futures Trading Commission, "Order Instituting Proceedings, In the matter of: Rabobank," *Independent*, October 29, 2013.
7. Depending on the security or financial contract being written, the reference rate might be the CPI, unemployment rates, or loan default rates. *Financial Times*, August 24, 2012; June 19, 2013. *The Guardian*, August 4, 2015. Carsella, "LIBOR: Immensely Important Little Understood," 46–48.
8. At year-end 2021, the New York Federal Reserve and U.K. regulators began the process of phasing out LIBOR and replacing it with SOFR. Earlier, in March 2021, New York State enacted the Libor Transition Bill (S. 297B, 2021 Leg., Reg. Sess. [N.Y. 2021]), which directed that by June 30, 2023, all contracts, including legacy contracts, that reference LIBOR be amended to instead reference the "recommended benchmark replacement," since determined to be SOFR. Keschner, "Goodbye LIBOR, Hello SOFR." Typically, an adjustable-rate mortgage might be two to three percentage points over the six-month LIBOR rate. *Wall Street Journal* (online), August 3, 2012.

New York Times, June 28, 2012, Late Edition (East Coast), July 10, 2012; July 11, 2012, Late Edition (East Coast); August 7, 2012, Late Edition (East Coast); DealBook, *New York Times*, November 16, 2013, Late Edition (East Coast). Murphy, "LIBOR: Frequently Asked Questions," 309–315.

9. Kennedy, "Balance of Payments," 44. O'Shaughnessy, "Reconsideration of United States Overseas Direct Investment Controls," 14. Johnson, "Governing Certain Capital Transfers Abroad," 47. Lascelles, *The Story of Minos Zombanakis*, 78.

10. The purpose of this account is to sketch the rise and spread of LIBOR, rather than how London regained its primacy as the center of world finance. Many factors contributed to the resurgence of London, and a considerable body of scholarship has grown up around the topic. A good bibliography can be found in Bellringer and Michie, "Big Bang in the City of London." O'Shaughnessy, "Reconsideration of United States Overseas Direct Investment Controls," 14.

11. N. Ferguson, *High Financier*, 216. Burn, "The State, the City and the Euromarkets," 235–236. Schenk, "Origins of the Eurodollar Market in London," 234. "Special Report: International Banking," *The Economist* (London), November 15, 1969, 14–16. The Edge Act, 1919. The impetus for the act was to give U.S. firms more flexibility to compete with foreign firms. Before 1919, U.S. institutions were not permitted to own foreign banks.

12. Higonnet, "Eurobanks, Eurodollars and International Debt," 28. The timing of the first Eurodollar deposit is uncertain. The two most common—but uncorroborated—origin stories are that (1) the Chinese People's Republic made the first Eurodollar deposit in 1949 or (2) the Soviet Union did so in about 1957. In both stories, the motive was the same, namely, fear that the country's funds held in U.S. banks would be frozen because of heightened international tension (either the Chinese Communist revolution or the Hungarian revolt). George Goodman, writing as Adam Smith, has written that the first significant Eurodollar loan was made in the late 1950s, when a Soviet-controlled bank in Paris, Banque Commercial pour l'Europe du Nord, placed $800,000 with international borrowers. The term "Eurodollar" came from the bank's Telex name, EUROBANK. Garson, *Money Makes the World Go Around*, 29. A. Smith, *Paper Money*, 122. Friedman, "The Euro-Dollar Market," 2, 7–9. *The Economist* (London), July 11, 1959, 109–110. Chesquiere, "Causes and Implications of the Growth of the Eurodollar Market," 1.

13. When the *Economist* article came out in July 1959, London banks offering 3–3¼ percent for large deposits; New York banks offered 2.5 percent. New York charged 4 percent for loans; Eurobanks charged less. The Kennedy-Johnson capital movement controls kept U.S. firms out of the London commercial paper market. Chesquiere, "Causes and Implications of the Growth of the Eurodollar Market," 2, 7, 116. Higonnet, "Eurobanks, Eurodollars and International Debt," 29.

14. Zombanakis was from Kalives, Chania, Greece. Lascelles, *The Story of Minos Zombanakis*, 13–15, 80, 84. Manufacturers Hanover Limited was formed February 1969. Eighty-five percent of the $44 billion total (US$37.5 billion) was in U.S. dollars. Chesquiere, "Causes and Implications of the Growth of the Eurodollar Market," 124, referencing data from BIS annual reports.

15. *New York Times*, August 16, 1969, 42. *Wall Street Journal*, August 18, 1969, 17.

16. *New York Times*, August 16, 1969, 42. *Wall Street Journal*, 18 August 1969, 17. Wellons, *Borrowing by Developing Countries on the Eurocurrency Market*, 26. *Bankers Trust New York Corporation 1968 Annual Report*, 13. Wiseman, "Syndicated Facilities," 259. Lascelles, *The Story of Minos Zombanakis*, 85–88. *New York Times*, August 16, 1969, 42. *Financial Times*, March 27, 2012. "A Greek Banker, the Shah, and the Birth of LIBOR," *Reuters Hedgeworld*, August 8, 2012.

17. At that time, Bankers Trust put together a syndicate of New York and European banks to extend an $80 million medium-term floating-rate loan to Austria. Eurobonds also originated in London, under the leadership of Siegmund Warburg of S. G. Warburg & Company. The first such issue was to the Italian toll road company, Autostrade, in 1963, $15 million for six years. In 1964, a total of forty-four dollar-denominated Eurobond issues cumulatively raised $681 million, an average of $15.5 million per issue. For the year 1967, 104 new Eurobond issues in all currencies raised a total of $2,338 million, an average of $22.5 million per issue. N. Ferguson, *High Financier*, 202, 211, 214–216, 219–221. Wiseman, "Syndicated Facilities," 259. *Wall Street Journal*, January 4, 1967, 19. Wellons, *Borrowing by Developing Countries on the Eurocurrency Market*, 26. *Bankers Trust New York Corporation 1968 Annual Report*, 13. Richebächer, "The Problems and Prospects of Integrating European Capital Markets," 344.

18. Higonnet, "Eurobanks, Eurodollars and International Debt," 28. Carsella, "LIBOR: Immensely Important Little Understood," 46–48. Burn, "The State, the City and the Euromarkets," 227.

19. Park, "Currency Swaps as a Long-Term International Financing Technique," 47. "Swapping Currencies with the World Bank," *Institutional Investor*, December 1981, 98–101.

20. Wellons, *Borrowing by Developing Countries on the Eurocurrency Market*, 23. *New York Times*, July 11, 2012, Late Edition (East Coast). *Financial Times*, October 27, 1986; December 20, 2012.

21. A major milestone occurred in 1996, when CME started using LIBOR to price its popular Eurodollar contract. Business exploded—from average daily volume of 394,348 contracts in 1997 to a peak of 2.5 million in 2007. Until then, almost all U.S. consumer transactions and many commercial ones were tied to the prime rate of a major U.S. bank, as was much of the capital base of U.S. banks. Prime rates, on the other hand, move in sync

with the FFTR, which is set by the Federal Reserve. Mollenkamp et al., "How Gaming LIBOR Became Business as Usual." *Financial Times*, December 31, 1996. Hull and Basu, *Options, Futures, and Other Derivatives*, 1. Marton, "How LIBOR Became a Fixture of the U.S. Financial System," 1112. Carsella, "LIBOR: Immensely Important Little Understood," 46–48. *Global Financial Centres Index 1*, *March 2007*, 9.

22. Section 15 of the Securities Act of 1933 contained prohibitions on fraud in the sale of securities that were greatly strengthened by the Securities Exchange Act of 1934. The term "insider trading" (or "dealing") has been used in British law since 1980. After several aborted tries to pass legislation through the Parliament, on June 23, 1980, sections 69–73 contained in Part V of the Companies Act 1980 came into force and made "insider dealing" a criminal offense. Later this was reenacted in the Company Securities (Insider Dealing) Act 1985 and amended by the Financial Services Act 1986. *Wall Street Journal*, July 6, 2012, Eastern Edition. In 2007, City firms employed 354,000 (in London), which by 2013 had fallen to 237,000. *Financial Times*, February 11, 2013.

23. The ten currencies were U.S. dollar, euro, pound sterling, Japanese yen, Swiss franc, Canadian dollar, Australian dollar, Danish kroner, Swedish krona, and New Zealand dollar. By year-end 2013, the four largest London banks, RBS, Lloyds, Barclays, and HSBC, would cut their global headcount by 24 percent to a nine-year low of 606,000, compared with their pre-crisis peak of 795,000 in 2008. Figures compiled by Bloomberg. When the financial crisis of 2007–2008 began, the fifteen maturities, or "tenors," were one day, one week, two weeks, and one to twelve months. By 2013, the number of tenors has been reduced to seven: one day, one week, one month, two months, three months, six months, and twelve months. To be precise, the panel was the BBA's Foreign Exchange and Money Markets Committee. *The Guardian*, May 29, 2013. *Financial Times*, July 20, 2012. Murphy, "LIBOR: Frequently Asked Questions," 309–315. Carsella, "LIBOR: Immensely Important Little Understood," 46–48. *Business Insider*, July 13, 2012.

24. Hou and Skeie, "LIBOR: Origins, Economics, Crisis, Scandal, and Reform," 2.

25. United States Commodity Futures Trading Commission, "Order Instituting Proceedings, In the matter of: ICAP Europe Limited," September 25, 2013, 4–5. EURIBOR Rates, "Euribor Interest Rates 2007." Rates trading figures include cash rates (govies), derivatives (swaps and options), short-term interest-rate trading (STIRT-MM), and exotic and structured rates. The figure excludes municipal bonds (munis). The 37 percent figure is Coalition's figure for the top twelve global banks, per an October 19, 2016, email to the author. According to the *Coalition Index for Investment Banking*, the top twelve global banks at the time were Bank of America Merrill Lynch, Barclays, BNP Paribas, Citigroup, Credit Suisse, Deutsche Bank,

Goldman Sachs, JP Morgan Chase, Morgan Stanley, Royal Bank of Scotland, Societe Generale, UBS. Data provided courtesy of Coalition Development Ltd. For the 2012 Citigroup study otherwise cited here, the figure is 36 percent. Heckinger et al., "Over-the-Counter Derivatives," 34. Most of these contracts were priced in dollars, and over 80 percent traded in the OTC market. One year later, in June 2008, three months after the forced merger of Bear Stearns with JPMorgan Chase, worldwide total notional value of outstanding swaps contracts peaked at $673 trillion worldwide. Bank for International Settlements, "Graph D.1. Global OTC Derivatives Markets."

26. "Canary Wharf Singing a Red-Hot Tune," *Globe and Mail*, June 19, 2007. In June 2007, GBP 1 = USD 1.985594. Sudjic, *The Edifice Complex*, 2005.

27. Enrich, *The Spider Network*, 51. Duff, "A $20,000 Bottle of Wine? Welcome to Wall Street." Abolafia, *Making Markets*, 30.

28. Transcript of message dated June 4, 2007, in United States Commodity Futures Trading Commission, "Order Instituting Proceedings, In the Matter of: ICAP Europe Limited," 18.

29. Message of September 18, 2008, released by the U.K. Financial Services Authority, quoted in "Libor Lies Revealed in Rigging of $300 Trillion Benchmark," *Bloomberg*, February 6, 2013.

30. *Business Insider*, May 20, 2015.

31. The early cases mostly concerned the private interests of corporate directors coming into conflict with the directors' duties to shareholders. A list of pertinent cases to 1859 can be found in Gardner, *Institutes of International Law*, 321–323. U.K. National Archives, *Gower Report on Investor Protection* (1984). *Big Bang 20 Years On*, iii.

32. On February 27, 2007: Freddie Mac press release, cited by St. Louis Federal Reserve, "The Financial Crisis: Full Timeline." Singh, "The 2007–08 Financial Crisis in Review."

33. Dolmetsch, "Subprime Collapse to Global Financial Meltdown: Timeline." BNP Paribas press release, SEC filing, and U.K. Treasury Department press release, cited in St. Louis Federal Reserve, "The Financial Crisis: Full Timeline." DealBook, *New York Times*, December 30, 2007. In the GFCI ranking for March 2007, Shanghai and Dubai were numbers 24 and 25, respectively. Mumbai was number 39, just ahead of Warsaw. *Global Financial Centres Index 1, March 2007*, 13.

34. Federal Reserve Bank of New York, "New York Fed Responds to Congressional Request for Information on Barclays–LIBOR Matter," 6. *Wall Street Journal*, September 4, 2007, Eastern Edition. Gyntelberg and Wooldridge, "Interbank Rate Fixings during the Recent Turmoil," 73–74. *Wall Street Journal*, September 4, 2007, Eastern Edition. Gilbert, "Barclays LIBOR Woes." Gilbert, "Barclays Takes a Money-Market Beating." *Financial Times*, September 25, 2007, 1. Meeting of November 15, 2007, the first known Bank of England discussion of LIBOR problems. House of Commons

Treasury Committee, *Fixing LIBOR*, 1:28. *New York Times*, July 21, 2012, Late Edition (East Coast). "Timeline: LIBOR-Fixing Scandal," BBC, February 6, 2013.

35. Additional Barclays mass emails sent to New York Fed, October 3, 3007, November 29, 2007. *New York Times*, July 21, 2012, Late Edition (East Coast). "Timeline: LIBOR-Fixing Scandal," BBC, February 6, 2013. *Financial Times*, May 1, 2013. Mollenkamp et al., "How Gaming LIBOR Became Business as Usual." Federal Reserve Bank of New York, "New York Fed Responds to Congressional Request for Information on Barclays–LIBOR Matter," 6. Gyntelberg and Wooldridge, "Interbank Rate Fixings during the Recent Turmoil," 73–74. *Wall Street Journal*, September 4, 2007, Eastern Edition. Dolmetsch, "Subprime Collapse to Global Financial Meltdown: Timeline." Simone Foxman, "Central Banks Knew about LIBOR Manipulation for Years," *Business Insider*, July 13, 2012. U.K. Treasury Department press release, cited in St. Louis Federal Reserve, "The Financial Crisis: Full Timeline."

36. Earlier that month, on the tenth, a Citigroup analyst questioned LIBOR's strange behavior in an investment newsletter. The *Wall Street Journal* article on the sixteenth got much more attention, however. Peng, Gandhi, and Tyo, "Special Topic: Is LIBOR Broken?" *Wall Street Journal*, April 16, 2008; April 17, 2008, Eastern Edition. Federal Reserve Bank of New York, "New York Fed Responds to Congressional Request for Information on Barclays—LIBOR Matter." *New York Times*, July 21, 2012, Late Edition (East Coast). *The Guardian*, July 13, 2012; July 21, 2012. "Timeline: LIBOR-Fixing Scandal," BBC, February 6, 2013. *Financial Times*, December 19, 2012.

37. *Wall Street Journal*, May 29, 2008, Eastern Edition. Finch and Gotkine, "LIBOR Banks Misstated Rates, Bond at Barclays Says," *Bloomberg*, May 29, 2008, cited in House of Commons Treasury Committee, *Fixing LIBOR: Some Preliminary Findings*, 1:26n80. Finch and Livesey, "BBA Refrains from LIBOR Changes in Favor of Greater Oversight," *Bloomberg*, May 30, 2008. *Financial Times*, June 2, 2008.

38. The prosecution was a joint CFTC–Department of Justice undertaking, settled 2007–2008. *United States Commodity Futures Trading Commission v. American Electric Power Co., Inc., and AEP Energy Services.* The investigation resulted in criminal settlements and prison terms of up to fourteen years. The Department of Justice eventually exacted fines of $91 million from twenty companies; the CFTC reached civil settlements with over twenty energy companies for $300 million. *Financial Times*, September 7, 2011. Section 9(a)(2), Commodities Exchange Act. *United States of America v. James Brooks, Wesley C. Walton, James Patrick Phillips; United States of America v. Michelle M. Valencia.* Also *United States Commodity Futures Trading Commission v. Denette Johnson, et al.*, cited in United States Commodity Futures Trading Commission, "Order Instituting Proceedings, In the Matter of: UBS AG," 52. *The Economist* (London), September 3, 2009. Enrich, *The Spi-*

der Network, xii. "Timeline: LIBOR-Fixing Scandal," BBC, February 6, 2013. Borak, "Bernanke Defends Regulators' Actions in LIBOR Scandal," *American Banker*, July 18, 2012. *Wall Street Journal*, July 6, 2012, Eastern Edition. Federal Reserve Bank of New York, "New York Fed Responds to Congressional Request for Information on Barclays—LIBOR Matter." *New York Times*, August 7, 2012, Late Edition (East Coast); August 13, 2012, Late Edition (East Coast).

39. The three vanishing banks were Bear Stearns, Lehman Brothers, and Merrill Lynch. According to the Bank of England, the spot rate for British pounds to U.S. dollars on October 15, 2008 (midmonth), was 1:1.7456. The cost of the global financial crisis in 2008 U.S. dollars was therefore £4,473 billion * 1.7456 = US$7,808 billion. Enrich, *The Spider Network*, xii, 257, 261–262. "Timeline: LIBOR-Fixing Scandal," BBC, February 6, 2013. *New York Times*, August 13, 2012, Late Edition (East Coast). Borak, "Bernanke Defends Regulators' Actions in LIBOR Scandal," *American Banker*, July 18, 2012. *Wall Street Journal*, July 6, 2012, Eastern Edition. Federal Reserve Bank of New York, "New York Fed Responds to Congressional Request for Information on Barclays—LIBOR Matter." Polk, *For the Love of Money*, 224, 226. FDIC press release, Federal Reserve press release, and Treasury Department press release, cited in St. Louis Federal Reserve, "The Financial Crisis: Full Timeline." Dolmetsch, "Subprime Collapse to Global Financial Meltdown: Timeline." On September 7, 2008: *Wall Street Journal*, June 28, 2008; September 16, 2008. *Financial Times*, July 18, 2012. Bank of England, *Financial Stability Report* 24 (October 2008): 33. Pound Sterling Live, "British Pound / US Dollar Historical Reference Rates from Bank of England for 2008."

40. Polk, *For the Love of Money*, 224, 226. Read, "Stocks Turn in Worst Performance for New President." Oatley and Petrova, "Banker for the World."

41. *New York Times*, November 16, 2013, Late Edition (East Coast). In April 2021, Gensler was appointed chairman of the SEC.

42. "LIBOR: Twin Conundrums," *Wrightson ICAP Newsletter*, September 3, 2007, noted in Federal Reserve Bank of New York, "New York Fed Responds to Congressional Request for Information on Barclays—LIBOR Matter."

43. *Financial Times*, January 1, 2013. *The Economist* (London), July 20, 2013, 64.

44. The LIBOR trials exposed many weaknesses in British banking regulation. Among many other problems, it emerged that the U.K. FSA had no rule that required the banks to submit accurate and fair LIBOR quotes. *Financial Times*, July 26, 2012; December 21, 2012. Mollenkamp et al. "How Gaming LIBOR Became Business as Usual." *Wall Street Journal*, July 6, 2012, Eastern Edition. *New York Times*, June 5, 2014, Late Edition (East Coast); May 25, 2015, Late Edition (East Coast). *The Independent*, August 1, 2012.

45. *New York Times*, May 27, 2015, Late Edition (East Coast). "Drama of LIBOR Scandal Recounted in Trader's Book," *International Herald Tribune*,

February 21, 2013. United States Commodity Futures Trading Commission, "CFTC Orders UBS to Pay $700 Million Penalty to Settle Charges of Manipulation," 2. La Roche, "Instant Messages Allegedly Reveal How Brokers Would 'Fudge' Libor Rates for a Client." United States Commodity Futures Trading Commission, "Order Instituting Proceedings, In the matter of: Royal Bank of Scotland PLC," 6. Tan et al. "RBS Instant Messages Show Libor Rates Skewed for Traders." Armstrong, "Ex-RBS Trader Says Brevan Howard Sought LIBOR Rate Change." *Financial Times*, December 21, 2012; February 7, 2013; April 23, 2015. *The Guardian*, December 20, 2012. *Wall Street Journal*, July 24, 2012, Eastern Edition.

46. "Barclays Bosses 'Sent Trader to Rig Rate in New York,' " *The Times* (London), April 8, 2016.

47. Tan Chi Min (RBS Singapore–based head of delta trading for Asia) in an August 19, 2007, conversation with traders at other banks, including Mark Wong (Deutsche Bank Singapore–based cohead of rates and FX trading for Asia). Tan et al. "RBS Instant Messages Show Libor Rates Skewed for Traders."

48. For example, *New York Herald*, January 29, 1866, 2.

49. Exchange dated September 15, 2009. *Washington Post*, February 6, 2013.

50. Exchange dated November 29, 2006, in United States Commodity Futures Trading Commission, "Order Instituting Proceedings, In the Matter of: Rabobank," 11.

51. "If You Aint Cheating, You Aint Trying," *Business Insider*, May 20, 2015. Title quote is from a Forex trader.

52. United States Commodity Futures Trading Commission, "Order Instituting Proceedings, In the Matter of: Royal Bank of Scotland PLC," 25–26. Most of the cliques discovered in the LIBOR and related investigations were all male, but there were exceptions. "The Mean Girls," a group of London-based foreign-exchange traders, apparently more than held its own. Jamie McGeever, "A Bunch of London Traders Allegedly Started a 'Mean Girls' Clique to Dominate FX Markets," *Business Insider*, June 19, 2014.

53. Hodges, "Ex-Barclays Trader Says Bosses Must've Known about LIBOR Fix." United States Commodity Futures Trading Commission, "CFTC Orders UBS to Pay $700 Million Penalty." *Washington Post*, July 7, 2012. *Wall Street Journal*, May 29, 2015, Eastern Edition. The CEO was Bob Diamond of Barclays. *New York Times*, May 2, 2013.

54. Joe Rennison, "The End of LIBOR Is (Finally) Here," *New York Times*, June 30, 2023.

55. " 'Put Guilty Bankers in Orange Jumpsuits,' Says Andrew Tyrie," *Money Marketing*, October 11, 2012, 3. *Wall Street Journal* (online), July 27, 2012. *The Guardian*, December 17, 2012; June 19, 2013. Stephenson, "Goldman's Blankfein: Libor Scandal Undermines Financial System." Denning, "Rethinking Capitalism."

56. *Financial Times*, June 19, 2013; October 1, 2014; October 2, 2014.

57. *Arthur Andersen LLP v. United States.* By one account, in the wake of the 2002 court judgment against Arthur Andersen, twenty thousand of the firm's employees immediately lost their jobs. Enrich, *The Spider Network*, 266. *Lehman Brothers Holdings, Inc. 2007 Annual Report*, 2. To convert to 2022 dollars, see note 13 in chapter 2. Lehman's 2007 total assets of $691,063 million therefore equals ($691,063) * 1.41 = $974,399 million in 2022 dollars. Bank of America: at December 31, 2012, $2.2 trillion and 267,000 full-time equivalent (FTE) employees. *Bank of America Corporation 2012 Annual Report*, 21. Citigroup: $1.87 trillion in assets and 259,000 FTE employees. *Citi 2012 Annual Report*, 3. JP Morgan Chase: $2.4 trillion in assets and 260,000 employees. *JP Morgan Chase & Company 2012 Annual Report*, 2 (inside cover), 11.

58. Giudice et al., *U.K. Economy*, 205. McWilliams and Said, "The Importance of the City of London to the UK Economy," 11–23. "UBS to Cut Thousands of Jobs in London," *Sunday Times* (London), October 28, 2012. *Financial Times*, February 11, 2013. "Barclays Caves into Criticism and Closes Tax Avoidance Unit," *The Observer* (U.K.), February 10, 2013. *Financial Times*, October 29, 2015. *Businessline*, January 23, 2013. CEOs and/or board chairmen at Deutsche Bank, Barclays, Rabobank, Royal Bank of Scotland, StanChart, ICAP, and the Bank of Cyprus all lost their jobs over LIBOR. From Barclays: Jerry del Missier, the bank's chief operating officer. "Diamond and Del Missier Resign from Barclays," *Risk* 25, no. 7 (July 2012): 12. Ritankar Pal, head of U.S. interest rates trading in New York. *Derivatives Week*, September 3, 2012. Iain Abrahams, head of Barclays' structured capital markets unit. *The Guardian*, October 5, 2012. Chief financial officer Christopher G. Lucas and general counsel Mark Harding. *New York Times*, February 4, 2013, Late Edition (East Coast). Rich Ricci, head of Barclays' investment bank. *The Guardian*, April 19, 2013. Chris Lucas, former finance director. *Financial Times*, August 14, 2013. Hans-Jorg Rudloff, chairman of Barclays' investment bank. *Financial Times*, February 25, 2014. Hugh E. McGee III, head of Barclays in the United States. *New York Times*, April 30, 2014, Late Edition (East Coast). Matthew Ginsburg, former head of Barclays investment banking for Asia. *International New York Times*, May 16, 2014. From Deutsche Bank: General Counsel Richard Walker. *Wall Street Journal* (online), August 7, 2015. Colin Fan, cohead of the investment bank; Michele Faissola, head of asset and wealth management; Stefan Krause, former chief financial officer; Stephan Leithner, formerly head of European business outside the U.K. and Germany. *Financial Times*, October 18, 2015. From HSBC: Joe Garner, head of the U.K. bank. *Financial Times*, September 13, 2012. From ICAP: finance chief Iain Torrens. *Wall Street Journal*, October 1, 2014, Eastern Edition. From RBS: Ron Teerlink, head of back-office systems. *The Herald* (Glasgow), October 6, 2012. RBS Jezri Mohideen (suspended), head of rates trading in Europe and Asia Pacific. *Financial Times*, October 15, 2012. Ryusuke Otani, chief executive of RBS Securities

Japan. *Financial Times*, April 11, 2013. From UBS: onetime investment bank chief Carsten Kengeter. *Wall Street Journal* (online), February 12, 2013; June 14, 2013. *Financial Times*, July 17, 2015. Since 2013, the FCA has been the successor agency to the FSA.

59. Hayes's sentence was later reduced to twelve years. *The Guardian*, December 20, 2012. Matthew Boesler, "Traders under Investigation for Libor Rigging Keep Turning Up at Swiss Hedge Funds," *Business Insider*, July 19, 2012. *The Guardian*, July 4, 2012. *Financial Times*, December 7, 2013; December 17, 2013; April 8, 2014; November 26, 2014; August 4, 2015; March 23, 2016. "Bob Diamond Storms Back to Wall Street," *Sunday Times* (London), August 16, 2015. *The Economist* (London), August 8, 2015, 61. *New York Times*, December 22, 2015, Late Edition (East Coast).

60. *Financial Times*, May 20, 2015; November 21, 2015. *BNP Paribas 2018 Annual Report*, 6 (total assets of €2,040,836 million converted at December 31, 3018, exchange rate: EUR 1 = USD 1.1492); *Bank of America Merrill Lynch 2018 Annual Report*, 32; *SBC 2018 Annual Report*, 2, 16; *JPMorgan Chase & Company 2018 Annual Report*, 2. At year-end 2018, the four largest banks were BNP Paribas, Bank of America Merrill Lynch, HSBC, and JPMorgan Chase.

61. International Swaps and Derivatives Association, "A Seminal Milestone for LIBOR." "Federal LIBOR Legislation: Five Things Financial Market Participants Need to Know," *Reuters*, March 23, 2022.

62. Less than twelve months after operations began, SWIFT had processed a total of ten million messages. As of June 2019, SWIFT has over eleven thousand member institutions, and traffic has risen to 3.5 billion messages over the course of the year (34.41 million messages per day). SWIFT, "Swift History." Alper and Pelton, *The INTELSAT Global Satellite System*, 2. *SWIFT 2007 Annual Report*, 3.

63. The Riegle-Neal Interstate Banking and Branching Efficiency Act of 1994 allowed banks that met capitalization requirements to acquire other banks in any other state after October 1, 1995. The Riegle-Neal Act permitted truly nationwide interstate banking for the first time. The number of securities and commodities firms increased from 11,279 in 1980 to 18,843 in 1985, a 60 percent rise. United States Bureau of the Census, *Statistical Abstract of the United States, 1988*, 446. Total employment in "security, commodities brokers, services" nearly doubled between 1980 and 1988, going from 259,000 to 509,000. United States Bureau of the Census, *Statistical Abstract of the United States, 1990*, 490. The preceding 1980 and 1988 industry statistics are not directly comparable to the later statistics cited in the introduction. In 1997, the U.S., Canada, and Mexico adopted the North American Industry Classification System (NAICS), a significant change from the previous industry classification system. United States Securities and Exchange Commission (SEC), *Study of Unsafe and Unsound Practices of Brokers and Dealers*, 18. In 2018, average daily NYSE volume ranged be-

tween two and six billion shares. Hulbert, "Here's What Low NYSE Trading Volume Is Telling Us about the Stock Market's Direction." Reichman, "Insider Trading," 55–96.

64. Weber et al., "Policy as Myth and Ceremony?," 1319–1347. World Bank, *Private Capital Flows to Developing Countries*, 16.

65. Presciently, Michel Abolafia predicted in 1996 that personal relationships among market regulars would weaken as satellites and computers replaced personal contact. Abolafia, *Making Markets*, 189–190.

66. M. Lewis, *Flash Boys*, loc. 1507.

Chapter Five. New York, 2015–2022

Chapter subtitle: Goldman senior swaps trader to his team, quoted in "U.S. Settlements Bare the 'Off-Channel' World of Bankers," *Financial Times*, September 30, 2022.

1. *In the Matter of BofA Securities, Inc.* (SEC), 10. *In the Matter of Barclays Capital Inc.* (SEC), 10. *In the Matter of Citigroup Global Markets Inc.* (SEC), 10. *In the Matter of Credit Suisse Securities (U.S.A.) LLC.* (SEC), 10. *In the Matter of Deutsche Bank Securities Inc.* (SEC), 10. *In the Matter of Goldman Sachs & Co. LLC* (SEC), 10. *In the Matter of Morgan Stanley & Co. LLC and Morgan Stanley Smith Barney LLC* (SEC), 10. *In the Matter of UBS Financial Services, Inc.* (SEC), 10. *In the Matter of Cantor Fitzgerald & Co.* (SEC), 10. *In the Matter of Jefferies LLC* (SEC), 10. *In the Matter of Nomura Securities International, Inc.* (SEC), 10. *In the Matter of Bank of America, N.A.* (CFTC), 12. *In the Matter of Barclays Bank PLC and Barclays Capital Inc.* (CFTC), 10. *In the Matter of Citibank, N.A.* (CFTC), 10. *United States of America Before the Commodity Futures Trading Commission. In the Matter of Credit Suisse International and Credit Suisse Securities (USA)* (CFTC), 10. *In the Matter of Deutsche Bank AG and Deutsche Bank Securities Inc.* (CFTC), 9. *In the Matter of Goldman Sachs & Co. LLC, f/k/a Goldman Sachs & Co.* (CFTC), 9. *In the Matter of Morgan Stanley & Co. LLC, Morgan Stanley Capital Services LLC, Morgan Stanley Capital Group Inc., and Morgan Stanley Bank, N.A.* (CFTC), 10. *In the Matter of UBS AG, UBS Financial Services, Inc., and UBS Securities LLC* (CFTC), 9. *In the Matter of Cantor Fitzgerald & Co.* (CFTC), 7. *In the Matter of Jefferies Financial Services, Inc. and Jefferies LLC* (CFTC), 9. *In the Matter of Nomura Global Financial Products Inc., Nomura Securities International, Inc., and Nomura International PLC* (CFTC), 12. "The 6 Best Apps for Keeping Your Private Messages Safe from Hackers, Spies, and Trolls," *Business Insider*, May 23, 2018. "Wall Street to Pay $1.8 Billion in Fines over Traders' Use of Banned Messaging Apps," *Wall Street Journal*, September 27, 2022.

2. "Wall Street Texts: Signal Not Noise," *Financial Times*, September 29, 2022.

3. Investigation periods were 2018 to 2022 for the SEC and 2015 to 2022 for the CFTC. "U.S. Settlements Bare the 'Off-Channel' World of Bankers," *Financial Times*, September 30, 2022. *In the Matter of BofA Securities, Inc.*

(SEC). *United States of America Before the Commodity Futures Trading Commission. In the Matter of Bank of America, N.A.* "The 6 Best Apps for Keeping Your Private Messages Safe from Hackers, Spies, and Trolls," *Business Insider*, May 23, 2018. "The Deli Was Allegedly a Fraud. Also Illegal Texting and DJ D-Sol's Golf Game," *Bloomberg*, September 28, 2022. "Banks Fined in Probe of Messages," *Wall Street Journal*, September 28, 2022.

4. *JPMorgan Chase & Company 2022 Annual Report.* "SEC Sends Bankers a $1bn Message about Encrypted Communications," *Financial Times*, September 3, 2022. "JPMorgan Bosses Hooked on WhatsApp Fuel $200 Million Penalty," *Bloomberg*, December 17, 2021.

5. "Banks Fined in Probe of Messages," *Wall Street Journal*, September 28, 2022. "The Court Case That Dragged Bankers into the Snapchat Generation," *Financial Times*, May 23, 2015. "Trading Scandals: The Final Nail in Chat Rooms' Coffins?," CNBC, November 11, 2013.

6. "Exclusive: The Rags-To-Riches Tale of How Jan Koum Built WhatsApp into Facebook's New $19 Billion Baby," *Forbes*, February 2, 2014. "WhatsApp Hits 600 Million Active Users, Founder Says," *Forbes*, August 25, 2014. "WhatsApp Partners with Open Whispersystems to End-to-End Encrypt Billions of Messages a Day," *TechCrunch*, November 18, 2014. "WhatsApp Completes End-to-End Encryption Rollout," *TechCrunch*, April 5, 2016. "Here's the 15-Page Pitch Deck a Fintech Helping Wall Street Keep Tabs on Employees' Use of Messengers like WhatsApp and Signal Used to Raise $22 Million," *Business Insider*, April 3, 2023. "Wall Street Is Losing Its Battle against Encrypted Apps like WhatsApp and WeChat as It Tries to Police Employee Communications—and Even Regulators Are Stumped," *Business Insider*, March 27, 2019. "Banks Face a WhatsApp Reckoning as Regulators Clamp Down on Messaging Apps," *Computerworld*, August 8, 2022. "You Can Now Record Video Messages on WhatsApp," Meta Newsroom, July 27, 2023.

7. "Wall Street's New Favorite Way to Swap Secrets Is against the Rules," *Bloomberg*, March 30, 2017. "Wall Street Sends Regulators a Poop Emoji," *Reuters*, September 27, 2022. "Inside Wall Street's War on WhatsApp: Why Traders Just Won't Quit Messaging Apps, Even as Heads Roll," *Business Insider*, November 10, 2020. "WhatsApp Crackdown Signals Tougher Approach," *Financial Times*, February 11, 2023. "Wall Street: Whoopsapp," *Business Insider*, June 15, 2022. "U.S. Settlements Bare the 'Off-Channel' World of Bankers," *Financial Times*, September 30, 2022.

8. "The Messaging Dilemma: Grappling with Employees' Off-System Communications," *Reuters*, February 3, 2023. "JPMorgan Suspends Trader for WhatsApp Use," *Financial Times*, January 14, 2020. "JPMorgan Chase Suspends Credit Trader for WhatsApp Messages," *Financial Times*, January 13, 2020. "Here's the 15-Page Pitch Deck a Fintech Helping Wall Street Keep Tabs on Employees' Use of Messengers like WhatsApp and Signal Used to Raise $22 Million," *Business Insider*, November 10, 2020. "The Court Case

That Dragged Bankers into the Snapchat Generation," *Financial Times*, May 23, 2015. "WhatsApp Is Off-Limits to Bankers. So Why Do They Keep Using It?," *American Banker*, March 14, 2022. "Wall Street Is Losing Its Battle against Encrypted Apps like WhatsApp and WeChat as It Tries to Police Employee Communications—and Even Regulators Are Stumped," *Business Insider*, March 27, 2019. "Wall Street's New Favorite Way to Swap Secrets Is against the Rules," *Bloomberg*, March 30, 2017.

9. "WhatsApp Is Off-Limits to Bankers. So Why Do They Keep Using It?," *American Banker*, March 14, 2022. "Texting on Private Apps Costs Wall Street Firms $1.8 Billion in Fines," *New York Times*, September 28, 2022, B4. "JPMorgan Nears Deal over Staff Texts Fine," *Wall Street Journal*, December 14, 2021. "Inside Wall Street's War on WhatsApp: Why Traders Just Won't Quit Messaging Apps, Even as Heads Roll," *Business Insider*, November 10, 2020. "U.S. Regulators Crack Down on Retention of Electronic Communications," *Reuters*, April 12, 2022. "SEC Sends Bankers a $1bn Message about Encrypted Communications," *Financial Times*, September 3, 2022.

10. "A Timeline of the Coronavirus Pandemic," *New York Times*, March 17, 2021.

11. "Split Trading Desks, Clorox May Follow Banks' Travel Bans," *Bloomberg*, February 28, 2020. " 'The Best Run I've Ever Had': Inside Wall Street's Coronavirus-Fueled Trading Frenzy, Where Historic Shocks of Volatility Are Creating Massive Paydays," *Business Insider*, March 30, 2020. "U.S. Yields Hurtle toward Zero With Thin Market Stunning Traders," *Bloomberg*, 6 March 2020. "JPMorgan Analysts Say Work-from-Home May Hit Funding Markets," *Bloomberg*, March 10, 2020. "Chaos of 2020 Can't Match 2008 but the Gut Punch Feels Familiar," *Bloomberg*, March 10, 2020. " 'Trying Not to Panic': The Collapse in U.S. Markets Spared No One," *Bloomberg*, March 10, 2020. The previous VIX record of 80.74 was set November 21, 2008. "Wall Street's Fear Gauge Closes at Highest Level Ever, Surpassing Even Financial Crisis Peak," *CNBC*, March 16, 2020. " 'The Best Run I've Ever Had': Inside Wall Street's Coronavirus-Fueled Trading Frenzy, Where Historic Shocks of Volatility Are Creating Massive Paydays," *Business Insider*, March 30, 2020. The VIX is also known as the "fear index."

12. "Inside Wall Street's War on WhatsApp: Why Traders Just Won't Quit Messaging Apps, Even as Heads Roll," *Business Insider*, November 10, 2020. "Inside a 38,000-Person Remote Work Rollout at Goldman Sachs: Sleepless Nights, Assembly Lines, and an Amazon-Like Hub on a Manhattan Trading Floor," *Business Insider*, April 16, 2020.

13. "Credit Suisse Joins Firms Scrapping Events on Virus Outbreak," *Bloomberg*, February 4, 2020. "Morgan Stanley Is Still Hosting Hong Kong Summit, Just Virtually," *Bloomberg*, February 19, 2020. "Wall Street Traders Are Still Going into Offices—for Now. Here's How WFH Could Set Off a Tech Scramble at the Worst Possible Time," *Business Insider*, March 18,

2020. "Financial Traders Are Getting Their Coronavirus Test," *Bloomberg*, March 3, 2020. "Inside a 38,000-Person Remote Work Rollout at Goldman Sachs: Sleepless Nights, Assembly Lines, and an Amazon-Like Hub on a Manhattan Trading Floor," *Business Insider*, April 16, 2020. "Wall Street's Disaster Playbook Never Included Work-from-Home Trading. Insiders Explain How Banks Rapidly Adjusted during One of the Most Chaotic Markets in History," *Business Insider*, April 1, 2020 "Wall Street Gets a Break from Regulator on Work-at-Home Traders," *Bloomberg*, March 9, 2020. United States Commodity Futures Trading Commission, "CFTC Provides Relief to Market Participants in Response to COVID-19." "A Timeline of the Coronavirus Pandemic," *New York Times*, March 17, 2021. " 'The Best Run I've Ever Had': Inside Wall Street's Coronavirus-Fueled Trading Frenzy, Where Historic Shocks of Volatility Are Creating Massive Paydays," *Business Insider*, March 30, 2020.

14. "What We Learned from the Work-from-Home Experiment," *Bloomberg*, March 27, 2020. "A UBS Exec Lays Out the Benefits and Pain Points of All-Electronic Trading after Coronavirus Concerns Cleared the Floor at NYSE," *Business Insider*, March 29, 2020. "SEC's Focus on Enforcement Actions for Record-Keeping Violations Ensnares JP Morgan: Who Else Will Be Swamped?," *Reuters*, January 5, 2022.

15. "Inside Wall Street's War on WhatsApp: Why Traders Just Won't Quit Messaging Apps, Even as Heads Roll," *Business Insider*, November 10, 2020. "Banks Face a WhatsApp Reckoning as Regulators Clamp Down on Messaging Apps," *Computerworld*, August 8, 2022. "Banks Grow Wary of Zoom Meetings," *American Banker*, April 24, 2020. Prodoscore, "Prodoscore Research from March/April 2020: Productivity Has Increased, Led by Remote Workers." "Wall Street's Disaster Playbook Never Included Work-from-Home Trading. Insiders Explain How Banks Rapidly Adjusted during One of the Most Chaotic Markets in History," *Business Insider*, April 1, 2020. "US Settlements Bare the 'Off-Channel' World of Bankers," *Financial Times*, September 30, 2022.

16. "Leaked Screenshots: JPMorgan Is Tracking Office Attendance Using 'Dashboards' and 'Reports'—and Some Employees Are Threatening to Quit," *Business Insider*, April 20, 2022. "Wall Street's New Virtual Workplace May Outlast the Virus," *Bloomberg*, March 17, 2020. "For Certain Corners of Wall Street, Dealmaking Is Happening Faster than Ever. That Could Mean a Permanent Lifestyle Change for Some Investment Bankers," *Business Insider*, May 8, 2020.

17. "Barclays Made $250 Million in One Day of Trading Last Week as Banks Raked in Money on Market Volatility," *Business Insider*, March 23, 2020.

18. "Global Banks Rake in Record Corporate Bond Fees amid Pandemic," *Reuters*, May 1, 2020. "For Certain Corners of Wall Street, Dealmaking Is Happening Faster than Ever. That Could Mean a Permanent Lifestyle Change for Some Investment Bankers," *Business Insider*, May 8, 2020. " 'The

Best Run I've Ever Had': Inside Wall Street's Coronavirus-Fueled Trading Frenzy, Where Historic Shocks of Volatility Are Creating Massive Paydays," *Business Insider*, March 30, 2020.

19. "Goldman Sachs Offices Are Open. But Getting Junior Bankers to Return Full Time Is Proving Tough," *Business Insider*, February 24, 2021. "Morgan Stanley CEO James Gorman Wants U.S. Employees Back in the Office by Labor Day: 'If You Can Go into a Restaurant in New York City, You Can Come into the Office,' " *Business Insider*, June 14, 2021. "Goldman Bankers Lead City of London's Uneven Return to Office," *Bloomberg*, June 11, 2021. "What We Learned from the Work-from-Home Experiment," *Bloomberg*, March 27, 2020. Gallup, "How Coronavirus Will Change the 'Next Normal' Workplace." "Europe's Time-Starved Traders Want to Keep Working from Home," *Bloomberg*, June 12, 2020.

20. "JPMorgan Staff Irked over Order to Save Texts on Personal Phones," *Bloomberg*, June 11, 2021. "WhatsApp Is Off-Limits to Bankers. So Why Do They Keep Using It?," *American Banker*, March 14, 2022. "Wall Street Bankers Are 'Livid' at Having to Hand Over Their Personal Cell Phones for the SEC's Texting Probe. 'I Have No Idea What Might Pop Up,' " *Business Insider*, May 18, 2022. "Wall Street Bankers Are Freaking Out over the Ouster of a Credit Suisse Exec over WhatsApp Messaging—and Worrying They Could Be Next," *Business Insider*, June 30, 2022. Steeleye, "85% of Firms Not Monitoring WhatsApp." "Morgan Stanley Duo Lose Jobs over WhatsApp," *Financial Times*, 2020. "Credit Suisse Banker Exits over Unauthorized Message App Use," *Bloomberg*, June 14, 2022.

21. "Societe Generale Drawn by U.S. SEC into Its Widening Messaging Probe," *Reuters*, February 8, 2023. "Months after Wall Street Hit with $1.8 Billion in Fines over WhatsApp, Wells Fargo Says It's under Investigation over Retaining Electronic Records," *MarketWatch*, March 22, 2023. "WhatsApp Crackdown Signals Tougher Approach," *Financial Times*, February 11, 2023. "Private-Equity Giants Are Latest Targets of SEC's Record-Keeping Probes," *DJ Institutional News*, November 8, 2022. "U.S. News: Hefty Wall Street Fines Surge under Biden's SEC," *Wall Street Journal*, October 29, 2022. "SEC's Focus on Enforcement Actions for Record-Keeping Violations Ensnares JP Morgan: Who Else Will Be Swamped?," *Reuters*, January 5, 2022.

22. "The Messaging Dilemma: Grappling with Employees' Off-System Communications," *Reuters*, February 3, 2023. "Inside the Little-Known Tool That Gives JPMorgan Chase the Power to Collect Data about Everything Its Employees Do at Work," *Business Insider*, May 27, 2022. "U.S. SEC Opens Inquiry into Wall Street Banks' Staff Communications—Sources," *Reuters*, October 12, 2021. In a 2012 decision, *U.S. v. Jones*, the justices said that planting a GPS tracker on a car for twenty-eight days without a warrant created such a comprehensive picture of the target's life that it violated the public's reasonable expectation of privacy. Similarly, the court's 2014 de-

cision in *Riley v. California* found that cellphones contain so much personal information that they provide a virtual window into the owner's mind and thus necessitate a warrant for the government to search. "Palantir Knows Everything about You," *Bloomberg*, April 19, 2018.

23. The fines would come out of the banks' profits rather than net income before taxes. The Internal Revenue Service does not allow tax deductions for expenses incurred to commit a crime. For Bank of America, 0.8% of $27.5 billion. *Bank of America 2022 Annual Report*, 75. Morgan Stanley's fine of $200 million was 5.5 percent of the firm's 2022 after-tax profits of $3.6 billion. *Morgan Stanley Bank, N.A. Annual Report as of and for the Years Ended December 31, 2022 and 2021*, 42. *Coalition Index for Investment Banking*, FY2022, 3.

24. Alex Morrell, "For Certain Corners of Wall Street, Dealmaking Is Happening Faster than Ever. That Could Mean a Permanent Lifestyle Change for Some Investment Bankers," *Insider*, May 8, 2020.

Conclusion

1. Petram, *The World's First Stock Exchange*, loc. 162–309.
2. Prodoscore, "Prodoscore Research from March/April 2020." Alex Morrell, "For Certain Corners of Wall Street, Dealmaking Is Happening Faster than Ever. That Could Mean a Permanent Lifestyle Change for Some Investment Bankers," *Insider*, May 8, 2020.
3. Front-office head count at the world's top twelve banks peaked at 64,500 in mid-2007, dropped sharply during the crisis, then rebounded to 65,600 in 2012. *Coalition Index for Investment Banking*, 1Q 2017, 6. The exact number for the total front-office head count in 2022 is 48,900. *Coalition Index for Investment Banking*, FY2022, 7. The exact number is 24,900. *Coalition Index for Investment Banking*, 1Q 2017, 6. The exact number for the total FICC head count in 2022 is 15,900. *Coalition Index for Investment Banking*, FY2022, 7. *Coalition Index for Investment Banking*, FY2021, 9. FICC head count dropped from 16,300 in 2019 to 15,900 in 2022. *Coalition Index for Investment Banking*, FY2021, 8. *Coalition Index for Investment Banking*, FY2022, 7, 8.
4. Also, though program trading was erroneously blamed for the 1987 Black Monday crash, it did drive the 2010 Flash Crash and market shocks in 2014 and 2015 and could produce more of the same. Program trading also caused the extreme volatility in Treasury markets on October 15, 2014, as well as the August 24, 2015, market crash. On that August day, the Dow Jones Industrial Average fell by more than one thousand points in early trading. Miller and Shorter, "High Frequency Trading," 2. Catarina et al. "How Cognitive Technologies Are Transforming Capital Markets," 2. "AI Annihilates the Stock Market Achieving Eye-Popping Returns, Study Shows," *Wall Street Pit*, March 23, 2017. Krauss et al. "Deep Neural Net-

works, Gradient-Boosted Trees, Random Forests," 689–702. "March of the Machines—The Stockmarket Is Now Run by Computers, Algorithms and Passive Managers," *The Economist* (London), October 3, 2019. "Each day around 7bn shares worth $320bn change hands on America's stock market. High-frequency traders, acting as middlemen, are involved in half of the daily trading volumes." Yellen, "Interconnectedness and Systemic Risk," 17. As of 2015, the notional principal value of outstanding financial derivatives, $63,312 billion exchange-traded (11 percent), and $532,344 billion OTC (89 percent). Total: $595,656 billion. *SIMFA 2016 Fact Book*, 62. *The Economist* (London), May 1, 2017.

5. "Rogues Gallery: Traders Who Lost Big from Unauthorized Deals," *Bloomberg*, September 20, 2019. "The London Whale." *Bloomberg*, February 23, 2016. "Here's the Story of How a Guy Making $66,000 a Year Lost $7.2 Billion for One of Europe's Biggest Banks," *Business Insider*, May 8, 2016. *Societe Generale Annual Financial Report*, 2017, 5. €6713 million, per Societe Generale's 2007 annual report, converted at EUR 1 = USD 1.46 (as of December 31, 2007).

6. Ho, *Liquidated*, 44, 49, 55, 58. Binder, "Why Are Harvard Grads Still Flocking to Wall Street?," 3.

7. Mandis, *What Happened to Goldman Sachs*, 144–146. Miller and Shorter, "High Frequency Trading," 2, 5.

8. Banner, *Anglo-American Securities Regulation*, 32–36, 198–217. Werner and Smith, *Wall Street*, 14–18.

9. Ashforth and Kreiner, "Dirty Work and Dirtier Work," 81–108.

10. Trollope, *The Way We Live Now*, 1:136.

11. Ashforth and Kreiner, "Dirty Work and Dirtier Work," 81–108. "Money in the Movies," *The Economist* (London), December 22, 2015.

12. "Why I Am Leaving Goldman Sachs," *New York Times*, March 14, 2012.

13. Augustin et al., "Informed Options Trading Prior to M&A Announcements." Polk, *For the Love of Money*, 152. Jeff Guo, "The Jobs That Really Smart People Avoid," *Washington Post*, January 12, 2017. Shu, "Innovating in Science and Engineering or 'Cashing In' on Wall Street?," iv, 3–5, 24–25. Ho, *Liquidated*, 55, 58. Frank and Schulze, "Does Economics Make Citizens Corrupt?," 101–113. Pinto et al., "Corrupt Organizations or Organizations of Corrupt Individuals?," 685–709. Gioia, "Business Education's Role in the Crisis of Corporate Confidence," 142–144. In the survey of five hundred executives, the percentages in the U.S. and the U.K. were 30 percent and 24 percent, respectively. "Many Wall Street Execs Say Wrongdoing Is Necessary," *Reuters Hedgeworld*, July 10, 2012. Cohn et al. "Business Culture and Dishonesty in the Banking Industry," 86–89.

14. Colman, *A Dictionary of Psychology*. Diener, et al. "Effects of Deindividuation Variables on Stealing among Halloween Trick-or-Treaters," 178–183.

15. Pinto et al. "Corrupt Organizations or Organizations of Corrupt Individuals?," 685–709. Ashforth and Anand, "The Normalization of Corruption in Organizations," 1–52. Sherman, "Three Models of Organizational Corruption

in Agencies of Social Control," 478–491. Hollinger and Clark, *Theft by Employees*. Kappeler et al., *Forces of Deviance*. Sykes and Matza, "Techniques of Neutralization," 664–670. Trice and Beyer, *The Cultures of Work Organizations*. Oliver, "The Antecedents of Deinstitutionalization," 563–588. Zucker, "The Role of Institutionalization in Cultural Persistence," 726–743. Baucus, "Pressure, Opportunity and Predisposition," 699–721. Sonnenfeld and Lawrence, "Why Do Companies Succumb to Price Fixing?," 145–157, 149. Not all top executives have avoided jail time. Those who have not include Bernard Madoff, Michael Milken, and Raj Rajaratnam.

16. Enrich, *The Spider Network*, 29.
17. Scher, "Importance of Human Resources Stressed by Swedish Auto-Maker," 7.

Appendix 1

1. As of mid-2023, the most recent complete sets of figures are from 2021.
2. United States Department of Labor, Bureau of Labor Statistics, "Quarterly Census of Employment and Wages: Employment and Wages Data Viewer." In 2021, Sector 52 finance and insurance had average annual employment of 6,147,933. For industries 523110 + 523130: (142,217 + 13,885) = 156,102. (156,102/6,147,933) = 0.0254 = 2.5 percent. United States Department of Labor, Bureau of Labor Statistics, "Quarterly Census of Employment and Wages: Employment and Wages Data Viewer." In September 2022, Walmart employed 1.6 million in the U.S. and 2.3 million worldwide. Walmart, "Company Facts." Statistics are incomplete after 2018, owing to noncompliance with reporting standards by the firms polled. United States Department of Labor, Bureau of Labor Statistics, "Private, NAICS17 523110 Investment banking and securities dealing, National; 2018–2019 First Quarter, All establishment sizes," in "Quarterly Census of Employment and Wages Data Viewer." Ho, *Liquidated*, 44.
3. According to CRISIL Coalition, a market intelligence firm, the top twelve global banks in 2022 were Bank of America Merrill Lynch, Barclays, BNP Paribas, Citigroup, Credit Suisse, Deutsche Bank, Goldman Sachs, HSBC, JPMorgan Chase, Morgan Stanley, Société Générale, and UBS. "Table One, GFCI 32 Top Ranks and Ratings," in *Global Financial Centres Index 32: September 2022*, 4–5. H. Jones, "New York Still Top, Moscow Sinks in Finance Centre Ranking."
4. As of December 31, 2022 full-time equivalent (FTE) employees of the twelve largest investment banks were as follows: Bank of America Merrill Lynch, 217,000 (*Bank of America Merrill Lynch 2022 Annual Report*, 74); Barclays, 87,400 (*Barclays PLC 2022 Annual Report*, 430); BNP Paribas, 190,000 (*BNP Paribas 2022 Annual Report*, 4); Citigroup, 240,000 (*Citi 2022 Annual Report*, 1); Credit Suisse, 50,480 (*Credit Suisse 2022 Annual Report*, 2); Deutsche Bank, 84,736 (*Deutsche Bank 2022 Annual Report*, 6); Goldman

Sachs, 48,500 [*Goldman Sachs Group, Inc. Annual Report 2021*, 7); HSBC, 219,000 (*HSBC Holdings PLC Annual Report and Accounts 2022*, 4); JPMorgan Chase, 293,723 (*JP Morgan Chase & Company 2022 Annual Report*, ii); Morgan Stanley, 82,000 (*Morgan Stanley Form 10-Q For the Quarterly Period Ended March 31, 2023*, 4); Societe Generale, 117,000 (*Societe Generale Universal Registration Document-EN*, 8); UBS, 74,022 (*UBS Group AG Annual Report 2022*, 4). Total: 1,687,261. *Coalition Index for Investment Banking*, FY2022, 7. American Bar Association, "About the American Bar Association." FINRA, *FINRA 2022 Industry Snapshot*, 2.

Appendix 2

1. Dodd, "Markets: Exchange or Over-the-Counter." World Federation of Exchanges, "Membership & Events." The sixty-one million figure assumes a 365-day year; 22,339,142,900 trades for calendar year 2016, being the total of electronic order book, negotiated deals, and reported trades. It excludes trades in fixed income, derivatives, trades by WFE nonmember exchanges, and transactions on proprietary trading platforms (dark pools) or in the OTC market. World Federation of Exchanges, *WFE Annual Statistics Guide 2016*.
2. World Federation of Exchanges, "Membership & Events."
3. Hilt, "Wall Street's First Corporate Governance Crisis," 13–14, 25–27, 30. Werner and Smith, *Wall Street*, 32–33. In 1865, when the first case in this book commences, the constitution and bylaws of the New York Stock Exchange and Board ran to twenty-four pages. Hamon, *New York Stock Exchange Manual*, 8–31. For the Chicago Board of Trade, the 1883 constitution and bylaws ran to a hundred pages, covering everything from smoking to the cut and packing of hog products. CBOT, *Act of Incorporation, 1883*.
4. CBOT, *Fifty-Third Annual Report (1910)*, 220.

Bibliography

Archival Sources

American Bar Association. "About the American Bar Association." http://www.americanbar.org.

Baker Library, Harvard Business School, Cambridge, Mass. R. G. Dun & Co. Credit Report Volumes.

Bank for International Settlements. "Graph D.1. Global OTC Derivatives Markets." In *Semiannual OTC Derivatives Statistics*. http://www.bis.org/statistics/derstats.htm.

Bank of America Merrill Lynch. "Our Global Workforce." https://about.bankofamerica.com/en-us/what-guides-us/our-global-workforce.html#fbid=10JgOwdxIdp.

Biographical Directory of the United States Congress. 1774–present. http://bioguide.congress.gov/scripts/biodisplay.pl?index=M000954.

BNP Paribas. "BNP Paribas Worldwide." https://group.bnpparibas/en/group/bnp-paribas-worldwide.

Chicago Historical Society, Chicago, Ill. Charles L. Hutchinson papers.

EURIBOR Rates. "Euribor Interest Rates 2007." http: www.euribor-rates.eu/en/euribor-rates-by-year/2007/.

ExchangeRates.org. "GPB to USD Historical Chart 2007." https://exchangerates.org/gbp/usd/in-2007.

FINRA. *FINRA 2022 Industry Snapshot: A Report from the Financial Industry Regulatory Authority*. https://www.finra.org/rules-guidance/guidance/reports-studies/2022-industry-snapshot.

Harvard College. "Admissions Statistics." https://college.harvard.edu/admissions/admissions-statistics.

Harvard University Archives, Cambridge, Mass.

Intercontinental Exchange (ICE). "ICE LIBOR." https://www.theice.com/iba/libor.

Lindert, Peter H., and Robert A. Margo, eds. *Historical Statistics of the United States*. Millennial Edition Online. Cambridge: Cambridge University Press, 2006. http://hsus.cambridge.org.proxy.uchicago.edu/HSUSWeb/search/searchTable.do?id=Cc1-2.

London Metals Exchange. "The Ring." https://www.lme.com/Trading/Trading-venues/The-Ring.

Massachusetts, Town and Vital Records, 1620–1988. http://search.ancestry.com/search/db.aspx?dbid=2495.

MeasuringWorth. "The Annual Consumer Price Index for the United States, 1774 to Present." https://www.measuringworth.com/datasets/uscpi/.

Museum of the City of New York, image collection. "New York Stock Exchange and Board, 1850s." Original from the *New-York Illustrated News*, October 15, 1853, 215.

NYSE (New York Stock Exchange) Market Data, NYSE website. http://www.nyxdata.com/Data-Products/NYSE-Closing-Prices?rfrby=sum#summaries.

Pound Sterling Live. "British Pound / US Dollar Historical Reference Rates from Bank of England for 2008." https://www.poundsterlinglive.com/bank-of-england-spot/historical-spot-exchange-rates/gbp/GBP-to-USD-2008.

Reference for Business. New Street Capital Inc. company profile. https://www.referenceforbusiness.com/.

Reference for Business website. http://www.referenceforbusiness.com.

Russell 3000 Index. "FTSE Russell." http://www.russell.com/indexes/data/fact_sheets/us/russell_3000_index.asp.

Saint Petersburg, Russia. "Administrative and Government Buildings." http://www.saint-petersburg.com/.

Securities and Exchange Commission. " 'Pump-and-Dumps' and Market Manipulations." http://www.sec.gov/answers/pumpdump.htm.

Securities and Exchange Commission website. http://www.sec.gov.

Sibley, John Langdon. Private Journal, 1846–1882. Papers of John Langdon Sibley, Harvard University Archives. https://hollisarchives.lib.harvard.edu/repositories/4/archival_objects/3489303.

Stock Exchange [London] Benevolent Fund website. http://www.sebf.co.uk/.

SWIFT (Society for Worldwide Interbank Financial Transfer). "Swift FIN Traffic & Figures." https://www.swift.com/about-us/swift-fin-traffic-figures.

SWIFT (Society for Worldwide Interbank Financial Transfer). "Swift History." https://www.swift.com/about-us/history.

U.K. National Archives. *Gower Report on Investor Protection* (1984). http://discovery.nationalarchives.gov.uk/details/r/C14391212.

United States Census. "Number of Firms, Number of Establishments, Employment, and Annual Payroll by Enterprise Employment Size for the United States, All Industries: 2016." https://www2.census.gov/programs-surveys/susb/tables/2016/us_6digitnaics_2016.xlsx?

United States Census. *Population Schedules for the Seventh, Eighth, Ninth, Tenth, and Fourteenth, 1850, 1860, 1870, 1880, 1920.* National Archives Microfilm Series. Ancestry.com.

United States Commodity Futures Trading Commission. "About the CFTC." https://www.cftc.gov/About/AboutTheCommission.

United States Department of Labor, Bureau of Labor Statistics. "Consumer Price Index Research Series Using Current Methods (CPI-U-RS): U.S. city average. Updated CPI-U-RS, All items, 1977–2016." https://www.bls.gov/cpi/researchseries_allitems.

United States Department of Labor, Bureau of Labor Statistics. "Data by Enterprise Employment Size, U.S., 6-digit NAICS." https://www.census.gov/data/tables/2014/econ/susb/2014-susb-annual.html. uscensus_2014_naics_52_1.xlsx, 'US_naics_52311_only' tab.

United States Department of Labor, Bureau of Labor Statistics. "The Employment Situation—March 2019." News Release, April 5, 2019. https://www.bls.gov/news.release/archives/empsit_04052019.pdf.

United States Department of Labor, Bureau of Labor Statistics. "Industries at a Glance—Finance and Insurance: NAICS 52, Quarterly Census of Employment and Wages." https://www.bls.gov/iag/tgs/iag52.htm.

United States Department of Labor, Bureau of Labor Statistics. "Private, NAICS17 523110 Investment banking and securities dealing, National; 2018–2019 First Quarter, All establishment sizes." In "Quarterly Census of Employment and Wages Data Viewer." https://data.bls.gov/cew/apps/table_maker/v4/table_maker.htm#type=20&from=2018&to=2019&qtr=1&ind=523110&size=0&supp=1.

United States Department of Labor, Bureau of Labor Statistics. "Quarterly Census of Employment and Wages." https://www.bls.gov/cew/bls_naics/v1/bls_naics_app.htm#tab=search&naics=2012&keyword=523110&searchType=indexes&filter=6_filter&sort=text_asc&resultIndex=0.

United Sates Department of Labor, Bureau of Labor Statistics. "Quarterly Census of Employment and Wages: Employment and Wages Data Viewer." https://data.bls.gov/cew/apps/data_views/data_views.htm#tab=Tables.

Walmart. "About." https://corporate.walmart.com/about.

Walmart. "Company Facts." http://corporate.walmart.com/newsroom/company-facts.

Wikimedia Commons. Canary Wharf photograph by Adrian Pingstone, June 2005. https://commons.wikimedia.org/wiki/File:Canary.wharf.from.thames.arp.jpg.

World Bank Open Data. https://data.worldbank.org/.

World Federation of Exchanges. "Membership & Events." https://www.world-exchanges.org/home/index.php/members/wfe-members.

World Federation of Exchanges. *WFE Annual Statistics Guide 2016.* Downloaded March 28, 2018. https://www.world-exchanges.org/home/index.php/statistics/annual-statistics.

Zombanakis, Andreas. Personal papers.

Periodicals

Abrantes-Metz, Rosa M., Michael Kraten, Albert D. Metz, and Gim S. Seow. "LIBOR Manipulation?" SSRN-id1201389, August 4, 2008.

Adams, Charles F., Jr. "A Chapter of Erie." *North American Review* 109, no. 224 (July 1869): 30–106.

Adler, Jerry. "Raging Bulls: How Wall Street Got Addicted to Light-Speed Trading." *Wired*, August 3, 2002.

Adler, Paul S. and Seok-Woo Kwon. "Social Capital: Prospects for a New Concept." *Academy of Management Review* 27 (2002): 17–40.

"AI Annihilates the Stock Market Achieving Eye-Popping Returns, Study Shows," *Wall Street Pit*, March 23, 2017.

Akerlof, George A. The Market for 'Lemons': Quality Uncertainty and the Market Mechanism," *Quarterly Journal of Economics* 84, no. 3 (1970): 488–500.

Albany (NY) Evening Journal, October 13, 1853, 2.

Alton (IL) Evening Telegraph, December 22, 1931, 1.

American Elevator and Grain Trade 28, no. 1 (July 15, 1909): 38.

American Railroad Journal, October 3, 1863.

Armstrong, Rachel. "Ex-RBS Trader Says Brevan Howard Sought LIBOR Rate Change." *Reuters*, March 30, 2012.

Ashforth, Blake E. and Vikas Anand. "The Normalization of Corruption in Organizations." *Research in Organizational Behavior* 25 (2003): 1–52.

Ashforth, Blake E. and Glen E. Kreiner. "Dirty Work and Dirtier Work: Differences in Countering Physical, Social, and Moral Stigma." *Management and Organization Review* 10, no. 1 (March 2014): 81–108.

Atchison (KS) Daily Globe, various issues, 1884–1888.

Augustin, Patrick, Menachem Brenner, and Marti G. Subrahmanyam. "Informed Options Trading Prior to M&A Announcements: Insider Trading?" (May 24, 2014). Available at SSRN: http://ssrn.com/abstract=2441606.Informed-Options-Trading_June-12-2014.

" 'Ay Shepherds Pie': The Libor Broker Trial in a Dozen Quotes." *Bloomberg*, January 27, 2016.

Baker, Wayne E. "The Social Structure of a National Securities Market."*American Journal of Sociology* 89, no. 4 (January 1984): 775–811.

Bank of England. *Financial Stability Report*, no. 24 (October 2008).

"Banks Face a WhatsApp Reckoning as Regulators Clamp Down on Messaging Apps." *Computerworld*, August 8, 2022.

"Banks Grow Wary of Zoom Meetings." *American Banker*, April 24, 2020.

Barabási, Albert-László and Réka Albert. "Emergence of Scaling in Random Networks." *Science* 286, no. 5439 (1999): 509–512.

"Barclays Agrees to Pay $100 Million over State Libor Probes." *Bloomberg*, August 8, 2016.

"Barclays Bosses 'Sent Trader to Rig Rate in New York.' " *The Times* (London), April 8, 2016.

"Barclays Caves into Criticism and Closes Tax Avoidance Unit." *The Observer* (U.K.), February 10, 2013.

"Barclays May Move Hundreds of Jobs to India: Report." *Times of India*, January 23, 2013.

"Barclays Paying $453m Fine to Settle Libor Probe." *Reuters Hedgeworld*, June 27, 2012.

Baucus, Melissa S. "Pressure, Opportunity and Predisposition: A Multivariate Model of Corporate Illegality." *Journal of Management* 20 (1994): 699–721.

Baucus, M. S. and J. P. Near. "Can Illegal Corporate Behavior Be Predicted? An Event History Analysis." *Academy of Management Journal* 34 (1991): 9–36.

Bellringer, Christopher and Ranald Michie. "Big Bang in the City of London: An Intentional Revolution or an Accident?" *Financial History Review* 21, no. 2 (2014): 111–137.

"Big Banks Reassure Staff About Potential Job Cuts." *Reuters*, March 26, 2020.

Binder, Amy J. "Why Are Harvard Grads Still Flocking to Wall Street?" *Washington Monthly*, September–October 2014.

Bismarck (Dakota Territory) Weekly Tribune, November 20, 1888.

Bismarck (ND) Daily Tribune, July 10, 1892, 4.

Blume, Marshall E. and Donald B. Keim. "Institutional Investors and Stock Market Liquidity: Trends and Relationships." Working paper, the Wharton School, University of Pennsylvania (August 21, 2012). Available at http://finance.wharton.upenn.edu/~keim/research/ChangingInstitutionPreferences_21Aug2012.pdf.

"Bob Diamond Storms Back to Wall Street." *Sunday Times* (London), August 16, 2015.

Borak, Donna. "Bernanke Defends Regulators' Actions in LIBOR Scandal." *American Banker*, July 18, 2012.

Borgatti, Stephen P., Ajay Mehra, Daniel J. Brass, and Giuseppe Labianca. "Network Analysis in the Social Sciences." *Science* 323 (2009): 892–895.

Boston Evening Journal, September 19, 1879, 2.

Boston Globe, various issues, 1888–1899.

Boston Traveler, April 1, 1831, 3.

"B. P. Hutchinson, 'Old Hutch,' the Great Chicago Wheat Operator during a Trading Session." *Harper's Weekly*, May 10, 1890, 1.

Brass, Daniel J., Kenneth D. Butterfield, and Bruce C. Skaggs. "Relationships and Unethical Behavior: A Social Network Perspective." *Academy of Management Review* 23, no. 1 (1998): 14–31.

Breiger, R. L. "The Duality of Persons and Groups." *Social Forces* 53, no. 2 (1974): 181–190.

"Britain to Scrap Libor Rate Benchmark from End-2021." *Reuters*, July 27, 2017.

Burn, Gary. "The State, the City and the Euromarkets." *Review of International Political Economy* 6, no. 2 (Summer 1999): 225–261.

Burt, Ronald S. "Models of Network Structure." *Annual Review of Sociology* 6 (1980): 79–141.

Burt, Ronald S. "The Network Structure of Social Capital." *Research in Organizational Behaviour* 22 (2000): 345–423.

Business Insider, various issues, 2012–2023.

Businessline, January 23, 2013.

Butts, Carter T. "Social Network Analysis: A Methodological Introduction." *Asian Journal of Social Psychology* 11, no. 1 (2008): 13–41.

"Canary Wharf Singing a Red-Hot Tune." *Globe and Mail,* June 19, 2007.

Carsella, Mike. "LIBOR: Immensely Important Little Understood." *Secured Lender* 65, no. 5 (July 2009): 46–48.

"Chaos of 2020 Can't Match 2008 but the Gut Punch Feels Familiar." *Bloomberg,* March 10, 2020.

Chicago (Daily) Inter-Ocean, various issues, 1888.

Chicago Daily News, various issues, 1888.

Chicago (Daily) Tribune, various issues, 1859–1988.

Chicago Herald, various issues, 1888.

Chicago Press and Tribune (the name of the *Chicago Tribune* between 1858 and 1860), various issues, 1859–1860.

Chicago Times, various issues, 1888.

Christensen, E. W. and G. G. Gordon. "An Exploration of Industry, Culture, and Revenue Growth." *Organization Studies* 20 (1999): 397–422.

Claro, Danny Pimentel and Sílvio Abrahão Laban Neto. "Sales Managers' Performance and Social Capital: The Impact of an Advice Network." *Brazilian Administration Review* 6 no. 4 (October–December 2009): 316–330.

"Clearing Members Analyze the Resolution of Central Counterparties in New White Paper." International Swap Dealers Association (ISDA) press release, May 24, 2016.

Cohn, Alain, Ernst Fehr, and Michel André Maréchal. "Business Culture and Dishonesty in the Banking Industry." *Nature* 516, no. 7529 (December 4, 2014): 86–89.

Coleman, James. "Social Capital in the Creation of Human Capital." *American Journal of Sociology* 94 (1988): S95—S121.

"Credit Market Endures Worst Day in a Decade on Virus Rout." *Bloomberg,* March 6, 2020.

"Credit Suisse Banker Exits over Unauthorized Message App Use." *Bloomberg,* June 14, 2022.

"Credit Suisse Joins Firms Scrapping Events on Virus Outbreak." *Bloomberg,* February 4, 2020.

"Daniel Drew, Esq., of New York." *Harper's Weekly,* April 27, 1867, 1.

Darley, J. M. "The Cognitive and Social Psychology of Contagious Organizational Corruption." *Brooklyn Law Review* 70 (2005): 1177–1194.

"The Deli Was Allegedly a Fraud. Also Illegal Texting and DJ D-Sol's Golf Game." *Bloomberg,* September 28, 2022.

Denning, Steve. "Rethinking Capitalism: Sandy Weill Says Bring Back Glass-Steagall." *Forbes*, July 25, 2012.

Derivatives Week, December 12, 2011; September 3, 2012.

"Deutsche Bank Slashes 18,000 Jobs." *Bloomberg*, July 7, 2019.

"Diamond and Del Missier Resign from Barclays." *Risk* 25, no. 7 (July 2012): 12.

"Dictionary of Commercial Terms: Usual Form of an Inland Bill. New-York." *Bankers' Magazine and Statistical Register* 10, no. 7 (January 1861): 545.

Dieleman, Marleen and Wladimir Sachs. "Oscillating between a Relationship-Based and a Market-Based Model: The Salim Group." *Asia Pacific Journal of Management* 23 (2006): 521–536.

Diener, Edward, Scott C. Fraser, Arthur L Beaman, and Roger T. Kelem. "Effects of Deindividuation Variables on Stealing among Halloween Trick-or-Treaters." *Journal of Personality and Social Psychology* 33, no. 2 (February 1976): 178–183.

Dodd, Randall. "Markets: Exchange or Over-the-Counter." International Monetary Fund, July 29, 2017. http://www.imf.org/external/pubs/ft/fandd/basics/markets.htm.

Dolmetsch, Chris. "Subprime Collapse to Global Financial Meltdown: Timeline." *Bloomberg*, October 13, 2008.

"Drama of LIBOR Scandal Recounted in Trader's Book." *International Herald Tribune*, February 21, 2013.

Duff, Turney. "A $20,000 Bottle of Wine? Welcome to Wall Street." CNBC, March 8, 2016. https://www.cnbc.com/2016/03/08/a-20000-bottle-of-wine-welcome-to-wall-street-commentary.html.

The Economist (London), various issues, 1870–2023.

European Commission. "Antitrust: Commission Fines Banks € 1.71bn for Participating in Cartels in the Interest Rate Derivatives Industry." Press release, December 4, 2013.

"Europe's Time-Starved Traders Want to Keep Working from Home." *Bloomberg*, June 12, 2020.

"Ex-Barclays Trader Told SFO His Bosses Knew about LIBOR Fix." *Bloomberg*, April 7, 2016.

"Exclusive: The Rags-to-Riches Tale of How Jan Koum Built WhatsApp into Facebook's New $19 Billion Baby." *Forbes*, February 2, 2014.

Fama, Eugene F. "Efficient Capital Markets: A Review of Theory and Empirical Work." *Journal of Finance* 25, no. 2 (1970): 383–417.

Fama, Eugene F. and Kenneth R. French. "Common Risk Factors in the Returns on Stocks and Bonds." *Journal of Financial Economics* 33, no. 1 (1993): 3–56.

Farley, Ryan, Eric K. Kelley, and Andy Puckett. "Dark Trading Volume and Market Quality: A Natural Experiment, 13th Annual Mid-Atlantic Research Conference in Finance (MARC), March 16, 2018. Available at SSRN: https://ssrn.com/abstract=3088715.farley_r_2018_1.

"Federal LIBOR Legislation: Five Things Financial Market Participants Need to Know." *Reuters*, March 23, 2022.

Federal Reserve Bank of New York. "New York Fed Responds to Congressional Request for Information on Barclays–LIBOR Matter." Press release, July 13, 2012.

Feld, Scott. "The Focused Organization of Social Ties." *American Journal of Sociology* 86 (1981): 1015–1035.

Financial Services Agency (Japan). "Administrative Action on Citigroup Global Markets Japan Inc." Press release, December 16, 2011.

Financial Services Agency (Japan). "Administrative Actions against UBS Securities Japan Ltd and UBS AG, Japan Branches, Japan." Press release, December 16, 2011.

Financial Services Authority (UK). "Barclays Fined £59.5 Million for Significant Failings in Relation to Libor and Euribor." Press release, June 27, 2012.

Financial Times, various issues, 1986–2023.

"Financial Traders Are Getting Their Coronavirus Test." *Bloomberg*, March 3, 2020.

Finch, Gavin and Elliott Gotkine. "LIBOR Banks Misstated Rates, Bond at Barclays Says." *Bloomberg*, May 29, 2008.

Finch, Gavin and Ben Livesey. "BBA Refrains from LIBOR Changes in Favor of Greater Oversight." *Bloomberg*, May 30, 2008.

"Former Stamford UBS Building's Mortgage Sells at Deep Discount." *Stamford (CT) Advocate*, April 19, 2017.

Fort Worth (TX) Gazette, various issues, 1888–1889.

Frank, Björn and Günther G. Schulze. "Does Economics Make Citizens Corrupt?" *Journal of Economic Behavior & Organization* 43 (2000): 101–113.

Frank Leslie's Illustrated Newspaper, October 21, 1871; March 27, 1886; December 22, 1888.

Freeman, Linton C. "Centrality in Social Networks: Conceptual Clarification." *Social Networks* 1 (1979): 215–239.

"FTC Capital Sues Over Libor." *Fund Action*, April 18, 2011.

"The Future of ETFs." *Barron's*, March 11, 2017.

Gallup. "How Coronavirus Will Change the 'Next Normal' Workplace." May 1, 2020.

"Gambling in Stocks." *Harper's Weekly*, May 7, 1864, 299.

Gilbert, Mark. "Barclays LIBOR Woes Began When It Broke Ranks." *Bloomberg*, May 18, 2016.

Gilbert, Mark. "Barclays Takes a Money-Market Beating." *Bloomberg*, September 9, 2007.

Gilmore, Stephen J. "Control Strategies for Endemic Childhood Scabies." *PloS ONE* 6, no. 1 (2011): e15990. https://doi.org/10.1371/journal.pone.0015990. Copyright: © 2011 Stephen J. Gilmore. This is an open-access article distributed under the terms of the Creative Commons Attribution License, which permits unrestricted use, distribution, and reproduction in any medium, provided the original author and source are credited.

Gioia, Dennis A. "Business Education's Role in the Crisis of Corporate Confidence." *Academy of Management Executive* 16, no. 3 (2002): 142–144.

"Global Banks Rake in Record Corporate Bond Fees amid Pandemic." *Reuters*, May 1, 2020.

"Goldman Bankers Lead City of London's Uneven Return to Office." *Bloomberg*, June 11, 2021.

"Goldman Sachs Gets Record Intern Applications—Despite 'Hellhole' Work Conditions." *New York Post*, April 5, 2022.

"Goldman Sachs Is Ordering Employees Back to the Office 5 Days (Or More) a Week. Inside CEO David Solomon's Mission to End Hybrid Work." *Fortune*, March 10, 2022.

Granovetter, Mark. "The Strength of Weak Ties." *American Journal of Sociology* 78 (1973): 1360–1380.

"A Great Operator." *Harper's Weekly*, May 10, 1890, 367.

"A Greek Banker, the Shah, and the Birth of LIBOR." *Reuters Hedgeworld*, August 8, 2012.

The Guardian, various issues, 2012–2019.

Gyntelberg, Jacob and Philip Wooldridge. "Interbank Rate Fixings during the Recent Turmoil." *Bank for International Settlements Quarterly Review* 70 (March 2008): 73–74.

Hawe, Penelope, Cynthia Webster, and Alan Shiell. "A Glossary of Terms for Navigating the Field of Social Network Analysis." *Journal of Epidemiology and Community Health* 58 (2004): 971–975.

Hayek, Friedrich A. von. "The Trend of Economic Thinking," Inaugural lecture delivered at the London School of Economics, March 1, 1933. *Economica* 40 (May 1933): 121–137.

Hayek, Friedrich A. von. "The Use of Knowledge in Society." *American Economic Review* 35, no. 4 (September 1945): 519–530.

The Herald (Glasgow), October 6, 2012.

Hilt, Eric. "Wall Street's First Corporate Governance Crisis: The Panic of 1826." NBER Working Paper 14892, April 2009.

Hilt, Eric. "When Did Ownership Separate from Control? Corporate Governance in the Early-Nineteenth Century." *Journal of Economic History* 68, no. 3 (September 2008): 645–685.

Hilt, Eric and Jacqueline Valentine. "Democratic Dividends: Stockholding, Wealth, and Politics in New York, 1791–1826." *Journal of Economic History* 72, no. 2 (June 2012): 332–363.

"The History of Wall-Street Corners." *Bankers Magazine and Statistical Register* 36 (October 1881): 309.

Hodges, Jeremy. "Ex-Barclays Trader Says Bosses Must've Known about LIBOR Fix." *Bloomberg*, May 20, 2016.

Homans, George C. "Bringing Men Back In." *American Sociological Review* 29 (1964): 809–818.

Hou, David and David Skeie. "LIBOR: Origins, Economics, Crisis, Scandal, and Reform." Staff Report No. 667, Federal Reserve Bank of New York, March 2014.

Hulbert, Mark. "Here's What Low NYSE Trading Volume Is Telling Us about the Stock Market's Direction." *MarketWatch*, January 20, 2019. https://www.marketwatch.com/story/heres-what-low-nyse-trading-volume-is-telling-us-about-the-stock-markets-direction-2019-01-18.

Illustrated London News, March 25, 1854, 268–269.

The Independent, August 1, 2012.

Insider (alternate name for *Business Insider*), various issues, 2016–2023.

International Swaps and Derivatives Association. "A Seminal Milestone for LIBOR." June 29, 2023.

"Items of General News." *Maine Farmer*, March 20, 1880, 2.

"Jacob Little, Esq." *Harper's Weekly*, September 18, 1858, 1.

Jones, Huw. "New York Still Top, Moscow Sinks in Finance Centre Ranking." *Reuters*, September 9, 2022. https://www.reuters.com/business/finance/new-york-still-top-moscow-sinks-finance-centre-ranking-2022-09-22/.

Jones, Jeffrey M. "In U.S., Real Estate Still Leads Stocks as Best Investment." Gallup, May 7, 2019.

"JPMorgan Analysts Say Work-from-Home May Hit Funding Markets." *Bloomberg*, March 10, 2020.

"JPMorgan Bosses Hooked on WhatsApp Fuel $200 Million Penalty." *Bloomberg*, December 17, 2021.

"JPMorgan Staff Irked over Order to Save Texts on Personal Phones." *Bloomberg*, June 11, 2021.

Keschner, Jason R. "Goodbye LIBOR, Hello SOFR." *Fordham Journal of Corporate and Financial Law*, April 14, 2022. https://news.law.fordham.edu/jcfl/2022/04/14/goodbye-libor-hello-sofr/.

Krauss, Christopher, Xuan Anh Do, and Nicolas Huck. "Deep Neural Networks, Gradient-Boosted Trees, Random Forests: Statistical Arbitrage on the S&P 500." FAU [Friedrich-Alexander-Universität Erlangen-Nürnberg] Discussion Papers in Economics, no. 03/2016. Later published in the *European Journal of Operational Research* 259, no. 2 (June 1, 2017): 689–702.

Kuprianov, Anatoli. "Money Market Futures." *Federal Reserve Bank of Richmond Economic Review*, November–December 1992.

Kurtzleben, Danielle. "While Trump Touts Stock Market, Many Americans Are Left out of the Conversation." Delmarva Public Radio, Mary 1, 2017.

Labaton, Stephen. "Drexel Burnham Charged by S.E.C. with Stock Fraud." *New York Times*, September 8, 1988, 1.

Lancaster (PA) Daily Intelligencer, May 3, 1890, 3.

Lavalle, Irving H. "A Bayesian Approach to an Individual Player's Choice of Bid in Competitive Sealed Auctions." *Management Science* 13, no. 7, Series A, Sciences (March 1967): 584–597.

"Lewis S. Ranieri: Your Mortgage Was His Bond." *Bloomberg BusinessWeek*, November 29, 2004.

"Libor Lies Revealed in Rigging of $300 Trillion Benchmark." *Bloomberg*, February 6, 2013.

"Libor Scandal: Counting the Cost of the Fix." *Euromoney*, August 2012.

"LIBOR: Twin Conundrums." *Wrightson ICAP Newsletter*, September 3, 2007.

"Liquidity Angst Builds in Bond Market on Surging Risk Indicators." *Bloomberg*, March 6, 2020.

Livermore, Shaw. "Unlimited Liability in Early American Corporations." *Journal of Political Economy* 43, no. 5 (October 1935): 674–687.

"London Metals Trading Floor Is Fighting to Survive." *Bloomberg*, October 13, 2021.

Los Angeles Times, September 30, 1888, 4.

"Many Wall Street Executives Say Wrongdoing Is Necessary: Survey." *Reuters Hedgeworld*, July 10, 2012.

Marion (IA) Sentinel, May 25, 1893.

Marton, Andrew. "How LIBOR Became a Fixture of the US Financial System." *American Banker Magazine* 122, no. 10 (October 2012): 1112.

McCarthy, Justin. "Just Over Half of Americans Own Stocks, Matching Record Low." Gallup.com, April 20, 2016.

McDonald, Robert and Anna Paulson. "AIG in Hindsight." *Journal of Economic Perspectives* 29, no. 2 (Spring 2015): 81–106.

McGrath, Charles, "80% of Equity Market Cap Held by Institutions," *Pensions and Investments*, 20170425.

McPherson, J. Miller, Lynn Smith-Lovin, and James M. Cook. "Birds of a Feather: Homophily in Social Networks." *Annual Review of Sociology* 27 (2001): 415–444.

Medbery, James K. "The Great Erie Imbroglio." *The Atlantic*, July 1868, 111–121.

Merchants' Magazine and Commercial Review, June 1, 1866, 54.

Merton, Robert C. "Theory of Rational Option Pricing." *Bell Journal of Economics and Management Science* 4, no. 1 (Spring 1973): 141–183.

Merton, Robert K. "The Matthew Effect in Science: The Reward and Communication Systems of Science Are Considered." *Science* 159 (January 5, 1968): 56–63.

"The Messaging Dilemma: Grappling with Employees' Off-System Communications." *Reuters*, February 3, 2023.

Michigan Farmer, October 6, 1888, 4.

Milgram, Stanley. "The Small-World Problem." *Psychology Today* 1, no. 1 (May 1967): 61–67.

Milwaukee (WI) Daily Journal, September 28, 1888; October 1, 1888.

Milwaukee (WI) Sentinel, various issues, 1886–1899.

Mizruchi, Mark S. "Social Network Analysis: Recent Achievements and Current Controversies." *Acta Sociologica* 37 (1994): 329–343.

Mollenkamp, Carrick, Jennifer Ablan, and Matthew Goldstein. "How Gaming LIBOR Became Business as Usual." *Reuters*, November 20, 2012.

"Months after Wall Street Hit with $1.8 Billion in Fines over WhatsApp, Wells Fargo Says It's under Investigation over Retaining Electronic Records." *MarketWatch*, March 22, 2023.

"Morgan Stanley Is Still Hosting Hong Kong Summit, Just Virtually." *Bloomberg*, February 19, 2020.

Morris, Ken. "Mike Milken and Warren Buffet: The Two Sides of Wall Street." 2011. http://www.kennethmorris.net/twosides.html.

Murphy, Edward V. "LIBOR: Frequently Asked Questions." *Journal of Current Issues in Finance, Business and Economics* 5, no. 3 (2012): 309–315.

The Nation, various issues, 1866.

New York Commercial Advertiser, various issues, 1861–1867.

New York (Daily) Tribune, various issues, 1856–1879.

"The New York Grain Trade." *Farmer's Magazine* (London) 18, 3rd ser. (July–December 1860): 431.

New York Evening Post, various issues, 1854–1868.

New York Herald, various issues, 1848–1868.

"The New York Stock Exchange." *Harper's New Monthly Magazine*, November 1885, 829–853.

New York Sun. various issues, 1888.

New York Times, various issues, 1858–2023.

New York World, August 27, 1890, 2.

Oatley, Thomas and Bilyana Petrova. "Banker for the World: Global Capital and America's Financialization." Unpublished paper, 2016.

Odle, T. "Entrepreneurial Cooperation on the Great Lakes: The Origin of the Methods of American Grain Marketing." *Business History Review* 38, no. 4 (Winter 1964): 439–455.

"Oil Stock Excitement." *Scientific American* 12 (January 2, 1865): 8.

Oliver, Christine. "The Antecedents of Deinstitutionalization." *Organization Studies* 13 (1992): 563–588.

Omaha (NE) Daily Bee, various issues, 1888.

"Palantir Knows Everything about You." *Bloomberg*, April 19, 2018.

Park, Yoon S. "Currency Swaps as a Long-Term International Financing Technique." *Journal of International Business Studies* 15, no. 3 (Winter 1984): 47–54.

Payne, Will. "The Chicago Board of Trade." *Century Illustrated Magazine* 65, no. 5 (March 1903): 745–654.

Pendleton (OR) East Oregonian, October 10, 1888, 1.

Peng, Scott, Chintan Gandhi, and Alexander Tyo. "Special Topic: Is LIBOR Broken?" *Citigroup US Rate Strategy Focus* 10 (April 10, 2008).

Philadelphia Evening Telegraph, April 2, 1867, 1.

Philadelphia Inquirer, July 6, 1866, 5.

Pinto, Jonathan, Carrie R. Leana, and Frits K. Pil. "Corrupt Organizations or Organizations of Corrupt Individuals? Two Types of Organization-Level Corruption." *Academy of Management Review* 33, no. 3 (2008): 685–709.

Pollock, Ian. "LIBOR Scandal: Who Might Have Lost?" BBC News, June 28, 2012.

Prairie Farmer, October 6, 1888, 646.

"Private-Equity Giants Are Latest Targets of SEC's Record-Keeping Probes." *DJ Institutional News*, November 8, 2022.

Prodoscore. "Prodoscore Research from March/April: Productivity Has Increased, Led by Remote Workers." May 19, 2020.

"Punch-Drunk Traders Focus Simply on 'Survival, Not Returns.' " *Bloomberg*, February 28, 2020.

" 'Put Guilty Bankers in Orange Jumpsuits,' Says Andrew Tyrie." *Money Marketing*, October 11, 2012, 3.

"Rabobank Faces Second Biggest Fine in Libor Scandal." *Reuters Hedgeworld*, October 23, 2013.

"Rabobank Hit with Over $1bn of Libor Fines." *FOWeek*, October 7, 2013.

"RBS Back-Office Systems Chief to Quit Bank in 2013." *(Glasgow) Herald*, October 6, 2012.

"RBS to Pay $612m in Rate-Fixing Settlement." *International Herald Tribune*, February 7, 2013.

Read, Madlen. "Stocks Turn in Worst Performance for New President." *The Street*, March 10, 2009.

Reichman, Nancy. "Insider Trading." *Crime and Justice* 18 (1993): 55–96.

Richebächer, Kurt. "The Problems and Prospects of Integrating European Capital Markets," *Journal of Money, Credit and Banking* 1, no. 3 (August 1969): 336–346.

Riddiough, Timothy J. and Howard E. Thompson. " "Déjà Vu All Over Again: Agency, Uncertainty, Leverage and the Panic of 1857." HKIMR Working Paper No.10/2012, April 19, 2012.

Robins, Garry, Philippa Pattison, and Jodie Woolcock. "Small and Other Worlds: Global Network Structure from Local Processes." *American Journal of Sociology* 110 (2005): 894–936.

"Robots, Rogues and Regulation." *Bloomberg*, June 6, 2016.

"Rogues Gallery: Traders Who Lost Big from Unauthorized Deals," *Bloomberg*, September 20, 2019.

Rose, Arnold. "A Social Psychological Approach to the Study of the Stock Market." *Kyklos* 19 (1966): 267–287.

Rousseau, Denise M., Sim B. Sitkin, Ronald S. Burt, and Colin Camerer. "Not So Different After All: A Cross-Discipline View of Trust." *Academy of Management Review* 23, no. 3 (1998): 393–404.

Saint Paul (MN) Daily Globe, various issues, 1888–1899.

Saint Paul (MN) Pioneer Press, October 3, 1888.

San Francisco Chronicle, various issues, 1888.

San Francisco Morning Call, various issues, 1891.

Schelling, Thomas. "Dynamic Models of Segregation." *Journal of Mathematical Sociology* 1, no. 2 (July 1971): 143–186. Originally published May 1969 by RAND Corporation, RM-6014-RC.

Schenk, Catherine R. "The Origins of the Eurodollar Market in London: 1955–1963." *Explorations in Economic History* 35 (April 1998): 221–238.

Scher, Robert H. "Importance of Human Resources Stressed by Swedish Auto-Maker." *Daily Pennsylvanian* 90, no. 32 (March 29, 1974): 7.

"SEC's Focus on Enforcement Actions for Record-Keeping Violations Ensnares JP Morgan: Who Else Will Be Swamped?" *Reuters*, January 5, 2022.

Seeking Alpha, August 29, 2019. Citing data from *Bloomberg* Market Cap Indices. https://seekingalpha.com/article/4202768-u-s-of-world-stock-market-cap-tops-40-again.

Shen, Allan. "Updated: Vanguard Group Founder John C. Bogle '51 Passes Away at 89." *Daily Princetonian*, 20190116.

Sherman, L. W. "Three Models of Organizational Corruption in Agencies of Social Control." *Social Problems* 27 (1980): 478–491.

Sherwood, Robert M. "The Unseen Elephant: What Blocks Judicial System Improvement?" Working Paper No. 050207-11, University of California Berkeley Program in Law and Economics, Berkeley, Calif., 2007.

"16 Wall Street Firms Fined $1.8B for Using Private Text Apps, Lying about It." *Computerworld*, September 28, 2022.

Snowden, Kenneth A. "Covered Farm Mortgage Bonds in the United States during the Late Nineteenth Century." *Journal of Economic History* 70, no. 4 (December 2010): 783–812.

"Societe Generale Drawn by U.S. SEC into Its Widening Messaging Probe." *Reuters*, February 8, 2023.

Sonnenfeld, Jeffrey A. and Paul R. Lawrence. "Why Do Companies Succumb to Price Fixing?" *Harvard Business Review* 56, no. 4 (1978): 145–157.

"Split Trading Desks, Clorox May Follow Banks' Travel Bans." *Bloomberg*, February 28, 2020.

Spread Networks, Inc. "Spread Networks and Seaborn Team up to Provide Seaspeed™: Brazil's First Dedicated Ultra-Low Latency Subsea Route." Press release, May 8, 2017.

"Spread Networks, LLC—Company Overview." *Bloomberg*, May 6, 2018.

Steeleye. "85% of Firms Not Monitoring WhatsApp—Bank of America Latest Firm to Face Fine." July 19, 2022.

Stephenson, Emily. "Goldman's Blankfein: Libor Scandal Undermines Financial System." *Reuters Hedgeworld*, July 18, 2012.

Stephenson, Karen and Marvin Zelen. "Rethinking Centrality: Methods and Examples." *Social Networks* 11 (1989): 1–31.

Stevens, Albert C. " 'Futures' in the Wheat Market." *Quarterly Journal of Economics* 2 (October 1, 1887): 37–63.

St. Louis Federal Reserve. "The Financial Crisis: Full Timeline." n.d. http://stlouisfed.org/financial-crisis/full-timeline.

St. Louis (MO) Globe-Democrat, April 29, 1885, 4.

"Swapping Currencies with the World Bank." *Institutional Investor*, December 1981, 98–101.

Sykes, Gresham M. and David Matza. "Techniques of Neutralization: A Theory of Delinquency." *American Sociological Review* 22 (1957): 664–670.

Sylla, Richard E., Robert E. Wright, and David J. Cowen. "Alexander Hamilton, Central Banker: Crisis Management during the U.S. Financial Panic of 1792." *Business History Review* 83, no. 1 (Spring, 2009): 61–86.

Tan, Andrea, Gavin Finch, and Liam Vaughan. "RBS Instant Messages Show Libor Rates Skewed for Traders." *Bloomberg*, September 25, 2012.

Tempkin, Adam. "1977: US$100m Deal for Bank of America: The First Private-Label MBS." *International Financial Review (IFR)*, 2000 issue Supplement, February 26, 2014.

"These Are the Brokers Cleared of Helping Tom Hayes Rig Libor." *Bloomberg*, January 28, 2016.

"This Is the Last Photo We'll Ever Run of the NYSE Trading Floor." *Market-Watch*, October 1, 2014.

"Timeline: LIBOR-Fixing Scandal." BBC, February 6, 2013.

Tomes, Robert. "The Fortunes of War: How They Are Made and Spent." *Harper's New Monthly Magazine*, June 1864, 227–231.

Tonello, Matteo and Stephan Rahim Rabimov. "The 2010 Institutional Investment Report: Trends in Asset Allocation and Portfolio Composition." The Conference Board Research Report, No. R-1468-10-RR, November 11, 2010. Available at SSRN: https://ssrn.com/abstract=1707512.

"Trading Scandals: The Final Nail in Chat Rooms' Coffins?" CNBC, November 11, 2013.

Treviño, L. K. and S. A. Youngblood. "Bad Apples in Bad Barrels: A Causal Analysis of Ethical Decision-Making Behavior." *Journal of Applied Psychology* 75 (1990): 378–385.

"Trump Adviser from Wall St. Backs U.S. Bank Breakup Law." *Reuters*, April 6, 2017.

" 'Trying Not to Panic': The Collapse in U.S. Markets Spared No One." *Bloomberg*, March 9, 2020.

"Try to Kill Book about Daniel Drew: Son of Drover and Financier Says It Misrepresents His Father and Could Not Be Founded on His Writings." *Carmel (NY) Putnam County Courier*, April 29, 1910.

"Twenty Years Ago: Reminiscences of a Few Famous Sound Steamers." *New London (CT) Day*, September 21, 1883, 2.

"UBS Fined $1.5 Billion, 2 Charged in Libor Rigging Probe." *Investor's Business Daily*, December 19, 2012.

"UBS to Cut Thousands of Jobs in London." *Sunday Times* (London), October 28, 2012.

United States Commodity Futures Trading Commission. "CFTC Orders Barclays to Pay $200 Million Penalty for Attempted Manipulation of and False Reporting Concerning LIBOR and Euribor Benchmark Interest Rates." Press release pr6289-12, June 27, 2012.

United States Commodity Futures Trading Commission. "CFTC Orders UBS to Pay $700 Million Penalty to Settle Charges of Manipulation, Attempted

Manipulation and False Reporting of LIBOR and Other Benchmark Interest Rates." Press release PR6472-12, December 19, 2012.

United States Commodity Futures Trading Commission. "United States Commodity Futures Trading Commission Launches Multiple Federal Actions Against a Total of Fifteen Energy Traders, Charging Them with False Reporting and Attempted Manipulation." Press release 5045-05, February 1, 2005.

United States Commodity Futures Trading Commission. "United States Commodity Futures Trading Commission Settles Natural Gas Attempted Manipulation Lawsuit with Joseph P. Foley, a Former American Electric Power Company, Inc. Trader." Press release PR 5236-06, October 2, 2006.

"U.S. Justice Dept. Toughens on Corporate Crime, Will Pursue More Individuals." *Reuters*, October 28, 2021.

"U.S. Regulators Crack Down on Retention of Electronic Communications." *Reuters*, April 12, 2022.

"U.S. SEC Opens Inquiry into Wall Street Banks' Staff Communications-Sources." *Reuters*, October 12, 2021.

"U.S. Yields Hurtle toward Zero with Thin Market Stunning Traders." *Bloomberg*, March 6, 2020.

Uzzi, Brian. "The Sources and Consequences of Embeddedness for the Economic Performance of Organizations: The Network Effect." *American Sociological Review* 61, no. 4 (August 1996): 674–698.

"Wall Street Bank Investors in Dark on Libor Liability." *Bloomberg*, July 5, 2012.

"Wall Street Gets a Break from Regulator on Work-at-Home Traders." *Bloomberg*, March 9, 2020.

Wall Street Journal, various issues, 1968–2023.

"Wall Street Sends Regulators a Poop Emoji." *Reuters*, September 27, 2022.

"Wall Street's Fear Gauge Closes at Highest Level Ever, Surpassing Even Financial Crisis Peak." CNBC, March 16, 2020.

"Wall Street's New Favorite Way to Swap Secrets Is against the Rules." *Bloomberg*, March 30, 2017.

"Wall Street's New Virtual Workplace May Outlast the Virus." *Bloomberg*, March 17, 2020.

"Wall Street's Return-to-Office Gulf Exposed by Goldman, Citi." *Bloomberg*, June 14, 2021.

"Wall Street Traders Are Tethered to the Desk with Virus Arriving." *Bloomberg*, March 4, 2020.

"Wall Street Worries about Risk Running Amok with Traders at Home." *Bloomberg*, March 6, 2020.

Washington Post, various issues, 1888–2017.

Watts, Duncan. J. "Networks, Dynamics and the Small World Phenomenon." *American Journal of Sociology* 195 (1999): 493–527.

Watts, Duncan. J. "The 'New' Science of Networks." *Annual Review of Sociology* 30 (2004): 243–270.

Watts, Duncan J. and Steven H. Strogatz. "Collective Dynamics of 'Small-World Networks." *Nature* 393 (1998): 440–442.

Weber, Klaus, Gerald F. Davis, and Michael Lounsbury. "Policy as Myth and Ceremony? The Global Spread of Stock Exchanges, 1980–2005." *Academy of Management Journal* 52, no. 6 (December 2009): 1319–1347.

Wells, Wyatt. "Certificates and Computers: The Remaking of Wall Street, 1967 to 1971." *Business History Review* 74, no. 2 (Summer 2000): 193–235.

"What It Costs to Corner Wall Street." *Harper's Weekly*, April 14, 1866, 227.

"WhatsApp Completes End-to-End Encryption Rollout." *TechCrunch*, April 5, 2016.

"WhatsApp Hits 600 Million Active Users, Founder Says." *Forbes*, August 25, 2014.

"WhatsApp Is Off-Limits to Bankers. So Why Do They Keep Using It?" *American Banker*, March 14, 2022.

"WhatsApp Partners with Open Whispersystems to End-to-End Encrypt Billions of Messages a Day." *TechCrunch*, November 18, 2014.

"What We Learned from the Work-from-Home Experiment." *Bloomberg*, March 27, 2020.

White, Z. L. "Western Journalism." *Harper's New Monthly Magazine* 77, no. 461 (October 1888): 678.

The White House, Office of the Press Secretary. "President Clinton Names Gary Gensler as Under Secretary for Domestic Finance at the Department of the Treasury." Press release, October 8, 1998.

"Who's Hiring." *BusinessWeek.com*, June 14, 2006.

"Why Wall Street Is in Hot Water for Using WhatsApp." *Bloomberg*, March 14, 2022.

Wichita (KS) Daily Eagle, various issues, 1888.

Williams, Jeffrey C. "The Origin of Futures Markets." *Agricultural History* 56, no. 1 (January 1982): 306–316.

Withers, Hartley. "The London Stock Exchange." *Quarterly Review* 217 (July 1912): 88–109.

World Bank. "Market Capitalization of Listed Domestic Companies (Current US$) | Data." data.worldbank.org. Retrieved September 20, 2021.

"You Can Now Record Video Messages on WhatsApp." Meta Newsroom, July 27, 2023. https://about.fb.com/news/2023/07/video-messages-on-whatsapp/.

Zheng, Tian, Matthew J. Salganik, and Andrew Gelman. "How Many People Do You Know in Prison? Using Overdispersion in Count Data to Estimate Social Structure in Networks." *Journal of the American Statistical Association* 101 (2006):409–423.

Zucker, Lynne G. "The Role of Institutionalization in Cultural Persistence." *American Sociological Review* 42 (1977): 726–743.

Printed Sources

Abolafia, Mitchel Y. *Making Markets: Opportunism and Restraint on Wall Street.* Cambridge, Mass.: Harvard University Press, 1996.

"An Act in Relation to Railroads Held under Lease." Passed April 3, 1867. In *Laws of the State of New York, 1867*, 444–445.

"An Act Relative to Incorporations for Manufacturing." Passed March 22, 1811. In *Laws of the State of New-York, 1811*, 111–114.

Acts of the Forty-Ninth General Assembly of the State of New-Jersey, at a Session Begun at Trenton, the Twenty-Eighth Day of October, One Thousand Eight Hundred and Twenty-Four. Princeton (NJ): D. A. Borrenstein, 1824.

"An Act to Amend Chapter One Hundred and Forty of the Laws of Eighteen Hundred and Fifty, Entitled 'An Act to Authorize the Formation of Railroad Corporations and to Regulate the Same.' " Passed June 25, 1887. *General Statutes of the State of New York for the Year 1887*, 284.

"An Act to Authorize the Formation of Railroad Corporations, and to Regulate the Same." Passed April 2, 1850. Chapter 140, *Laws of the State of New-York, 1850*, 225.

"An Act to Incorporate a Company to Form an Artificial Navigation between the Passaic and Delaware Rivers." Passed December 31, 1824. *Acts of the Forty-Ninth General Assembly of the State of New-Jersey*, 1824, 159.

"An Act to Prohibit Certain Sales of Gold and Foreign Exchange." *U.S. Statutes at Large*, 38th Cong., 1st sess., 13:132.

"An Act to Repeal the Act of the Seventeenth of June, Eighteen Hundred and Sixty-Four, Prohibiting the Sales of Gold and Foreign Exchange." *U.S. Statutes at Large*, 38th Cong., 1st sess., 13:344.

Adams, Charles Francis, Jr., et al. *High Finance in the Sixties: Chapters from the Early History of the Erie Railway*. New Haven, Conn.: Yale University Press, 1929.

Adler, Patricia A. and Peter Adler, eds. *The Social Dynamics of Financial Markets*. Greenwich, Conn.: JAI, 1984.

Akerlof, George and Robert Shiller. *Phishing for Phools: The Economics of Manipulation and Deception*. Princeton, N.J.: Princeton University Press, 2015.

Alper, Joel and Joseph N. Pelton, eds. *The INTELSAT Global Satellite System: Progress in Astronautics and Aeronautics*. Vol 93. Martin Summerfield, series editor in chief. New York: American Institute of Aeronautics and Astronautics, 1984.

Angell, Joseph K. and Samuel Ames. *The Law of Private Corporations Aggregate*. Boston: Hilliard, Gray, Little and Wilkins, 1832.

Annual Report of the State Engineer and Surveyor of the State of New York, and of the Tabulations and Deductions from the Reports of the Rail Road Corporations for the Year Ending September 30th, 1865. Albany, N.Y.: Weed, Parsons, 1866.

Annual Report of the State Engineer and Surveyor of the State of New York, and of the Tabulations and Deductions from the Reports of the Rail Road Corporations for the Year Ending September 30th, 1866. Albany, N.Y.: Weed, Parsons, 1867.

Annual Report of the State Engineer and Surveyor of the State of New York, and of the Tabulations and Deductions from the Reports of the Rail Road Corporations for the Year Ending September 30th, 1868. Albany, N.Y.: Weed, Parsons, 1869.

Aristotle. *Aristotle Metaphysics: Books Z and H.* Translated by David Bostock. Oxford, UK: Clarendon, 1994.

Armstrong, William (pseud. A Reformed Stock Gambler). *Stocks and Stock-Jobbing in Wall-Street, with Sketches of the Brokers, and Fancy Stocks.* New York: New York Publishing, 1848.

Arthur Andersen LLP v. United States, 544 U.S. 696 (2005). Legal Information Institute, Cornell University Law School. https://www.law.cornell.edu/supct/html/04-368.ZS.html.

Ayers, Andrew. *The Architecture of Paris.* London: Edition Axel Menges, 2003.

Baker, Wayne. "Floor Trading and Crowd Dynamics." In Patricia A. Adler and Peter Adler, eds., *The Social Dynamics of Financial Markets*, 107–128. Greenwich, Conn.: JAI, 1984.

Bakken, Henry H. "Historical Evaluation, Theory and Legal Status of Futures Trading in American Agricultural Commodities." In H. H. Bakken et al., eds., *Futures Trading Seminar*, vol. 1, *History and Development*, 1–60. Madison, Wis.: Mimir, 1960.

Bankers Trust New York Corporation 1968 Annual Report.

Banking Act of 1933 (Glass-Steagall Act). Public Law 73-66, 73d Cong., H.R. 5661.

Bank of America 2012 Annual Report.

Bank of America 2021 Annual Report.

Bank of America 2022 Annual Report.

Bank of America Merrill Lynch 2018 Annual Report.

Bank of America Merrill Lynch 2022 Annual Report.

Bank of England Financial Stability Report 24, October 2008.

Banner, Stuart. *Anglo-American Securities Regulation, 1690–1860.* New York: Cambridge University Press, 1998.

Barclays PLC 2021 Annual Report.

Barclays PLC 2022 Annual Report.

Benwell, John. *An Englishman's Travels in America: His Observations of Life and Manners in the Free and Slave States.* London: Binns and Goodwin, 1853.

Big Bang 20 Years On: New Challenges Facing the Financial Services Sector. London: Centre for Policy Studies, 2006.

Blaine, James G. "War Debts of the Loyal States, to Accompany H.R. Bill 282." February 16, 1866. U.S. Congress, House Report, 39th Cong., 1st sess., 1866. House Document 16, *U.S. Congressional Serial Set*, vol. 1272, 1866.

BNP Paribas 2018 Annual Report.

BNP Paribas 2021 Annual Report.

BNP Paribas 2022 Annual Report.

Box, George E. P. and Norman R. Draper. *Empirical Model-Building and Response Surfaces.* Hoboken, N.J.: John Wiley, 1987.

Browder, Clifford. *The Money Game in Old New York: Daniel Drew and His Times.* Lexington: University Press of Kentucky, 1986.

Burk, James. *Values in the Marketplace: The American Stock Market under Federal Securities Laws.* New York: de Gruyter, 1988.

Burt, Ronald S. *Brokerage and Closure.* New York: Oxford University Press, 2005.

Burt, Ronald S. "Distinguishing Relational Contents." In Ronald S. Burt and Michael J. Minor, eds., *Applied Network Analysis,* 35–74. Beverly Hills, Calif.: Sage, 1983.

Burt, Ronald S. *Structural Holes: The Social Structure of Competition.* Cambridge, Mass.: Harvard University Press, 1992.

Catarina, Darshan, Fuad Faridi, Jared Moon, and Christina Schulz. "How Cognitive Technologies Are Transforming Capital Markets." McKinsey & Company Financial Services, July 2017.

Chesquiere, Henri. "Causes and Implications of the Growth of the Eurodollar Market." Ph.D. diss., Yale University, 1979.

Chicago Board of Trade. *Act of Incorporation and Rules and By-Laws of the Board of Trade of the City of Chicago, Also Rules for the Inspection of Provisions. Adopted September 19, 1871.* Chicago: Horton and Leonard, 1871.

Chicago Board of Trade. *Act of Incorporation, Rules and By-Laws of the Board of Trade, for the City of Chicago Adopted April 12, 1869.* Chicago: Horton and Leonard, 1869.

Chicago Board of Trade. *Act of Incorporation, Rules and By-Laws of the Board of Trade, for the City of Chicago Adopted March 18, 1875.* Chicago: Horton and Leonard, 1875.

Chicago Board of Trade. *Act of Incorporation, Rules, By-Laws and Inspection Regulations of the Board of Trade of the City of Chicago. Adopted August 29, 1883.* Chicago: Knight and Leonard, 1883.

Chicago Board of Trade. *Annual Statement of the Trade and Commerce of Chicago for the Year Ended December 31, 1858. Reported to the Chicago Board of Trade by Seth Catlin, Secretary.* Chicago: Hyatt Brothers, 1859.

Chicago Board of Trade. *Second Annual Statement of the Trade and Commerce of Chicago for the Year Ended December 31, 1859. Reported to the Chicago Board of Trade by Seth Catlin, Secretary.* Chicago: Hyatt Brothers, 1860.

Chicago Board of Trade. *Seventeenth Annual Report of the Trade and Commerce of Chicago for the Year Ended December 31, 1874. Compiled for the Board of Trade by Charles Randolph, Secretary.* Chicago: Knight and Leonard, 1875.

Chicago Board of Trade. *Eighteenth Annual Report of the Trade and Commerce of Chicago for the Year Ended December 31, 1875. Compiled for the Board of Trade by Charles Randolph, Secretary.* Chicago: Knight and Leonard, 1876.

Chicago Board of Trade. *Twentieth Annual Report of the Trade and Commerce of Chicago for the Year Ending December 31, 1877. Compiled for the Board of Trade by Charles Randolph, Secretary.* Chicago: Knight and Leonard, 1878.

Chicago Board of Trade. *Twenty-Fifth Annual Report of the Trade and Commerce of Chicago, for the Year Ending December 31, 1882. Compiled for the Board of Trade by Charles Randolph, Secretary.* Chicago: Knight and Leonard, 1883.

Chicago Board of Trade. *Twenty-Sixth Annual Report of the Trade and Commerce of Chicago, for the Year Ending December 31, 1883. Compiled for the Board of Trade by Charles Randolph, Secretary.* Chicago: Knight and Leonard, 1884.

Chicago Board of Trade. *Twenty-Seventh Annual Report of the Trade and Commerce of Chicago, for the Year Ending December 31, 1884. Compiled for the Board of Trade by George F. Stone, Secretary.* Chicago: Knight and Leonard, 1885.

Chicago Board of Trade. *Twenty-Eighth Annual Report of the Trade and Commerce of Chicago, for the Year Ending December 31, 1885. Compiled for the Board of Trade by George F. Stone, Secretary.* Chicago: Knight and Leonard, 1886.

Chicago Board of Trade. *Twenty-Ninth Annual Report of the Trade and Commerce of Chicago, for the Year Ending December 31, 1886. Compiled for the Board of Trade by George F. Stone, Secretary.* Chicago: Knight and Leonard, 1887.

Chicago Board of Trade. *Thirtieth Annual Report of the Trade and Commerce of Chicago for the Year Ending December 31, 1887. Compiled for the Board of Trade by George F. Stone, Secretary.* Chicago: Knight and Leonard, 1888.

Chicago Board of Trade. *Thirty-First Annual Report of the Trade and Commerce of Chicago for the Year Ending December 31, 1888. Compiled for the Board of Trade by George F. Stone, Secretary.* Chicago: J. M. W. Jones, 1889.

Chicago Board of Trade. *Thirty-Third Annual Report of the Trade and Commerce of Chicago for the Year Ending December 31, 1890. Compiled for the Board of Trade by George F. Stone, Secretary.* Chicago: J. M. W. Jones, 1891.

Chicago Board of Trade. *Forty-Second Annual Report of the Trade and Commerce of Chicago for the Year Ending December 31, 1899. Compiled for the Board of Trade by George F. Stone, Secretary.* Chicago: J. M. W. Jones, 1900.

Chicago Board of Trade. *Forty-Third Annual Report of the Trade and Commerce of Chicago for the Year Ending December 31, 1900. Compiled for the Board of Trade by George F. Stone, Secretary.* Chicago: J. M. W. Jones, 1901.

Chicago Board of Trade. *Fifty-Second Annual Report of the Trade and Commerce of Chicago for the Year Ending December 31, 1909. Compiled for the Board of Trade by George F. Stone, Secretary.* Chicago: Hedstrom-Barry, 1910.

Chicago Board of Trade. *Fifty-Third Annual Report of the Trade and Commerce of Chicago for the Year Ending December 31, 1910. Compiled for the Board of Trade by George F. Stone, Secretary.* Chicago: Hedstrom-Barry, 1911.

Chicago Board of Trade. *Sixty-Second Annual Report of the Trade and Commerce of Chicago for the Year Ended December 31, 1919. Compiled for the Board of Trade by John R. Mauff, Secretary.* Chicago: Hedstrom-Barry, 1920.

Chicago Board of Trade. *Sixty-Third Annual Report of the Trade and Commerce of Chicago for the Year Ended December 31, 1920. Compiled for the Board of Trade by John R. Mauff, Secretary.* Chicago: Hedstrom-Barry, 1921.

Chicago Board of Trade. *Seventy-Second Annual Report of the Trade and Commerce of Chicago for the Year Ended December 31, 1929. Compiled for the Board of Trade by Fred H. Clutton, Secretary.* Chicago: Hedstrom-Barry, 1930.

Chicago Board of Trade. *Seventy-Third Annual Report of the Trade and Commerce of Chicago for the Year Ended December 31, 1930. Compiled for the Board of Trade by Fred H. Clutton, Secretary.* Chicago: Lincoln, 1931.

Chicago Board of Trade. *Eighty-Second Annual Report of the Trade and Commerce of Chicago for the Year Ended December 31, 1939. Compiled for the Board of Trade by Fred H. Clutton, Secretary.* Chicago: Hedstrom-Barry, 1940.

Chicago Board of Trade. *Eighty-Third Annual Report of the Trade and Commerce of Chicago for the Year Ended December 31, 1940. Compiled for the Board of Trade by Fred H. Clutton, Secretary, and Lyman C. West, Statistician.* Chicago: Lincoln, 1941.

Citi Annual Report, various issues 2012–2022.

Clews, Henry. *Twenty-Eight Years in Wall Street.* New York: Irving, 1888.

Coalition Index for Investment Banking. CRISIL, various issues.

Code of Federal Regulations. U.S. Government Publishing Office.

Cohen, Lester. *The Great Bear.* New York: Boni and Liveright, 1927.

Colman, Andrew M. *Dictionary of Psychology.* 4th ed. New York: Oxford University Press, 2015.

Combe, William. *The Microcosm of London, or London in Miniature.* Vol. 3. London: Rudolph Ackerman, 1810. Reprint, London: Methuen, 1904.

Commodity Exchange Act, 1936. Public Law 74-675. 74th Cong., H.R. 6772.

Commons, John R. *Institutional Economics.* Madison: University of Wisconsin Press, 1959.

Companies Act 1980 (UK). http://www.legislation.gov.uk/ukpga/1980/22/contents/enacted.

Company Securities (Insider Dealing) Act 1985 (UK) (repealed 1.3.1994). http://www.legislation.gov.uk/ukpga/1985/8/contents.

Congressional Record: Containing the Proceedings and the Debates of the Forty-Seventh Congress, Second Session. Washington, D.C.: Government Printing Office, 1882.

Congressional Record: Containing the Proceedings and Debates of the Fiftieth Congress, First Session (House). Vol. 19. Washington, D.C.: Government Printing Office, 1888.

Cornwallis, Kinahan. *The Gold Room and the New York Stock Exchange and Clearing House.* New York: A. S. Barnes, 1879.

Cotton Futures Act of 1914. Public Law 63-174. 38 Stat. 693.

Cram's Standard American Atlas of the World. Chicago: George F. Cram, 1889. David Rumsey Historical Map Collection, https://www.davidrumsey.com.

Credit Suisse 2021 Annual Report.

Credit Suisse 2022 Annual Report.

Cronon, William. *Nature's Metropolis: Chicago and the Great West.* New York: Norton, 1992.

Davis, Joseph Stancliffe. "William Duer, Entrepreneur, 1747–1799." In *Essays in the Earlier History of American Corporations.* Cambridge, Mass.: Harvard University Press, 1917, 111–338. Reprint by Russell and Russell, 1965.

Davis, Lance, Larry Neal, and Eugene White. "Membership Rules and the Long Run Performance of Stock Exchanges: Lessons from Emerging Markets, Past and Present." Paper presented at the annual meeting of the ISNIE (International Society for the New Institutional Economics) Conference, Washington, D.C., September 17–19, 1999.

de la Vega, Joseph. *Confusion of Confusions*. Kress Library of Business and Economics 13. Boston: Baker Library of the Harvard Business School, 1957.

Deutsche Bank 2021 Annual Report.

Deutsche Bank 2022 Annual Report.

De Vries, J. and A. Van De Woude. *The First Modern Economy: Success, Failure and Perseverance of the Dutch Economy, 1500–1815*. Cambridge: Cambridge University Press, 1997.

Dreiser, Theodore. *The Financier*. New York: Harper and Brothers, 1912.

Dwyer, Patrick, et al. "Recent Developments in Short-Term Funding Markets." U.S. Department of the Treasury, May 6, 2008.

Eames, Francis L. *The New York Stock Exchange*. New York: Thomas G. Hall, 1894.

Edge Act, "Investments by United States Banking Organizations in Foreign Companies That Transact Business in the United States." Passed into law December 24, 1919. An amendment to the United States Federal Reserve Act of 1913. Codified as section 25(a) of the Federal Reserve Act, 12 U.S.C. 611.

Edmonds, John W., ed. *Statutes at Large of the State of New York, Comprising the Revised Statutes, as They Existed on the 1st Day of July 1862*. Vol. 1. Albany, N.Y.: Weare C. Little, 1863.

Enrich, David. *The Spider Network: The Wild Story of a Math Genius, a Gang of Backstabbing Bankers, and One of the Greatest Scams in Financial History*. New York: HarperCollins, 2017.

Fabozzi, Frank J. and Franco Modigliani, Franco. *Mortgage and Mortgage-Backed Securities Markets*. Boston: Harvard Business School Press, 1992.

Falloon, William D. *Market Maker: A Sesquicentennial Look at the Chicago Board of Trade*. Chicago: Board of Trade of the City of Chicago, 1998.

Ferguson, Adam. *Essay on the History of Civil Society*. Dublin: Boulter Grierson, 1767.

Ferguson, Niall. *High Financier: The Lives and Time of Siegmund Warburg*. New York: Penguin, 2010.

Fictitious Dealing in Agricultural Products: Testimony Taken before the Committee on Agriculture during a Consideration of Bills Nos. 392, 2699, and 3870, Restricting and Taxing Dealers in "Futures" and "Options" in Agricultural Products, and for Other Purposes. Submitted by Mr. Hatch from the Committee on Agriculture, U.S. House of Representatives. Washington, D.C.: U.S. Government Printing Office, 1892.

Financial Services Act 1986 (UK). http://www.legislation.gov.uk/ukpga/1986/60/contents/enacted.

Fowler, William Worthington. *Inside Life in Wall Street, or, How Great Fortunes Are Lost and Won: With Disclosures of Doings and Dealings on 'Change*. Hartford, Conn.: Dustin, Gilman, 1873.

Fowler, William Worthington. *Ten Years in Wall Street, or, Revelations of Inside Life and Experience on 'Change*. Hartford, Conn.: Dustin, Gilman, 1873.

Fowler, William Worthington. *Twenty Years of Inside Life in Wall Street, or Revelations of the Personal Experience of a Speculator, Including Sketches of the Leading Operators and Money Kings, the Great Rises and Panics, the Mysteries of the Rings, Pools, and Corners, and How Fortunes Are Made and Lost on 'Change*. New York: Orange Judd, 1880.

Freeman, Linton C. "The Development of Social Network Analysis—with an Emphasis on Recent Events." In John Scott and Peter Carrington, eds., *The Sage Handbook of Social Network Analysis*, 26–39. London: Sage. 2014.

Friedman, Milton. "The Euro-Dollar Market: Some First Principles." Selected Papers No. 34, Booth School of Business, University of Chicago. Originally published in the Morgan Guaranty Survey, October 1969.

Future Trading Act of 1921. Public Law 67-66. 42 Stat. 187.

Gardner, Daniel. *Institutes of International Law, Public and Private, as Settled by the Supreme Court of the United States, and by Our Republic, with References to Judicial Decisions*. New York: John S. Vorhees, 1860.

Garson, Barbara. *Money Makes the World Go Around*. New York: Viking, 2001.

General Statutes of the State of New York for the Year 1887. Albany, N.Y.: Weed, Parsons, 1887.

Giudice, Gabriele, Robert Kuenzel, and Tom Springbett. *UK Economy: The Crisis in Perspective: Essays on the Drivers of Recent UK Economic Performance and Lessons for the Future*. London: Routledge, 2012.

Global Financial Centres Index 1, March 2007. London: City of London Corporation, 2007.

Global Financial Centres Index 15, March 2014. Qatar Financial Centre Authority, 2014.

Global Financial Centres Index 20, September 2016. Z/Yen Group and the China Development Institute, 2016.

Global Financial Centres Index 31: March 2022. London: Long Finance and Financial Centre Futures, 2022.

Global Financial Centres Index 32: September 2022. London: Long Finance and Financial Centre Futures, 2022.

Goldgar, Anne. *Tulipmania: Money, Honor, and Knowledge in the Dutch Golden Age*. Chicago: University of Chicago Press, 2007.

Goldman Sachs Group, Inc. Annual Report 2021.

Goldman Sachs Group, Inc. Annual Report 2022.

Goldsmith, Raymond W., "The Historical Background: Financial Institutions as Investors in Corporate Stock before 1952." Chapter 2 in Raymond W. Goldsmith, ed., *Institutional Investors and Corporate Stock—A Background Study*. Studies in Capital Formation and Financing 13. New York: Columbia University Press for the NBER, 1973.

Graham, Benjamin and David L. Dodd. *Security Analysis*. New York: Whittlesey House, McGraw-Hill, 1934.

Gramm-Leach-Bliley Act (GLBA), also known as the Financial Services Modernization Act of 1999. Public Law 106-102. 113 Stat. 1338. Enacted November 12, 1999.

Hall, Oakley. *Warlock*. New York: Viking, 1958.

Hamilton, David L. and Sara A. Crump. "Entitativity." In Roy F. Baumeister and Kathleen D. Vohs, eds., *Encyclopedia of Social Psychology*. Thousand Oaks, Calif.: Sage, 2007.

Hamon, Henry. *New York Stock Exchange Manual, Containing Its Principles, Rules, and Its Different Modes of Speculation: Also, a Review of the Stocks Dealt in on 'Change, Government and State Securities, Railway, Mining, Petroleum, &c, &c.* New York: John F. Trow, 1865.

Hartley, L. P. *The Go-Between*. London: H. Hamilton, 1956.

Hastings v. Drew. In Nathan Howard, ed., *Practice Reports in the Supreme Court and Court of Appeals*, 50:257. Albany, N.Y.: William Gould and Son, 1876.

Heckinger, Richard, Ivana Ruffini, and Kirstin Wells. "Over-the-Counter Derivatives." Chapter 3 in *Understanding Derivatives: Markets and Infrastructure*, 27–38. Chicago: Federal Reserve Bank of Chicago, 2014.

H. Henry Baxter. New York: Atlantic, 1884.

Hieronymus, T. A. *Economics of Futures Trading for Commercial and Personal Profit*. New York: Commodity Research Bureau, 1977.

Higonnet, Rene P. "Eurobanks, Eurodollars and International Debt." In Paolo Savona and George Sujita, eds., *Eurodollars and International Banking*. New York: St. Martin's, 1985.

Ho, Karen. *Liquidated: An Ethnography of Wall Street*. Durham, N.C.: Duke University Press, 2009.

Hollinger, Richard C. and John P. Clark. *Theft by Employees*. Lexington, Mass.: Lexington Books, 1983.

Homer, Sidney and Richard Sylla. *A History of Interest Rates*. 4th ed. Hoboken, N.J.: Wiley, 2007.

Hou, David and David Skeie. "LIBOR: Origins, Economics, Crisis, Scandal, and Reform." Federal Reserve Bank of New York Staff Reports, March 2014.

House of Commons Treasury Committee. *Fixing LIBOR: Some Preliminary Findings. Second Report of Session 2012–13.* 3 vols. Report HC 481-1. August 18, 2012. London: Stationery Office, 2012.

HSBC Holdings PLC Annual Report and Accounts 2021.

HSBC Holdings PLC Annual Report and Accounts 2022.

Hull, John C. and Sankarshan Basu. *Options, Futures, and Other Derivatives.* 9th ed. Indian Subcontinent Adaptation. Delhi: Pearson India Education Services, 2016.

Hurd, Harvey B., comp. and ed. *Revised Statutes of the State of Illinois. A.D. 1874. Comprising the Revised Acts of 1871–2 and 1873–4, Together with All Other General Statutes of the State, in Force on the First Day of July 1874.* Springfield: Illinois Journal Company, 1874.

Insider Trading and Securities Fraud Enforcement Act of 1988 (ITSFA). *United States Statutes at Large*, 102 Stat. 4677.

International Monetary Fund. *Global Financial Stability Report: Meeting New Challenges to Stability and Building a Safer System.* Washington, D.C.: IMF, April 2010.

In the Matter of Bank of America, N.A., BofA Securities, Inc., and Merrill Lynch, Pierce, Fenner & Smith Incorporated, Respondents. Order Instituting Proceedings Pursuant to Section 6(c) and (d) of the Commodity Exchange Act, Making Findings, and Imposing Remedial Sanctions. CFTC, September 27, 2022.

In the Matter of Barclays Bank PLC and Barclays Capital Inc., Respondents. Order Instituting Proceedings Pursuant to Section 6(c) and (d) of the Commodity Exchange Act, Making Findings, and Imposing Remedial Sanctions. CFTC, September 27, 2022.

In the Matter of Barclays Capital Inc., Respondent. Order Instituting Administrative and Cease-And-Desist Proceedings, Pursuant to Sections 15(B) and 21c of the Securities Exchange Act of 1934, Making Findings, and Imposing Remedial Sanctions and a Cease-and-Desist Order. Administrative Proceeding File No. 3-21164. SEC, September 27, 2022.

In the Matter of BofA Securities, Inc. and Merrill Lynch, Pierce, Fenner & Smith Incorporated, Respondent. Order Instituting Administrative and Cease-and-Desist Proceedings, Pursuant to Sections 15(B) and 21c of the Securities Exchange Act of 1934, Making Findings, and Imposing Remedial Sanctions and a Cease-and-Desist Order. Administrative Proceeding File No. 3-21166. SEC, September 27, 2022.

In the Matter of Cantor Fitzgerald & Co. Order Instituting Proceedings Pursuant to Section 6(c) and (d) of the Commodity Exchange Act, Making Findings, and Imposing Remedial Sanctions. CFTC, September 27, 2022.

In the Matter of Cantor Fitzgerald & Co., Respondent. Order Instituting Administrative and Cease-and-Desist Proceedings, Pursuant to Sections 15(B) and 21c of the Securities Exchange Act of 1934, Making Findings, and Imposing Remedial Sanctions and a Cease-and-Desist Order. Administrative Proceeding File No. 3-21172. SEC, September 27, 2022.

In the Matter of Citibank, N.A., Citigroup Energy Inc., and Citigroup Global Markets Inc., Respondents. Order Instituting Proceedings Pursuant to Section 6(c) and (d) of the Commodity Exchange Act, Making Findings, and Imposing Remedial Sanctions. CFTC, September 27, 2022.

In the Matter of Citigroup Global Markets Inc., Respondent. Order Instituting Administrative and Cease-and-Desist Proceedings, Pursuant to Sections 15(B) and 21c of the Securities Exchange Act of 1934, Making Findings, and Imposing Remedial Sanctions and a Cease-and-Desist Order. Administrative Proceeding File No. 3-21165. SEC, September 27, 2022.

In the Matter of Credit Suisse International and Credit Suisse Securities (USA) LLC Respondents. Order Instituting Proceedings Pursuant to Section 6(C) and (D) of the Commodity Exchange Act, Making Findings, and Imposing Remedial Sanctions. CFTC Docket No. 22-47, September 27, 2022.

In the Matter of Credit Suisse Securities (U.S.A.) LLC, Respondent. Order Instituting Administrative and Cease-and-Desist Proceedings, Pursuant to Sections 15(B) and 21c of the Securities Exchange Act of 1934, Making Findings, and Imposing Remedial Sanctions and a Cease-and-Desist Order. Administrative Proceeding File No. 3-21171. SEC, September 27, 2022.

In the Matter of Deutsche Bank AG and Deutsche Bank Securities Inc., Respondents. Order Instituting Proceedings Pursuant to Section 6(c) and (d) of the Commodity Exchange Act, Making Findings, and Imposing Remedial Sanctions. CFTC, September 27, 2022.

In the Matter of Deutsche Bank Securities Inc., DWS Investment Management Americas, Inc., and DWS Distributors, Inc., Respondent. Order Instituting Administrative and Cease-And-Desist Proceedings, Pursuant to Sections 15(B) and 21c of the Securities Exchange Act of 1934, Making Findings, and Imposing Remedial Sanctions and a Cease-and-Desist Order. Administrative Proceeding File No. 3-21173. SEC, September 27, 2022.

In the Matter of Goldman Sachs & Co. LLC, f/k/a Goldman Sachs & Co., Respondents. Order Instituting Proceedings Pursuant to Section 6(c) and (d) of the Commodity Exchange Act, Making Findings, and Imposing Remedial Sanctions. CFTC, September 27, 2022.

In the Matter of Goldman Sachs & Co. LLC, Respondent. Order Instituting Administrative and Cease-and-Desist Proceedings, Pursuant to Sections 15(B) and 21c of the Securities Exchange Act of 1934, Making Findings, and Imposing Remedial Sanctions and a Cease-and-Desist Order. Administrative Proceeding File No. 3-21167. SEC, September 27, 2022.

In the Matter of Jefferies Financial Services, Inc. and Jefferies LLC, Respondents. Order Instituting Proceedings Pursuant to Section 6(c) and (d) of the Commodity Exchange Act, Making Findings, and Imposing Remedial Sanctions. CFTC, September 27, 2022.

In the Matter of Jefferies LLC, Respondent. Order Instituting Administrative and Cease-and-Desist Proceedings, Pursuant to Sections 15(B) and 21c of the Securities Exchange Act of 1934, Making Findings, and Imposing Remedial Sanctions and a Cease-and-Desist Order. Administrative Proceeding File No. 3-21168. SEC, September 27, 2022.

In the Matter of Morgan Stanley & Co. LLC and Morgan Stanley Smith Barney LLC, Respondent. Order Instituting Administrative and Cease-and-Desist Proceedings, Pursuant to Sections 15(B) and 21c of the Securities Exchange Act of 1934, Making Findings, and Imposing Remedial Sanctions and a Cease-and-Desist Order. Administrative Proceeding File No. 3-21169. SEC, September 27, 2022.

In the Matter of Morgan Stanley & Co. LLC, Morgan Stanley Capital Services LLC, Morgan Stanley Capital Group Inc., and Morgan Stanley Bank, N.A., Respondents. Order Instituting Proceedings Pursuant to Section 6(c) and (d) of the Commodity Exchange Act, Making Findings, and Imposing Remedial Sanctions. CFTC, September 27, 2022.

In the Matter of Nomura Global Financial Products Inc., Nomura Securities International, Inc., and Nomura International PLC, Respondents. Order Instituting Proceedings Pursuant to Section 6(c) and (d) of the Commodity Exchange Act, Making Findings, and Imposing Remedial Sanctions. CFTC, September 27, 2022.

In the Matter of Nomura Securities International, Inc., Respondent. Order Instituting Administrative and Cease-And-Desist Proceedings, Pursuant to Sections 15(B) and 21c of the Securities Exchange Act of 1934, Making Findings, and Imposing Remedial Sanctions and a Cease-and-Desist Order. Administrative Proceeding File No. 3-21170. SEC, September 27, 2022.

In the Matter of UBS AG, UBS Financial Services, Inc., and UBS Securities LLC, Respondents. Order Instituting Proceedings Pursuant to Section 6(c) and (d) of the Commodity Exchange Act, Making Findings, and Imposing Remedial Sanctions. CFTC, September 27, 2022.

In the Matter of UBS Financial Services, Inc. and UBS Securities LLC, Respondent. Order Instituting Administrative and Cease-And-Desist Proceedings, Pursuant to Sections 15(B) and 21c of the Securities Exchange Act of 1934, Making Findings, and Imposing Remedial Sanctions and a Cease-and-Desist Order. Administrative Proceeding File No. 3-21174. SEC, September 27, 2022.

Investigation into the Causes of the Gold Panic. Report of the Majority of the Committee on Banking and Currency. March 1, 1870. Washington, D.C.: Government Printing Office, 1870.

Jackson, Frederick (pseud. One Who Knows). *A Week in Wall Street.* New York: Published for the Booksellers, 1841.

Johnson, Lyndon. "Governing Certain Capital Transfers Abroad." Executive Order 11387, January 1, 1968. F. R. Doc 68-112. *Federal Register* 33 (January 3, 1968): 47.

JPMorgan Chase & Company 2012 Annual Report.
JPMorgan Chase & Company 2018 Annual Report.
JPMorgan Chase & Company 2021 Annual Report.
JPMorgan Chase & Company 2022 Annual Report.

Kadushin, Charles. *Understanding Social Networks: Theories, Concepts, and Findings.* New York: Oxford University Press, 2012.

Kappeler, Victor E., Richard D. Sluder, and Geoffrey P. Alpert. *Forces of Deviance: Understanding the Dark Side of Policing.* Prospect Heights, Ill.: Waveland, 1994.

Kellenbenz, Hermann. "Introduction." In Joseph de la Vega, *Confusion of Confusions.* Kress Library of Business and Economics 13. Boston: Baker Library of the Harvard Business School, 1957.

Kennedy, John F. "Balance of Payments." Message to House of Representatives on July 18, 1963, 88th Cong., 1st sess. Doc. No. 41. *Congressional Record,* vol. 106. Washington, D.C.: Government Printing Office, 1963.

Keynes, John Maynard. *The General Theory of Employment, Interest, and Money.* New Delhi: Atlantic, 2008.

Klein, Maury. *The Life and Legend of E. H. Harriman.* Chapel Hill: University of North Carolina Press, 2000.

Klein, Maury. *The Life and Legend of Jay Gould*. Baltimore: Johns Hopkins University Press, 1986.

Krackhardt, David. "Simmelian Ties: Super, Strong, and Sticky." In Roderick Kramer and Margaret Neale, eds., *Power and Influence in Organizations*, 21–38. Thousand Oaks, Calif.: Sage, 1998.

Kroeber, Alfred Louis and Clyde Kluckhohn. *Culture: A Critical Review of Concepts and Definitions*. Cambridge, Mass.: Peabody Museum of American Archaeology, 1952.

Lakeside Annual Directory of the City of Chicago, 1885. Chicago: Chicago Directory, 1885.

Lakeside Annual Directory of the City of Chicago, 1892. Chicago: Chicago Directory, 1892.

Langevoort, Donald C. *Insider Trading Regulation*. New York: Clark Boardman, 1991.

Lascelles, David. *The Story of Minos Zombanakis: Banking without Borders*. Athens, Greece: Kerkyra-Economia, 2011.

Launer, R. L and G. N. Wilkinson, eds. *Robustness in Statistics*. New York: Academic, 1979.

Laws of the State of New-York, Passed at the Thirty-Fourth Session of the Legislature, Begun and Held at the City of Albany the Twenty-Ninth Day of January, 1811. Albany, N.Y.: S. Southwick, 1811.

Laws of the State of New-York, Passed at the Seventy-Third Session of the Legislature, Begun the first Day of January and Ended the Tenth Day of April, 1850, at the City of Albany. Albany, N.Y.: Little, 1850.

Laws of the State of New-York, Passed at the Seventy-Sixth Session of the Legislature. The Regular Session Begun on the Fourth Day of January, and Ended the Thirteenth Day of April, 1853; and (After a Recess from the 15th of April to the 24th of May) Ended the Twenty-First Day of July, 1853, at the City of Albany. Albany, N.Y.: Gould, Banks, 1853.

Laws of the State of New York, Passed at the Ninetieth Session Legislature, Begun January First, and Ended April Twentieth, 1867, in the City of Albany. Vol. 1. Albany, N.Y.: Weare C. Little, 1867.

Lazonick, William. *Business Organization and the Myth of the Market Economy*. New York: Cambridge University Press, 1991.

Leech, Harper. *Armour and His Times*. New York: D. Appleton-Century, 1938.

Lehman Brothers Holdings, Inc. 2007 Annual Report.

Lewis, C. S. "The Inner Ring." Memorial Lecture at King's College, University of London, 1944. C. S. Lewis Society of California, http://www.lewissociety.org/innerring.php.

Lewis, Michael. *Flash Boys: A Wall Street Revolt*. New York: Norton, 2014. Kindle ed.

Lewis, Michael. *Liar's Poker: Rising through the Wreckage on Wall Street*. New York: Penguin, 1990.

Lo, Andrew W. "The Gordon Gekko Effect: The Role of Culture in the Financial Industry." NBER Working Paper No. 21267, June 2015.

Longworth's American Almanac, New-York Register, and City Directory for the Sixty-Fourth Year of American Independence. New York: Thomas Longworth, 1839.

Lurie, Jonathan. *The Chicago Board of Trade, 1859–1905: The Dynamics of Self-Regulation.* Urbana: University of Illinois Press, 1979.

Macaulay, Frederick R. *Some Theoretical Problems Suggested by the Movements of Interest Rates, Bond Yields and Stock Prices in the United States since 1856.* New York: National Bureau of Economic Research, 1938.

MacKenzie, Donald. *An Engine, Not a Camera: How Financial Models Shape Markets.* Cambridge, Mass.: MIT Press, 2006.

Mandis, Steven. *What Happened to Goldman Sachs: An Insider's Story of Organizational Drift and Its Unintended Consequences.* Cambridge, Mass.: Harvard Business Review Press, 2013.

McWilliams, Douglas and Jonathan Said, "The Importance of the City of London to the UK Economy." In *Big Bang 20 Years On: New Challenges Facing the Financial Services Sector*, 11–23. London: City of London Center for Policy Studies, 2006.

Medbery, James K. *Men and Mysteries of Wall Street.* Boston: Fields, Osgood, 1879.

Melamed, Leo, with Bob Tamarkin. *Escape to the Futures.* Hoboken, N.J.: Wiley, 1996.

Merrill Lynch, Pierce, Fenner & Smith 1971 Annual Report.

Miller, Rena S. and Gary Shorter. "High Frequency Trading: Overview of Recent Developments." Congressional Research Service Report R44443, i. Washington, D.C.: CRS, April 4, 2016.

Mitchell Map of New York City, 1860. In S. A. Mitchell Jr., *Mitchell's New General Atlas, Containing Maps of the Various Countries of the World, Plans of Cities, Etc. Embraced in Forty-Seven Quarto Maps, Forming a Series of Seventy-Six Maps and Plans, Together with Valuable Statistical Tables.* Philadelphia: S. Augustus Mitchell, Jr., 1860. https://commons.wikimedia.org/.

"Money Markets—What Is Happening to O/N USD Rates?" Internal memorandum. Federal Reserve Bank of New York, March 27, 2008.

Morgan Stanley Bank, N.A. Annual Report as of and for the Years Ended December 31, 2022 and 2021.

Morgan Stanley Form 10-K for the Year Ended December 31, 2021. Washington, D.C.: United States Securities and Exchange Commission, 2022.

Morgan Stanley Form 10-Q For the Quarterly Period Ended March 31, 2023.

Morris, Edward L. *Wall Streeters: The Creators and Corruptors of American Finance.* New York: Columbia Business School Press, 2015.

Morrison, John Harrison. *History of American Steam Navigation.* New York: W. F. Sametz, 1903.

Mott, Edward H. *Between the Ocean and the Lakes: The Story of Erie.* New York: J. S. Collins, 1901.

Murray, James M. *Bruges, Cradle of Capitalism, 1280–1390.* New York: Cambridge University Press, 2005.

Nelson, S. A. *ABC of Wall Street*. New York: S. A. Nelson, 1900.

New-York as It Is: Containing a General Description of the City of New-York; Lists of Officers, Public Institutions, and Useful Information: Including the Public Officers, &c, of the City of Brooklyn. 6th ed. New York: T. R. Tanner, 1840.

Nissen, Hans J., Peter Damerow, and Robert K. Englund. *Archaic Bookkeeping: Writing and Techniques of Economic Administration in the Ancient Near East.* Translated by Paul Larsen. Chicago: University of Chicago Press, 1993.

North American Industry Classification System: United States, 2017. Office of Management and Budget, Executive Office of the President, 2017. https://www.census.gov/eos/www/naics.

O'Shaughnessy, Robert Joseph. "Reconsideration of United States Overseas Direct Investment Controls." Ph.D. diss., George Washington University, 1971.

Ott, Julia. *When Wall Street Met Main Street: The Quest for Investor Democracy.* Cambridge, Mass.: Harvard University Press, 2011.

Oxford English Dictionary Online. http://www.oed.com/.

Pak, Susie J. *Gentlemen Bankers: The World of J. P. Morgan.* Cambridge, Mass.: Harvard University Press, 2013.

Penal Code of the State of New York, in Force May 1, 1882, with Notes of Decisions, a Table of Sources and a Full Index. New York: Banks and Brothers, 1881.

Perkins, Edwin J. *American Public Finance and Financial Services, 1700–1815.* Columbus: Ohio State University Press, 1994.

Petram, Lodewijk. *The World's First Stock Exchange.* Translated by Lynne Richards. New York: Columbia Business School Publishing, 2014. Kindle ed.

Polk, Sam. *For the Love of Money: A Memoir.* New York: Scribner, 2016.

Prell, Christina, *Social Network Analysis: History, Theory, and Method.* London: Sage, 2012.

Priest, William. *Travels in the United States of America; Commencing in the Year 1793 and Ending in 1797.* London: J. Johnson, 1802.

Ransom, Roger L. "The Economics of the Civil War." In Robert Whaples, ed., *EH.Net Encyclopedia of Economic and Business History.* Economic History Association, n.d. https://eh.net/encyclopedia-2/.

Report of the Comptroller of the Currency to the Third Session of the Fortieth Congress of the United States, December 7, 1868. Washington, D.C.: Government Printing Office, 1868.

Reports and Decisions of the Interstate Commerce Commission of the United States 116, September–November 1926.

Riegle-Neal Interstate Banking and Branching Efficiency Act of 1994 (IBBEA). Public Law 103-328. 108 Stat. 2338. Enacted September 29, 1994.

Robinson, S. L. and M. S. Kraatz. "Constructing the Reality of Normative Behavior: The Use of Neutralization Strategies by Organizational Deviants." In R. W. Griffin, A. O'Leary-Kelly, and J. M. Collins, eds., *Dysfunctional Behavior in Organizations: Violent and Deviant Behavior*, Monographs in Organizational Behavior and Industrial Relations 23, parts A and B, 203–220. Greenwich, Conn.: Elsevier Science/JAI Press, 1998.

Sageman, Marc. *Understanding Terror Networks*. Philadelphia: University of Pennsylvania Press, 2004.

Santos, Joseph M. "Grain Futures Markets: What Have They Learned?" *Proceedings of the NCCC-134 Conference on Applied Commodity Price Analysis, Forecasting, and Market Risk Management*. St. Louis, MO, 2009.

SBC 2018 Annual Report.

Scharf, J. Thomas. *History of Saint Louis City and County from the Earliest Periods to the Present Day Including Biographical Sketches of Representative Men*. 2 vols. Philadelphia: Louis H. Everts, 1883.

Schein, Edgar H. *Organizational Culture and Leadership*. San Francisco: Jossey-Bass, 2004.

Schelling, Thomas. *Micromotives and Macrobehavior*. New York: Norton, 1978.

Scott, J. *Social Network Analysis: A Handbook*. London: Sage, 1991.

Securities Act of 1933. Title I of Public Law 73-22, 48 Stat. 74, enacted May 27, 1933, codified at 15 U.S.C. § 77a et seq.

Securities Exchange Act of 1934. Section 10-b of Public Law 73-291, 48 Stat. 881, enacted June 6, 1934, codified at 15 U.S.C. § 78a et seq.

Senate Report No. 67: Reports of the Majority and Minority of the Select Committee of the Senate of the State of New York, Appointed under a Resolution of the Same, Passed March 5, 1868, Directing an Investigation into the Management and Condition of the Erie Railway Company. April 1, 1868. In *Documents of the Senate of the State of New York. Ninety-First Session.—1868. Vol. 5.—Nos. 50 to 76 Inclusive*. Albany, N.Y.: C. Van Benthuysen and Sons, 1868.

"Shaping an Interconnected World." G-20 Summit Documents, Pittsburgh, Pa., 2009.

Shapiro, Susan P. *Wayward Capitalists: Targets of the SEC*. New Haven, Conn.: Yale University Press, 1984.

Shiller, Robert J. "Investor Behavior in the October 1987 Stock Market Crash: Survey Evidence." National Bureau of Economic Research Working Paper 2246, November 1987.

Shu, Pian. "Innovating in Science and Engineering or 'Cashing In' on Wall Street? Evidence on Elite STEM Talent." Working Paper 16-067, Harvard Business School, November 2016.

SIMFA 2016 Fact Book. Securities Industry and Financial Markets Association, 2016.

Singh, Manoj. "The 2007–08 Financial Crisis in Review." http://www.investopedia.com/articles/economics/09/financial-crisis-review.asp.

Smith, Adam. *An Inquiry into the Nature and Causes of the Wealth of Nations*. 3rd ed. 3 vols. London: A. Strahan and T. Cadell, 1784.

Smith, Adam (George J. W. Goodman). *Paper Money*. London: Macdonald, 1982.

Smith, C. W. *The Mind of the Market*. Totowa, N.J.: Rowman and Littlefield, 1981.

Smith, Howard Irving. *Smith's Financial Dictionary*. 2nd ed. New York: Moody's Magazine, 1908.

Smith, Matthew Hale. *Twenty Years among the Bulls and Bears of Wall Street*. Hartford, Conn.: J. B. Burr, 1871.

Snowden, Kenneth A. *Mortgage Banking in the United States, 1870–1940*. Washington, D.C.: Research Institute for Housing America, 2013.

Sobel, Robert. *The Big Board: A History of the New York Stock Market*. New York: Free Press, 1965.

Societe Generale Annual Financial Report, 2017.

Societe Generale Universal Registration Document-EN.

Soros, George. *The Alchemy of Finance*. New York: John Wiley, 1987. Reprint, 1994.

Soros, George. "Financial Markets." Lecture at Central European University, October 27, 2009. Open Society Foundations, 2009.

Special Laws of the State of Connecticut. Compiled and Published under Authority of the General Assembly. Vol. 6, *From the Year 1866 to the Year 1870, Inclusive*. Hartford, Conn.: Case, Lockwood and Brainard, 1872.

Spender, J. C. *Industry Recipes: An Inquiry into the Nature and Sources of Managerial Judgments*. Cambridge, Mass.: Blackwell, 1989.

Stenfors, Alexis. "Determining the LIBOR: A Study of Power and Deception." PhD diss., School of Oriental and African Studies (SOAS), University of London, 2013.

Stewart, James B. *Den of Thieves*. New York: Simon and Schuster, 1992.

Stiles, T. J. *The First Tycoon: The Epic Life of Cornelius Vanderbilt*. New York: Knopf, 2009.

"Stock Exchange Practices." Report of the Committee on Banking and Currency Pursuant to Senate Relation 84 (72nd Cong.). Senate Report no. 1455. Washington, D.C.: Government Printing Office, 1934.

Stone, Dan G. *April Fools: An Insiders' Account of the Rise and Fall of Drexel Burnham*. New York: Donald Fine, 1990.

Strong v. Repide, 213 U.S. 419 (1909). https://supreme.justia.com/cases/federal/us/213/419/.

Sudjic, Deyan. *The Edifice Complex: How the Rich and Powerful Shape the World*. New York: Penguin, 2005.

SWIFT (Society for Worldwide Interbank Financial Telecommunication) 2007 Annual Report.

Sylla, Richard E., Jack W. Wilson, and Robert E. Wright. "Price Quotations in Early United States Securities Markets, 1790–1860." ICPSR04053-v1. Ann Arbor, Mich.: Inter-university Consortium for Political and Social Research, 2005.

Taylor, Charles H., ed. *History of the Board of Trade of the City of Chicago*. 3 vols. Chicago: Robert O. Law, 1917.

Testimony Taken before the Committee on Agriculture, during a Consideration of Bill Nos. 392, 2699, and 3870, Restricting and Taxing Dealers in "Futures" and "Options" in Agricultural Products, and for Other Purposes. Submitted by Mr. Hatch from the Committee on Agriculture. Washington, D.C.: Government Printing Office, 1892.

Timberlake, Richard H. *Monetary Policy in the United States: An Intellectual and Institutional History*. Chicago: University of Chicago Press, 1978.

Trice, Harrison M. and Janice M. Beyer. *The Cultures of Work Organizations*. Englewood Cliffs, N.J.: Prentice-Hall, 1993.

Trollope, Anthony. *The Way We Live Now*. 4 vols. London: Chapman and Hall, 1875.

UBS Group AG Annual Report 2021.

UBS Group AG Annual Report 2022.

UBS Group Annual Report 2016.

"Union Pacific Railroad." Executive Document No. 253. In *Executive Documents Printed by Order of the House of Representatives, during the Second Session of the Fortieth Congress, 1867–'68*, vol. 17. Washington, D.C.: Government Printing Office, 1868.

United States Bureau of the Census. *Abstract of the Fourteenth Census of the United States, 1920. General Report and Analytical Tables*. Washington, D.C.: Government Printing Office, 1922.

United States Bureau of the Census. *Statistical Abstract of the United States, 1988*. Washington, D.C.: U.S. Government Printing Office, 1988.

United States Bureau of the Census. *Statistical Abstract of the United States, 1990*. Washington, D.C.: U.S. Government Printing Office, 1990.

United States Commodity Futures Trading Commission. "CFTC Orders 11 Financial Institutions to Pay over $710 Million for Recordkeeping and Supervision Failures for Widespread Use of Unapproved Communication Methods." Release Number 8599-22. September 27, 2022.

United States Commodity Futures Trading Commission. "CFTC Provides Relief to Market Participants in Response to COVID-19." Release number 8132-20, March 17, 2020.

United States Commodity Futures Trading Commission. "Order Instituting Proceedings, In the matter of: ICAP Europe Limited." September 25, 2013.

United States Commodity Futures Trading Commission. "Order Instituting Proceedings, In the matter of: Rabobank." October 29, 2013.

United States Commodity Futures Trading Commission. "Order Instituting Proceedings, In the matter of: Royal Bank of Scotland PLC." February 6, 2013.

United States Commodity Futures Trading Commission. "Order Instituting Proceedings, In the matter of: UBS AG." December 19, 2012.

United States Commodity Futures Trading Commission v. American Electric Power Co., Inc., and AEP Energy Services, Defendants. Final judgment and consent order, U.S. District Court for the Southern District of Ohio, filed September 26, 2005.

United States Commodity Futures Trading Commission v. Denette Johnson, et al. 408 F. Supp. 2d 259, 267 (S.D. Tex. 2005).

United States of America Before the Commodity Futures Trading Commission. In the Matter of ICAP Europe Limited, Respondent. Order Instituting Proceedings Pur-

suant to Sections 6(c) and 6(d) of the Commodity Exchange Act Making Findings and Imposing Remedial Sanctions. September 25, 2013. CFTC Docket No. 13-38.

United States of America v. James Brooks, Wesley C. Walton, James Patrick Phillips. No. 09-20871, 2012 WL 1768061, *691 (5th Cir. May 18, 2012).

United States of America v. Paul Robson, Paul Thompson, Tetsuya Motomura. Exhibit of Facts. Department of Justice, January 13, 2014.

United States, Plaintiff-Appellant, v. Michelle M. Valencia, Defendant-Appellee. United States Court of Appeals, Fifth Circuit. No. 03-21217. Decided December 17, 2004.

United States Securities and Exchange Commission (SEC). *Study of Unsafe and Unsound Practices of Brokers and Dealers*. Report to the Committee on Interstate and Foreign Commerce of the U.S. Congress, 92nd Cong., 1st sess., 1971.

United States Securities and Exchange Commission v. Drexel Burnham Lambert Incorporated, et al. Litigation Release No. 11859/September 7, 1988. *SEC Docket* 41, no.15 (September 1988): 1047–1053.

United States Securities and Exchange Commission v. Drexel Burnham Lambert Incorporated, et al. No. 88 Civ. 6209. U.S. District Court for the Southern District of New York, filed September 7, 1988.

United States Securities and Exchange Commission v. Texas Gulf Sulfur, 401 F.2d 833; 2 A.L.R. Fed. 190. Also 107 U.S. 666 (1969).

United States Statutes at Large. Library of Congress, Washington, D.C.

Wasserman, S. and K. Faust. *Social Network Analysis: Methods and Applications*. Cambridge: Cambridge University Press, 1994.

Waterman, Thomas W., ed. *Reports of Cases Argued and Determined in the Superior Court of the City of New York by the Hon. Lewis H. Sanford, One of the Justices of the Court*. 2nd ed. 5 vols. New York: Banks and Brothers, 1849.

Watts, Duncan J. *Six Degrees: The Science of a Connected Age*. New York: Norton, 2003.

Watts, Duncan J. "The Structure and Dynamics of Small-World Systems." Ph.D. diss., Cornell University, 1997.

Weber, Max. *From Max Weber: Essays in Sociology*. Translated, edited, and with an introduction by H. H. Gerth and C. Wright Mills. New York: Oxford University Press, 1946.

Wellman, Barry. "Structural Analysis: From Method and Metaphor to Theory and Substance." In B. Wellman and S. D. Berkowitz, eds., *Social Structures: A Network Approach*, 19–61. New York: Cambridge University Press, 1988.

Wellons, Philip A. *Borrowing by Developing Countries on the Eurocurrency Market*. Paris: Development Center of the OECD, 1977.

Werner, Walter and Steven T. Smith. *Wall Street*. New York: Columbia University Press, 1991.

White, Bouck. *The Book of Daniel Drew: A Glimpse of the Fisk-Gould-Tweed Regime from the Inside*. New York: Doubleday, 1910.

Williams, Marlene and Timothy Geithner, to Mervyn King. "LIBOR Recommendations." http://www.bankofengland.co.uk/publications/Documents/news/2012/nr068.pdf.

Williamson, Oliver. *The Economic Institutions of Capitalism: Firms, Markets, Relational Contracting*. New York: Free Press, 1985.

Wilson, H., comp. *Trow's New York City Directory for the Year Ending May 1, 1856*. New York: John F. Trow, 1855.

Wilson, H., comp. *Trow's New York City Directory for the Year Ending May 1, 1857*. New York: John F. Trow, 1856.

Wilson, H., comp. *Trow's New York City Directory for the Year Ending May 1, 1863*. New York: John F. Trow, 1862.

Wilson, H., comp. *Trow's New York City Directory for the Year Ending May 1, 1865*. New York: John F. Trow, 1864.

Wilson, H., comp. *Trow's New York City Directory for the Year Ending May 1, 1868*. New York: John F. Trow, 1867.

Wilson, Margaret Mary. "The Attack on Options and Futures, 1888–1894." Thesis, University of Kansas, 1932.

Wiseman, Peter. "Syndicated Facilities." Chapter 7 in Brian J. Terry, ed., *The International Handbook of Corporate Finance*, 3rd ed. Chicago: Glenlake, 1997.

Wolff, Edward N. "Household Wealth Trends in the United States, 1962–2013: What Happened Over the Great Recession?" NBER Working Paper 20733. National Bureau of Economic Research, 2014.

Wolff, Edward N. "Household Wealth Trends in the United States, 1962 to 2016: Has Middle Class Wealth Recovered?" NBER Working Paper 24085. National Bureau of Economic Research, November 2017.

World Bank. *Private Capital Flows to Developing Countries: The Road to Financial Integration*. Oxford: Oxford University Press, 1997.

Yellen, Janet. "Interconnectedness and Systemic Risk: Lessons from the Financial Crisis and Policy Implications." Remarks Delivered at the American Economic Association/American Finance Association Joint Luncheon, San Diego, Calif., January 4, 2013. Board of Governors of the Federal Reserve System, 2013.

Zaloom, Caitlin. *Out of the Pits: Traders and Technology from Chicago to London*. Chicago: University of Chicago Press, 2006.

Index

business schools, 158
Butler, Benjamin, 45

Canary Wharf, 121–124
Cantor Fitzgerald, 141
capital controls, 114
CDOR. *See* interest rates
Central Bank of Iran. *See* Bank Markazi
central banks, 3, 114–116, 118, 120, 128
Century Club, 44–46, 48, 59–61, 67, 75, 107
Chicago Board of Trade (CBOT): Appeals Committee, 104; Arbitration Committee, 104; connected noncore member class (CNC), 93–95, 97, 100–103, 105; core-component member class, 91, 93–97, 99–105; corn trading, 48–49, 57, 61, 66, 69, 74; Dec (December) wheat, 55, 57–60, 74, 81; four-fecta members, 100, 103–104; governance committees, 88, 93–94, 97, 104, 106; isolates member class, 91, 95, 97, 99, 104; Membership Committee, 97; provisions (dressed pork) trading, 48, 61, 69, 74; Sep (September) wheat, 48, 50, 53, 55–56, 58–62, 66–67, 69–71, 73–78; trifecta members, 95–96, 99–100, 102–104; wind wheat, 50, 53
Chicago Board of Trade (CBOT) building, 46–48, 82
Chicago Board Options Exchange (CBOE), 88, 110–111, 144
Chicago Fire (1871), 65
Chicago Mercantile Exchange (the Merc), 5, 106
Cincinnati, Ohio, 21, 43
City of London, ix, 4, 120, 134, 159
Clews, Henry, 69, 168
CME Group, 89
commercial banking, 155
Commodity Exchange Act of 1936, 128
compliance departments, 125, 141–142, 144–145, 148–149, 151

conflicts of interest, 124–125
Conspiracy One, 129–131, 134, 136
Conspiracy Two, 129–130, 134
consumer prices, 17
Corn Exchange Bank, 45
Cotton Futures Act of 1914, 80
Countrywide, 128
COVID, 140, 144–146, 148, 150, 153
Cowperwood, Frank, 106
Cudahy, Jack, 50–52, 78–80, 82

Dall, Robert, 5
Detroit, Michigan, 72
Deutsche Bank, 131, 133, 141, 153
Diamond, Bob, 135
diamond merchants, 111, 136
Docklands, 121–122
dot-com collapse, 153
Douglas, Michael, 13
Dow. *See* market indices
Drew, Daniel, 20–40, 79, 86, 106, 131, 168–169
Drew Theological Seminary, Drew University, 20
Duer, William, 11, 38
Duluth, Minnesota, 45, 61
Dun's credit service (R. G. Dun & Co.), 45
Dunn, William, 90

EBF-EURIBOR. *See* interest rates
economics students, 158
edge. *See* networks
edge (market performance). *See* trading strategies
Edge Act corporations, 115
edifice complex, 122
efficient market hypothesis, 29
Eggleston, Sandy, 59–60
electrical equipment suppliers, 6
emerging market country funds, 138
emerging markets debt crisis, 137
encryption, 141–143
energy companies, 128